The Transfigured Kingdom

THE
TRANSFIGURED
KINGDOM

*Sacred Parody and Charismatic
Authority at the Court of
Peter the Great*

Ernest A. Zitser

Cornell University Press

ITHACA AND LONDON

The author expresses appreciation to the University Seminars at Columbia University for their help in publication. Material in this work was presented to the University Seminar on Slavic History and Culture.

First published 2004 by Cornell University Press

Printed in the United States of America

Library of Congress Cataloging-in-Publication Data

Zitser, Ernest A.
    The transfigured kingdom : sacred parody and charismatic authority at the court of Peter the Great / Ernest A. Zitser.
        p. cm.
    Includes bibliographical references and index.
    ISBN 0-8014-4147-1 (cloth : alk. paper)
    1. Russia—History—Peter I, 1689–1725. 2. Peter I, Emperor of Russia, 1672–1725. 3. Russia—Court and courtiers. 4. Rites and ceremonies—Russia. I. Title: Sacred parody and charismatic authority at the court of Peter the Great. II. Title.
    DK133.Z58 2004
    947'.05—dc22   2004000816

Cornell University Press strives to use environmentally responsible suppliers and materials to the fullest extent possible in the publishing of its books. Such materials include vegetable-based, low-VOC inks, and acid-free papers that are recycled, totally chlorine-free, or partly composed of nonwood fibers. For further information, visit our website at www.cornellpress.cornell.edu.

Cloth printing   10 9 8 7 6 5 4 3 2 1

To the memory of my grandparents—both those who brought me to the Promised Land and those who stayed behind.

Contents

Acknowledgments

Acknowledging everyone who contributed to this project is the most pleasant task of the entire process, and also the most daunting. There are so many people to thank and so many debts to repay that despite my best efforts, this brief note of recognition cannot do justice to them all. Nevertheless, I must single out a few individuals and organizations without whose contributions my work would not have been possible. My year-long research trip to Moscow and St. Petersburg was funded by the Individual Advanced Research Opportunities in Eurasia (IARO) Program of the International Research and Exchanges Board (IREX). The Eurasia Program Dissertation Fellowship of the Social Science Research Council (SSRC), the Josephine De Kármán Foundation Fellowship, and the Junior Fellowship of the Harriman Institute at Columbia University provided financial support during the write-up stage. The revision of the book was started on the west coast, during my term as a postdoctoral research fellow at the Center for Seventeenth- and Eighteenth-Century Studies, University of California, Los Angeles, and completed on the east, during my stint as a postdoctoral fellow of the Davis Center for Russian and Eurasian Studies, Harvard University. Parts of an earlier draft of the introduction and Chapter 2 appeared in "Politics in the State of Sober Drunkenness: Parody and Piety at the Court of Peter the Great," *Jahrbücher für Geschichte Osteuropas* 51, no. 1 (2003), 1–15, at the very beginning of my tenure as a Center Associate.

It gives me great pleasure to thank my teachers at Columbia University, who freely shared their excitement for the study of things Russian. As both pedagogues and scholars, Leopold H. Haimson and Mark L. von Hagen helped create an exciting intellectual environment in which I could pursue my interests, wherever they might lead. In the best traditions of the Columbia history and Slavic literature departments, J. W. Smit and Irina Reyfman continuously challenged me to be more comparative and to think more broadly (and more theoretically) about the sources and the implications of my arguments. Robert O. Crummey's seminar on the history and culture of early modern Russia first sparked my interest in seventeenth-century Muscovy, and his encouragement of my earliest endeavors in this field fanned the flame. But it is Richard S. Wortman, my academic adviser and mentor, who has been and remains the greatest source of intellectual combustion. He has been a constant source of inspiration and guidance, and I thank him for his support throughout the entire process.

During the course of this project I have also had the privilege of discussing my work with scholars whose suggestions shaped the direction of my research in ways that they may not have been aware of, and for which, of course, they are not to blame. I am grateful to Paul Bushkovitch, Paul Hollingsworth, Lindsey Hughes, John P. LeDonne, Eve Levin, Marc Raeff, L. I. Sazonova, and V. M. Zhivov, all of whom graciously offered useful advice, generously shared valuable information, and left an indelible imprint on the final product. I must single out the input of James Cracraft, whose extensive comments on earlier drafts allowed me to engage in a virtual dialogue that taught me not only how I could revise my work but also what true collegiality is. Finally, I thank the director of Cornell University Press, John G. Ackerman, whose enthusiasm for this project was so genuine that I never once had to justify my aspiration to add yet another monograph to the already extensive literature on the reign of Peter the Great.

I am most grateful for the moral support of my parents, Larisa and Alexander Zitser, and of the entire gang in L.A., particularly Diane, Mark, and Leo Goldenberg. They gave me the freedom to discover what I really wanted, the desire to strive for it, and the determination to attain it. This book would not have been written without their encouragement. Fortunately for them, the responsibility for any errors is mine alone.

E.Z.

Abbreviations

ARCHIVES

IRLI	Institut russkoi literatury (Pushkinskii Dom) (Institute of Russian Literature [Pushkin House])
RGADA	Rossiiskii gosudarstvennyi arkhiv drevnikh aktov (Russian State Archive of Ancient Documents)
RGAVMF	Rossiiskii gosudarstvennyi arkhiv voenno-morskogo flota (Russian State Naval Archive)
RGIA	Rossiiskii gosudarstvennyi istoricheskii arkhiv (Russian State Historical Archive)
RGVIA	Rossiiskii gosudarstvennyi voenno-istoricheskii arkhiv (Russian State Military-Historical Archive)
RO BRAN	Rukopisnyi otdel, Biblioteka Rossiiskoi akademii nauk (Manuscript Division, Library of the Russian Academy of Sciences)
RO RNB	Rukopisnyi otdel, Rossiiskaia natsional'naia biblioteka (Manuscript Division, Russian National Library)
SPb F IRI RAN	Sankt-Peterburgskii filial, Institut russkoi istorii Rossiiskoi akademii nauk (St. Petersburg Branch, Institute of Russian History, Russian Academy of Sciences)

ARCHIVAL SUBSECTIONS

ch.	*chast'* (section)
ed. khr.	*edinitsa khraneniia* (storage unit)
f., ff.	*fond* (collection[s])
kn.	*kniga* (book)
koll.	*kollektsiia* (collection)

xi

l., ll.   *list, listy* (folio[s])
MS(S)   manuscript(s)
otd.   *otdelenie* (division)
op.   *opis'* (description)

OTHER SOURCES

Gordon, "Diary"   "Zhurnal ili dnevnaia zapiska (na Angliiskom iazyke)
                  byvshago v Rossiiskoi sluzhbe Generala Gordona, im samim
                  napisannyi," RGVIA, f. 846, op. 15
PiB   *Pis'ma i bumagi imperatora Petra Velikogo,* 13 vols. to date
                  (St. Petersburg, 1887–)
RBS   *Russkii biograficheskii slovar',* 25 vols. (St. Petersburg,
                  1896–1918)

The Transfigured Kingdom

Introduction

In a sensationalist political exposé about his brief stay in the land of the tsars, Johann Georg Korb (c. 1670–1741), the secretary of the 1698–99 Habsburg mission to Muscovy, offered his readers an account that fulfilled and at times even exceeded everything they had come to expect from the rulers of that "rude and barbarous kingdom."[1] In one famous passage of his travel diary, Korb described in deliberately exaggerated prose the ceremonies surrounding the dedication of Tsar Peter Alekseevich's new suburban pleasure palace—a public ceremony witnessed by the Russian court and at least some of the members of the foreign diplomatic corps. "Today," wrote Korb, in the entry for February 21, 1699,

> a sham Patriarch and a complete set of scenic clergy dedicated to Bacchus, with solemn festivities, the palace which was built at the Czar's expense, and which it has pleased him now to call Lefort's [after his chief foreign favorite]. A procession thither set out from the house of Colonel Lima [another of the tsar's foreign favorites]. He that bore the assumed honors of the Patriarch was conspicuous in the vestments proper to a bishop. Bacchus was decked with a miter, and went stark naked, to betoken lasciviousness to the lookers on. Cupid and Venus were the insignia on his crosier, lest there should be any mistake about what flock he was a pastor of. The remaining rout of Bacchanalians came after him, some carrying great bowls full of wine, others mead, others again beer and brandy, that last joy of the heated Bacchus. And as the wintry cold hindered their binding their brows with laurel, they carried great dishes of

1. On Korb and the sources of his travel diary, see Friedrich Dukmeyer, *Korbs Diarium itineris in Moscoviam und Quellen, die es ergänzen*, 2 vols., Historische Studien 70 and 80 (Berlin, 1909–10); Paul Bushkovitch, "Aristocratic Faction and the Opposition to Peter the Great: The 1690s," *Forschungen zur Osteuropäischen Geschichte* 50 (1995): 98–99, 117–20; and his *Peter the Great: The Struggle for Power, 1671–1725* (Cambridge, 2001), 204n85.

dried tobacco leaves, with which, when ignited, they went to the remotest corners of the palace, exhaling those most delectable odors and most pleasant incense to Bacchus from their smutty jaws. Two of those pipes . . . being set crosswise, served the scenic bishop to confirm the rites of consecration.

"Now, who would [ever] believe," Korb concluded melodramatically, "that the sign of the cross—that most precious pledge of our redemption—was held up to [such] mockery?"[2]

Who indeed? Certainly not the imperial court in Vienna, which just a few months before had toasted the young Orthodox tsar as a valuable partner in the new crusade against the Islamic Ottoman Porte. And certainly not those Russian Orthodox moralists who boldly proclaimed their disapproval of the "childish amusements" of Peter Alekseevich and his dissolute royal favorites.[3] In fact, when confronted with what one outraged contemporary described as the tsar's "apostasy-like deeds" (*otstupnicheskie dela*), most Russian commentators echoed Korb's bewilderment at the fact that a self-described Christian monarch would choose to display his royal authority by means of spectacles that parodied the sacraments established by "our God, Christ Himself."[4] Yet for more than three decades that is precisely what the tsar did. Indeed, from the very beginning of his independent reign (in 1689) until almost the day of his death (in 1725), Peter and his courtiers repeatedly and quite deliberately engaged in what many God-fearing Christians regarded as offensive and dissolute behavior more appropriate to a gang of rogues than to the entourage of a pious Orthodox tsar.[5]

Adapting the indecent language, dress, and games of traditional Yuletide

2. J.-G. Korb, *Diary of an Austrian Secretary of Legation*, ed. and trans. Count MacDonnell, 2 vols. (1863; rpt. London, 1968), 1:255–56.

3. See the comments by Abbot Avraamii of the Andreevskii Monastery, in N. A. Baklanova, "Tetradi startsa Avraamiia," *Istoricheskii arkhiv* 6 (1951): 145, 148; for a transcript of Avraamii's interrogation, see "Delo o podannykh tsariu tetradiakh stroitelia Andreevskogo monastyria Avraamiem [1697 g.]. Doprosy Avraamiia, Pososhkova, i dr.," in B. B. Kafengauz, *I. T. Pososhkov: Zhizn' i deiatel'nost'*, 173–81 (Moscow and Leningrad, 1950); and M. Ia. Volkov, "Monakh Avraamii i ego 'Poslanie Petru I,'" in *Rossiia v period reform Petra I*, 311–36 (Moscow, 1973). See also N. B. Golikova, *Politicheskie protsessy pri Petre I* (Moscow, 1957), 79–81; and James Cracraft, *The Church Reform of Peter the Great* (London, 1971), 19–20.

4. "Otryvok oblicheniia na vseshuteishii sobor. Ok. 1705 g.," in *Materialy dlia russkoi istorii*, ed. S. A Belokurov (Moscow, 1888), 539. Despite Belokurov's tentative date, the internal evidence suggests that this anonymous denunciation must have been written sometime between 1692 and 1700. This suggestion is confirmed by Golikova, *Politicheskie protsessy*, 132, who has located the original document in RGADA, f. Sekretnykh del, kn. 2, *pis'mo* 12 "e."

5. The author of the anonymous denunciation of Peter's Yuletide amusements described the annual caroling processions as the work of "Mikita" [*sic*] Zotov, a lowborn "rogue" (*plut*) who encouraged the tsar and his courtiers to "carry on like devils" (*besitsia*) and to curse God under the guise of "singing praises to Christ" (*slavit'*). See "Otryvok," in Belokurov, *Materialy dlia russkoi istorii*, 539–40. On literary rogues in late seventeenth-century Russian literature and their connection to "devilish" Yuletide amusements, see E. V. Dushechkina, *Russkii sviatochnyi rasskaz: Stanovlenie zhanra* (St. Petersburg, 1995), 56–64.

mummers to their own ends,[6] the tsar and his companions would, in the words of a contemporary denunciation, "ordain a false patriarch in the same manner as [one] ordains [a real] patriarch. Likewise [they would ordain false] metropolitans of Kiev, Novgorod, and other [famous Russian eparchies] and make for them counterfeit hierarchical vestments. . . . Taking as their example [the ceremony of ordination found in] the [Orthodox] service book [*vzem s chinovnoi knigi obraz*], in order [both] to subvert it and to curse and renounce God they [would] swear with all their faith to call upon and to believe in someone named Bach (*nekoego Baga*)"—an obvious and very telling misreading (on the part of the anonymous author of the denunciation) of the Russian calque of "Bacchus" (*Bag*), which is pronounced like the word for "God" (*Bog*).[7] And for two or three weeks after the Nativity of Christ, the tsar and his entire "devilish host" would ride around the houses of "all the royal counselors," as well as the members of the Holy Council of the real Russian Orthodox patriarch, in the guise of mock ecclesiastics. Singing Christmas carols and extorting gifts from their hosts, this "unholy council" would carouse at the expense of the very people they mocked, while the properly ordained ecclesiastical officials "not only would do nothing to forbid" the tsar and his retinue from carrying on in this way but would even "drink and act merry along with them."[8] For the outraged author of this anonymous denunciation, such Yuletide spectacles went far beyond the traditional caroling visits by royal choristers and clerics of the Kremlin cathedrals and chapels. According to him, Peter's Bacchanalia not only were indecent, they were downright blasphemous.[9]

In this book I seek to explain why the monarch who has been credited with creating modern Russia routinely organized and personally took part

6. For an analysis of Yuletide celebrations in seventeenth-century Muscovy, see N. V. Ponyrko, "Russkie sviatki XVII veka," *Trudy otdela drevnerusskoi literatury* 32 (1977): 84–99; idem, "Sviatochnyi smekh," in D. S. Likhachev et al., *Smekh v drevnei Rusi*, 154–74 (Leningrad, 1984); and Dushechkina, *Russkii sviatochnyi rasskaz*, 48–56. For the culture of Yuletide mummery in Russia, see L. M. Ivleva, *Riazhen'e v russkoi traditsionnoi kul'ture* (St. Petersburg, 1994).

7. "Otryvok," in Belokurov, *Materialy dlia russkoi istorii*, 539–40. For a reading that situates this text within the context of early modern Russian appropriations of classical mythology, see V. M. Zhivov and B. A. Uspenskii, "Metamorfozy antichnogo iazychestva v istorii russkoi kul'tury XVII–XVIII veka," in *Iz istorii russkoi kul'tury*, ed. A. D. Koshelev (Moscow, 1996), 4:482.

8. "Otryvok," in Belokurov, *Materialy dlia russkoi istorii*, 540.

9. For references to earlier seventeenth-century Yuletide caroling visits by royal choristers (*pevchie diaki*), see I. E. Zabelin, *Domashnii byt russkogo naroda*, 2nd ed. (Mosocw, 1872), 1:331–32; M. D. Khmyrov, *Grafinia Ekaterina Ivanovna Golovkina i ee vremia (1701–1791). Istoricheskii ocherk po arkhivnym dokumentam* (St. Petersburg, 1867), 34; and A. P. Bogdanov, "Fedor Alekseevich," *Voprosy istorii* 7 (1994): 69. The records of gifts made to priests and deacons of the Kremlin cathedrals and chapels for singing indicate that at the end of Peter's reign mock carolers still coexisted with the traditional variety. See *Obshchii arkhiv Ministerstva Imperatorskogo Dvora. Opisanie vysochaishikh povelenii po pridvornomu vedomstvu (1701–1740 gg.)* (St. Petersburg, 1888), 87, 97–101; and Lindsey Hughes, *Russia in the Age of Peter the Great* (New Haven, 1998), 254, 517n55.

in such carnivalesque spectacles. I do so by exploring the connection between the staging of sacred parodies and the enactment of charismatic authority at the court of Peter the Great.[10] The book details how over the course of Peter's long and turbulent reign the tsar and his close political advisers used Muscovite royal amusements (*potekhi*) to create a countercultural play world that was, I contend, playful in name only. Centered first in the suburban royal estate of Novo-Preobrazhenskoe (literally, New Transfiguration) and subsequently in the new imperial capital of St. Petersburg, this play world—with its mock kings, knights, and clerics, its extravagant ceremonies of solidarity, and its imaginary and ever-expanding topography—served as an important point of reference for every member of the tsar's inner circle. Simultaneously a geographical and a rhetorical commonplace (*topos*),[11] the "Transfigured Kingdom" (as I have dubbed it) delineated the boundaries between those courtiers who belonged to Peter's select "company" (*kompaniia*) and those who did not.[12] Continuously invoked, presented, and re-presented by the organizers of Petrine court spectacles, both in public ceremonies and in private correspondence, this imaginary realm marked off those who had come to believe in Peter's personal gift of grace (charisma, in its original, religious sense—the one that will be used throughout this book)[13] from those who remained unconvinced or hostile

10. Rhetoric manuals of the time defined "parody" (Lat. *parodia*) as a type of translation or imitation, not as ridicule (Lat. *ridiculum*), which signified simply a generic type of humorous story. Thus "sacred parody" (Lat. *parodia sacra*) characterized any imitation of a sacred text, whether scriptural, liturgical, or homiletic, no matter the purpose to which it was put. This formal, scholastic definition did not explicitly condemn what we would now call satire against ecclesiastics, but that was not its original purpose. Indeed, until well into the eighteenth century, even the most rabidly anticlerical parodies did not necessarily signify the rejection of religious tradition. See Paulina Lewin, "Jan Kochanowski: The Model Poet in Eastern Slavic Lectures on Poetics of the Seventeenth and Eighteenth Centuries," in *The Polish Renaissance in Its European Context,* ed. Samuel Fiszman (Bloomington, 1988), 442n44; Ernst Robert Curtius, "Jest and Earnest in Medieval Literature," in his *European Literature and the Latin Middle Ages,* trans. Willard R. Trask (New York, 1953), 433n35, 435n40; and B. A. Uspenskii, *Kratkii ocherk istorii russkogo literaturnogo iazyka (XI–XIX vv.)* (Moscow, 1994), 103–5.

11. For the distinction between topographical common place and topical commonplace, see Svetlana Boym, *Common Places: Mythologies of Everyday Life in Russia* (Cambridge, 1994); cf. *Realms of Memory: Rethinking the French Past,* trans. Arthur Goldhammer, 3 vols. (New York, 1996–98).

12. For a pioneering attempt to determine the membership of Peter's company, based on the informal networks established (and celebrated) during Petrine court spectacles, see A. I. Zaozerskii, *Fel'dmarshal B. P. Sheremetev,* ed. B. V. Levshin (Moscow, 1989), 173, 200–208, 210. See also N. I. Pavlenko, *Petr Velikii* (Moscow, 1990), 36–37; and Bushkovitch, *Peter the Great,* 177–83. For a prosopographical study of Peter's court, see Robert O. Crummey, "Peter and the Boyar Aristocracy, 1689–1700," and Brenda Meehan-Waters, "The Russian Aristocracy and the Reforms of Peter the Great," *Canadian-American Slavic Studies* 8, no. 2 (Summer 1974): 274–87, 288–99; John P. LeDonne, "Ruling Families in the Russian Political Order," pt. 1, "The Petrine Leadership, 1689–1725," *Cahiers du monde russe et soviétique* 28, no. 3–4 (1987): 233–322; and esp. I. Iu. Airapetian, "Feodal'naia aristokratiia v period stanovleniia absoliutizma v Rossii" (Kand. diss. ist. nauk, M. V. Lomonosov State University, Moscow, 1987).

13. Like Max Weber's famous sociological analysis of charisma, my discussion relies on St. Paul's definition (I Cor. 12:4–7; cf. Rom. 12:6–8; and Matt. 25:15) of the workings of di-

to the tsar's leadership style and his version of the reform project inaugurated, but not completed, during the reign of his father, Tsar Aleksei Mikhailovich Romanov (r. 1645–76).

The political sacraments associated with Peter's Transfigured Kingdom sought to elevate the tsar's persona above internal court factions and clan politics, to guarantee his prerogatives over ecclesiastical affairs, and to bind his entourage into an ecumenical community of true believers. By implicating courtiers in taboo-breaking bacchanalian mysteries, the tsar and his advisers also attempted to induct select members of the Muscovite elite into a new order of distinctions between nobility and baseness, sacrality and profanity, tradition and modernity, thereby challenging them to confront, internalize, and implement Peter's charismatic scenario of power.[14] In this view, much of the courtiers' sense of mission and their commitment to imperial expansion, administrative reorganization, and moral renewal antedated the tsar's first visit to the West (1697–98) and derived, at least in part, from their belief in Peter's personal election for the task of transfiguring the Muscovite realm. Indeed, I suggest that the tsar and his advisers continually returned to the alternatively sacred and sacrilegious male bonding rituals associated with the Transfigured Kingdom precisely because these royal spectacles constituted an integral part of the company's attempt to articulate and enact its reformist political vision.

The Petrine scenario of power could not have been formulated, much less enforced, without the active collaboration of those courtiers who kept up the illusion—a word that literally means "in play"[15]—of royal absolutism. The fact that from the very beginning some of the most important political figures of the reign—men such as F. Iu. Romodanovskii (head of Peter's secret police), F. A. Golovin (head of the Foreign Affairs Chancellery), T. N. Streshnev (head of Crown Appointments), I. A. Musin-Pushkin (de facto administrator of the Russian Orthodox Church), and N. M. Zotov (Peter's former tutor, longtime personal secretary, and chief financial administrator)—also held mock ranks in the ecclesiastical synod of the Transfigured Kingdom supports the contention that Peter's acolytes

vine grace (Greek *charis*). Max Weber, "The Sociology of Charismatic Authority," in *From Max Weber: Essays in Sociology,* trans. and ed. by H. H. Gerth and C. Wright Mills (New York, 1946), 245–52. See also B. A. Uspenskii, *Tsar' i patriarkh: kharizma vlasti v Rossii (Vizantiiskaia model' i ee russkoe peroosmyslenie)* (Moscow, 1998).

14. In his magisterial work on the self-presentation of Russian monarchs, Richard Wortman defined royal "scenarios of power" as the "individual modes of performance of the imperial myth" enacted in Russia from Peter's time onward. See Richard S. Wortman, *Scenarios of Power: Myth and Ceremony in Russian Monarchy,* 2 vols. (Princeton, 1995, 2000), 1:6–7. On the process of "elevation," defined as "an intentional and often painstaking effort to present the ruler as supreme and to vest him or her with sacral qualities," see ibid., 4; and, more generally, Clifford Geertz, "Centers, Kings, and Charisma: Reflections on the Symbolics of Power," in *Rites of Power: Symbolism, Ritual, and Politics since the Middle Ages,* ed. Sean Wilentz (Philadelphia, 1985), 13–16.

15. Johan Huizinga, *Homo Ludens: A Study of the Play Element in Culture* (New York, 1970), 11.

gave an appearance of stability to the fragile construct known as the "well-ordered police state."[16] I say "fragile" because despite its nascent bureaucratic pretensions, Peter's government, like those of his early modern European contemporaries, was still very much a personal affair. The ability to mobilize a royalist party through familial and clientage ties was the surest way of guaranteeing that a ruler's will would be done—even if that will was to realize the ideals of the cameralist *Polizeistaat.*[17] The complicated mechanism of the well-ordered police state required a divinely inspired (if not divine) creator to set it in motion;[18] and that kind of authority depended on the willingness of the monarch's followers to partake of his gift of grace.

By presenting themselves as an antinomian elite, empowered by God to go against the previously existing laws in order to perform redemptive if seemingly strange acts, the tsar's companions expressed their belief in the power of a monarch who could turn the world upside down in order to institute a radically new dispensation.[19] The origins of Russia's well-ordered police state were thus inextricably linked to the assertion of personal, ex-

16. For a classic definition of this term, see Marc Raeff, "The Well-Ordered Police State and the Development of Modernity in Seventeenth- and Eighteenth-Century Europe: An Attempt at a Comparative Approach," *American Historical Review* 80 (December 1975): 1221–43; and his *Well-Ordered Police State: Social and Institutional Change through Law in the Germanies and Russia, 1600–1800* (New Haven, 1983). See also B. I. Syromiatnikov, *"Reguliarnoe" gosudarstvo Petra I i ego ideologiia* (Moscow and Leningrad, 1943).

17. For a good introduction to work on the patronage networks and clientage systems that did much to define the limits of early modern Russian absolutism, see Bushkovitch, *Peter the Great,* 3–5; Valerie Kivelson, "Kinship Politics/Autocratic Politics: A Reconsideration of Early-Eighteenth-Century Political Culture," in *Imperial Russia: New Histories for the Empire,* ed. Jane Burbank and David L. Ransel, 5–31 (Bloomington, 1998); and Don Ostrowski, "The Façade of Legitimacy: Exchange of Power and Authority in Early Modern Russia," *Comparative Studies in Society and History* 44, no. 3 (2002): 534–63. For a cogent critique of the absolutist paradigm, see Nicholas Henshall, *The Myth of Absolutism: Change and Continuity in Early Modern European Monarchy* (London, 1992).

18. An undated cameralist memorandum that was presented to the tsar at the beginning of the eighteenth century made the case for a system of government that would work like a well-oiled machine without any need for the intervention of its inventor by specifically invoking the Almighty: "God, as a God of order, rules everything wisely and in an orderly manner with his invisible hand. The Gods of this world, or the likenesses of God's power (I am thinking of the absolutist monarchs), have to establish their forms of government in accordance with this order if they wish to enjoy the sweet fruits of a flourishing state for their great effort." A. Voskresenskii, ed., *Zakonodatel'nye akty Petra I* (Moscow and Leningrad, 1945), 1:270, cited in Hughes, *Russia,* 107.

19. By "antinomian" I mean to designate the behavior and self-understanding of those actors who believe that their special religious qualities allow them to transgress against (anti-) the established moral, political, or religious law (*nomos*) of the community in which they live. For a sociological definition of religious antinomianism, see Stephen Sharot, "The Sacredness of Sin: Antinomianism and Models of Man," *Religion* 13 (1983): 37–54. See also the historical literature about Orthodox "fools in Christ" (*iurodivye*), who transgress the communal boundaries between the sacred and the profane in order "to awaken the indifferent to eternal truths" by the "shock value" of their "performance, which is essentially a reenactment of Christ's walk with the cross." George P. Fedotov, "The Holy Fools," in *The Russian Religious Mind,* 2 vols. (Belmont, MA, 1975), 2:chap. 12; A. M. Panchenko, "Smekh kak zrelishche," in *Smekh v drevnei Rusi,* ed. D. S. Likhachev, 72–153 (Leningrad, 1984); and Richard W. F. Pope, "Fools and Folly in Old Russia," *Slavic Review* 39, no. 3 (1980): 476–81, esp. 479.

tralegal, and God-given authority; in fact, at least in this case, the flamboyant flaunting of royal charisma helped to promote, not to undermine, the ideals of modern bureaucracy. Indeed, for many of Peter's courtiers, the transformation of Muscovy into imperial Russia was as much a leap of faith as a matter of bureaucratic restructuring—that is, as much transfiguration (*preobrazhenie*) as reform (*preobrazovanie*).

Sources

The evidence on which the argument of this book is based consists of four kinds of primary sources: eyewitness accounts, official administrative documents, visual representations, and letters between the tsar and his intimates. First, and most traditional, are the narrative sources written by contemporary eyewitnesses (both native and foreign) to the burlesque spectacles staged at the court of Peter the Great. Despite the evidently biased analyses offered by uncomprehending foreign diplomats or disaffected Russian courtiers, such sources remain valuable as much for their often detailed descriptions as for their embarrassed silences; indeed, a carefully contextualized reading of these sources can provide one of the best opportunities for gauging how contemporaries understood (or misunderstood) the spectacles associated with Peter's Transfigured Kingdom.[20] The second type of source used in this book consists of the administrative paperwork related to the preparation and staging of these ceremonies. The fact that most of these records do not appear before the first decade of the eighteenth century suggests that until the court settled more or less permanently in St. Petersburg, Peter's play world was sustained by much less formal means than administrative directives or royal decrees. Like my third source—the official engravings, paintings, and drawings representing some of the ceremonies and participants of the tsar's imaginary realm—these documents illustrate the tension between the need to induct believers by means of secret ceremony and the desire to dramatize that belief in elaborate public spectacles. Particularly important for my analysis of the relationship between court spectacle and royal charisma, however, is the voluminous correspondence between the tsar and his advisers, some of which has appeared in the ongoing collection of Petrine "Letters and Papers," but much of which remains in manuscript.[21] The way I use these epistolary sources to reconstruct the relationships between the tsar and his entourage, as well as the political discourse

---

20. For a sustained defense of the importance of foreign diplomatic sources, see Bushkovitch, *Peter the Great*, 7–10.

21. *PiB*, 13 vols. to date (St. Petersburg, 1887–). Nineteenth-century copies of many of the unpublished letters can be found in SPb F IRI RAN, f. 279. For the publication history of the "Letters and Papers of Peter the Great," see E. P. Pod''iapol'skaia, "Ob istorii i nauchnom znachenii izdaniia 'Pis'ma i bumagi imperatora Petra Velikogo,'" in *Arkheograficheskii ezhegodnik za 1972 god*, 56–70 (Moscow, 1974).

by which these relationships are expressed, is perhaps the most method-
ologically innovative (and potentially most controversial) aspect of this
study, and therefore requires further commentary.

Before I undertook my archival research, I had assumed that the so-called
Most Comical and All-Drunken Council (*vseshuteishii i vsep'ianeishii
sobor*) of Peter the Great was a sort of playful institution, with a more or
less fixed staff and its own archival holdings, and hence that it could be approached in the traditional ways in which previous historians had approached other Petrine institutions. That sense was reinforced by both his-
toriographical convention and the existence of a separate file in the Moscow
Archive of Ancient Documents specifically devoted to the "Prince-Pope and
His Council."[22] As I quickly discovered, however, this file was not the long-
lost archive of the Most Drunken Council but an idiosyncratic and rather
haphazard selection of letters between the tsar and his courtiers (dating
from around 1708 to 1724), which gained its sense of coherence from the
fact that it was organized into a separate file (*delo*) by an eighteenth-century
archivist, Prince M. M. Shcherbatov,[23] and published as a separate case
study by a nineteenth-century popular historian, M. I. Semevskii.[24] After
reading this file, as well as a plethora of other letters and documents associated with Petrine court spectacles, I came to realize that the Drunken Council was not an institution at all, parodic or otherwise; it was a discourse,

22. RGADA, f. 9, otd. I, kn. 67.
23. Prince M. M. Shcherbatov (1733–90) put the letters together in the course of his work
as Catherine II's court historiographer. By creating a separate, topical collection of "merry letters" (*uveselitel'nye pis'ma*) Prince Shcherbatov violated the general chronological organization of the Cabinet Archive (based on a division between incoming and outgoing correspondence) and contributed to this collection's peculiar position among the business papers of
Peter's personal chancellery. Now they stood out as archival evidence of, at best, the private in-
dulgence and, at worst, the personal vice of a great man of public virtue. In adopting this particular cataloging strategy, Prince Shcherbatov reproduced on the level of archival organization his ambivalent personal and professional evaluation of the "great" monarch and his
"civilizing" reforms, a position that was most clearly articulated in his unpublished critique of
Catherinian court society, "On the Decline of Morals in Russia" (1787). For Shcherbatov's unpublished explanatory "Notice [*izvestie*] about the Prince-Pope and the Letters of His Council," see RO RNB, f. 450, ll. 10–11. Prince M. M. Shcherbatov was the grandson of one of
Peter's mock arch-hierarchs, Prince Iu. F. Shcherbatov (1686–1737). See Appendix 2.
24. A selection of the documents collected by M. M. Shcherbatov was published in a heavily expurgated version by M. I. Semevskii, the editor of *Russkaia starina*. See M. I. Semevskii,
"Petr Velikii—kak iumorist (Novye materialy dlia kharakteristiki Petra)," *Svetoch''* 9, no. 2
(1861): 1–50 (second pagination); this article later appeared in expanded and revised form in
Semevskii's own journal as "Shutki i potekhi Petra Velikago. Petr Velikii—kak iumorist,"
Russkaia starina 6 (June 1872): 855–92; and then again as "Petr Velikii kak iumorist" in his
collected essays on eighteenth-century Russia, *Ocherki i razskazy iz russkoi istorii XVIII v.:
Slovo i delo! 1700–1725*, 2nd rev. ed., 278–334 (St. Petersburg, 1884; rpt. Moscow, 1991).
The publication of Semevskii's article was perhaps the most important milestone in the histori-
ographical institutionalization of the Unholy Council since Shcherbatov's discovery of the
Council of the Prince-Pope; for not only did Semevskii coin the collective term by which Peter's
burlesque amusements came to be known in Russian historiography, but he also helped publi-
cize and defend the idea that Peter had founded an institution (*uchrezhdenie*) called the Most
Comical and All-Drunken Council.

that is, a way of speaking about royal authority that was constitutive of political relations as much as a reflection of the way power was actually distributed and organized at the court of Peter the Great. Consequently, it did not lend itself to a clear-cut institutional history; any attempt to explore it would have to engage with the languages of power and the discursive practices employed by Peter and his courtiers.[25]

The nature of the sources also allowed me to address two of the most stubborn methodological problems raised by Richard Wortman's approach to Russian imperial scenarios: the questions of authorship and reception.[26] Anyone who has worked with the rare and notoriously reticent autobiographical accounts of early modern Russian courtiers knows how difficult it is to document all assertions of motive on the part of contemporary actors, not to mention all assertions of reception (or perception) of those original intentions. Even the most conscientious source study will not always yield this kind of information, and scholars must often content themselves with the most plausible of possible interpretations. This is particularly true in the case of the carnivalesque ceremonies associated with the Transfigured Kingdom, which remain opaque to those who were not inducted into the brotherhood of believers in the charismatic authority of Peter the Great and who therefore are not in on the seriousness of the game being played. Consequently, even such personally authored documents as the letters between the tsar and his intimates do not provide conclusive evidence of Peter's intentions. They do, however, offer a rich base from which to reconstruct what Ernst H. Kantorowicz once described as the mutually binding "double-edged" language of a "court coterie"—a language that is "by turns veiling and revealing," self-conscious of both its playful theatricality and its political significance. In Kantorowicz's apt formulation, "if the phrase of the worshipper is taken too seriously it immediately becomes a jest, but if it is treated as a courtly game it suddenly is fully and literally intended."[27]

Peter's correspondence with his courtiers, and in particular with the members of his company, demonstrates just this kind of self-conscious and ironic wordplay on the part of both the letter writer and the addressee.[28] In

25. My definition of "discourse" relies (at least in part) on Michel Foucault's discussion of the "mechanics of power." See Michel Foucault, "Truth and Power," in *Power/Knowledge: Selected Interviews and Other Writings, 1972–1977,* ed. Colin Gordon, 115–16 (New York, 1980).

26. For an excellent summary of the methodological issues raised by Wortman's approach to the Russian monarchy, see Mikhail Dolbilov, "The Political Mythology of Autocracy: Scenarios of Power and the Role of the Autocrat," *Kritika: Explorations in Russian and Eurasian History* 2 (Fall 2001): 773–95; Richard Wortman, "Reply to Mikhail Dolbilov," ibid., 797–801; and the roundtable discussion "Kak sdelana istoriia: Obsuzhdenie knigi R. Uortmana," in *Novoe literaturnoe obozrenie* 56 (2002): 42–66.

27. E. H. Kantorowicz, *Frederick the Second, 1194–1250,* trans. E. O. Lorimer (London, 1931), 522.

28. The unique qualities of the epistolary genre in general and Petrine correspondence in particular are the topic of N. I. Gainulina, *Epistoliarnoe nasledie Petra Velikogo v istorii russkogo literaturnogo iazyka XVIII veka (Istoriko-lingvisticheskii aspekt)* (Almaty, 1995).

such an intimate epistolary exchange, a playful allusion to a specific sacred text reveals as much as an annotated reference in a biblical concordance. For in addition to demonstrating that Peter was well versed in the Bible (an important fact in itself, considering the oft-repeated descriptions of Peter as an irreligious secularizer), such casual asides demonstrate the degree to which biblical and liturgical references were taken for granted in the shared discourse of the in-group. A reader does not have to agree fully with a particular interpretation of a specific allusion invoked in an epistolary exchange to understand the importance of this discourse as a source of collective self-assertion and male bonding for the denizens of a peripatetic, martial, and libertine court; or to acknowledge the fact that the religious allusions in these texts are fundamental to the rhetorical transfer of sacrality by which the members of Peter's entourage come to view themselves as a secular priesthood of believers in the tsar's charismatic authority. This type of symbolic transference from things ecclesiastical to things monarchical has been described by other scholars (most notably in Kantorowicz's magisterial study of medieval political theology) without eliciting the criticism that the author was reading too much into the sources.[29] I suggest that the same can be said of the private correspondence between Peter and his courtiers. Indeed, it is precisely their familiarity with the language of the in-group that distinguished Peter's company from other courtiers, and that demonstrated their intimate knowledge of the bacchanalian mysteries of state that lay at the heart of Peter's Transfigured Kingdom.[30]

Historiography

By highlighting the fact that the tsar and his entourage relied on court spectacles to assert the sacrality of royal authority, my study not only provides a needed corrective to the secularist bias of the historiography on the reforms of Peter the Great, but also contributes to the growing literature about the role of ritual in the creation of political order in early modern Europe. My understanding of the relationship between power and spectacle at the late Muscovite court derives partly from Norbert Elias's insights into the

29. E. H. Kantorowicz, *The King's Two Bodies: A Study in Medieval Political Theology* (Princeton, 1957). Kantorowicz's methodological innovations were applied to Russian monarchy by his student Michael Cherniavsky, *Tsar and People: Studies in Russian Myths* (New Haven, 1961); and taken up, with a renewed focus on the sacralization of the tsar, by B. A. Uspenskii and V. M. Zhivov, " 'Tsar' i Bog': Semioticheskie aspekty sakralizatsii monarkha v Rossii," in B. A. Uspenskii, *Izbrannye trudy*, 2nd ed., 1:205–337 (Moscow, 1996); Stephen L. Baehr, *The Paradise Myth in Eighteenth-Century Russia: Utopian Patterns in Early Secular Russian Literature and Culture* (Stanford, 1991); and Iurii Kagarlitskii, "Sakralizatsiia kak priem: Resursy ubeditel'nosti i vliiatel' nosti imperskogo diskursa v Rossii XVIII veka," *Novoe literaturnoe obozrenie* 38 (1999): 66–77.

30. For the notion of "mysteries of state," see E. H. Kantorowicz, "Mysteries of State: An Absolutist Concept and Its Late Mediaeval Origins," *Harvard Theological Review* 48 (January 1955): 65–91.

functioning of European court society—a spatially and temporally bounded set of social relations that, Elias argued, could be approached with the same analytical tools as other historical figurations, such as the village, the city, and the nation-state.[31] My argument also owes much to the work of those literary and art historians who elucidate the underlying connections between art and power, that is, between the staging of royal festivities and the political organization of court society (and, by implication, of the early modern state as well). Scholars such as Frances Yates and Roy Strong have suggested that when the aristocratic participants in the cults of absolutist patron-rulers sang the praises and danced to the glory of their respective monarchs, they literally embodied, replayed, and reinforced the dependence of court society, and by metonymic extension the realm as a whole, on the person of the monarch. In this interpretation, royal spectacles served as much to discipline the bodies of courtiers as to enlighten participants/viewers about the values and methods of their official patrons.[32]

In the social figuration described by scholars of the early modern European court, even such strange (to our eyes) comparisons as that between a Christian monarch and the Roman god of wine could be interpreted as apposite political allegories about royal rule.[33] This is precisely how, for example, Diego Velásquez, the most famous artist at the court of the Spanish Habsburgs, intended his painting *Bacchus in Iberia* to be interpreted by his royal patron, King Philip IV. In Velásquez's painting, executed in the first half of the seventeenth century, the Catholic king appeared in the allegorical guise of Bacchus, offering a glass of wine to his loyal followers. This painting represents not a dissolute bunch of drunkards, as the popular title of this work (*Los Borrachos*) would indicate, but rather a virtuous company (or confraternity) that champions the cause of a higher being—a being who, in turn, rewards them for their devotion.[34] Similarly, we know that in his youth even the fastidious Louis XIV appeared alongside the Roman god of wine at a court ballet called *The Festivals of Bacchus*. Here the young

31. Norbert Elias, *The Court Society,* trans. Edmund Jephcott (New York, 1983); and his *Civilizing Process: A History of Manners,* trans. Edmund Jephcott (New York, 1978). For an insightful critique, see Jeroen Duindam, *Myths of Power: Norbert Elias and the Early Modern European Court* (Amsterdam, 1999).

32. Frances A. Yates, *Astraea: The Imperial Theme in the Sixteenth Century* (London, 1985); Roy Strong, *Art and Power: Renaissance Festivals, 1450–1650* (Woodbridge, Suffolk, 1984), 185–215; Mark Franko, *Dance as Text: Ideologies of the Baroque Body* (Cambridge, 1993); and Kristiaan P. Aercke, *Gods of Play: Baroque Festive Performances as Rhetorical Discourse* (Albany, 1994), 253–70. My thinking on spectacles of power has also been shaped by David Starkey, "Representation through Intimacy: A Study in the Symbolism of Monarchy and Court Office in Early-Modern England," in *Symbols and Sentiments: Cross-Cultural Studies in Symbolism,* ed. Ioan Lewis, 187–224 (London, 1977); and Clifford Geertz, *Negara: The Theatre State in Nineteenth-Century Bali* (Princeton, 1980).

33. For the notion of political allegory, see Paul Kléber Monod, *The Power of Kings: Monarchy and Religion in Europe, 1589–1715* (New Haven, 1999), 54–57, 340n74; for an example of a specifically bacchanalian political allegory, see ibid., 363n192.

34. Steven N. Orso, *Velásquez, "Los Borrachos," and Painting at the Court of Philip IV* (Cambridge, 1993).

Sun King was playing out a well-established tradition in French royal pane-gyrics, according to which Bacchus, "the world-conquering God of the East," embodied the theme of France's imperial expansion.[35] In fact, the po-litical appropriation of the image of Bacchus was not confined to the courts of these classically minded European monarchs; for by the third quarter of the seventeenth century the Roman god of wine already appeared in a Yule-tide theatrical production staged in front of none other than the "most pious" (*tishaishii*) Russian Orthodox tsar Aleksei Mikhailovich himself. It was but a short step from this initial foray into the discursive practices as-sociated with Baroque appropriations of Bacchus to the bacchanalian tri-umph witnessed by the imperial diplomat Korb during the dedication of Peter's suburban pleasure palace in the winter of 1699.[36]

Indeed, I propose that the war games, mock religious processions, and carnivalesque inversions of the political order staged at Peter's court fit into the context of the pan-European Baroque court culture described by schol-ars of early modern monarchy.[37] As I see it, Peter used the institutions of his personal household to surround himself with a new group of people, chosen according to his own inclinations and to the contemporary ideas of specta-cle.[38] In the process, he reorganized the typical amusements of a seven-teenth-century monarch—court theater, war games, dwarves, and jesters—and transformed them into means of mobilizing support for royal policies, keeping courtiers in line by means of informal sanctions, and policing (and if necessary punishing) those in disfavor. But in the cultural context of Mus-covite Russia the royal amusements organized by Peter and his closest polit-ical advisers did more than that: they highlighted the need for and justified the transfiguration of the realm by presenting the monarch's strange acts as the creative deeds of a demiurge bringing order out of chaos. Thus the war games and religious burlesques of Peter the Great, like the court spectacles

35. Charles Blitzer, *Age of Kings* (New York, 1967), 129; Yates, *Astraea*, 140–46.

36. For another example of a royalist bacchanalian triumph, see Thomas Jordan, "Bacchus Festival, or a New Medley . . ." (1660), in *Illustrations of Early English Popular Literature*, ed. J. P. Collier, vol. 2, no. 6 (London, 1864), a "musical representation" staged by the wine mer-chants of London in honor of General George Monck (the commanding officer of the royalist troops, whose march on and occupation of the capital facilitated the peaceful restoration of the English monarchy after more than a decade of civil war and religious strife).

37. For a pioneering attempt to situate Peter's reign within the context of the Russian Baroque, see A. A. Morozov, "Problema barokko v russkoi literature XVII–nachala XVIII veka (sostoianie voprosa i zadachi izucheniia)," *Russkaia literatura* 3 (1962): 3–38; and D. S. Likhachev, "Byla li epokha petrovskikh reform pereryvom v razvitii russkoi kul'tury?" in *Sla-vianskie kul'tury v epokhu formirovaniia i razvitiia slavianskikh natsii XVIII–XIX vv. Materi-aly mezhdunarodnoi konferentsii IuNESKO*, 170–74 (Moscow, 1978), published in English as "The Petrine Reforms and the Development of Russian Culture," trans. Avril Pyman, *Cana-dian-American Slavic Studies* 13, no. 1–2 (1979): 230–34. See also L. I. Sazonova, *Poeziia russkogo barokko (vtoraia polovina XVII–nachalo XVIII v.)* (Moscow, 1991).

38. For a discussion of contemporary notions of spectacle in late Muscovite Russia, see P. N. Berkov, "Iz istorii russkoi teatral'noi terminologii XVII–XVIII vekov ('Komediia,' 'inter-mediia,' 'dialog,' 'igrishche' i dr.)," *Trudy otdela drevnerusskoi literatury* 11 (1955): 280–99; and, more generally, Sazonova, *Poeziia russkogo barokko*, passim.

of his early modern European contemporaries, were neither frivolous diversions nor Enlightenment propaganda, but rather the very stuff of rule.

Bringing together (as I do) such disparate phenomena as war games and religious parodies under the rubric of the Transfigured Kingdom and making these spectacles an essential part of the Petrine scenario of power challenges previous interpretations, which tend to fall into two general types: the utilitarian and the propagandistic.[39] When not simply dismissing the "clownish" and "brutish" spectacles staged at Peter's court as "disgusting ritual" too "foul" to appear in print,[40] the utilitarian interpretation stresses the extent to which Peter's so-called childhood amusements prefigured the serious reforms he undertook as an adult. Not surprisingly, scholars who espouse this view focus almost exclusively on the war games carried out by Peter and his "toy soldiers" (*poteshnye*) at the end of the seventeenth century, rather than on the contemporaneous and inextricably linked organization of the mock ecclesiastical council. In this view, the military maneuvers staged on the grounds of the royal estates outside of Moscow modeled the eventual reorganization of the Russian imperial army and provided the training grounds for the troops that went on to expand the Russian realm.[41] Indeed, there is some contemporary evidence from no less an authority than Peter himself that the maneuvers at Kozhukhovo (1694), the biggest war games of his entire reign, served precisely such a purpose. "We jested at Kozhukhovo; now we are going to play [for real] at Azov" (*Shutili pod Kozhukhovym, a teper' pod Azov igrat' edem*), the tsar wrote in a letter to one of the members of his company on the eve of the first, unsuccessful siege of that Turkish fortress. As we will see in Chapter 2, however, neither this nor any other of Peter's

39. For a succinct but thorough summary of the historiography on Petrine amusements in general and the Drunken Council in particular, see Hughes, *Russia*, 249–57; and her *Playing Games: The Alternative History of Peter the Great*, SSEES Occasional Papers no. 41 (London, 2000). See also Russell Zguta, "Peter I's 'Most Drunken Synod of Fools and Jesters,'" *Jahrbücher für Geschichte Osteuropas* 21 (1973): 18–28; Paul Hollingsworth, "The 'All-Drunken, All-Joking Synod': Carnival and Rulership in the Reign of Peter the Great," paper presented at the seminar "The Image of Peter the Great in Russian History and Thought," University of California, Berkeley, 1982; and idem, "Carnival and Rulership in the Reign of Peter the Great," paper presented at the national convention of the American Historical Association, December 1985. V. M. Zhivov deserves special mention for returning to the archival sources and for emphasizing the special symbolic and historical significance of Peter's so-called amusements for a proper understanding of the tsar's cultural reforms. See V. M. Zhivov, "Kul'turnye reformy v sisteme preobrazovanii Petra I," in *Iz istorii russkoi kul'tury*, ed. A. D. Koshelev, 3:528–83 (Moscow, 1996); and his "Dopolnitel'nye primechaniia," in *Razyskaniia v oblasti i predistorii russkoi kul'tury*, 427–35 (Moscow, 2002), esp. 428–30.

40. B. H. Sumner, *Peter the Great and the Emergence of Russia* (London, 1958), 29.

41. This connection was originally made in Russian historiography by G.-F. M[iller]., "Izvestie o nachale Preobrazhenskogo i Semenovskogo polkov gvardii," in *Sobranie raznykh zapisok i sochinenii, sluzhashchikh k dostavleniiu polnago svedeniia o zhizni i deianiiakh gosudaria imperatora Petra Velikago*, 7:299–328 (St. Petersburg, 1787). This view was shared by the dean of Soviet Petrine studies, N. I. Pavlenko, "Petr I (K izucheniiu sotsial'no-politicheskikh vzgliadov)," in *Rossiia v period reform Petra I*, 40–102 (Moscow, 1973), and *Petr Velikii*, 26, 47.

war games can be understood apart from the sacred parodies associated with the court's antinomian religious rhetoric—a fact brought home most forcefully when we realize that the tsar signed this very missive as "humble deacon Peter" (*smirennyi diakon Petr*), appending his pseudonymous nickname alongside that of another prominent member of his mock ecclesiastical council, the "Most Holy Metropolitan Gideon of Kiev" (*preosviashchennyi mitropolit Kievskii Gideon*).[42]

When this side of Petrine political discourse is addressed, the utilitarian explanation imperceptibly shades off into the propagandistic one. In this interpretation, Peter's parodies of Russian Orthodox ritual appear as important hallmarks in the tsar's program of secularization, an enlightened (if not yet Enlightenment) project directed against the supposedly obscurantist church and its nominal head, the patriarch.[43] However, the fact that the Unholy Council first appeared in 1691–92, long before Peter ever contemplated abolishing the patriarchate, and lasted some four years after Peter decided to institute the government-controlled Ecclesiastical College (in 1721), suggests that there is no straight line between this parody of the Muscovite Holy Council and Peter's supposedly secularizing religious reforms.[44] As if to answer this objection, a much more sophisticated version of the propagandistic argument treats Peter's sacred parodies as examples of "antibehavior,"[45] a form of semiotic violence by which the tsar attempted to ridicule and thereby discredit the tradition-bound, religious Russian past in order to propagandize the bright, secular, and Westernized future. However, the binary nature of the divisions implied in this formulation (past and future, traditional and modern, Russian and Western) betrays the degree to which this interpretation is indebted not only to structuralist polarities but also to modern debates about Russia's special path, debates that have less to do with how Peter and his contemporaries understood their world than with contemporary ideological constructions. Even the very Soviet notion

42. Peter to F. M. Apraksin, c. April 1695, in *PiB*, 1:28 (no. 35); cf. Peter to Apraksin, April 16, 1695, ibid., 29 (no. 36). For an insightful discussion of this quote in relation to the organization and planning of the 1694 war games, see Richard H. Warner, "The Kozhukhovo Campaign of 1694; or, The Conquest of Moscow by Preobrazhenskoe," *Jahrbücher für Geschichte Osteuropas* 13 (1965): 487–96, esp. 493–94.

43. For the classic statement of this position, see I. I. Golikov, *Dopolnenie k "Deianiiam Petra Velikogo"* . . . (Moscow, 1794), 12:325. The most sophisticated restatement of this interpretation can be found in Reinhard Wittram, "Peters des Grossen Verhältnis zur Religion und den Kirchen: Glaube, Vernunft, Leidenschaft," *Historische Zeitschrift* 173 (1952): 266; and his *Peter I, Czar und Kaiser: Zur Geschichte Peters des Grossen in seiner Zeit* (Göttingen, 1964), 1:106–11.

44. This important point was first made in Cracraft, *Church Reform*, 13. See also V. M. Zhivov, "Church Reforms in the Reign of Peter the Great," trans. W. Gareth Jones, in *Russia in the Reign of Peter the Great: Old and New Perspectives*, ed. Anthony Cross, 1:65–75 (Cambridge, 1998).

45. For a definition of this notion, see B. A. Uspenskii, "Anti-povedenie v kul'ture drevnei Rusi," in his *Izbrannye trudy*, 2nd rev. ed., 1:460–76 (Moscow, 1996); as well as his "Historia sub specie semioticae," ibid., 71–82.

of parody as a form of propaganda assumes the existence of a public often missing during the staging of the most important of Petrine political sacraments (such as the installation of the first mock patriarch in 1692), an assumption more appropriate to the arena of modern mass politics than to that of the early modern court.[46]

Neither of these two major approaches is wrong. Indeed, both capture important aspects of the spectacles staged at the court of Peter the Great, most notably their intensely political, deliberate, and persistent nature. Both the utilitarian and the propagandistic interpretations, however, condense the polyvalent (that is to say, Baroque) complexity of Petrine political theology to a few anachronistic antinomies (such as seriousness vs. play or religiosity vs. secularism). At the same time, by reifying Peter's parodies as the activities of a Drunken Council, such approaches reduce a discourse that permeated nearly every aspect of the reign to a peripheral if not downright psychopathological phenomenon. But any interpretive strategy that attributes the persistence and intensity of these spectacles merely to Peter's psyche, whether playful or damaged, only begs the questions of how this particular discourse came to inform the actions of the tsar and his company in the first place and why Russian courtiers played along for so long.[47] Indeed, none of the previously cited interpretations convincingly explains why Peter and his company continued to engage in this so-called play for more than thirty years, well after the tsar had abandoned his childhood amusements, reached maturity as a self-conscious reformer, and begun institutionalizing his famous reforms.

Recognizing the significant lacunae in our understanding of Petrine political theology, I place such supposedly marginal phenomena as the spectacles associated with the Transfigured Kingdom at the center of the story of Peter's reforms. Taking an anthropologically and semiotically informed view of Muscovite court society allows us to see two things: first, that war games and sacred parodies constituted an important part of Petrine court culture, and second, that they served as a means of both personal and collective empowerment, giving the tsar and his company the ability to articulate, move forward, and eventually carry out the projects they at first only dreamed about. As we will see, even when things went completely against Peter and his entourage, they succeeded in staging spectacles that celebrated moments of divine favor, when (in their interpretation) God broke through everyday reality to show them that Peter was the man whom they should

46. Zhivov, "Kul'turnye reformy," 529. For a cogent critique of the propagandistic approach to court spectacles, as well as a discussion of how this approach is often allied with the absolutist paradigm, see John Adamson, "The Making of the *Ancien-Régime* Court, 1500–1700," in *The Princely Courts of Europe: Ritual, Politics and Culture under the Ancien Régime, 1500–1750,* ed. Adamson (London, 1999), 34–35, 40.

47. For an interpretation that stresses Peter's undeniable dark side, see Cracraft, *Church Reform,* 18–19; and M. S. Anderson, *Peter the Great,* 2nd ed. (London, 1995), 121–22. On Peter's black sense of humor, see Semevskii, "Petr Velikii—kak iumorist," 279–334.

follow, that their cause was just, and that his mission was right. Such spectacles helped to commemorate moments of epiphany and to reinforce the shared experience of belonging to a chivalrous brotherhood of true believers in Russia's own anointed one.[48] Indeed, far from being a sign of Peter's irreligion or drive toward secularization, these spectacles demonstrated how fundamentally Peter and his company were indebted to late Muscovite religious justifications of political rule.

This enormous debt is the topic of the first two chapters, which examine the highly charged allegorical language in which the distaff sides of the Russian royal house conducted the succession struggle that culminated in the equivocal triumph of Tsar Peter Alekseevich, the Naryshkin candidate. Focusing on the rhetoric of Peter's most ardent supporters, Chapter 1 shows how a particular set of notions about family honor and royal charisma came to justify his candidacy at a time when his claims to the throne were vulnerable on both counts. Peter's subversion of this exaggerated emphasis on Muscovite family values and the resultant foundation of the Transfigured Kingdom form the subject of Chapter 2. The next three chapters analyze the spread of the Transfigured Kingdom in both its geographical and rhetorical aspects, demonstrating how, over the course of the Great Northern War (1700–1721), the discursive practices that had originally served as a way of asserting the charisma of a youthful monarch and his retinue against the Muscovite establishment became part and parcel of the effort to create a chivalrous new elite, committed to the ideals enshrined during the founding of St. Petersburg. The reason why the apotheosis of Russia's new imperial capital, its cosmopolitan elite, and its royal namesake took the form of an elaborate jester wedding, which until then had served primarily as a private joke among the members of Peter's entourage, is the subject of Chapter 4. This chapter also includes a discussion of the tsar's own dynastic scenario, a family drama that sets the stage for the tragic denouement of the book, which ends with an analysis of the connection between the mock ceremonies immediately preceding the trial of the heir apparent, the abolition of the patriarchate, and Peter's assumption of the title "Father of the Fatherland" (Chapter 5).

In sum, the organization of the book reflects my conviction that an investigation of the language employed by the tsar and his advisers in ritual, visual, and epistolary texts offers a fruitful way of analyzing the processes of political legitimation at the court of Peter the Great. Focusing on the rhetorical mobilization and spectacular dramatization of royal charisma, I look closely at the way Peter and his entourage transformed the evolving Muscovite discourse on the sanctity of royal authority into a bold assertion of the tsar's personal election and their own sense of belonging to a commu-

48. For an explicit defense of the idea that tsars deserve to be referred to as "gods (*bozi*) and christs (*khristy*) [i.e., the anointed ones]," see Feofan (Prokopovich), "Slovo v nedeliu osmuiunadesiat' . . ." (October 23, 1717), in his *Sochineniia*, ed. I. P. Eremin (Moscow and Leningrad, 1961), 84–85.

nity of true believers. I suggest that this community appears as an instantiation of a new form of sociability, one focused less on family or clan ties than on individual merit and personal allegiance to God's chosen military leader. These two elements of the new legitimizing language initially associated with Peter's play world—the charismatic and the chivalrous—are the leitmotivs of my investigation into the ideological underpinnings of royal absolutism at the late Muscovite and early imperial Russian court.

If this book succeeds in demonstrating that Petrine parodies were not trivial or embarrassing asides in the teleology of Russia's modernization but rather crucial constituents of a distinctively Petrine court culture—a culture that is more complicated and more interesting, I would say more Baroque, than traditional descriptions of its supposed Westernizing and secularizing character would allow—it will have accomplished its purpose.

I   *The Naryshkin Restoration*

The discursive practices associated with the Transfigured Kingdom of Peter the Great can be traced back to the late seventeenth-century struggle for succession, an extremely volatile situation in which court factions vied to enthrone their own candidate and of which the young Peter Alekseevich was largely the unwitting beneficiary. The historical example of the Time of Troubles (*smuta*)—a period of foreign invasion and civil war that immediately preceded the "miraculous" restoration of royal rule through the divinely inspired election of the Romanov dynasty—informed the actions of nearly all the leading political actors during this period of instability.[1] Even the conspirators who organized the court coups of 1682 and 1689, who had less reason than anyone else to see their opportunistic political tactics as unconscious echoes of the events of a century ago, sought to take advantage of the historical paradigm according to which violence served as divine retribution for the sins of unruly subjects, wicked counselors, and heretical pretenders to the throne—the scapegoats of an original holy community of Russian Orthodox Christians.[2]

In this context, the question of who would inherit the throne of Moscow appeared much more than a family quarrel between the in-laws of Tsar

---

1. Chester S. L. Dunning, *Russia's First Civil War: The Time of Troubles and the Founding of the Romanov Dynasty* (University Park, PA, 2001). For a discussion of late Muscovite interpretations of this formative period see Daniel Rowland, "The Problem of Advice in Muscovite Tales about the Time of Troubles," *Russian History/Histoire russe* 6, no. 2 (1979): 259–83.

2. Maureen Perrie, *Pretenders and Popular Monarchism in Early Modern Russia* (Cambridge, 1995). For an insightful analysis of the relationship between scapegoating and the assertion of religious community, see René Girard, *Violence and the Sacred,* trans. Patrick Gregory (Baltimore, 1977); and Paul Kléber Monod, *The Power of Kings: Monarchy and Religion in Europe, 1589–1715* (New Haven, 1999), 14–15, 71, 88–89, 127.

Aleksei Mikhailovich. Or rather, the dispute between the Miloslavskiis, Aleksei's in-laws by his first marriage, and the Naryshkins, his in-laws by his second marriage, replayed and served to symbolize the much larger generational, political, and religious conflicts taking place within the Muscovite elite as a whole.[3] Both sides of the succession struggle understood that the resolution of the family quarrel involved taking a particular stance vis-à-vis the reformist legacy of Tsar Aleksei Mikhailovich. Whether this legacy was understood literally, as the real estate bequeathed by Russia's royal father, or figuratively, as the grace bestowed by the divine Father, the post-Alekseevan succession necessarily touched upon the social and ideological bases of Romanov rule. In practice the struggle for the throne took the form of a dispute over which of Aleksei Mikhailovich's children could oversee the "restoration" of his legacy. The men who organized the court coup that secured the succession for the Naryshkin line of the Russian royal family used a criminal investigation into the alleged conspiracy against Tsar Peter Alekseevich to present the overthrow of the regency of his half sister, Tsarevna Sof'ia Alekseevna, as the restoration of divinely ordained paternal order to a royal house disrupted by the topsy-turvy rule of a female usurper. By parodying what they described as the pompous and hypocritical conventions of the regent and her government, the supporters of the candidacy of Peter Alekseevich sought to impugn Sof'ia Alekseevna's commitment to the program of imperial renovation and religious enlightenment begun under Aleksei Mikhailovich and to demonstrate their own candidate's impeccable qualifications for the post.

In view of the highly charged figurative language used to legitimate (some would say sacralize) the new Muscovite ruling house from at least the middle of the seventeenth century,[4] it is not surprising that the criteria by which one could distinguish which candidate was divinely chosen to rule and what constituted his or her "election" was articulated most clearly during the course of an ecclesiastical debate over the central mystery of the Christian faith, the Eucharist. This court-sponsored theological debate was the crucible in which the loose coalition that put the future Peter the Great on the Muscovite throne forged its own legitimation as well as a critique of the religious and foreign policies of its opponents in the succession struggle. Indeed, we can understand neither the rhetoric in which the leaders of the Naryshkin restoration justified the legitimacy of their coup nor the criteria by which they determined the charismatic status of their candidate for the

3. For an excellent survey of these larger issues, see Nancy Shields Kollmann, *By Honor Bound: State and Society in Early Modern Russia* (Ithaca, 1999), chaps. 4–6, Epilogue.

4. For an argument that places the sacralization of royal authority squarely within the context of the Russian Baroque, see V. M. Zhivov and B. A. Uspenskii, "Tsar' i Bog: Semiotich-eskie aspekty sakralizatsii monarkha v Rossii," in Uspenskii, *Izbrannye trudy*, 2nd ed., 1:205–337 (Moscow, 1996); and their "Zur Spezifik des Barock in Russland: Das Verfahren der Äquivokation in der russischen Poesie des 18. Jahrhunderts," trans. A. Kaiser, in *Slavische Barockliteratur II: Gedenkschrift für Dmitrij Tschizewskij (1894–1977)*, ed. Renate Lachmann, 25–56 (Munich, 1983).

Muscovite throne without analyzing the seemingly irrelevant and abstruse theological question of the exact moment during the Orthodox liturgy when the sacramental bread and wine is transformed into the mystical body and blood of the Saviour—the so-called moment of transubstantiation.

The Compromise of 1682

In April 1682, immediately after the unexpected death of Aleksei Mikhailovich's hand-picked successor (his eldest son, Tsar Fedor), a cabal of conspirators led by the Naryshkin side of the royal family attempted to put Tsarevich Peter Alekseevich on the throne of Muscovy, ahead of his elder half brother, Ivan Alekseevich. On April 27 Patriarch Ioakim (Savelov) and the Naryshkins presented Tsarevich Peter Alekseevich as the next Orthodox tsar in front of a hastily convoked and largely ceremonial *zemskii sobor* (assembly of the land) consisting of royal courtiers, chancellery clerks, and Moscow merchants.[5] However, this halfhearted attempt to invoke the waning tradition of popular acclamations (and thereby to forestall any possible questions about the legitimacy of the Naryshkin candidate) could not stifle the growing unrest among the rank-and-file members of the plebeian musketeer (*strel'tsy*) units garrisoned in and around Moscow or quell the increasingly persistent rumors that the elder (and hence more legitimate) "true" tsar had been murdered by a Naryshkin "usurper."[6] Indeed, despite the apparent pragmatism of the coup plotters, their concerted effort to bypass the mentally and physically handicapped Ivan in favor of his ten-year-old half brother, Peter, turned out to be a miserable failure. For many of the Naryshkin conspirators and their supporters, it also turned out to be fatal.

The timing of the urban uprising sparked by the machinations of Patriarch Ioakim and the Naryshkins—the uprising began on May 15, the same day as the murder of Tsarevich Dmitrii of Uglich, the grand prince whose suspicious death triggered the original Time of Troubles—demonstrates the degree to which the privileged military units of Moscow musketeers shared in the founding myths of the Romanov dynasty.[7] Shrewdly exploiting the factional divisions within the ruling elite to press their claims against the Russian government, which was then pursuing a highly unpopular program

5. For the best summary of these developments, see Lindsey Hughes, *Sophia, Regent of Russia, 1657–1704* (New Haven, 1990), 52–53.

6. Equating I. K. Naryshkin with Boris Godunov, the usurper who was reputed to have murdered the last Riurikid heir and sparked the original Time of Troubles, popular rumors accused Naryshkin of trying on the royal regalia, insulting the Russian royal family, and plotting against the life of the Miloslavskii tsarevich. See ibid., 59–60, 285n43.

7. Ibid., 62. One of the official contemporary accounts of the events of May 1682, compiled in the Crown Appointments Department (Razriad), was even titled "Time of Troubles" ("Smutnoe vremia"). See "Zapisnaia kniga razriadnogo prikaza za 15 maia–konets dek. 1682," cited ibid., 285n64.

of military reorganization—a program that prefigured the reforms eventually introduced during the reign of Peter the Great—several regiments of musketeers rose up against their noble commanders.[8] Encouraged by the supporters of the still very much alive elder tsarevich, the mutinous troops invaded the inner sanctum of the Muscovite Kremlin, dispatched several of their most hated governors (as well as some innocent bystanders), and finally, after three days of terrible bloodshed, called for Ivan's coronation alongside his younger half brother. In this way the lower-class rebels sought to sanction through religious ceremony what they had accomplished through force of arms. Usurping the electoral power so jealously guarded by the defenders of Russian monarchical absolutism, the rebels thus reenacted the original, founding moment of the covenant between the Romanov dynasty and its Orthodox subjects.

Frightened into submission, the Naryshkins acceded to the demands of their political rivals, the Miloslavskiis, and the latter's (temporary) lower-class allies. In exchange for sparing their lives, the few surviving members of the Naryshkin clan were forced to retire from the arena of Muscovite politics, and the Russian Orthodox patriarch was forced to perform an unheard-of dual coronation.[9] The ruling elite's accession to this unprecedented coronation of both half brothers represented a pragmatic political expedient, which attempted to double the chances that at least one young Romanov tsar would live long enough to father a viable heir to the throne. Reason of state, however, was not a legitimate justification for the religious ceremony that was intended to invoke God's grace upon the mortal body of his earthly representative—the man officially empowered to rule alone.[10] Nor could this expedient political solution quell the self-righteous anger of the mutinous soldiers and rioters, many of whom pushed for a much more radical reconfiguration of the Russian body politic, a revision that drew at

8. On the causes of the *strel'tsy* mutiny, see ibid., 54–55; and P. V. Sedov, "Sotsial'no-politicheskaia bor'ba v Rossii v 70kh–80kh gg. XVII v. i otmena mestnichestva" (avtoreferat diss. kand. ist. nauk, A. A. Zhdanov State University, 1985). On Peter's debt to these earlier military reforms, see Richard Hellie, "The Petrine Army: Continuity, Change, and Impact," *Canadian-American Slavic Studies* 8, no. 2 (Summer 1974): 237–53; and Carol B. Stevens, "Evaluating Peter's Military Forces," in *Russia in the Reign of Peter the Great: Old and New Perspectives*, ed. Anthony Cross, 2:89–103 (Cambridge, 1998).

9. The killing of three Naryshkins during the 1682 mutiny was followed by the political emasculation of the survivors. After the maternal grandfather of Tsar Peter Alekseevich was forcibly tonsured and exiled to a monastery in the far north, the clan lost its last representative in the Muscovite royal council. See A. S. Lavrov, *Regentstvo tsarevny Sof'i Alekseevny: Sluzhiloe obshchestvo i bor'ba za vlast' v verkhakh Russkogo gosudarstva v 1682–1689 gg.* (Moscow, 1999), 125–26. For the text of the double coronation, dated June 25, 1682, see *Polnoe sobranie zakonov Rossiiskoi imperii s 1649 goda* (St. Petersburg, 1830), 2:412–39 (no. 931).

10. On the sanctity of Russian royal coronations, see B. A. Uspenskii, *Tsar' i patriarkh: Kharizma vlasti v Rossii (Vizantiiskaia model' i ee russkoe pereosmyslenie)* (Moscow, 1998); and, more generally, Marie-Karine Schaub, "Les couronnements des tsars en Russie du XVIe au XVIIIe siècle: Essai d'historiographie," in *La royauté sacrée dans le monde chrétien (Colloque de Royaumont, mars 1989)*, ed. Alain Boureau and C. S. Ingerflom, 137–48 (Paris, 1992).

least some of its inspiration from the millenarian ideals of social justice advocated by the sectarian proponents of Old Belief—the growing if still inchoate movement of opposition against the liturgical reforms introduced during the reign of Tsar Aleksei Mikhailovich.[11] And it is precisely because of the threat that popular insurrection posed to both the natural and political bodies of the two young tsars that the entire court fled the turbulent politics of the Russian capital. Eventually the court took refuge behind the fortified walls of the Trinity–St. Sergius Monastery, from which it issued a decree calling up all the hereditary provincial servitors of Muscovy to come and save the two royal brothers from the "seditious" and "schismatic" politics of their own subjects.

The choice to retire behind the fortified walls of the Trinity Monastery complex was neither as arbitrary nor as purely pragmatic as it may seem. As the final resting place of the preeminent national saint—St. Sergius of Radonezh—this monastery had long been seen as the main bastion of defense against those infidels and heretics who would subvert the confessional purity of the Russian Orthodox realm and overthrow its divinely appointed rulers. Most recently the monastery had quite literally served as the bastion against the Catholic armies of the Polish-backed pretender to the Muscovite throne, who had succeeded in crowning himself as the tsar of Russia during the Time of Troubles.[12] Indeed, the Trinity monastery was one of the best-known historical sites in the Muscovite political imagination, a symbol of confessional purity and military might that could serve as a powerful focus for mobilizing public opinion in favor of anyone who sought refuge behind its walls.[13] By making an unscheduled "pilgrimage" to the Trinity Monastery, the court of Moscow had thus won an important ideological battle against the mutineers and the Old Believers who had driven it from the capital during the new Time of Troubles.

The Royal Trinity

Despite such familiar historical parallels, however, the reassertion of Romanov rule after the 1682 uprising was anything but traditional. The court's return to Moscow did not mean a return to the same kind of monarchical rule as had prevailed before the new Time of Troubles. If anything, it

11. For an insightful discussion of the origins and institutionalization of this movement, see S. A. Zen'kovskii, *Russkoe staroobriadchestvo: Dukhovnye dvizheniia semnadtsatogo veka* (Moscow, 1995); and the revisionist study of Georg Bernhard Michels, *At War with the Church: Religious Dissent in Seventeenth-Century Russia* (Stanford, 1999).

12. On the first False Dmitrii, see R. G. Skrynnikov, *Samozvantsy v Rossii v nachale XVII veka: Grigorii Otrep'ev* (Novosibirsk, 1987); and Chester Dunning, "Who Was Tsar Dmitrii?" *Slavic Review* 60, no. 4 (2001), 705–29.

13. On the importance of the Trinity–St. Sergius Monastery in the political, economic, and spiritual life of medieval Russia, see Pierre Gonneau, *La Maison de la Sainte Trinité: Un grand monastère russe au Moyen Age tardif (1345–1533)* (Paris, 1993).

signaled the dispersal of royal charisma rather than its concentration in a single ruler. As a result of the political compromise hammered out between the feuding sides of the Russian royal family during the course of the Moscow uprising, Tsarevich Ivan Alekseevich had acceded to the throne alongside his half brother, while the Miloslavskiis and their supporters among the Muscovite political elite assumed control of what was, in essence, an informal regency council. In fact, for more than seven years (1682–89) one of Aleksei Mikhailovich's daughters, Tsarevna Sof'ia Alekseevna, ruled in the name of the two tsars, neither of whom was deemed fit to rule by himself (Peter by reason of age, Ivan by reason of his health). Tsarevna Sof'ia assumed the responsibility of her deceased mother, Tsaritsa Maria Il'inichna Miloslavskaia, Tsar Aleksei Mikhailovich's first wife, despite the fact that Aleksei's second wife (and the mother of the younger co-tsar), Tsaritsa Natal'ia Kirillovna Naryshkina, was still very much alive. Sof'ia's controversial role reflected the actual balance of power between the distaff sides of the royal house. It also demonstrated that even after his coronation, Peter remained a secondary figure in an inherently unstable political compromise brokered by the Russian Orthodox patriarch.

The unprecedented situation that prevailed after the 1682 Moscow uprising prompted Muscovite and Ruthenian (that is, Ukrainian and Belorussian Orthodox) panegyrists to create an innovative theology of rule based on their (often conflicting) interpretations of what we may call the Alekseevan heritage of religious enlightenment. For example, Sil'vestr (Medvedev), the abbot of the Moscow Zaikonospasskii Monastery and one of the earliest and most outspoken Russian advocates of the 1682 compromise, used the theological associations of the female regent's Christian name, Sof'ia, to popularize the mystical trope of Holy Wisdom, the Divine Omniscience of the three hypostases of the Trinity, as the most important allegorical image of the entire regency.[14] Like his more famous predecessor Simeon of Polotsk, the chief panegyrist at the court of Tsar Aleksei Mikhailovich, Sil'vestr sought to use the biblical imagery associated with the cult of the "wise" ruler to draw an analogy between the microcosm of the Muscovite realm and the macrocosm of the kingdom of God. However, applying such imagery to the complicated political situation of the regency was a much

14. Biographical information on Abbot Sil'vestr (Simeon Agafonnikovich Medvedev) can be found in I. P. Kozlovskii, *Sil'vestr Medvedev. Ocherk iz istorii russkogo prosveshcheniia i obshchestvennoi zhizni v kontse XVII veka* (Kiev, 1895); A. [A.] Prozorovskii, *Sil'vestr Medvedev (Ego zhizn' i deiatel'nost').* *Opyt tserkovno-istoricheskogo izsledovaniia* (Moscow, 1896); A. P. Bogdanov, "Sil'vestr Medvedev," *Voprosy istorii* 2 (1988): 84–98; and idem, "Razum protiv vlasti," *Pero i krest: Russkie pisateli pod tserkovnym sudom* (Moscow, 1990), 231–383. For his role in advocating the cult of Sophia–Holy Wisdom, see Elizabeth Kristofovich Zelensky, "Sophia the Wisdom of God as a Rhetorical Device during the Regency of Sof'ia Alekseevna, 1682–1689" (Ph.D. diss., Georgetown University, 1992), chap. 4; A. P. Bogdanov, "Sofiia-Premudrost' Bozhiia i tsarevna Sof'ia Alekseevna: Iz istorii russkoi dukhovnoi literatury i iskusstva XVII veka," *Germenevtika russkoi literatury* 7, no. 2 (1994): 399–428; and Isolde Thyrêt, *Between God and Tsar: Religious Symbolism and the Royal Women of Muscovite Russia* (DeKalb, IL, 2001), chap. 5.

more controversial enterprise, if for no other reason than that Tsarevna Sof'ia Alekseevna was not a crowned head of state and, according to Muscovite customary law, could never assume the crown in her own right. Nevertheless, this inconvenient fact did not deter Sil'vestr from addressing his new royal patron in the elaborate allegorical style of the Moscow Baroque. Following the abbot of the Zaikonospasskii Monastery, several other Muscovite panegyrists, as well as some of the leading Orthodox hierarchs of the metropolitanate of Kiev, began to apply Wisdom imagery to Tsarevna Sof'ia Alekseevna.[15] Indeed, after the regency government committed Muscovite forces to the defense of the Orthodox population of the southwestern borderlands against the incursions of the Crimean vassals of the Ottoman Porte—a consequence of the regency's controversial diplomatic rapprochement with the Catholic Polish-Lithuanian Commonwealth[16]—the image of Holy Wisdom became the cornerstone of all the literary and visual panegyrics concerning the personal virtues of the regent and the policies of her government, both in Muscovy and in Ukraine. Paradoxically, the person who owed her sudden appearance on the political stage to the divisive succession struggle between the distaff branches of the Russian royal house was thus invoked by clerical panegyrists as the symbol of Orthodox unity.[17]

In this politically tense period, those clerical factions that sought to counterbalance the influence of the patriarch appealed more and more often to the divine wisdom of Tsarevna Sof'ia Alekseevna. Exploiting the dynastic instability at the Muscovite court in order to defend the independent status of the Kievan metropolitanate against the centralizing policies of the Russian Orthodox Church, Ruthenian hierarchs sought to offer their own version of religious and political renewal. The patriarch claimed to have a monopoly on the power to authorize changes in the Orthodox canon and the religious imagery that legitimated Muscovite imperial rule. But Ruthenian Orthodox hierarchs took advantage of their reputation for erudition and their access to the most modern printing technology to promote their own interpretation of Muscovite political theology. Over the course of the regency, literary and visual panegyrics, such as the books and engravings printed at the press of Lazar' (Baranovich), the archbishop of Chernigov and Novgorod-Seversk, increasingly depicted the Muscovite regent as the most important figure in the entire Orthodox realm. For example, just a

15. A. P. Bogdanov, "Politicheskaia graviura v Rossii perioda regenstva Sof'ii Alekseevny," in *Istochnikovedenie otechestvennoi istorii. Sbornik statei za 1981 g.,* ed. V. I. Buganov (Moscow, 1982), 225, 229.

16. For a discussion of the geopolitical implications of the regency's diplomatic efforts vis-à-vis the Polish-Lithuanian Commonwealth, see Hughes, *Sophia,* chap. 8; Z. Wójcik, "From the Peace of Oliwa to the Truce of Bakhchisarai: International Relations in Eastern Europe, 1660–1681," *Acta Poloniae Historica* 34 (1976): 255–80; and I. K. Babushkina, "Mezhdunarodnoe znachenie Krymskikh pokhodov 1687 i 1689 gg.," *Istoricheskie zapiski* 33 (1950): 159–61.

17. To some extent, Sof'ia's unique position can be explained by her handlers' respect for traditional gendered notions about the special piety of Muscovite royal women. See Thyrêt, *Between God and Tsar,* 162.

year after the political compromise that resulted in the creation of the informal regency of Tsarevna Sof'ia Alekseevna, Archbishop Lazar' wrote an exegetical apologia for dual rule called *Grace and Truth*. The title of the book evoked the virtues of the young tsars' heavenly namesakes, the apostles John and Peter; but, as the accompanying engraving implied, it was the counsel of Sophia—the Wisdom of God, the namesake of Tsarevna Sof'ia—that would guide the new government to act in the interests of religious enlightenment and imperial renovation. The archbishop appealed to the royal triumvirate of Ivan, Peter, and Sof'ia, as the rightful protectors of what we may call the Kievan religious enlightenment, urging the regency government to send troops to protect the newly incorporated southwestern territories, but to refrain from subordinating the local religious establishment to its Muscovite counterpart. At the end of his learned treatise, Lazar' appended a large engraving that was meant to offer a visual summary (*conclusio*) of the book's arguments and conclusions.[18] This engraving attempted to illustrate the argument that only a sovereignty based on adherence to the "true science of government—Divine Wisdom—and one ultimately based on the source of all wisdom—the Trinity" could ensure victory against the Islamic infidels and protect all of Rus'. Like other panegyrical productions during the regency, the engraving appended to Lazar''s book relied on the iconographic convention of depicting Sophia the Wisdom of God reigning over the world in order to make a point about the political organization of the Muscovite realm. The Ruthenian engraver depicted the unstable political compromise of 1682 as part of the divine order, in a chain of perfection stretching from the Holy Trinity to the three patron saints of the rulers and finally to the rulers' earthly intercessors, the metropolitan of Kiev and the patriarch of Moscow. In this view, the new Muscovite government would act most wisely if it followed its divine prototype, the Divine Wisdom of the Holy Trinity.[19]

As long as the 1682 compromise held, even those clerics allied with the Russian patriarch and the factions opposed to the regency council of Tsarevna Sof'ia invoked the rhetorical trope of Sophia as the Wisdom of God to describe the political situation of the newly restored Romanov dynasty. The power of this courtly convention helps to explain why, for example, Sophronios and Ioannikos Leichoudes—the two Greek monks called to Russia by Patriarch Ioakim to undermine Sil'vestr (Medvedev), who hoped to use his position as Sof'ia's chief panegyrist to become the rector of the projected theological academy in Moscow—invoked the Wis-

---

18. On the genre of *conclusio*, which was very popular in the Orthodox brotherhood schools of Ukraine and Ruthenia, see M. A. Alekseeva, "Zhanr konkliuzii v russkom iskusstve kontsa XVII–nachalo XVIII veka," in *Russkoe iskusstvo barokko. Materialy i issledovaniia*, 7–29 (Moscow, 1977).

19. My interpretation of Metropolitan Lazar''s *Grace and Truth* (Chernigov, 1683) and the so-called Shchirskii engraving is indebted to Zelensky, "Sophia the Wisdom of God," 307–12; and Thyrêt, *Between God and Tsar*, 157–61.

dom of God in a laudatory oration to the regent on the occasion of her birthday.[20] Unlike Abbot Sil'vestr and the Ruthenian hierarchs, however, the Leichoudes brothers did not use the trope of Sophia as the Wisdom of God to make Tsarevna Sof'ia Alekseevna the leading person in the political and mystical perfection supposedly embodied by the Muscovite royal trinity. Although they did refer to the tsarevna as "empress" (*imperatrix*), the regent's claim to the Byzantine imperial heritage was expressed in a very attenuated way. Relying on the Greek Orthodox iconographic image of the Holy Virgin as the Wall, the two Greek monks drew attention to the intercessory role performed by the regent in the then current Muscovite campaign against the Crimean khanate. The Leichoudes brothers limited her role to praying to the Mother of God for the success and welfare of the "virile" troops of Muscovy. In their presentation the royal trinity appeared as a divinely appointed but essentially passive figurehead for the manly exploits of Russian troops against the infidel Turk. The humiliating failure of these troops during the Crimean campaigns of 1687–89 would occasion the collapse of the broad coalition behind the 1682 compromise and lead to a drastic re-visioning of the place of the three persons of the Muscovite royal trinity.

The Naryshkin Manifesto

It was very characteristic of the covert methods by which the political coalition that put the future Peter the Great on the throne conducted its business that the youngest son of Tsar Aleksei Mikhailovich played no more than a symbolic role in the second palace coup staged in his favor.[21] Following the ideological conventions and the informal rules of engagement elaborated during the two previous Times of Troubles, Peter's maternal relatives did not shrink from using falsification, coercion, and political manipulation to press the claims of their candidate in August and September 1689. As in 1682, the court of a Romanov tsar made an unexpected pilgrimage to the Trinity Monastery in order to escape the threat of violence; as was the case during the previous Time of Troubles, the appeals issued from behind the safety of the Trinity Monastery walls called for the restoration of legitimate royal authority; and finally, just as before, this move was

20. For the Russian translation of the Latin oration delivered on September 17, 1686, see *Pokhval'noe slovo Likhudov tsarevne Sof'e Alekseevne*, ed. E. L. Lermontova (Moscow, 1910). On the Leichoudes brothers, see Nikolaos A. Chrissidis, "Creating the New Educated Elite: Learning and Faith in Moscow's Slavo-Greco-Latin Academy, 1685–1694" (Ph.D. diss., Yale University, 2000).

21. For an insightful discussion of the domestic and geopolitical determinants of the 1689 coup, see Lavrov, *Regentstvo tsarevny Sof'i Alekseevny*, 15–16, 92, 96; and Hughes, *Sophia*, chap. 9.

an ingenious way of branding one's political opponents as rebels, usurpers, and heretics.

However, whereas in 1613 (and to a lesser extent in 1682) the self-proclaimed royalists really did seek to quell an armed popular insurgency, the coup organized by the Naryshkins in 1689 can more accurately be described as a preemptive strike against the supporters of the regency of Tsarevna Sof'ia Alekseevna. Taking advantage of a suspicious mobilization of Moscow musketeers in the Kremlin, Peter's advisers persuaded the tsar to flee the suburban royal estate of Novo-Preobrazhenskoe and seek shelter at the Trinity Monastery. This tactical relocation was timed to coincide with the feast day of the Transfiguration of the Saviour (which, as we will see, was an important holiday at Novo-Preobrazhenskoe, the royal estate controlled by the supporters of the young Naryshkin candidate). Shortly after taking refuge behind the fortified walls of the Trinity Monastery, a representative of the hastily assembled armed retinue of the seventeen-year-old co-tsar informed the court of Ivan Alekseevich of several faits accomplis: the execution of Moscow's police chief, F. L. Shaklovityi, for allegedly conspiring against the life of Peter and his maternal relatives; the removal of the name of the regent, Tsarevna Sof'ia Alekseevna, from the official royal title used in diplomatic and intragovernmental correspondence; and the sacking of chancellery personnel loyal to the Miloslavskii-led regency and their replacement by officials loyal to the new Naryshkin regime.[22]

The organizers of the 1689 palace coup that finally overthrew the regency of Tsarevna Sof'ia Alekseevna attempted to depict their actions as the rightful restoration of the diarchy of the sons of Tsar Aleksei Mikhailovich and, by implication, as a repudiation of female rule. This tactic was clearly revealed in a letter supposedly written by Tsar Peter Alekseevich to his half brother and co-ruler, Tsar Ivan Alekseevich, on September 12, 1689.[23] I say "supposedly" because although the letter was made to appear as if it had come from the pen of the younger co-tsar, it was neither composed nor signed by Peter himself.[24] In fact, it is unknown what role, if any, the younger co-tsar had in drafting what was, in essence, an unofficial proclamation of the de facto beginning of his independent reign. Judging by his familiarity with the secret transcripts of the official criminal proceedings against Shaklovityi, the anonymous author of the 1689 letter to Tsar Ivan was actually a member of the royal commission charged with conducting the investigation into the alleged plot that had sparked the Naryshkin coup.

Even a brief look at the composition of the commission entrusted with the sensitive job of making the case against the former head of the Moscow police force, and implicitly against the regency and person of Tsarevna

---

22. Lavrov, *Regentstvo tsarevny Sof'i Alekseevny,* 167–68, 182–90.
23. *PiB,* 1:13–14.
24. Ibid., 488; Lavrov, *Regentstvo tsarevny Sof'i Alekseevny,* 167, 244n50.

Sof'ia Alekseevna, reveals that it was headed up by men who had a personal stake in the success of the Naryshkin candidate.[25] For example, Prince I. B. Troekurov (d. 1703), the father of one of Peter's earliest companions, not only served as one of the official witnesses at Tsar Peter's wedding to E. F. Lopukhina in January 1689 but by his own marriage to A. F. Lopukhina, the sister of the tsar's bride, managed to ally himself with both the Lopukhin and the Naryshkin clans, who formed the main contingent of the courtiers at the Trinity Monastery.[26] Although the second member of the Trinity troika, Prince B. A. Golitsyn (1654–1714), held the relatively low court rank of official drink attendant (*kravchii*) and privy chamberlain (*komnatnyi stol'nik*) to Tsar Peter Alekseevich, he was one of the master-minds behind the 1689 coup and perhaps one of the staunchest supporters of the tsar's charismatic claims; in fact, Golitsyn was so willing to die for *his* anointed one that Sof'ia's chief adviser once mocked his loyalty by snidely comparing him to the apostles, none of whom ever offered "to die for Christ at the crucifixion."[27] Besides being one of Peter's legally appointed guardians (*diad'ki*), T. N. Streshnev (1649–1719), the third and final member of the commission, was one of the leading figures of the Naryshkin group, related by marriage to both the Golitsyn clan and the Russian royal family.[28] Thus all three men in charge of the Trinity investigative commission were not only members of Peter Alekseevich's personal entourage but related to either the Romanov dynasty, the Naryshkin clan, or the young tsar himself. Together with some of their lower-born, professionally trained administrative assistants—most notably the chancellery clerk (*d'iak*) N. M. Zotov (1643/44–1718), the future Prince-Pope of Peter's mock ecclesiastical council[29]—they would go on to form the core group of the Transfigured Kingdom.

25. For the composition of the Trinity investigative commission, see Lavrov, *Regentstvo tsarevny Sof'i Alekseevny*, 168–69, 245n70.
26. For I. B. Troekurov's court rank and family connections, see ibid., 169; and I. Iu. Airapetian, "Feodal'naia aristokratiia v period stanovleniia absoliutizma v Rossii" (diss. kand. ist. nauk, M. V. Lomonosov State University, 1987), 319; on his service career, see *PiB*, 1:538; and Robert O. Crummey, "Peter and the Boiar Aristocracy, 1689–1700," *Canadian-American Slavic Studies* 8 (Summer 1974): 284. On Troekurov's role in Peter's wedding, see the official account in *Drevniaia Rossiiskaia Vivliofika*, ed. N. I. Novikov, 2nd ed. (1789), 11:196. Prince I. B. Troekurov was the father of privy chamberlain (*komnatnyi stol'nik*) F. I. Troekurov, one of Peter's closest intimates, who was fatally wounded during a mock military maneuver in 1695. See Peter to F. Iu. Romodanovskii, September 8, 1695, in *PiB*, 1:49. On Fedor Troekurov's role in Peter's company, see *PiB*, 1:26, 32, 503. As a member of that company he was buried "like the Saviour [himself]" (*pokhoronili iako spassa*) (Prince B. A. Golitsyn to Peter, November 1695, in *PiB*, 1:538–39).
27. The comment was made in April 1685 by none other than V. V. Golitsyn, the chief adviser to the regent Sof'ia and Prince B. A. Golitsyn's first cousin. See Paul Bushkovitch, *Peter the Great: The Struggle for Power, 1671–1725* (Cambridge, 2001), 144.
28. On T. N. Streshnev, see Airapetian, "Feodal'naia aristokratiia," 99, 154–55, 335; Lavrov, *Regentstvo tsarevny Sof'i Alekseevny*, 168–69; and Lindsey Hughes, *Russia in the Age of Peter the Great* (New Haven, 1998), 418. For his rank in the mock ecclesiastical council of Peter the Great, see Appendix 2.
29. This lowborn chancellery clerk (*dumnyi diak*) became an intimate member of the Naryshkin party thanks partly to his appointment as personal tutor to Tsar Peter Alekseevich. Zotov's participation in the case against Shaklovityi is attested to by his signature on two im-

The fact that the members of the Trinity investigative commission decided to draft a letter from "Tsar Peter" (*tsar' Pëtr*) to his "brother sovereign" (*bratets gosudar'*) suggests that their use of a folksy, familial address represented an epistolary attempt to maintain the fiction of a diarchy while shifting the actual control of the regency from the Miloslavskiis to the Naryshkins. The anonymous author of the 1689 letter struggled to depict the palace coup staged by Peter's maternal relatives and supporters as the restoration of the piety and justice associated with the reign of the co-tsars' late father. Putting the religious and allegorical language favored at the court of Tsar Aleksei Mikhailovich into the mouth of his youngest son and heir, the author of this document had the epistolary Tsar Peter stress, in very traditional Muscovite fashion, that the royal brothers had been chosen by God to fulfill the obligations of earthly sovereigns: "The scepter by which the two of us govern the Russian tsardom of our ancestors has been entrusted to us by the grace of God, as is evidenced by the [7]190 [i.e., 1682] decision of the ecclesiastical council of our Mother, the Eastern Church, as well as by [the tacit consent of] our [royal] brotherhood, the neighboring sovereigns." By invoking the "scepter of governance" (*skipetr pravleniia*)—a synecdoche first used by Simeon of Polotsk to justify Aleksei's program of religious enlightenment (and religious persecution)[30]—the author of the 1689 letter asserted that Aleksei's sons had become the legal and spiritual guardians of the largest community of Orthodox Slavs in the world. Their accession to this divinely ordained duty was confirmed by the actions of their "mother," the Eastern Orthodox Church assembled in council; it was also tacitly acknowledged by the divinely ordained "fraternity" (*bratiia*) of neighboring sovereign princes, who signaled their agreement to offer diplomatic recognition to the unstable political compromise of 1682 by addressing the Muscovite tsars with their full royal titles.

The problem with this definition of what constituted a legitimate claim to the Muscovite throne was that according to these criteria, all three official Muscovite heads of state at the end of the 1680s could claim to have fulfilled these requirements. Both the tsars and the regent were the children of

---

portant documents, both of which are reproduced in *Rozysknye dela o Fedore Shaklovitom i ego soobshchnikakh*, 4 vols. (St. Petersburg, 1884–93), 1:263–64, 270. For the genealogy of the Zotov clan, see S. Liubimov, *Opyt istoricheskikh rodoslovii: Gundorovy, Zhizhemskie, Nesvitskie, Sibirskie, Zotovy i Ostermany* (Petrograd, 1915), 80–90; "Grafy Zotovy," in *Gerboved*, ed. S. N. Troitskii, 131–35 (September 1914); and Airapetian, "Feodal'naia aristokratiia," 121, 366–67. On N. M. Zotov's career in the Muscovite civil service before the 1689 coup, see M. M. Bogoslovskii, "Detstvo Petra Velikogo," *Russkaia starina* 1 (1917): 27–29; his *Petr I: Materialy dlia biografii* (Moscow and Leningrad, 1940), 1:34–37, 55–56; and V. Korsakov, "Zotov, gr. Nikita Moiseevich," in *RBS* (New York, 1962), 7:476–77. For his rank in the mock ecclesiastical council, see Appendix 2.

30. The "scepter of governance" echoes the title of Simeon's polemical religious treatise, *The Staff of Governance*, written to defend the irreconcilable position taken by the church council of 1666–67 against the Old Believers. For a discussion of Simeon's *Zhezl pravleniia* (Moscow, 1667), see Paul Bushkovitch, *Religion and Society in Russia: The Sixteenth and Seventeenth Centuries* (New York, 1992), 166; and Cathy Jean Potter, "The Russian Church and the Politics of Reform in the Second Half of the Seventeenth Century" (Ph.D. diss., Yale University, 1993), 217n66.

Tsar Aleksei Mikhailovich; their right to rule had been affirmed by the mother church; and their legitimacy had been recognized by their brother sovereigns, most notably by the Polish king, during the "Eternal Peace" between Muscovy and the Polish-Lithuanian Commonwealth, negotiated during Sof'ia's regency.[31] Clearly another reason why the "scepter of rule" belonged only to the royal brothers had to be found. In an attempt to exclude the regent and by implication the Miloslavskii clan as a whole from the royal succession, the author of the 1689 letter implicitly appealed to the Muscovite political elite's traditional conceptions of patrilineal inheritance, which held that elder daughters were entitled to a share of the patrimony in the form of a dowry and could even act as guardians during the minority of their brothers but could not assume the entire inheritance for themselves.[32] The "scepter of rule" could be handed down only from father to son. This was especially the case within the Romanov royal house, which in its two generations on the Russian throne had devised the practice of keeping its female members as secluded and celibate as nuns. This policy was an expedient way of elevating the Romanov clan above the other clans of hereditary military servitors who constituted the political and social elite of Muscovy. By keeping their sisters and nieces out of the marriage market, seventeenth-century Romanov tsars could avoid the messy and potentially destabilizing problems associated with unequal marriages, especially that of integrating new royal in-laws into the matrimonial alliances that shaped the politics within the Muscovite elite.[33]

In the brief preamble to the 1689 Naryshkin manifesto, the author skillfully managed to insinuate that the regent had violated these common law notions about familial obligations and "willfully" overstepped her traditional gender role. According to this interpretation, Tsarevna Sof'ia unceremoniously usurped her brothers' personal responsibility for securing domestic tranquility, guaranteeing the fair administration of justice, and defending the Orthodox faith, traditionally the most important tasks of Russian tsars, for which they were ultimately to be accountable before the Supreme Judge himself.[34] In what appears to have been intended as a subtle

31. L. R. Lewitter, "The Russo-Polish Treaty of 1686 and Its Antecedents," *Polish Review* 9, nos. 3–4 (1964): 5–29, 21–37.

32. For a discussion of female inheritance practices among the Muscovite hereditary military elite, see N. L. Pushkareva, *Women in Russian History: From the Tenth to the Twentieth Century*, trans. and ed. Eve Levin (Armonk, NY, 1997), 44–49, 106–12; and Michelle Lamarche Marrese, *A Woman's Kingdom: Noblewomen and the Control of Property in Russia, 1700–1861* (Ithaca, 2002).

33. Nancy Shields Kollmann, "The Seclusion of Elite Muscovite Women," *Russian History* 10, no. 2 (1983): 170–87; and Russell Edward Martin, "Dynastic Marriage in Muscovy, 1500–1729" (Ph.D. diss., Harvard University, 1996).

34. On the discourse about responsibilities of Muscovite tsars, see Douglas Joseph Bennett, "The Idea of Kingship in Seventeenth-Century Russia" (Ph.D. diss., Harvard University, 1967); and Rowland, "Problem of Advice"; on the use of this discourse in the 1689 letter to Tsar Ivan Alekseevich, see Barbara Joyce Merguerian, "Political Ideas in Russia during the Period of Peter the Great (1682–1730)" (Ph.D. diss., Harvard University, 1970), 103.

distinction between governance (*pravlenie*), the legitimate authority exercised by the sovereign over his realm, and possession (*vladenie*), the illegitimate rule of a usurper who illegally appropriates the patrimony of the rightful property owners, the author of the 1689 letter managed to attack the legitimacy of Sof'ia's regency council as well as the integrity of the regent herself: "There was never any mention [in the previously cited proofs of the legitimacy] of our sovereignty of a third person having an equal share with us in governance. But you already know about what happened after our sister . . . began to rule our realm of her own will, [how] her rule was against our own persons, [how it put ever more] burdens on the people, and how we [were forced to] put up with it."[35] By including her own name in the royal titulature alongside that of the anointed and crowned heads of Muscovy, the regent could be said to have asserted that she was equally entitled to govern the Russian tsardom and thereby illegally took possession (*uchela vladet'*) of her brothers' patrimony.

By subverting the patrilineal principle and usurping the hereditary property rights of her brothers, Sof'ia had appropriated the symbols of their sovereignty as well as their masculinity. As a result of her self-willed act, the virgin tsarevna began to wield political authority, which, as we have seen, was represented in the Naryshkin manifesto by the brothers' "scepter of rule." The regent's usurpation of this symbol of public and ancestral trust infringed on the benevolent, paternal authority of God himself. Indeed, employing the same underhanded techniques as those of the Miloslavskii sympathizers who had fabricated the story that I. K. Naryshkin had tried on the crown in 1682, the author of the 1689 letter insinuated that the co-tsars' passivity in the face of (in this case, metaphorical) rough handling of the royal regalia was explained by the suspicion that Tsarevna Sof'ia had some kind of supernatural control over her brothers. Playing on the multiple meanings of the word "possession" (*vladenie*), the anonymous courtier from the retinue of Tsar Peter Alekseevich implied that the regent was also a witch—an accusation that was not unusual at the seventeenth-century Muscovite court. As the recorded cases of words and deeds (*slovo i delo gosudarevo*) against the majesty of the tsar demonstrate, such practices as putting the evil eye, casting magic spells, and invoking unclean spirits to send wasting diseases on one's political rivals were quite regularly invoked in Muscovite political disputes.[36] If the male co-tsars did not seem to be performing their duties; if justice and domestic tranquility were being perverted; if, in other words, the rightful Muscovite tsars had lost the use (or

---

35. *PiB*, 1:13.

36. For the Naryshkins' accusations against those involved in the case of F. L. Shaklovityi, see A. N. Truvorov, "Volkhvy i vorozhei na Rusi, v kontse XVII veka," *Istoricheskii vestnik* 6 (1889): 710–15; and W. F. Ryan, *The Bathhouse at Midnight: An Historical Survey of Magic and Divination in Russia* (University Park, PA, 1999), 77, 173, 415–16; in the same volume, see 38–39, 165, 375, and chap. 16 for the political dimension of witchcraft accusations more generally, and 8, 41, and 78 on demonic possession in Russia, which is also discussed in A. S. Lavrov, *Koldovstvo i religiia v Rossii, 1700–1740 gg.* (Moscow, 2000).

possession) of their (phallic) royal scepters, then they must have been at the mercy of forces beyond their control—forces that the author of the 1689 Naryshkin manifesto associated with the "self-willed" female regent. If this reading of the letter is correct, then Tsarevna Sof'ia Alekseevna appeared to her opponents as one of the most potent (and anxiety-producing) figures of all: the carnivalesque harridan who inverted the traditional gender roles of the patriarchal political establishment.[37]

Foreshadowing the conclusion of the special report compiled by the Trinity investigative commission, the author of these scurrilous innuendoes went on to argue that the time had finally come when the co-tsars could dispense with the regency government altogether.

> And now, sovereign brother, the time has come for both of our persons to control for ourselves the tsardom entrusted to us by God, for we have come into the fullness of our age. We should not permit that extraneous [literally, "third"] reprehensible person, our sister ts. S. A., to [appear] alongside our masculine persons in the titulature or in the administration of affairs. And you too, my sovereign brother, should bend your will [to this purpose], because [not only did] she begin to get involved in government affairs and to include her name in the official royal titulature without our permission, but, to add the ultimate insult to our injury, she wanted to be crowned with the royal wreath. [We have finally attained our] majority and at our age, sovereign, it is shameful for this reprehensible person to control the realm in our stead.[38]

Urging his "brother sovereign" to recognize their "shameful" (*sramno*) passivity and prove that he was no longer subject to the charms of his sister, "Tsar Peter" demanded that his elder co-tsar demonstrate that he could still "bend his will" to the exercise of his own legitimate royal authority. Only if they were both able to break free of the spell cast over the diarchy by the female regent—that extraneous, "reprehensible," and literally unmentionable third person ("S. A."), who wielded their royal scepters for them—could the co-tsars assert their God-given right to rule as mature men. In what seems to be a veiled reference to the pregnancy of Peter's young bride, the author of the 1689 letter hinted at the most visible sign that the regent's evil machinations had failed to prevent Peter from reaching the "fullness" of his age and becoming a real man. And now that the Naryshkin coup had exorcised the influence of the regent, the letter's author seemed to be saying, the youngest son of Tsar Aleksei Mikhailovich had also come of age politically.

The fact that the term "reprehensible person" (*zazornoe litso*) appears in

---

37. For a discussion of this carnivalesque image, which was one of the most important cultural tropes in the language of early modern European popular festivals, see Natalie Zeman Davis, "Women on Top," in her *Society and Culture in Early Modern France*, 124–51 (Stanford, 1975); and, more generally, Peter Burke, *Popular Culture in Early Modern Europe* (New York, 1978).

38. *PiB*, 1:13.

two consecutive sentences underlines its ideological significance in the compositional structure of the Naryshkin manifesto about the restoration of legitimate masculine royal authority. For this term referred mostly to individuals, and particularly to unmarried women, with whom it was "blameworthy" (*zazorno*) for ecclesiastics to have relations. No matter how holy or celibate, the cleric who had to deal with a woman was necessarily exposed to moral reproof, because even the most innocent relations carried the danger of sexual temptation and ritual pollution. Indeed, in using this loaded term in a sense already anachronistic by the end of the seventeenth century,[39] the author of the 1689 letter implied that Tsarevna Sof'ia Alekseevna's untoward actions vis-à-vis her brothers—the rightful, divinely ordained tsars of Russia—had subverted the ideal of (almost monastic) purity that Tsar Aleksei Mikhailovich had attempted to establish at court and within his royal house.[40]

In order to parody the supposedly vain and unnatural ambitions of the regent, the author of the 1689 letter resorted to familiar literary models. By the end of the seventeenth century, accusations of sexual impropriety on the part of monks and nuns, ecclesiastics who had taken vows of chastity and had self-consciously adopted the "angelic form," had become a stock example of hypocrisy in the polemical literature directed against the vices of the Russian Orthodox clergy. The number of humorous stories, poems, and parodies about licentious monks and nuns was matched only by the number of literary examples of gluttony and intemperance. Such accusations constituted an integral part of the rhetoric of seventeenth-century Orthodox ecclesiastical reformers and laity and contributed to the larger project to restore the purity of the one true Orthodox faith, which supposedly had become corrupted by noncanonic and "pagan" as well as foreign accretions.[41] The Naryshkins' allegations about Tsarevna Sof'ia's improprieties vis-à-vis her brothers, as well as about her supposed plans to get married, take on the crown of Russia, and unite with Rome—a line of argument only hinted at in the letter's reference to her insulting desire to be "crowned with the royal wreath," a term that applied both to coronations and the wreaths

39. *Slovar' russkogo iazyka XI–XVII vv.* (Moscow, 1978), 5:199.

40. For an argument that emphasizes the similarity between courtly etiquette and religious decorum (*chin*) during the reign of Tsar Aleksei Mikhailovich, see A. N. Robinson, *Bor'ba idei v russkoi literature XVII veka* (Moscow, 1974), chap. 2; L. N. Pushkarev, *Obshchestvenno-politicheskaia mysl' Rossii. Vtoraia polovina XVII veka. Ocherki istorii* (Moscow, 1982), chap. 3; and V. V. Bychkov, *Russkaia srednevekovaia estetika, XI–XVII veka* (Moscow, 1995), chap. 8, esp. 530–42. For an assessment of the "nightmarish religiosity" of Aleksei's court, see Michael Cherniavsky, *Tsar and People: Studies in Russian Myths* (New Haven, 1961), 63.

41. For a discussion of seventeenth-century *parodia sacra* as popular criticism of the vices of the Orthodox clergy, see V. P. Adrianova-Peretts, *Russkaia demokraticheskaia satira XVII veka*, 2nd ed. (Moscow, 1977); L. A. Chernaia, "Parodiia na tserkovnye teksty v russkoi literature XVII veka," *Vestnik Moskovskogo universiteta*, ser. 8, *Istoriia*, 2 (1980): 53–63; and, more generally, D. S. Likhachev, "Smekh kak mirovozzrenie," in his *Smekh v drevnei Rusi*, 7–71 (Leningrad, 1984), esp. 50–57.

worn by bride and groom during an Orthodox wedding service[42]—relied on this confessional critique, which effectively struck at the heart of the regent's claim to be the best defender of the religious and political orthodoxy of the Romanov royal house. In reply to that claim, the author of the 1689 Naryshkin manifesto asserted that by overthrowing the regency of Tsarevna Sof'ia Alekseevna the retinue of Tsar Peter Alekseevich was bent on restoring the religious, political, and sexual order confused during the topsy-turvy rule of a woman. "Tsar Peter" thus concluded his epistle by calling upon his elder brother sovereign to help him return to the harmonious, patriarchal ideal elaborated during the reign of their father.[43] What he described was a Romanov restoration, not a Naryshkin coup d'état.

In reality, of course, the September 1689 letter, like the investigation and execution of the supposed plotters against the life of Tsar Peter Alekseevich, was itself an important means of legitimating the palace coup. Even before the Naryshkin manifesto was delivered to Tsar Ivan and his handlers, the members of the Trinity investigative commission had opened an inquest into the plot against Peter's life, the ostensible reason for his flight to the Trinity Monastery. The investigators had no problem locating a scapegoat on whom to put the blame for the violence lurking just beneath the surface of the post-Alekseevan succession struggle. Seeking to underline the similarity between the 1689 coup and the last Time of Troubles, Peter's advisers put all the blame on F. L. Shaklovityi, the relatively lowborn royal secretary who was entrusted to run the Musketeer Chancellery during Sof'ia's regency.[44] As an important political figure at the regent's court, Moscow's new police chief was a perfect person to reprise the role of I. A. Khovanskii, the former head of the Musketeer Chancellery and the person whose name served as an eponym for the violence that was perpetrated against the Naryshkin clan in 1682.[45]

Tortured into submission on the orders of the pro-Naryshkin Trinity commission, Shaklovityi eventually confessed to knowing about and concealing the "evil intentions" of the musketeers, who supposedly had contemplated launching an attack on the royal regiments guarding Novo-Preobrazhenskoe. He confirmed the allegation that he had personally instructed the musketeers to set fire to the Naryshkins' suburban estate in order to capture and then kill the young co-tsar, his mother, their relatives, high-ranking political supporters, and Peter's royal favorites (in particular, Prince B. A. Golitsyn and the boyar L. K. Naryshkin, the tsar's maternal uncle). Finally, Shaklovityi also admitted that he was aware of Tsarevna Sof'ia Alekseevna's plans to have herself crowned and even expressed support for a

42. For a discussion of Sof'ia's alleged matrimonial plans, see the "amazing rumors" recorded by the Czech Jesuit Irzhi (Georgius) David, cited in Hughes, *Sophia*, 263–64, 310n6.

43. *PiB*, 1:14.

44. On the career of F. L. Shaklovityi, see Lavrov, *Regentstvo tsarevny Sof'i Alekseevny*, 142, 236n301; and Lindsey Hughes, "Shaklovityi, Fedor," in *The Modern Encyclopedia of Russian and Soviet History*, ed. Joseph L. Wieczynski, 34:146–48 (Gulf Breeze, FL, 1983).

45. For a discussion of the "time of Khovanskii" (*Khovanshchina*), see Hughes, *Sophia*, chap. 3, esp. 80, 82–84.

plot to assassinate the Moscow patriarch.[46] For all their sensationalism, however, the "confessions" of Shaklovityi served as a better guide to the fears entertained by the Naryshkins and their allies than to any actual conspiracy on the part of Tsarevna Sof'ia and her lowborn favorite. Indeed, the hastily organized execution of Shaklovityi and his alleged co-conspirators was meant to allay fears and end speculations, not to open up other lines of inquiry into the meaning of the new Time of Troubles.[47]

Tsar by Sacrament

Although the members of the Trinity investigative commission ultimately failed to prove any direct connections between Shaklovityi and the Miloslavskiis (beyond the unsubstantiated rumors of an illicit affair between the doomed police chief and the virgin tsarevna),[48] they did succeed in linking him with Sof'ia's ecclesiastical protégé, Sil'vestr (Medvedev), the monk whom the Trinity troika branded as the main ideologue of the regency regime and whom they eventually executed as the second leader of the conspiracy against the Naryshkins. In fact, the Trinity investigative commission did not officially disband until it had succeeded in capturing and interrogating Sil'vestr, who supposedly had direct proof that the former regent had planned to get herself crowned, and who was himself rumored to have had designs on the patriarchal throne. The amount of time, energy, and manpower devoted to tracking down and returning the fugitive monk suggests that the Naryshkins and their supporters were determined to have Abbot Sil'vestr share the burden of Shaklovityi's "conspiracy." Indeed, if we now turn to the commission's case against Sil'vestr (Medvedev), we will see how Peter's kinsmen used contemporary theological debates to garner support for the Naryshkin candidate and demonstrate his divine election.

The fact that the only concrete evidence against Abbot Sil'vestr, aside from some contradictory and coerced testimony from Shaklovityi and his co-conspirators, consisted of two panegyrical engravings that asserted Tsarevna Sof'ia Alekseevna's divine election underscores the political significance of the figurative language in which the competing sides of the theological controversies at the late seventeenth-century Muscovite court conducted their debates. Indeed, the high-stakes showdown between the entourage of the Russian Orthodox patriarch, a coterie of independent-minded Ukrainian Orthodox hierarchs, and Sof'ia's ecclesiastical protégé over the moment of transubstantiation of the Host during the Eucharist echoed and in many ways shaped the succession struggle between the

46. For the text of Shaklovityi's deposition, see *Rozysknye dela*, 1:165–78.
47. Lavrov, *Regentstvo tsarevny Sof'i Alekseevny*, 178–81, 247n98, 268.
48. On rumors of an illicit affair between the regent and her chief of police, see the memoir of Tsar Peter's brother-in-law, Prince B. I. Kurakin, "Gistoriia o tsare Petre Alekseeviche (1682–1694)," in *Petr Velikii. Vospominaniia. Dnevnikovye zapisi. Anekdoty*, ed. L. Nikolaeva (Moscow, 1993), 66.

Naryshkins and the Miloslavskiis. In the course of this dispute it became apparent, for example, that the Eucharistic controversy was as much about who had the power to interpret the signs of the tsars' divine election as about the correct exegesis of the sacramental liturgy. In other words, the transubstantiation debate constituted an important element in the political programs of competing court factions, each of which sought to institutionalize its own particular definition of divine kingship.[49]

The highly charged rhetoric of the Russian Orthodox patriarch and other participants in these religious and educational debates necessarily intertwined theology and politics. For, in the decades after the fateful church council of 1666–67—which approved Aleksei Mikhailovich's controversial and far-reaching liturgical reforms and thereby inaugurated the schism (*raskol*)—subjects throughout the far-flung Muscovite realm were forced to confront the uncomfortable fact that when almost every question was about the "true faith" of the only independent Orthodox kingdom in the world, there was ample room for charges of both heresy and treason. This was bound to be especially the case in respect to such politically sensitive issues as the reform of the liturgy regarding the Eucharist, the central mystery of Orthodox Christianity. Indeed, from the moment the court of Tsar Aleksei Mikhailovich embarked on its ambitious program of imperial expansion and religious renewal, the question about the proper and uniquely Orthodox way of conducting the divine liturgy became one of the most important and highly controversial issues of Muscovite political theology. This politicization of the Eucharist provoked a bitter rebuke from both the supporters and the opponents of Aleksei's religious reforms. In response to such criticisms, as well as to the continuing reform of the Orthodox liturgy, the leaders of the Russian church commissioned several important official statements on the question. They included both official translations of classic theological texts, such as the *Skrizhal* of Arsenii the Greek, as well as original contributions by foreign Orthodox experts, such as Paisius Ligarides and Simeon of Polotsk.[50] For most of the seventeenth century, however, the Russian Orthodox Church did not have a clearly defined theological position on the moment of transubstantiation. Only during the debate against

---

49. For a discussion of the divine nature of monarchy in early modern Europe, see Monod, *Power of Kings*, passim; and the section on the "Eucharistic prince" in John Adamson, "Introduction: The Making of the *Ancien-Régime* Court, 1500–1700," in *The Princely Courts of Europe: Ritual, Politics and Culture under the* Ancien Régime, *1500–1750*, ed. Adamson (London, 1999), 27–33; cf. the discussion of the "king by sacrament" in Louis Marin, *Portrait of the King*, trans. Martha M. Houle (Minneapolis, 1988). On divine kingship in Russian monarchy, see Zhivov and Uspenskii, "Tsar' i Bog"; Uspenskii, *Tsar' i patriarch*, 14–29, 109–210; Richard S. Wortman, "The Redefinition of the Sacred: Eighteenth-Century Russian Coronations," in *La royauté sacrée dans le monde chrétien (Colloque de Royaumont, mars 1989)*, ed. Alain Boureau and C. S. Ingerflom, 149–56 (Paris, 1992); and his *Scenarios of Power: Myth and Ceremony in Russian Monarchy*, 2 vols. (Princeton, 1995, 2000), vol. 1.

50. See M. Smentsovskii, *Brat'ia Likhudy. Opyt izsledovaniia iz istorii tserkovnogo prosveshcheniia i tserkovnoi zhizni kontsa XVII i nachala XVIII vekov* (St. Petersburg, 1899), 109–10, 115–16.

Sil'vestr (Medvedev), in the tense political atmosphere of the succession struggle for the Alekseevan heritage, did the entourage around the Russian Orthodox patriarch come up with an official line on this question.

The Eucharist controversy played an important role in the elaboration of the conflict between the defenders of the regent's right to rule in the name of her two brothers and those who pressed for the independent rule of the two co-tsars. Well before the fatal split within the broad coalition that supported the compromise of 1682, the retinue of Patriarch Ioakim (Savelov) and the supporters of the Naryshkin candidate for the Muscovite throne had become embroiled in a theological debate against Abbot Sil'vestr and several important Ukrainian Orthodox hierarchs who were the leading apologists for the religious and foreign policies of the regency of Tsarevna Sof'ia, particularly her government's long-sought and much-trumpeted rapprochement with the Catholic Polish-Lithuanian Commonwealth. In an attempt to reassert his authority over the program of religious enlightenment, the Russian Orthodox patriarch recruited two classically trained Greeks from the University of Padua to head the Epiphany monastery school, the site of Abbot Sil'vestr's main competitor in the educational and religious debates at the Muscovite court.[51] On March 15, 1685, just nine days after Sophronios and Ioannikos Leichoudes arrived in Moscow, the entourage around Patriarch Ioakim and the court of the tsaritsa dowager Marfa Matveevna (*née* Apraksina, the young widow of Tsar Fedor Alekseevich) sponsored an academic "disputation" about the moment of transubstantiation of the Host during the Eucharist.[52]

Like the 1666–67 church council's orchestrated condemnation of the "schismatic" Old Believers, the organizers of the informal religious disputation of 1685 intended to show off the erudition of the Leichoudes brothers while impugning the Orthodoxy and political loyalty of their opponent. During this disputation, the Leichoudeses confronted a self-professed philosopher named Jan (Andrei) Belobodskii, a Polish Catholic convert to Orthodoxy who had come to Muscovy on his own initiative in the hope of securing an important educational post.[53] By attacking Belobodskii, Abbot Sil'vestr's former rival in the struggle for the rectorship of the projected Moscow academy, the Leichoudes brothers announced their intention to take on Medvedev himself while at the same time accusing the regent's ec-

51. For a discussion of Patriarch Ioakim's version of Orthodox religious enlightenment, see Potter, "Russian Church," chaps. 6–9; on the educational background of the Leichoudes brothers, see Chrissidis, "Creating the New Educated Elite."

52. Smentsovskii, *Brat'ia Likhudy*, 62–63; Prozorovskii, *Sil'vestr Medvedev*, 242–44. On Marfa Matveevna Apraksina (b. 1667) and her brief marriage to Tsar Fedor Alekseevich (in 1682), see Bushkovitch, *Peter*, 123–24. On the culture of religious disputations at the Muscovite court, see A. M. Panchenko, "Russkaia kul'tura v kanun petrovskikh reform," in *Iz istorii russkoi kul'tury*, ed. A. D. Koshelev (Moscow, 1996), 3:199–202.

53. For Belobodskii's biography, see A. Kh. Gorfunkel', "Andrei Belobodskii—poet i filosof kontsa XVII–nachala XVIII veka," *Trudy otdela drevnerusskoi literatury* 18 (1962): 188–213; and his " 'Pentateugum' Andreia Belobodskogo (Iz istorii pol'sko-russkikh literaturnykh sviazei)," ibid., 21 (1965): 39–64, esp. 39–40.

clesiastical protégé of "Latin heresy." By implication rather than by direct attack, the Leichoudes brothers thus publicly declared that the regent's choice for the position of rector was fundamentally flawed, and that the regency's Polonophile foreign policy and its lenient treatment of foreign (especially Catholic-leaning) clerics were having a deleterious effect on Russian Orthodoxy.

Sil'vestr had already denounced Belobodskii's views in front of Patriarch Ioakim, who had condemned the Polish philosopher's critique of the validity of the doctrine of transubstantiation at the 1681 Moscow church council. At the time, the Russian Orthodox patriarch and the entire Holy Council had agreed with the position paper submitted by Abbot Sil'vestr, who had persuasively argued that on this question the positions of the Greek Orthodox and Roman Catholic churches were identical: the bread and wine are transformed into the body and blood of Christ during the moment in the liturgy when the officiating priest pronounces the Words of the Institution: "This is my body. . . . This is my Blood" (cf. Matt. 26:26–28). Now, barely four years later, Ioakim's entourage had reversed themselves on the issue, branding as idolatry the "Latin heresy" that they had formerly avowed as official Orthodox dogma.[54] Using the Leichoudes brothers as their own liturgical specialists, the patriarch's party encouraged their Greek protégés to argue that all three sections of the Eucharistic prayer in the Orthodox liturgy formed an integral part of the one act of consecration of the sacramental bread and wine. In this view, the exact moment when the bread and wine are transformed into the actual body and blood of Christ does not occur until the last amen of the Invocation Prayer (*epiklesis*), which "calls down" the Spirit on the Holy Gifts: "Send down thy Holy Spirit upon us and upon these gifts set forth: And make this bread the Precious Body of thy Christ, And that which is in this cup, the Precious Blood of thy Christ, Changing them by thy Holy Spirit. Amen, amen, amen." To argue, as Sil'vestr (Medvedev) had done just four years earlier, that transubstantiation occurs when the priest repeats the words said by Christ during the Last Supper was to commit the heresy of "artolatry" and to indulge in "bread worship," the idolatrous reverence of the sacramental elements before their consecration.[55]

The impression that the disputation of March 1685 was organized by factions hostile to the regency is supported by the list of the prominent people (*znatnye liudi*) and royal counselors (*boiare*) who supposedly had presided over it. The only source for this list is the Leichoudes brothers' own literary *Cure* for Belobodskii's "harmful" doctrines, a polemical treatise whose arguments were later interpolated into the manuscripts of Sil'vestr's main en-

54. See Sil'vestr's written response to Belobodskii's "Confession of Faith," esp. the section "On the Holy Eucharist or Communion," in *Pamiatniki k istorii protestanstva v Rossii,* ed. Dm. Tsvetaev, 1:219–40 (Moscow, 1888), esp. 227–31. Also see the discussion in Smentsovskii, *Brat'ia Likhudy,* 118–19; and Prozorovskii, *Sil'vestr Medvedev,* 240–41.
55. Timothy Ware, *The Orthodox Church* (Baltimore, 1963), 287–90.

emies during the Eucharist debates.[56] In this self-serving version, written two years after their disputation with Belobodskii, the Leichoudeses were careful to record the fact that they had the full support of Patriarch Ioakim and a powerful group of Muscovite grandees around the court of tsaritsa dowager Marfa Matveevna. In particular, they singled out the tsaritsa's brothers, all of whom would later assume some of the most prominent positions at the court of Peter the Great;[57] N. G. Milescu-Spafarios (1636–1708), an important chancellery official, translator, and scholar, who was patronized by several leading members of the Naryshkin faction;[58] and the boyar I. A. Musin-Pushkin (1661–1729), Patriarch Ioakim's nephew-in-law and future head of the Monastery Chancellery, who was rumored to be Tsar Aleksei Mikhailovich's illegitimate son and hence Peter's half brother.[59] The unofficial academic nature of this religious disputation, as well as its contemporary political significance, is confirmed by the fact that even after the Leichoudeses had defeated their clerical opponent and supposedly demonstrated their ability to take over the leadership of the Moscow academy, the regency's foreign affairs chancellery still demanded that the Greek brothers present proofs of their educational qualifications.[60]

The theological dispute of 1685 became the opening salvo in a bitter and protracted controversy at the Muscovite court over the moment of transubstantiation. Sil'vestr (Medvedev), who was not one to back down from a theological debate, especially when both his principles and his career were on the line, eagerly entered the fray. By-passing official ecclesiastical channels, he appealed directly to Tsarevna Sof'ia's wisdom as a way of seeking royal support for his theological positions as well as for his candidacy as rector of the projected academy. Going beyond the customary invocation of the monarch's role in the religious enlightenment of his realm—another trope first applied to a Romanov tsar by his teacher, Simeon of Polotsk—

---

56. The relevant excerpt from the Leichoudeses' "Akos, ili vrachevaniie . . ." was published in Tsvetaev, *Pamiatniki*, 240–42, from the original held in the Moscow Synodal Library, kn. 440, ll. 36–37.

57. Like the Streshnevs, the Apraksins were a long-time *boyar* family, with marital links to the Russian royal house and ready access to the quarters of Tsar Peter Alekseevich; in fact, at the time of the 1685 disputation, all three Apraksin brothers served as Peter's privy counselors (*komnatnye stol'niki*). See Airapetian, "Feodal'naia aristokratiia," 99, 329, 321, 316; Hughes, *Russia*, 115, 418–19; and Appendix 2.

58. See O. A. Belobrova, "Lichnost' i nauchno-prosvetitel'skie trudy Nikolaia Spafariia," in *Nikolai Spafarii. Esteticheskii traktaty*, ed. A. M. Panchenko (Leningrad, 1978), 4; and Smentsovskii, *Brat'ia Likhudy*, 130–31. Belobrova also comments on his patronage network, 15n38.

59. For a genealogy of the Musin-Pushkins, see *Istoriia rodov russkogo dvorianstva*, ed. P. N. Petrov (St. Petersburg, 1886), 1:293; and L. M. Savelov, *Rod dvorian Savelovykh (Savelkovy)* (Moscow, 1895), 32–33. For his service career, see Airapetian, "Feodal'naia aristokratiia," 97, 317; Crummey, "Peter and the Boiar Aristocracy," 283n18; D. N. Bantysh-Kamenskii, *Slovar' dostopamiatnykh liudei Russkoi zemli* (Moscow, 1836), 3:385–87; and M. Gorchakov, *Monastyrskii prikaz (1649–1725)* (St. Petersburg, 1868), 121–22. On the question of illegitimacy, see *PiB*, 2:91; and Hughes, *Russia*, 418, 553n18. For his role in the mock ecclesiastical council of Peter the Great, see Appendix 2.

60. Smentsovskii, *Brat'ia Likhudy*, 64.

Sil'vestr's numerous contributions to the Eucharist debate included pointed political references to Sof'ia as the leading member of the Russian royal family, the receptacle of grace, and the true inheritor of royal authority. According to Sil'vestr, as the earthly representative of Divine Wisdom, the tsarevna did not need to be consecrated in order to have the right to oversee the enlightenment of her realm, just as he did not need the permission of the patriarchal administration in order to qualify for the position of rector of the Moscow academy. This appeal to Divine Wisdom without the mediation of the church hierarchy questioned the power of the ordained authorities, undermining the patriarch's control over the official program of enlightenment as well as her brothers' right to rule on their own.[61]

Sil'vestr's insistence on the centrality of the Words of the Institution during the Eucharist, as well as his attempts to equate Tsarevna Sof'ia with Christ in his liminal, Sophic aspect, was clearly intended to justify the regent's claims to royal rule despite the fact that she was not anointed. For example, in his "Presentation to the Noble and Christ-Loving Great Sovereign Lady, the Divinely Wise Tsarevna, the Merciful Sof'ia Alekseevna of the Charter to the Academy" (1685), Sil'vestr asserted that "it is not given for people to know who from among them is chosen as the vessel for the spirit of grace." Referring to the Pentecostal imagery from the Acts of the Apostles and the Prayer of Invocation, Sil'vestr proposed that "the Holy Spirit makes a sign" of its presence in a soul by its portents, "as a flame appears above" the heads of Christ's true disciples. "Then the soul is filled by the activity of three graces"—an indirect reference to Faith, Hope, and Charity, the daughters of St. Sophia, who was another of the regent's divine namesakes.[62] According to Sil'vestr, the regent was just such a vessel of God's grace, which made its presence known not through consecration but through Sof'ia's virtuous and wise actions, including her patronage of him. Only people such as Abbot Sil'vestr himself, who were able to correctly interpret the scriptures and to see in the regent's acts signs of divine election, realized that hers was a soul graced by the Holy Spirit.[63]

During the protracted Eucharistic debate, the abbot of the Zaikonospasskii Monastery challenged the church's control over grace and enlightenment, asserting his patron's (and by implication his own) unmediated access to the divine. According to Sil'vestr's interpretation of the Eucharist, the power of the divine resided in the Word, specifically the phrase pronounced by Christ during the Last Supper, "Take . . . eat"; conse-

61. My interpretation of Sil'vestr's position is greatly indebted to the analyses of his writings by Prozorovskii, *Sil'vestr Medvedev;* Smentsovskii, *Brat'ia Likhudy;* Zelensky, "Sophia the Wisdom of God"; and Potter, "Russian Church."

62. Tsarevna Sof'ia Alekseevna was born September 17, the name day of the martyred St. Sophia and her daughters. See Zelensky, "Sophia the Wisdom of God," 203–5; and Hughes, *Sophia,* chap. 1.

63. For the text of Sil'vestr's panegyrical "Charter" (January 21, 1685), see A. M. Panchenko, *Russkaia sillabicheskaia poeziia XVII–XVIII vv.* (Leningrad, 1970), 191–97; and the discussion in Zelensky, "Sophia the Wisdom of God," 285.

quently, mere human words and actions, such as the ones performed by the clergy during the Eucharist, had no power to transform the bread and wine into the body and blood of Christ. The clergy enjoyed no special relationship with the divine; they were simply men, and their only power was to perform and maintain the cult. Consequently, grace and enlightenment did not require consecration.[64] Similarly, the female regent did not need to be crowned or anointed by the patriarch in order to exercise royal authority. Her mandate to rule came from the fact that in her liminal position as the earthly counterpart of Divine Wisdom, she was above and beyond all established hierarchies, whether of gender, church, or state.[65]

Responding to Sil'vestr's challenge to patriarchal authority, Ioakim's team of experts (the brothers Leichoudes and the patriarch's ghost writer, Evfimii Chudovskii)[66] argued that God's grace could not be bestowed on the Eucharistic elements, or, for that matter, on the tsar, without the mediation of the ordained members of the ecclesiastical hierarchy. Only the recitation of the Prayer of Invocation can transform the sacramental bread and wine into the body and blood of Christ. Similarly, only the patriarch's invocation of the Holy Spirit—particularly during the ceremony in which the leading hierarch anoints a newly crowned tsar—symbolically elevated the body of the earthly monarch to the level of the Heavenly King. Furthermore, they linked anointment, like Communion during the coronation service, with the special sacerdotal quality of Muscovite tsars. Invoking the authority of Greek theologians such as Archbishop Symeon of Thessalonica, Evfimii Chudovskii defended the practice of taking Communion as a priest, behind the closed gates that hid the altar from the laity during the Eucharistic service—a practice that was explicitly modeled on the coronation of Byzantine emperors and seems to have been introduced during the reign of Tsar Aleksei Mikhailovich as a way of highlighting the tsar's divine election.[67] Since a woman could neither receive Communion at the altar nor be ordained as a priest, this practice also ensured and legitimated succession by primogeniture exclusively through the male line of the royal family. The patriarchalism of the Russian Orthodox Church on the issue of the royal succession thus fitted in well with the customary laws regarding property relations among the hereditary landowning service elites. Taken together, both could be used to challenge the legitimacy of Tsarevna Sof'ia's rule. And, as we have seen, that is precisely what the Trinity investigative commission attempted to accomplish.

64. For a discussion of this important point, see Potter, "Russian Church," 443–44, 463, 458.

65. On the interstitial nature of the Wisdom ideogram and its relation to Tsarevna Sof'ia Alekseevna's "gender-based marginality," see Zelensky, "Sophia the Wisdom of God," 8, 27.

66. On the life and career of Evfimii Chudovskii, see Olga B. Strakhov, "The Reception of Byzantine and Post-Byzantine Culture and Literature in Muscovite Rus': The Case of Evfimii Chudovskii (1620s–1705)" (Ph.D. diss., Brown University, 1996).

67. For a discussion of this liturgical innovation, see Uspenskii, *Tsar' i patriarkh*, 174, 170, 164, 156, 185, 23n20.

The religious debate, like the succession struggle with which it was intimately intertwined, was settled by force of arms. After the coup of 1689, the patriarch personally authorized a search of Abbot Sil'vestr's monastic cell for any damaging evidence about his participation in the Shaklovityi plot.[68] A search of the premises turned up two engravings that served as the visual apotheosis of Tsarevna Sof'ia Alekseevna's claims to the leading position in the Muscovite royal trinity. In an engraving commissioned in 1688 by Shaklovityi for the glorification of his embattled patron, the Ukrainian artist A. Tarasevich depicted an allegorical representation of the triumvirate in Moscow. This visual panegyric, which was modeled on the *conclusio* appended to Lazar' Baranovich's *Grace and Truth,* was to accompany Iakov Bogdanovskii's book in honor of the regent, *The Gifts of the Holy Spirit.*[69] In the engraving, which illustrated the main proposition of the book, Tarasevich portrayed "the descent of the seven gifts of the Holy Spirit . . . above that of her great sovereign majesty"; above the figures of the two co-tsars he pointedly excluded everything but their patronymics. In the words of Abbot Sil'vestr, who was shown a copy of this engraving, "all the glory and praise went to the great sovereign lady alone."[70] By emphasizing that the gifts of the Holy Spirit descended on the tsarevna, and on her alone, the engraver followed the author in designating the regent as more than first among equals. Referring to a biblical verse often used in the regent's panegyrics, the author of this visual composition underlined the connotations of God-chosen charismatic rulership, standing above and beyond the natural laws of inheritance or gender.[71] Just as the Holy Spirit descended upon the "holy gifts" of the Eucharistic bread and wine, miraculously transforming them into the body and blood of Christ, so the descent of the "gifts of the Holy Spirit" transformed a woman, traditionally excluded from political rule, into the earthly embodiment of God-given sovereignty.

Sil'vestr's personal participation in the creation of the second engraving discovered during the search of his premises demonstrated his continued reliance on the gifts of the Holy Spirit as the main distinguishing sign of the regent's divine election. In this print, Tsarevna Sof'ia Alekseevna is pictured with scepter, orb, and crown (but without the pectoral cross) of the Romanov tsars as they were portrayed in the official Book of Royal Titles (*Tituliarnik*), whose oval portraits seem to have been the prototype for this engraving. The regent's title as full-fledged sovereign, as well as a panegyric by Sil'vestr, is located in a cartouche at the bottom of the page. In these verses Sil'vestr enumerates the personal qualities that demonstrate that Sof'ia has

68. *Rozysknoe delo,* 1:829–30.

69. On A. Tarasevich and his engraving, see M. A. Alekseeva, *Graviura petrovskogo vremeni* (Leningrad, 1990), 8, 12. Unlike I. Bogdanovskii's *Dary dukha sviatogo* (Chernigov, 1688), the Tarasevich engraving has not been preserved. See Bogdanov, "Politicheskaia graviura," 241n70.

70. *Rozysknoe delo,* 1:660, 595–96.

71. See the analysis in Zelensky, "Sophia the Wisdom of God," 280, 315–16.

been blessed with the divine grace and power of Sophia the Wisdom of God.[72] The oval portrait appeared on the chest of the two-headed eagle of the Muscovite grand princely seal, surrounded by medallions depicting the allegorical representations of the seven gifts of the Holy Spirit (wisdom, piety, virginity, mercy, justice, fortitude, and meekness) mentioned in the abbot's panegyric to his patron. In the words of Shaklovityi, who had commissioned this engraving, the whole layout was supposed to echo the seal of the Holy Roman Emperor (also a two-headed eagle, with the seven medallions originally representing the seven imperial electors).[73] But although he thereby suggested that this engraving may simply have been part of the regency's efforts to prop up its declining international prestige after the failed Crimean campaign, the investigators from the Trinity commission clearly saw this as part of a treasonous attempt to crown the tsarevna alongside her brothers.[74]

To the Naryshkins and the retinue of the patriarch, Sil'vestr's participation in the creation of these engravings served as direct evidence of the abbot's crimes against the majesty of the tsar, the piety of the faithful, and the stability of the Russian Orthodox Church. Such crimes called for the harshest possible penalties from both the secular and spiritual authorities. A massive manhunt launched by the Trinity investigative commission resulted in Sil'vestr's capture in a monastery near Smolensk, on the border between Muscovy and the Polish-Lithuanian Commonwealth. The fleeing abbot was quickly returned to Moscow and incarcerated in the Trinity–St. Sergius Monastery, where just a few weeks before Shaklovityi and the other "co-conspirators" had met their bloody end. At the same time, Patriarch Ioakim quickly organized a rump church council to reassert his authority over the program of religious enlightenment and signal the defeat of what came to be branded as the "Latin" party within the Russian and Ukrainian Orthodox churches.[75] By defrocking Abbot Sil'vestr and forcing him to renounce his views on the Eucharist, the patriarch and his entourage succeeded not only in cowing the Ukrainian prelates into accepting what soon became the official Russian Orthodox dogma on the moment of transubstantiation,[76] but also in diverting the blame for the violent outcome of the succession struggle within the royal family to another scapegoat.

Polemical pamphlets and manuscripts produced in the wake of the

72. For a translation of the text, see ibid., 317–18.

73. *Rozysknye dela*, 1:596.

74. Even now this engraving is often referred to as a "coronation portrait." See Bogdanov, "Politicheskaia graviura," 242. For a discussion of the origins and symbolism of the engraving, see Zelensky, "Sophia the Wisdom of God," 318–22.

75. On the church council of 1690, see Prozorovskii, *Sil'vestr Medvedev*, 370–76; and Potter, "Russian Church," 504–5. The partisan terms ("Latinophile" and "Grecophile") for the different sides of the educational and theological debates in the second half of the seventeenth century appear to have been applied consistently only after this council, i.e., a couple of years after the conclusion of the debates that supposedly gave rise to them. See Strakhov, "Reception," 55; Potter, "Russian Church," 453.

76. Potter, "Russian Church," 468–69.

church council of 1690, such as "The Dagger" of Evfimii Chudovskii and "The Shield of Faith" of Archbishop Afanasii of Kholmogory, depicted Sil'vestr (Medvedev) as another in a long line of heretical priests and rabble-rousers whose nefarious activities and crypto-Catholic views shook the foundations of Muscovy. It is not surprising, therefore, that the (as yet unidentified) author of one of these manuscripts compared the abbot's actions with those of the early seventeenth-century renegade who was popularly identified with the False Dmitrii. Having betrayed his Orthodox faith and committed treason against the tsar, "like the former false and defrocked monk Grishka Otrep'ev," Abbot Sil'vestr had fled to Poland "to create more trouble [*smushchenie*], to evoke the scorn of the Catholic Church for our Eastern Orthodox faith, and to cause harm to our most pious Russian tsardom."[77] In this view, "Sen'ka Medvedev" was yet another Grishka Otrep'ev, a defrocked priest who had made a pact with the Catholic Poles in order to stir up a new Time of Troubles. However, just as the unanimous election of the Romanov tsar put an end to the period of unrest heralded by the collapse of the Riurikid dynasty, so the restoration of the diarchy and the imposition of unanimity within the church signaled the providential resolution of the new dynastic crisis. In this typological reading of Muscovite history, the formative moment of the reigning Romanov dynasty foreshadowed and clarified the outcome of the succession struggle three generations later. Thus, according to the politically motivated and self-serving interpretations offered by the apologists of the 1689 coup, divine intervention, not religious repression and political violence, ensured the success of the Naryshkins' restoration of Romanov rule.

The overthrow of the regency and the condemnation of Abbot Sil'vestr's teachings silenced all assertions about Tsarevna Sof'ia Alekseevna's unmediated access to the divine. Nevertheless, the fact that this principle of political legitimation had already been broached created the possibility for yet another way of describing the charisma of the tsar. In fact, as we will see, Peter's increasingly self-confident attempts to free himself from the constraints imposed on him by the Naryshkin restoration and declare his independence from the political coalition that had put him on the throne would rely, at least in part, on the ideas put forward by his former enemies. Simultaneously, the notion of unmediated royal charisma would inform the relations between the tsar and his entourage and would lead to the formation of Peter's own company, a socially heterogeneous and ecumenical coterie based less on familial and clan ties than on belief in his divine election for the task of transfiguring the Russian realm. This unconsecrated company— unconsecrated in both senses of the word, as not needing clerical sanctification and as something blasphemous and unholy—would become the cornerstone of Peter's Transfigured Kingdom.

77. Cited in Prozorovskii, *Sil'vestr Medvedev,* 330. On Grish'ka Otrep'ev, see Skrynnikov, *Samozvantsy v Rossii,* passim; and Dunning, "Who Was Tsar Dmitrii?" passim.

2   An Unconsecrated Company

On September 16, 1689, the Sunday immediately after the execution of F. L. Shaklovityi and his alleged co-conspirators, the armed retinue of Tsar Peter Alekseevich finally departed from the Trinity–St. Sergius Monastery, the fortified complex that had sheltered them during the coup against the regency of Tsarevna Sof'ia Alekseevna. Instead of returning to the newly pacified Russian capital, however, the leaders of the new, Naryshkin-led regime undertook yet another politically significant pilgrimage, this one to a nunnery near Aleksandrovskaia sloboda, a suburban royal estate some thirteen miles (twenty versts) outside of Moscow. The decision to visit this particular estate so soon after successfully carrying out the palace coup in favor of the Naryshkin line of the Russian royal house was significant in several respects. First, the trip guaranteed that the young tsar would be away from the capital on September 17, the name day of his half sister, the deposed regent. So while Tsar Ivan Alekseevich commemorated this day by dutifully toasting the health of his sister, his stepbrother and co-ruler was off in the country, demonstratively inspecting "a Monastery of Nunnes" who, in the words of General Patrick Gordon (1635–99), were reputed to keep "a very strict Lyfe, and admit no sort of male persons" into their company.[1] Judging by the rumors about Sof'ia Alekseevna's loose morals, secret liaisons,

---

1. *Dvortsovye razriady* (St. Petersburg, 1855), 4:486; Gordon, "Diary," RGVIA, f. 846, op. 15, kn. 4, l. 260 (September 16, 1689). Gordon was the most senior foreign officer in Muscovite service and the acknowledged head of Moscow's Catholic community. During the 1689 court coup, Gordon threw in his lot with the Naryshkins by dutifully bringing his troops to the Trinity–St. Sergius Monastery—an action to which he (rather immodestly) attributed decisive significance in the final showdown between the Naryshkins and the regency of Tsarevna Sof'ia Alekseevna. The most important source for Gordon's career in Muscovite service is his "Diary"; in addition, see M. O. Bender, "Patrick Gordon i ego dnevnik," RGVIA, f. 846, op. 15, kn. 8, ll. 1–53; and G. Herd, "General Patrick Gordon of Auchleuchries: A Scot in Seventeenth-Century Russian Service" (Ph.D. thesis, Aberdeen University, 1994).

and marriage plans, as well as by the Naryshkins' later decision to jail her in the Novodevich'i (New Maidens) Convent, this visit was a prelude to the forcible confinement of the "willful" tsarevna.[2]

Second, and just as important for understanding the political significance of the tsar's unscheduled pilgrimage to Aleksandrovskaia sloboda, was its historical value as the site of the infamous countercourt (*oprichnina*) of Tsar Ivan Vasil'evich (1530–84), better known as Ivan the Terrible.[3] From this suburban estate the sixteenth-century Russian monarch had launched his violent campaign of intimidation against the "traitors" within the established political elite in an attempt to realize the "autocratic" ideal signified by his earlier adoption of the Byzantine imperial title of tsar.[4] As the alternative site to the old Muscovite capital, Aleksandrovskaia sloboda represented the center of monastic purity from which the tsar and his closest advisers would sweep away corruption from the land and reinstitute the glory of Moscow, the Third Rome.[5] By implicitly invoking the image of Ivan Vasil'evich's terrible wrath against those members of the elite who supposedly had plotted against him during his minority, the organizers of the 1689 coup made a pointed historical reference, with menacing contemporary overtones for any potential political opposition to the newly installed relatives of Tsar Peter Alekseevich.[6]

2. The leaders of the Naryshkin-led regime confined Tsarevna Sof'ia Alekseevna in 1689, but she was not forced to take the veil until after the *strel'tsy* uprising of 1698. See Lindsey Hughes, *Sophia, Regent of Russia, 1657–1704* (New Haven, 1990), 133, 255, 310n41.

3. In addition to the nearby "Monastery of Nunnes," Gordon's attention was drawn to the fact that "here the Tzaar Ivan Vasiliovits (commonly called by strangers [i.e., foreigners] the tyrant) did usually reside, taking great delight in this solitary place, he had a large palace here, built of stone or brick rather environed with a thick and high earthen wall, the small River on the South syde thereof, giveing good convenience for ponds and meadows." See Gordon, "Diary," RGVIA, f. 846, op. 15, kn. 4, l. 260 (September 16, 1689).

4. For the ideological significance of Ivan Vasil'evich's 1547 coronation as tsar, see David B. Miller, "The Coronation of Ivan IV," *Jahrbücher für Geschichte Osteuropas* 15, no. 4 (1967): 559–74; Margarita E. Bychkova, "Obriady venchaniia na prestol 1498 i 1547 godov: Voploshchenie idei vlasti gosudaria," *Cahiers du monde russe et soviétique* 34, no. 1–2 (1993): 245–56; and B. A. Uspenskii, *Tsar' i patriarkh: Kharizma vlasti v Rossii (Vizantiiskaia model' i ee russkoe pereosmyslenie)* (Moscow, 1998), 13, 14, 20–22, 62–64, esp. 109–13.

5. See A. L. Dvorkin, *Ivan the Terrible as a Religious Type: A Study of the Background, Genesis and Development of the Theocratic Idea of the First Russian Tsar, and His Attempts to Establish "Free Autocracy" in Russia*, Oikonomia, 31 (Erlangen, 1992). The brooms carried by the tsar's personal bodyguards (the so-called *oprichniki*) symbolized the projected purification of the realm. For a discussion of the symbolism involved in Ivan's mock court (which appears to have been modeled on a religious military order), see D. S. Likhachev," Litsedeistvo Groznogo (k voprosu o smekhovom stile ego proizvedenii)," in Likhachev et al., *Smekh v drevnei Rusi*, 25–35 (Leningrad, 1984); and A. M. Panchenko and B. A. Uspenskii, "Ivan Groznyi i Petr Velikii: Kontseptsii pervogo monarkha," *Trudy otdela drevnerusskoi literatury* 37 (1983): 54–78.

6. The image of Ivan's terrible wrath was quite familiar to seventeenth-century Muscovites from various sources, including contemporary chronicles, the polemical correspondence between Ivan the Terrible and Prince Andrei Kurbskii, and historical accounts of the Time of Troubles. On the popularity of the epistolary exchange between the autocrat and the boyar, see Edward L. Keenan, *The Kurbskii-Groznyi Apocrypha: The Seventeenth-Century Genesis of the "Correspondence" Attributed to Prince A. M. Kurbskii and Tsar Ivan IV* (Cambridge, 1971). For the purposes of my argument, it does not really matter whether this correspondence

However, the fact that the supporters of the Naryshkin candidate enacted this threat thirteen miles from Moscow, and in the form of a previously unheard-of "field ballet military"—General Gordon's own term for the martial spectacles he helped to organize at the late seventeenth-century Russian court[7] —suggests that the military maneuvers that took place during Peter's stay at Aleksandrovskaia sloboda were intended more for the members of the new regime who participated in this expedition than for their foes back in Moscow. Indeed, the origins of the Transfigured Kingdom of Peter the Great owed as much to the esprit de corps fostered by such playful war games as to the evocative allegorical language in which seventeenth-century Muscovite courtiers and clerics had come to express their commitment to the divinely ordained person of the Russian Orthodox tsar. As we shall see, the Petrine court's antinomian stance toward the Muscovite establishment—a stance taken most clearly on the grounds of the royal suburban estate of Novo-Preobrazhenskoe during the tsar's supposedly innocent childhood amusements—served to emphasize the fact that the young Naryshkin candidate was the only person to possess the authority necessary to transfigure his realm on the basis of principles derived solely in accordance with the wishes of his father (both mortal and divine). In turn, the tsar's active participation in these suburban court spectacles demonstrated that at first his charismatic scenario of power could be formulated, understood, and enacted only in the small, self-selected company of his most trusted intimates.

The war games that took place at Aleksandrovskaia sloboda immediately after the 1689 palace coup were the first in a series of spectacular military maneuvers organized by General Gordon. But they were by no means the first martial ceremonies staged on the grounds of suburban royal estates by Peter's political supporters, nor were they the last in the line of politically significant royal amusements ever staged at the Muscovite court. Indeed, before we can understand the origins of Peter's new scenario of power and the way his pastimes could be used to assert his personal charisma, we must analyze the serious role that such private suburban royal spectacles assumed for the court of Peter's father. As even a brief survey of the prominent place of royal pastimes in Muscovite court culture will demonstrate, at least from the second half of the seventeenth century the suburban estates of Russian tsars served as alternative sites in the cultural geography of the capital and played an important role in the Romanovs' attempt to ground monarchical authority in the realm of the sacred.[8] Indeed, if we are to understand the full

---

is a forgery; what is important is the fact that these and other manuscript sources about the life and times of the last great Riurikid tsar undoubtedly circulated at the late Muscovite court. On the popularity of this epistolary exchange, see *Perepiska Ivana Groznogo s Andreem Kurbskim*, ed. Ia. S. Lur'e and Iu. D. Rykov (Leningrad, 1979), 248.

7. For Gordon's use of this term, see, e.g., the entry for October 14, 1691, in "Diary," RGVIA, f. 846, op. 15, kn. 5, l. 101.

8. For the growing importance of suburban pleasure palaces in the life of the Muscovite elite in general and the royal family in particular, see A. F. Smith, "Prince V. V. Golitsyn: The Life of an Aristocrat in Muscovite Russia" (Ph.D. diss., Harvard University, 1987), chap. 6; Iu. A. Tikhonov, "Podmoskovnye imeniia russkoi aristokratii vo vtoroi polovine XVII–nachale

significance of Novo-Preobrazhenskoe in the evolution of Peter's charismatic scenario of power, we must examine the way his father, Tsar Aleksei Mikhailovich, used *his* suburban royal estates as political statements.

Autocracy in the Suburbs

Article 6 of Aleksei Mikhailovich's Law Code of 1649, the first substantive legal definition of the Muscovite royal court as an institution, built a ceremonial fence of honor around any place His Majesty happened to be in the course of the customary pilgrimages through his Orthodox realm.[9] To infringe on this exclusive if peregrinating sacred spot was tantamount to encroaching on the house of God—the church. Equating ceremonial order, religious orthodoxy, and public tranquility, the compilers of the Law Code of 1649 did not hesitate to stipulate similarly severe punishments for blasphemers, schismatics, and other disturbers of the peace and decorum in church and at court.[10] In both ritual environments, the correct performance of ceremonies ensured that divine majesty and regal splendor radiated outward from the royal throne, whether it happened to be the Orthodox altar or the tsar's ceremonial seat of power.[11] Hierarchically arranged and legally enforced, proximity to either spot determined one's access to the powers of the divine.

Like Louis XIV's contemporaneous move to the hunting lodge of Versailles, the Muscovite court's withdrawal behind the guarded fences of elaborately organized suburban estates represented more than a flight from the often turbulent politics of the capital. Trips to the pleasure palaces outside Moscow, like pilgrimages and royal processions more generally, were also intended as the extension of a celestial order and harmony associated with the consecrated, immortal body of the tsar to the rest of his realm.[12] Whereas Aleksei Mikhailovich had to share the capital's ritual environment with the rest of the Muscovite political elite, his suburban estates gave him the opportunity to create his own personal space, one that embodied his tastes, ambitions, and personal vision of rule. From the mid-1660s, when

XVIII v.," in *Dvorianstvo i krepostnoi stroi Rossii XVI–XVIII vv. Sbornik statei, posviashchennyi pamiati A. A. Novosel'skogo,* ed. N. I. Pavlenko, 135–58 (Moscow, 1975); and O. R. Khromov, "Podmoskovnye votchiny Alekseia Mikhailovicha. Predvaritel'nye tezisy k vospriatiiu stilia tsarskikh usadeb," *Germenevtika drevnerusskoi literatury* 4 (1992): 285–301. For an insightful sociological analysis of the sacred as a product of ritual emplacement, see Jonathan Z. Smith, *To Take Place: Toward Theory in Ritual* (Chicago, 1987), 104–5.

9. For the text of the Law Code of Tsar Aleksei Mikhailovich, see *The Muscovite Law Code (Ulozhenie) of 1649,* ed. and trans. Richard Hellie (Irvine, CA, 1988).

10. Ibid., 1:1–9; Khromov, "Podmoskovnye votchiny," 288, 297.

11. For a semiotic interpretation positing the symbolic equivalence of the altar and the throne, see Uspenskii, *Tsar' i patriarkh,* 144–50.

12. Nancy S. Kollmann, "Pilgrimage, Procession, and Symbolic Space in Sixteenth-Century Russian Politics," in *Medieval Russian Culture,* California Slavic Studies 19, ed. Michael S. Flier and Daniel Rowland, 2:163–81 (Berkeley, 1994).

the tsar began to refurbish existing royal estates and acquired several new ones around the capital, his estates began to be ranked in accordance with the royal favor bestowed upon them and decorated to illustrate the image that the tsar wished to project. Just as a Muscovite courtier's honor was determined by a complicated system of place ranking (*mestnichestvo*), which combined pedigree and service, so the amount of attention, resources, and time lavished on one locale usually depended on both its function and its position in the royal hierarchy of status and prestige. In this way, royal suburban estates not only reflected the tsar's role as head of state, private individual, and leader of Muscovite court society, but also doubled for Aleksei Mikhailovich himself.[13] They thus served both of the tsar's two bodies, satisfying the personal needs of the mortal man and the dynastic and religious requirements of his body politic.[14]

Aleksei's suburban estates therefore presented the perfect arena for the tsar to escape the social and ideological constraints of Moscow and enact his particular political vision. Samuel Collins (1619–70), an Englishman who was privy to some of these intimate and personally meaningful demonstrations of royal power, thanks to his role as the tsar's personal physician, described the layout of one particularly memorable site on Aleksei Mikhailovich's annual pilgrimage circuit:

> Every year towards the latter end of May the Czar goes three miles out of Moscow, to an house of pleasure call'd Obrasausky [Preobrazhenskoe]: In English Transfiguration, being dedicated to the Transfiguration in the Mount. And according to that, Master 'tis good for us to be here, let us make three Tabernacles [Matt. 17:4; Mark 9:5; Luke 9:33]; So the Emperour has most magnificent Tents. . . . His and Czaritsa's, with those of his eleven children and five Sisters, stand in a circle with the Church-Tent in the middle, the most glorious show in its kind that ever I saw. There are Rails and Guards set Musquet shoot from them, beyond which no man may pass without order: For the Czar will have none of the vulgar people to be eye-witnesses of his pastimes.[15]

Although he was aware of the biblical proof texts on which this scene of royal deification was obviously modeled, Collins did not draw out the political implications of his observations. Nor was that his job. As the tsar's physician, he was hired to tend to the health of Aleksei's natural body. The

13. For a useful comparative discussion of the various roles a contemporary European monarch could assume on his suburban estates, see Samuel J. Klingensmith, *The Utility of Splendor: Ceremony, Social Life, and Architecture at the Court of Bavaria, 1600–1800* (Chicago, 1993), 7.

14. On the notion of the king's two bodies and the application of religious imagery to the monarch, see Ernst H. Kantorowicz, *The King's Two Bodies: A Study in Medieval Political Theology* (Princeton, 1957). For the Russian case, see Michael Cherniavsky, *Tsar and People: Studies in Russian Myths* (New Haven, 1961); and Stephen L. Baehr, *The Paradise Myth in Eighteenth-Century Russia: Utopian Patterns in Early Secular Russian Literature and Culture* (Stanford, 1991).

15. Samuel Collins, *The Present State of Russia . . .* (London, 1671), 113–14.

task of extolling the tsar's mystical body and ministering to his spiritual needs was in the hands of the official court preacher, Simeon of Polotsk (1629–80).[16] Not coincidentally, this academically trained Ruthenian Orthodox monk offered the best explanation of the way the allegorical spectacles staged on Aleksei Mikhailovich's suburban estates modeled the transfiguration of the tsar's body politic.

In a cycle of poems written to celebrate the dedication of the suburban royal estate at Kolomenskoe—one of the oldest hereditary possessions of the Muscovite grand princes and, before the cultivation of Preobrazhenskoe, the site of Aleksei's unofficial second capital—Simeon of Polotsk attempted to situate this architectural embodiment of the tsar's piety and political ambitions within the new imperial discourse that he helped to create.[17] By linking typically Baroque figurative conventions with imagery from the Old and New Testaments, Simeon depicted Aleksei Mikhailovich's pleasure palace, and by metaphoric extension his entire royal house, as a magnificent architectural reflection of metaphysical wisdom, celestial order, and heavenly light. Although Simeon's poetic evocation of Kolomenskoe is based on its explicit comparison with the royal palace of the biblical King Solomon, it also includes stylized descriptions of the actual architectural and iconographic wonders of Aleksei Mikhailovich's suburban estate, all of which served to underline the wisdom and taste of Simeon's royal patron.[18] Using the common rhetorical convention of comparing the garden with heaven—a tradition dating back to King Solomon's Song of Songs and popular in seventeenth-century moralistic, didactic, and religious works— Simeon thus sought to depict the tsar's exclusive suburban estate as a special paradisiacal spot and thereby to effect a (rhetorical) merger between the tsar's two bodies.[19]

16. For an analysis of Simeon's contribution to the formation of early modern Russian court culture, see A. N. Robinson, *Bor'ba idei v russkoi literature XVII veka* (Moscow, 1974); L. I. Sazonova, *Poeziia russkogo barokko (vtoraia polovina XVII–nachalo XVIII v.)* (Moscow, 1991); Paul Bushkovitch, *Religion and Society in Russia: The Sixteenth and Seventeenth Centuries* (New York, 1992), 163–72.

17. On Kolomenskoe, see *Podmoskov'e: Pamiatnye mesta v istorii russkoi kul'tury XIV–XIX vekov*, ed. S. V. Veselovskii et al., 2nd ed. (Moscow, 1962), 167–89; I. L. Bruseva-Davydova, "Ob ideinom zamysle Kolomenskogo dvortsa," *Arkhitektura mira* 2 (1993); idem, "Tsarskie usad'by XVII v.," *Russkaia usad'ba* 1 (1994): 140–44; and D. Zheludkov and O. Trubnikova, "Dereviannoe chudo v Kolomenskom," *Moskovskii arkhiv. Istoriko-kraevedcheskii al'manakh* 1 (1996): 12–28; for the notion of Kolomenskoe as second capital, see Khromov, "Podmoskovnye votchiny," 293. The ceremonial greeting in honor of Tsar Aleksei Mikhailovich has been published in two collections: *Simeon Polotskii. Izbrannye sochineniia*, ed. I. P. Eremin, 103–8 (Moscow and Leningrad, 1953); and *Russkaia sillabicheskaia poeziia XVII–XVIII vekov*, ed. V. P. Adrianova-Peretts, 108–11 (Leningrad, 1970). For the text of the "ceremonial greetings" composed in honor of the other members of the royal family, as well as an insightful analysis of the cycle as a whole, see O. R. Khromov, " 'Tsarskii dom' v tsikle Simeona Polotskogo na novosel'e," *Germenevtika drevnerusskoi literatury* 2 (1989): 217–43.

18. Khromov, " 'Tsarskii dom,' " 219–22.

19. On the sources and use of the motif of the heavenly "enclosed garden" (Lat. *hortus conclusus*) in the moral-didactic poetry of Simeon of Polotsk, see Sazonova, *Poeziia russkogo barokko,* chap. 5. On the merging of the tsar's two bodies in seventeenth-century Muscovite royal panegyrics, see Cherniavsky, *Tsar and People,* chap. 2.

Simeon's poetic evocation of Kolomenskoe did as much to emplace the sacrality of the house of Romanov as the architectural construction and ceremonial dedication of the tsar's pleasure palace. Alluding to the parable recounted in the Gospels (Mark 12:41–44; Luke 21:1–4), Simeon expressed the hope that Aleksei Mikhailovich would accept his poetic contribution to the housewarming celebrations, just as Christ the King (in Russian, *tsar'*) not only deigned to accept the poor widow's mite but also taught his disciples that her selfless act of charity meant more than all the gold cast in by the rich. Similarly, Simeon of Polotsk urged his royal patron not only to reward his poetic efforts with generosity but also to recognize the evangelical meaning contained in his poem (*slovo*, "word" or "sermon"). After wishing long life to the new homeowner, Simeon spelled out the implicit comparison between the earthly and heavenly tsars:

> In this new house, with the New Man
> invested, live till the end of [your] days.
> The New Man is Christ, the Tsar of Glory,
> He is also the crown on your head.

As Simeon's "word" is fleshed out during the recitation of this ceremonial greeting, the royal suburban estate where Aleksei Mikhailovich was poetically invested and crowned with Christ became the site of the tsar's deification. Indeed, the monk's poem seems intended to perform the same kind of mystery as the priest officiating at mass; for in the presence of believers, both public rituals transform the "host" into God. And just as the tsar becomes equated with Christ, so the estate at Kolomenskoe, in Simeon's highly stylized depiction, takes on the eschatological overtones of Mount Tabor, the site of Christ's transfiguration.[20] By arguing that the royal estate of Kolomenskoe was imbued with the celestial light of the Transfiguration, which passed from Godlike monarch to his radiant wife and children, illuminating the entire royal house and endowing his realm with an eschatological meaning, Simeon greatly expanded the iconographic boundaries of Muscovite political discourse.

But it was Preobrazhenskoe, the estate that actually bore the name of Christ's Transfiguration (after its first church, which was dedicated to the feast of the Transfiguration of the Saviour), that eventually came to play the most significant role in modeling the projected deification of the ruler, and therefore, by metaphoric extension, of his entire realm. Throughout the reign of Aleksei Mikhailovich, and even beyond, the position occupied by this royal estate in the courtly hierarchy of prestige evolved to reflect the changing political circumstances within the Muscovite royal house. Initially the village of Preobrazhenskoe was merely a convenient rest stop on the road to the royal estate of Izmailovo and the Trinity–St. Sergius monastery; it also served as a home base for those times when the tsar's hunting trips in

20. Khromov, " 'Tsarskii dom,' " 223.

the fields and groves around Elk Forest took him across the Iauza, a tributary of the Moscow River, to the small royal estate of Semenovskoe, the settlement of the royal falconers and the training ground for Aleksei Mikhailovich's extensive collection of hunting birds. By the end of the 1660s, however, after the tsar ordered the construction of a small wooden church dedicated to the Ascension (presumably to commemorate the death of his first wife and to accommodate even more of his retinue), the estate became a much more frequent stop on the court's annual itinerary.[21]

Preobrazhenskoe was extensively remodeled in the 1670s, after Aleksei Mikhailovich's second marriage and the birth of another male heir, the future Peter the Great. These dynastic developments, which sowed the seeds of the political rivalry between the supporters of the two distaff sides of the Russian royal family, were also linked to the timing of the first theatrical productions staged at the Muscovite court. This unprecedented royal amusement took place in a special playhouse constructed on the Preobrazhenskoe estate. The first play, based on the biblical story of Esther, was performed on October 17, 1672, just a few months after the birth of Peter Alekseevich, and represented the new in-laws' bid for power, as well as Aleksei Mikhailovich's attempt to ensure an orderly succession.[22] Indeed, the veiled allusions to contemporary events in this and other court dramas explain why in the last years of Aleksei's reign the court spent so much time in the relatively poor and undeveloped region around Preobrazhenskoe rather than in the more luxurious accommodations of some of the other royal estates.[23] For in the relative privacy of this secluded pleasure palace, Aleksei Mikhailovich was able both to stress his mediating leadership role as host to Muscovite court society in a new, dramatic fashion and to enact his own vision of personal rule in front of a captive audience (who, if need be, could be forced to attend).[24] In the latter years of his reign, Preo-

21. On Preobrazhenskoe, see I. E. Zabelin, "Istoriia i drevnosti Moskvy," in *Opyty izucheniia russkikh drevnostei i istorii. Issledovaniia, opisaniia i kriticheskie stat'i*, 2 vols., 2:107–53 (Moscow, 1872–73); idem, *Preobrazhenskoe ili Preobrazhensk: Moskovskaia stolitsa dostoslavnykh preobrazovanii pervogo imperatora Petra Velikogo* (Moscow, 1883); P. V. Sinitsyn, *Preobrazhenskoe i okruzhaiushchie ego mesta: Ikh proshloe i nastoiashchee* (Moscow, 1895); A. Bugrov, "Staro-Preobrazhenskii dvorets," *Moskovskii arkhiv. Istoriko-kraevedcheskii al'manakh* 1 (1996): 42–58.

22. For the text of the play, see A. N. Robinson et al., eds., *Pervye p'esy russkogo teatra* (Moscow, 1972). On the first Russian court theater, see S. K. Bogoiavlenskii, *Moskovskii teatr pri tsariakh Aleksee i Petre* (Moscow, 1914); and V. N. Vsevolodskii-Gerngross, *Russkii teatr: Ot istokov do serediny XVIII v.* (Moscow, 1957), chap. 5. For a discussion of the way Muscovite court theater reflected contemporary mores and referred to the latest political events, see Vsevolodskii-Gerngross, *Russkii teatr*, 102, 110; and O. A. Derzhavina, "Teatr i dramaturgiia," in *Ocherki russkoi kul'tury XVII v.*, ed. A. V. Artsikhovskii, 126–41 (Moscow, 1979).

23. Zabelin, *Preobrazhenskoe ili Preobrazhensk*, 17–18. Preobrazhenskoe was also conveniently located halfway between Moscow and the Foreign Settlement, which supplied the technical know-how for staging this new court spectacle.

24. Aleksei Veselovskii, *Starinnyi teatr v Evrope* (Moscow, 1870), 319–20, cited in A. S. Demin, "Russkie p'esy 1670-kh godov i pridvornaia kul'tura," *Trudy otdela drevnerusskoi literatury* 27 (1972): 282–83n17; Simon Karlinskii, *Russian Drama from Its Beginnings to the Age of Pushkin* (Berkeley, 1985), 43–44.

brazhenskoe was the only other suburban estate where Aleksei Mikhailovich celebrated important religious holidays and occasionally received foreign embassies, and it was therefore the only site that could rival Kolomenskoe as the capital of his own personal Transfigured Kingdom.

All Work and No Play

Despite Tsar Aleksei Mikhailovich's best efforts, the familial peace and social harmony symbolically enacted on the stage of Preobrazhenskoe failed to materialize in the political life of the court after his death in 1676. Indeed, after the untimely death of his eldest son and heir, Tsar Fedor Alekseevich in 1682, the political infighting between the Naryshkins and the Miloslavskiis escalated into a fierce succession struggle over the throne. As we have seen, in the course of that struggle each party put forth a candidate whom it claimed as the embodiment of Aleksei's vision of order and therefore the true heir to the throne of Moscow. Judging by their patronage strategies, as during the extensive remodeling of the Novodevich'i Convent, the architectural embodiment of the Sophia–Wisdom of God ideogram, the Miloslavskiis and their supporters chose to emphasize the exemplary piety of Tsar Ivan Alekseevich and his sister Sof'ia.[25] The Naryshkins, for their part, capitalized on the advice given in the introduction to Tsar Aleksei Mikhailovich's *Rules of Falconry* (1656): "These maxims are for your souls and bodies; but never forget truth and justice, and benevolent love and martial exercise; one must have enough time for work, and some hours of frolic."[26] Just as Aleksei Mikhailovich had playfully used his royal falconers to stage his personal vision of the well-ordered Orthodox realm on his favorite suburban estates,[27] so young Tsar Peter's relatives used the newly built estate of Novo-Preobrazhenskoe to stage politically significant court spectacles for their candidate's amusement.

Over the seven years of the succession struggle (1682–89) the Naryshkins and their allies mobilized the resources and symbolic practices associated with the discursive domain of the royal suburban estate as part of their attempt to put the young Peter Alekseevich on the throne.[28] Appealing to a tradition according to which royal estates could serve as the potential locus of political transformation and moral renewal, the tsar's maternal relatives

25. For a discussion of Tsarevna Sof'ia Alekseevna's patronage of the Novodevich'i Convent, see Hughes, *Sophia,* 124, 133, 152–54, 225, 243, 258–59; and E. K. Zelensky, " 'Sophia the Wisdom of God' as a Rhetorical Device during the Regency of Sof'ia Alekseevna, 1682–1689" (Ph.D. diss., Georgetown University, 1992), 323–31.

26. Serge A. Zenkovsky, ed., *Medieval Russia's Epics, Chronicles, and Tales,* 2nd ed. (New York, 1974), 521–22.

27. André Berelowitch, "Chasse et rituel en Russie au XVIIe siècle: Le *Règlement de la Fauconnerie* d'Alexis Mixajlovic," in *Russes, Slaves et Soviétiques. Pages d'histoire offertes à Roger Portal,* ed. C. Gervais-Francelle (Paris, 1992), 85–121.

28. On the formation of discursive domains, see Peter Stallybrass and Allon White, *The Politics and Poetics of Transgression* (Ithaca, 1986), 60–61.

sought to decenter the power of the regency of Tsarevna Sof'ia Alekseevna and to institutionalize their own opposition court. In the process of preparing for what must have seemed like an inevitable clash with the Miloslavskiis, Peter's entourage oversaw the militarization of the service staff responsible for administrating his amusements. Under the direction of Prince F. Iu. Romodanovskii (1640–1717)—head of the Preobrazhenskoe estate chancellery (*Poteshnaia izba*) responsible for recruiting, supplying, and administrating Peter's play regiments, as well as for policing the grounds of the estate—and some other courtiers around the tsaritsa dowager Natal'ia Kirillovna Naryshkina, royal falconers, grooms, and gunners joined foreign military specialists in staging salutes and firework displays on important family dates to symbolize the (frequently exaggerated) might of the Naryshkin faction.[29]

As early as May 30, 1683, on their candidate's eleventh birthday, the Naryshkins recruited a foreign mercenary named Simon Sommer to aid a team of master artisans and journeymen from the Moscow Artillery Chancellery in organizing a "playful firearms salute" (*ognestrel'nye poteshnye strel'by*) on the suburban estate of Vorob'evo.[30] A year later, in June 1684, Captain Sommer organized a similar display on the grounds of Preobrazhenskoe in anticipation of the young tsar's name day, which fell at the end of the month.[31] These demonstrations of advanced military firepower were a far cry from the wooden military toys traditionally assembled for the nursery of a young seventeenth-century Muscovite tsar, conveying the serious import that these royal amusements assumed on the estates outside of the Miloslavskii-controlled capital.[32] The military themes of the court spectacles staged by the Naryshkins presented their candidate as the rightful successor to the warlike imperial heritage of Tsar Aleksei Mikhailovich. The public demonstration of the young tsar's passion for fireworks and military spectacles thus asserted his role as the future commander in chief, a position

29. On Romodanovskii's role as head of the *Poteshnaia izba*, the precursor to the Preobrazhenskoe chancellery, see N. B. Golikova, *Politicheskie protsessy pri Petre I: Po materialam Preobrazhenskogo prikaza* (Moscow, 1957), 10.

30. On Simon Sommer, a professional soldier from Brandenburg then serving as a captain in Gordon's First Select Moscow Regiment, see G. V. Esipov, ed., *Sbornik vypisok iz arkhivnykh bumag o Petre Velikom*, 2 vols. (Moscow, 1872), 1:39. On the trip to Vorob'evo, see I. E. Zabelin, "Detskie gody Petra Velikogo," in *Opyty izucheniia russkikh drevnostei i istorii*, 43–45; idem, *Preobrazhenskoe ili Preobrazhensk*, 24–27; P. O. Bobrovskii, *Poteshnye i nachalo Preobrazhenskogo polka (Po ofitsial'nym dokumentam)* (St. Petersburg, 1899), 22.

31. Esipov, *Sbornik vypisok*, 1:46; and N. P. Astrov, "Pervonachal'noe obrazovanie Petra Velikogo," pt. 2, *Russkii arkhiv* 3, no. 8 (1875): 100.

32. On the traditional military nature of the toys in the Muscovite royal nursery, see E. F. Shmurlo, "Kriticheskie zametki po istorii Petra Velikogo," pt. 13, "Nachalo uchebnykh zaniatii Petra Velikogo," *Zhurnal Ministerstva Narodnogo Prosveshcheniia* 340 (1902): 435–36; P. V. Sedov, "Detskie gody tsaria Fedora Alekseevicha," in *Srednevekovaia Rus': Sbornik nauchnykh statei k 65-letiiu. . . . R. G. Skrynnikova*, 77–93 (St. Petersburg, 1995), esp. 80. On military toys in Peter's nursery, see Zabelin, "Detskie gody Petra Velikogo," 15–18, 42–43; and M. M. Bogoslovskii, *Petr I: Materialy dlia biografii* (Moscow and Leningrad, 1940), 1:18–20, 30–33.

to which neither of his Miloslavskii siblings could aspire, because of either health (Ivan) or gender (Sof'ia).

The construction of a small play city (*poteshnyi gorodok*) just across from Tsar Aleksei Mikhailovich's old Preobrazhenskoe palace was itself a significant step in the organization of the Naryshkins' countercourt and in the elaboration of its activist, political ideology. Early in February 1685, when the retinue of Tsar Peter Alekseevich first visited the site of the new suburban construction project, the play city consisted of nothing more than two small huts.[33] From such inauspicious beginnings, however, the play city went on to become the center of a bustling settlement of military units established for the tsar's amusement (*poteshnye polki*). Over the next decade, as part of the show of force favored by the entourage around Tsar Peter Alekseevich, this play city was transformed into the nucleus of a play kingdom, serious in all but name. At its center, on a manmade island in the middle of the Iauza River, stood a fortress, which was connected by floating bridges to the suburb of lower-class military servitors on one side and to Tsar Aleksei Mikhailovich's old royal palace on the other. The fort was defended by a mock army staffed by royal grooms from the old Preobrazhenskoe stables, the falconers from nearby Semenovskoe, and the children of the Muscovite noble elite, who served as Peter Alekseevich's royal chamberlains.[34] By 1687, court records indicate the appearance of "toy boats" (*poteshnye korabli*), such as those found in the garden ponds of the Kremlin and Izmailovo,[35] which could also be used to navigate the river. In the following years other buildings were erected within the city walls, including a stone church, living quarters for leading dignitaries and royal intimates— records for 1687 specifically mention the quarters of *kravchii* Prince B. A. Golitsyn and *spal'niki* L. K., M. K., and F. K. Naryshkin—and barns, stables, granaries, and storehouses for munitions.[36] In sum, by the end of the 1680s the Naryshkin faction had transformed Preobrazhenskoe from a bucolic site of Peter's childhood amusements to an alternative capital and the locus of a new transfiguration.

The deliberate addition of the adjective *Novo* (new) to the name of this particular royal estate demonstrates that the entourage of Tsar Aleksei Mikhailovich's youngest son intended to tap into the allegorical justifica-

33. Records for the new construction project began to be kept only in February 1685. See Esipov, *Sbornik vypisok*, 1:55–56, 345. On the royal visit, see *Dvortsovye razriady*, 4:327–29; Astrov, "Pervonachal'noe obrazovanie Petra Velikogo," pts. 2 and 3, *Russkii arkhiv* 3, nos. 8 (1875): 90–102, and 10 (1875): 213, 215–16.

34. For the memoirs of two prominent participants, see Prince B. I. Kurakin, "Gistoriia o tsare Petre Alekseeviche," in *Petr Velikii. Vospominaniia. Dnevnikovye zapisi. Anekdoty*, ed. L. Nikolaeva (Moscow, 1993), 67, 74–75; and A. A. Matveev, "Zapiski Andreia Artamonovicha, grafa Matveeva," in *Zapiski russkikh liudei: Sobytiia vremen Petra Velikogo*, ed. I. Sakharov (St. Petersburg, 1841), 48, 85n24. See also Bogoslovskii, *Petr I*, 1:20–21.

35. D. S. Likhachev, *Poeziia sadov. K semantike sadovo-parkovykh stilei: Sad kak tekst*, 2nd ed. (St. Petersburg, 1991), 116–17.

36. Astrov, "Pervonachal'noe obrazovanie Petra Velikogo," pt. 3, 217–18; Bogoslovskii, *Petr I*, 58–60, 63–64.

tions invoked to celebrate the construction of old Preobrazhenskoe, the suburban site of Aleksei's royal epiphany. That all sides of the succession struggle were aware of the special significance of Novo-Preobrazhenskoe is demonstrated by the fact that the coup of 1689 was started by a rumor that the musketeers loyal to the regent were about to descend upon and set fire to this suburban capital of the Naryshkin faction. Indeed, it is hardly a coincidence that the tsar's unscheduled pilgrimage to the Trinity–St. Sergius Monastery took place on the night of August 6–7, 1689, just one day before Tsar Peter Alekseevich and his kinsmen were to celebrate the feast of the Transfiguration of the Saviour (August 8), and not on September 25, the name day of St. Sergius and therefore the usual time for the court's annual pilgrimage to that monastic shrine.[37] If even foreigners could recognize that this church feast was "a great holiday at Preobrasinsky,"[38] so could the much better informed (and much more paranoid) warring factions at the Muscovite court. In that sense, one could even say that the Naryshkins' preparations for the feast of the Transfiguration in the summer of 1689 sparked the court coup in favor of their candidate. Ironically, once in power, the former Naryshkin candidate and his intimates would use some of the same tropes to distance Peter from the broad and necessarily temporary political coalition that had supported his candidacy in 1689 and to elevate his persona above the fray of Muscovite clan and ecclesiastical politics.

The Bellicose Kingdom of Peace

The war games organized by Peter and his advisers immediately after the 1689 coup signaled the elaboration of a new policy of royal access and evidenced the formation of the tsar's own retinue of intimates, mentors, and boon companions, better known as his company. Indeed, the fact that the tsar made a demonstrative effort to extend his patronage to foreign (and confessionally heterodox) military experts—such as General Patrick Gordon, the Roman Catholic Scottish mercenary who helped to stage these spectacular military maneuvers in the first place—underlined the changed basis of belonging to Peter's inner circle. Adopting an unprecedented imagery to represent the authority of a Russian Orthodox tsar, Peter Alekseevich and his personal entourage went on to stage a series of elaborate and realistic military maneuvers just outside of the estate named after the Trans-

---

37. On the timing of the Muscovite court's annual pilgrimages to the Trinity–St. Sergius Monastery, see E. F. Shmurlo, "Kriticheskie zametki po istorii Petra Velikogo," pt. 10, *Zhurnal Ministerstva Narodnogo Prosveshcheniia* 330 (July–August 1900): 225. For the timing of Peter's unscheduled pilgrimage, see A. S. Lavrov, *Regentstvo tsarevny Sof'i Alekseevny: Sluzhiloe obshchestvo i bor'ba za vlast' v verkhakh Russkogo gosudarstva v 1682–1689 gg.* (Moscow, 1999), 157–58.

38. Gordon, "Diary," RGVIA, f. 846, op. 15, kn. 4, ll. 22 (August 6, 1690), 260.

figuration, implementing their own interpretation of the fundamental transformation and renewal promised by that church holiday (a promise enacted most visibly in the tsar's "miraculous" rescue during the August 1689 coup). The special significance that the feast of the Transfiguration held for Peter and his courtiers may also help to explain why many of these spectacles emphasized the tsar's Christlike willingness to abandon the external attributes of power and don the coarse clothes of a common soldier, all for the salvation of his people and the welfare of his realm.[39] Thus, despite the fact that Peter skirmished alongside his courtiers as just another subject of his sham lord and liege, the Prince-Caesar—F. Iu. Romodanovskii, in his new role as the chivalrous king of the Transfigured Kingdom—no one could ever truly forget that these public demonstrations of the tsar's masculine virtues served only to underline his charisma and his divine calling.[40]

Peter's adoption of a military rank in the army of the mock king of the Transfigured Kingdom coincided with the reorganization of the entourage responsible for staging his childhood amusements. At the end of 1690, the tsar instructed General Gordon to reform the play regiments along the lines of the foreign-trained "new-style" regiments of professional soldiers.[41] This military reorganization was not completed until the end of 1692. By 1693, the year of the first surviving list of commanding officers for the Preobrazhensk regiment, Moscow had four regular regiments: two old ones, known as the First and Second Select, and two new ones, the Preobrazhensk and the Semenovsk, which were still occasionally referred to as the play regiments (*poteshnye polki*). The members of the tsar's entourage took all the leading command positions in the newly created regiments, while the court personnel who staffed the tsar's play regiments went on to form the core group of low-level cadres (sergeants, corporals, and bombardiers) of the Preobrazhensk regiment and the grenadier units.[42] The tsar himself became the official royal patron of the Preobrazhensk regiment, receiving a newly

---

39. In the Eastern Orthodox tradition, the feast of the Transfiguration emphasizes the humanity of Christ, as evidenced by the liturgical hymn that expresses "two aspects of Christ's humanity—his natural state and his state of voluntary submission to conditions of fallen humanity." See Vladimir Lossky, *The Mystical Theology of the Eastern Church*, trans. Fellowship of St. Alban and St. Sergius (London, 1957), 148–149. On Christ's kenosis as the voluntary assumption of "the form of a slave," see 148; and George Fedotov, "Russian Kenoticism," in *The Russian Religious Mind*, 3:94–131 (Belmont, MA, 1975).

40. For an insightful analysis of this kind of royal imposture, see B. A. Uspenskii, "Tsar and Pretender: *Samozvanchestvo* or Royal Imposture in Russia as a Cultural-Historical Phenomenon," in *The Semiotics of Russian Culture*, ed. Ann Shukman (Ann Arbor, 1984), 268–72.

41. Introduced in the reign of Peter's grandfather, Tsar Mikhail Romanov, to supplement the traditional levy of Muscovite noblemen and their retainers, the new-style regiments went on to become the most important component of the seventeenth-century Russian army. See John L. H. Keep, *Soldiers of the Tsar: Army and Society in Russia, 1462–1874* (Oxford, 1985), 80–92; Richard Hellie, "The Petrine Army: Continuity, Change, and Impact," *Canadian-American Slavic Studies* 8, no. 2 (Summer 1974): 237–53; and Carol B. Stevens, "Evaluating Peter's Military Forces," *Russia in the Reign of Peter the Great: Old and New Perspectives*, ed. Anthony Cross, 2:89–103 (Cambridge, 1998).

42. Bobrovskii, *Poteshnye i nachalo Preobrazhenskogo polka*, 13–14.

designed "sergeant's kaftan" from the Court Workshop at the beginning of 1691.[43]

The elaborate war games accompanying the militarization of the court of Tsar Peter Alekseevich were integral not only to the transformation of his personal entourage but also in the elaboration of its new self-conception. Although the former play regiments were named and divided on a strictly topographical basis, according to their place of quartering, this practical division soon acquired an added dimension of meaning as the competing realms of two mock kings, who acted as the main characters in the "field ballets military" organized by General Gordon, with "great pompe" and "formalities," in 1690 and 1691.[44] The mock-solemn tone of these war games, facetiously called the first and second Semenovskoe campaigns, is clearly expressed in a contemporary "Description of the Great and Terrible Battle in which His Highness, Generalissimo Friedrich Romodanovskii took part on the 6th, 7th, and 9th of October in the present 200th year [1691]."[45] This anonymous work, written from the point of view of a soldier in the army of "Generalissimo Friedrich," offers one of the first documented glimpses into the imagery and practices shaping the personal entourage of the young tsar, as well as insight into the structure of the imaginary Transfigured Kingdom that was being created on the grounds outside the Muscovite capital.

The mock armies that took part in the choreographed war games of 1691 were actually commanded by the two courtiers who headed the chancelleries responsible for administering the lands and supervising the personnel on the royal estates of Novo-Preobrazhenskoe and Semenovskoe. Judging by the title of the "Description," the leading role in the mock campaign was played by Prince F. Iu. Romodanovskii, a fifty-one-year-old privy chamberlain (*komnatnyi stol'nik*) who belonged to a clan that proudly traced its lineage to the founding of the Riurikid dynasty.[46] As we have seen, during the regency of Tsarevna Sof'ia Alekseevna, Romodanovskii had led the chan-

43. Ibid., 7; *Opisanie vysochaishikh povelenii po pridvornomu vedomstvu, 1701–1740 gg.* (St. Petersburg, 1888), iv–v.

44. Bobrovskii, *Poteshnye i nachalo Preobrazhenskogo polka*, 13; and "Kozhukhovskii pokhod. 1694. (Sovremennoe opisanie)," ed. M. I. Semevskii, *Voennyi sbornik* 11, no. 1 (1860): 54; Gordon, "Diary," RGVIA, f. 846, op. 15, kn. 5, 1. 101 (October 14, 1691).

45. "Opisanie velikogo i strashnogo boiu, kotoryi byl v nyneshnem 200 godu oktiabria 6 i v 7, i v 9 chislekh u ego presvetleishego Generalissimusa Fridrikha Romodanovskogo," in N. G. Ustrialov, *Istoriia tsarstvovaniia Petra Velikogo*, 2:486–90 (St. Petersburg, 1858); see the discussion in Bogoslovskii, *Petr I*, 1:125–30.

46. For the genealogy of the Romodanovskii clan, see *Istoriia rodov russkogo dvorianstva*, ed. P. N. Petrov (St. Petersburg, 1886), 1:139–41; and A. A. Dolgorukov, *Rossiiskaia rodoslovnaia kniga* (St. Petersburg, 1855), 51–52. For a brief biography of Prince F. Iu. Romodanovskii, see Lindsey Hughes, *Russia in the Age of Peter the Great* (New Haven, 1998), 423–24. On Romodanovskii's service career, see I. Iu. Airapetian, "Feodal'naia aristokratiia v period stanovleniia absoliutizma v Rossii" (Diss., kand. ist. nauk, M. V. Lomonosov State University, 1987), 78, 149–50; and [N. Tokarev], "Blizhniaia kantseliariia pri Petre Velikom i eia dela," in *Opisanie dokumentov i bumag khraniashchikhsia v Moskovskom arkhive Ministerstva Iustitsii* (Moscow, 1888), 5 (2): 43–101.

cellery that administered the Naryshkin-controlled Preobrazhenskoe and its service staff, especially the staff responsible for the royal amusements. During the military reorganization of the early 1690s, this estate chancellery assumed responsibility for administering the Preobrazhensk regiment and staging the tsar's war games, as well as for handling all cases of lèse-majesté.[47] Partly as a result of his new appointment as head of the dreaded "Chancellery of Transfiguration" (*Preobrazhenskii prikaz*), Romodanovskii became a virtual stand-in for Peter Alekseevich, not only during court entertainments but also within the political leadership during the young tsar's increasingly frequent absences from Moscow.[48] Indeed, although he had never been promoted to the Muscovite royal council (Boyar Duma), Romodanovskii was undoubtedly one of the most powerful men in the entourage of Peter the Great.

Romodanovskii's archrival was I. I. "the Elder" (*bol'shoi*) Buturlin (d. 1710), "tsar and sovereign of Semenovsk."[49] A royal chamberlain from a large and wealthy noble family,[50] Buturlin seems to have been given a prominent role in this royal amusement thanks largely to his official capacity as head of the chancellery responsible for administering the land and the personnel at Semenovskoe, the old falconry yard of Tsar Aleksei Mikhailovich.[51] In what may have been a tribute to the late tsar's favorite pastime, for the duration of the campaign Buturlin was referred to as "Vatupich," a nickname probably derived from the designation for a type of pigeon (*vatutin, vetiutin*).[52] To anyone familiar with the political significance of Tsar Aleksei Mikhailovich's amusements, particularly the stress he put in his *Rules for Falconry* on the beauty and harmony of orderliness, it was apparent that during the choreographed military maneuvers staged by the entourage of Tsar Peter Alekseevich, the irregular troops of the "King of Semenovsk" would inevitably fall prey to the superior training of those of his rival. As will soon become apparent, however, the skills of Generalissimo Friedrich and his army owed less to the injunctions of *The Rules of Falconry* than to the laws of contemporary military art and the tenets of European chivalry.

47. Golikova, *Politicheskie protsessy,* 10; Kurakin, "Gistoriia," 83–84.

48. Hughes, *Russia,* 98.

49. Although the "Description" does not mention the name of the rival generalissimo, he is identified by Kurakin, "Gistoriia," 75. In a letter to Peter dated July 31, 1695, I. I. Buturlin the Elder signed his name as "Iagan [Johann], Generalissimo of the Semenovsk regiment." See *PiB,* 1:523–24.

50. From 1682 until his accidental death (by a collapsed roof) in 1710, I. I. Buturlin the Elder served as privy chamberlain (*komnatnyi stol'nik*) to Tsar Peter Alekseevich; at the same time, fourteen other Buturlins served as rank-and-file chamberlains (*riadovye stol'niki*). See Airapetian, "Feodal'naia aristokratiia," 98, 329, 347. For the genealogy of the Buturlin clan, see "Rodoslovnaia rospis' Buturlinykh [April 6, 1682]. Zaverennaia kopiia 1798 g.," SPb F IRI RAN, koll. 238, op. 2, karton 264, no. 4, l. 347. For the date of his accidental death, see Airapetian, "Feodal'naia aristokratiia," 77.

51. Kurakin, "Gistoriia," 75; Golikova, *Politicheskie protsessy,* 10.

52. Kurakin, "Gistoriia," 75; Charles E. Gribble, *A Short Dictionary of 18th-Century Russian* (Columbus, OH, 1987), 15.

Judging by the fact that for the duration of this royal amusement the little fort across from Preobrazhenskoe received the name Pressburg (*Presh-pur*)—the name of the actual capital of the kingdom of Hungary—the model of these martial virtues seems to have been the Holy Roman Emperor of the German Nation, Leopold I.[53] The two symbolic acts that signaled the extension of Habsburg royal absolutism into Hungary after its devastation by the Ottoman Turks and a protracted civil war—the Magyar magnates' grudging acceptance of restrictions to their constitution and the unprecedented election of the emperor's heir as king of Hungary in 1687—both took place in Pressburg.[54] This absolutist project was devised with the input of some of the leading theorists of cameralism at the late seventeenth-century Habsburg court, the same economic advisers whose policies helped finance the royal building boom in the 1690s around Vienna—patronage that some contemporaries saw as the Holy Roman Emperor's reassertion of imperial ambitions.[55] With the help of the Vatican, Leopold I had organized a new crusade against the Muslim infidels, and during the regency of Tsarevna Sof'ia Alekseevna he arbitrated the Eternal Peace that paved the way for Muscovy's inclusion in the Holy Alliance against the Ottoman Porte. After the 1689 coup, imperial diplomats repeatedly sought to induce the new regime in Moscow to live up to its diplomatic responsibilities by launching yet another campaign against the Crimean Tatar vassals of the Porte; but in the early 1690s, the recently installed government continued to shy away from resuming the unsuccessful campaigns that had brought down the regency. The appearance of a "King of Pressburg" during the military maneuvers of 1691 thus may have had a contemporary geopolitical resonance for its participants. By pointing to the Habsburg emperor's difficulties in pacifying his own realm, the establishment of "Pressburg" appears to have been intended to mock the claims of one of the Muscovite leadership's main geopolitical and confessional rivals, while simultaneously signaling Peter's refusal to be bullied into any rash acts.

More important, the example of Leopold I's policies in Hungary appears to have served as a political allegory for the restoration of royal authority in

53. For the reference to Pressburg as the capital city (*stol'nyi gorod* or *grad*) of "His Highness" Romodanovskii, see "Opisanie," in Ustrialov, *Istoriia*, 490; and Peter to F. Iu. Romodanovskii, May 19, 1695, *PiB*, 1:29 (no. 37). For another argument linking the appearance of "Pressburg" and "Generalissimo Friedrich" to the example provided by the Holy Roman Emperor of the German Nation, see Elena Pogosian, *Petr I: Arkhitektor rossiiskoi istorii* (St. Petersburg, 2001), 210–13.

54. John P. Spielman, *Leopold I of Austria* (New Brunswick, 1977), 134, 136. During his trip to Vienna in 1698, Peter and his entourage made a special visit to Pressburg. See Pogosian, *Petr I*, 212.

55. Thomas DaCosta Kaufmann, *Court, Cloister, and City: The Art and Culture of Central Europe, 1450–1800* (Chicago, 1995), 290–300. Cameralist policies entailed the centralization of power and more efficient administration of royal lands to promote growth of commerce and industry in the kingdom as a whole, and hence the independent income and power of the monarch. See Leonard Krieger, *Kings and Philosophers, 1689–1789* (New York, 1970), 64; Marc Raeff, *The Well-Ordered Police State: Social and Institutional Change through Law in the Germanies and Russia, 1600–1800* (New Haven, 1983).

Muscovy. During the war games of the early 1690s, the divisive political struggle between the Naryshkins and Miloslavskiis was symbolically replayed on a battlefield that was purposely tilted against the reputed supporters of the recently deposed regent. Romodanovskii's troops, composed of the regular cavalry and infantry regiments, including the two new royal guards regiments, squared off against the Muscovite musketeers, whose support of the Miloslavskii candidate in 1682 resulted in a popular uprising reminiscent of the Muscovite Time of Troubles, if not of the Hungarian civil war.[56] The inevitability of the choreographed victory of the head of the Chancellery of Transfiguration, the security organ responsible for investigating and punishing all cases of rebellion against the tsar, hinted at the form the reassertion of Muscovite absolutism was to take. By assigning the playful role of King of Pressburg to a trusted old courtier who wielded extraordinary judicial power over the entire political elite and expected to be treated with the respect due to his office as the head of the secret police and generalissimo of the guards regiments, Peter and his advisers demonstrated that they took the cameralist ideals of subordination to the embodiment of centralized, absolute power very seriously. Generalissimo Friedrich's defense of his own Pressburg thus came to express a serious political message in the entertaining-didactic form of contemporary court amusements.

For Tsar Peter and his entourage, however, demonstrating the new rules of the game was perhaps even more important than replaying the battles that accompanied the recent succession struggle. The German pseudonym of the King of Pressburg, like the foreign name of his mock capital, hinted at the broader vision of the Transfigured Kingdom imagined by the tsar and his entourage. Romodanovskii's new Christian name, Friedrich, bore no direct relation to his real first name, Fedor; however, it pointed to something more significant than the fact that the tsar habitually showed off his knowledge of Dutch and German by sprinkling his speech with foreign words. Referring to the mock king by the German word for "peaceful," the tsar seems to have been designating the role that his old favorite was to play during the war games, as well as the way he was to play it. The German name of the King of Pressburg recalled the biblical prototype of King Solomon, the Prince of Peace, whose very name evoked messianic expectations and whose image was so important in the allegorical court culture of Tsar Aleksei Mikhailovich. As we saw, Simeon of Polotsk had compared the "wonders" of Aleksei's estate at Kolomenskoe to those of King Solomon's palace in an effort to extol the wisdom of his royal patron; in the poem of the court preacher, the ancient king of Israel, who built the Temple and presided over the reign of peace and plenty from his capital in Jerusalem, served as the

---

56. Kurakin, "Gistoriia," 66. These politics also informed the much more famous Kozhukhovo campaign of 1694. See Richard H. Warner, "The Kozhukhovo Campaign of 1694; or, The Conquest of Moscow by Preobrazhenskoe," *Jahrbücher für Geschichte Osteuropas* 13 (1965): 487–96.

model for the seventeenth-century Muscovite tsar. Simeon's panegyric partook of the exegetical tradition according to which Solomon was a type of Christ, the king who established peace not by the sword but by the Word of God.[57] Similarly, the anonymous author of the "Description" seems to have had the example of the Peaceful Prince in mind when he chose to emphasize that the mock King of Pressburg was spurred to take up arms only in response to the aggressive intentions of the enemy generalissimo.[58] Indeed, it appears that in the war games staged by Tsar Peter Alekseevich on the grounds of his father's royal estates, the wise and chivalrous character of Generalissimo Friedrich embodied the millenarian vision associated with the founding of a new, Petrine Transfigured Kingdom.

While F. Iu. Romodanovskii, the courtier entrusted with defending the royal dignity, took on the title of the mock king, Tsar Peter Alekseevich freed himself to play roles more in keeping with his attempts to demonstrate his divine calling. Following the rules of the game that he himself had helped to establish, Peter assumed a new name and rank in the army of Generalissimo Friedrich, commanding a company of foreign-style cavalry (*reitary*) under the nom de guerre of Captain (*rotmistr*) Peter Alekseev.[59] Derived from his patronymic, the tsar's pseudonymous last name emphasized the lengths to which the son of Aleksei went to demonstrate his charismatic status as Muscovy's rightful monarch. According to the "Description," despite the lowly rank of his adopted persona, the tsar actually performed the most heroic act of personal bravery during the whole mock campaign. By intercepting the reckless charge of Generalissimo Buturlin against His Highness Romodanovskii, cavalry captain Peter Alekseev foiled the enemy's attempt to kill Generalissimo Friedrich and thereby "to behead his troops."[60] The mock army, that miniature body politic that was the Transfigured Kingdom of the King of Pressburg, was thus saved from disorder, flight, and defeat by the actual head of the Muscovite realm. This prominent and public display of the tsar's personal bravery conveyed the redemptive role of God's anointed in the new rhetoric of religious chivalry, prefiguring the symbolic role that Peter's tricorne—shot through by an enemy bullet in the heat of battle—was later to play in the panegyrics produced during the Great Northern War.[61]

In the imaginary world revealed by the insider's account of the war games, God decided the outcomes of military engagements on the basis of

57. For the image of the "second Solomon" in Russian political thought before Simeon of Polotsk, see G. Stökl, "Der zweite Salomon. Einige Bemerkungen zur Herrschervorstellung im alten Russland," *Canadian-American Slavic Studies* 13, no. 1–2 (1979): 23–31.

58. "Opisanie," in Ustrialov, *Istoriia*, 486.

59. Bogoslovskii, *Petr I*, 1: 127.

60. "Opisanie," in Ustrialov, *Istoriia*, 487.

61. For the most famous interpretation of this episode, see Feofan (Prokopovich), "Slovo pokhval'noe nad voiskami Sveiskimi pobede . . . , v leto gospodne 1709 mesiatsa iunia dnia 27 bogom darovannoi," and his "Slovo pokhval'noe o batalii Poltavskoi . . . , iunia v 27 den' 1717," both in his *Sochineniia*, ed. I. P. Eremin (Moscow and Leningrad, 1961), 31–32, 56–57.

the competing sides' adherence to the code of chivalry and martial valor. The duplicitous and cowardly behavior of Generalissimo Buturlin only served to emphasize the magnanimity of the tsar's mock double, the chivalrous Christian sovereign of Pressburg. Taken prisoner, the enemy king was led into the camp of Generalissimo Friedrich, who received his rival with the honors befitting a worthy opponent. In a generous act of hospitality, which foreshadowed the treatment of the Swedish command staff captured after the decisive Russian victory at Poltava (1709), the King of Pressburg wined and dined his prisoner, while saluting the bravery of his own troops. Generalissimo Friedrich further demonstrated his nobility (*blagoutrobie*) as a Christian sovereign (*gosudar' khristianskii*) by honoring Buturlin's petition to be allowed to return to his troops in exchange for a pledge of friendship, peace, and obedience. The day after his release, however, the King of Semenovsk forgot his "promises and the mercy shown to him," and resumed his campaign against the King of Pressburg. In the words of the "Description," the ensuing defeat of the enemy's cavalry demonstrated "God's mercy" and the "injustice" of their cause.[62]

This playful religious rhetoric also extended to his account of the general battle that took place on the last day of the Semenovskoe campaign. The author of the "Description" equated this decisive engagement, a five-hour military maneuver involving both infantry and cavalry, with Judgment Day (*sudnyi den'*).[63] But in the witty, tongue-in-cheek style of the "Description," the eschatological battle between the forces of good and evil assumed the form of a mock epic, complete with a comic portrayal of the cowardly actions of the enemy generalissimo, who hid among the "corpses" of his own troops before he was located and brought to his knees, literally and figuratively, in front of Generalissimo Friedrich. And while the victory of this King of Peace did not inaugurate the reign of the Messiah, it did symbolize the triumph of the ideals of the Transfigured Kingdom imagined by the inner circle of Tsar Peter Alekseevich. And these new ideals could not help having an impact on the way the tsar and his entourage related to the conservative politicians who had put the young Naryshkin candidate on the Muscovite throne. Indeed, just two months after the conclusion of the first Semenovskoe campaign, the tsar went on to organize a much more private court spectacle that demonstrated how far Peter Alekseevich would go to assert his charismatic authority and left very little doubt about the radical antinomian thrust of his new scenario of power.

The New Gospel According to Peter

On Sunday, December 27, 1691, General Patrick Gordon recorded in his diary that he was present at a ceremony in the royal palace (literally,

---

62. "Opisanie," in Ustrialov, *Istoriia*, 488.
63. Ibid., 490.

"above," Gordon's translation of the traditional Muscovite term for the royal apartments in the Kremlin), where a number of people, making up the inner circle of Tsar Peter Alekseevich, "Choysed a Patr:." Five days later, on Friday, January 1, 1692, Gordon noted that he was "in Preobrasinsko, at the installing of the Patriarch."[64] Judging by these laconic entries, Gordon was as uncomfortable with recording all the details of these extraordinary events as he was with revealing the identity of the person concealed behind the idiosyncratic abbreviation "Patr:." Indeed, to someone who was un-aware that the Scottish general was describing the parodic ordination of Matvei Filimonovich Naryshkin—the first mock patriarch of the so-called Most Comical and All-Drunken Council of Peter the Great—it might have seemed that Gordon was talking about the election of the real head of the Russian Orthodox Church.[65]

In reality, of course, what Gordon witnessed was the promulgation of what could only half-jokingly be called the new Gospel According to Peter. For during the course of the Yuletide celebrations staged in Moscow and at Novo-Preobrazhenskoe, the young tsar and his courtiers elected and in-stalled a mock patriarch to act as the spiritual leader of the tsar's own fac-tion—an unconsecrated company based on intimate access to the person of the young Romanov tsar and committed to implementing in real life the re-ligious and chivalric ideals enacted during the court's war games. In direct opposition to the patrimonial politics of the party that had put Peter Alek-seevich on the Muscovite throne in 1689, the tsar and his intimates rau-cously asserted that to be a member of this "royal priesthood" (I Peter 2:9)

---

64. Gordon, "Diary," RGVIA, f. 846, op. 15, kn. 4, ll. 110 (December 27 1691), 154 (Jan-uary 1, 1692). On the Kremlin royal quarters (*verkh*), see I. E. Zabelin, *Domashnii byt russkogo naroda v XVI i XVII stoletiiakh,* ed. A. N. Sakharov (Moscow, 1990), 1:59–60.

65. In one sense, that is precisely the tactic adopted by Reinhard Wittram, "Peters des Grossen Verhältnis zur Religion und den Kirchen: Glaube, Vernunft, Leidenschaft," *Historische Zeitschrift* 173 (1952): 266; and his *Peter I, Czar und Kaiser: Zur Geschichte Peters des Grossen in seiner Zeit,* 2 vols. (Göttingen, 1964), 1:106–11. Although fully aware of the difference between the Prince-Pope and the Russian Orthodox patriarch, Wittram combined Gordon's vituperative comments about the ecclesiastical politics surrounding the election of Patriarch Adrian (1690) with his brief remark about the installation of the mock patriarch, and came up with an ingenious explanation for the origins of Peter's mock ecclesiastical coun-cil. Wittram suggested that the defeat of Markell of Pskov, the candidate supposedly favored by the young tsar against Adrian and formed the immediate background for the parodic ordination of his own mock patriarch. But as James Cracraft has pointed out, there is no evidence that the tsar and his allies interpreted the rejection of Markell of Pskov as a po-litical defeat. See James Cracraft, *The Church Reform of Peter the Great* (Stanford, 1971), 16–17. Indeed, as V. M. Zhivov has argued, immediately after the accession of Patriarch Adrian, the tsar and his entourage had even succeeded in scoring a victory against the intoler-ance and xenophobia expressed in the "Testament" of the late patriarch Ioakim by removing the article banning relations with heretics and marriages between Orthodox and other believ-ers from the "hierarchical vow" that all bishops had to swear upon their ordination. See V. M. Zhivov, "Church Reforms in the Reign of Peter the Great," in *Russia in the Reign of Peter the Great: Old and New Perspectives,* ed. Anthony Cross, 2 vols. (Cambridge, 1998), 1:66. What-ever the actual balance of power between the patriarch and the new regime may have been, the brevity and ambiguity of Gordon's diary entries about his participation in the ordination of the first mock patriarch shed less light on the tsar's motivations than on Gordon's own fastidious reaction to this monarchical rite of power.

one did not have to perform the rituals of Russian Orthodoxy or to be a royal relative, much less a native Muscovite; one simply had to believe in the divine gift of grace possessed by Russia's anointed one and, like the disciples at the moment of Jesus' transfiguration on Mount Tabor, bask in the marvelous light of his deified nature. This arguably was the true meaning of the private political sacrament originally enacted in the apartments of the Kremlin and on the grounds of Novo-Preobrazhenskoe during the memorable Yuletide of 1691–92.

As if to make up for the reticence of Gordon's laconic entries, the only other contemporary eyewitness to have written about the ceremony in question left a very detailed and highly unfavorable description of the election of the first "patriarch" of Peter's Transfigured Kingdom. The author of this piece was none other than Prince B. I. Kurakin (1676–1727), a disgruntled Russian courtier who at the time was not only a member of the inner circle of Tsar Peter Alekseevich but also his brother-in-law.[66] Before his appointment as ambassador to the courts of Europe, Kurakin was very well placed within the clique that controlled the Muscovite government after the coup of 1689. He was certainly present in the Trinity Monastery during the political standoff between the distaff branches of the royal house.[67] And he clearly took part in the war games staged in the early 1690s by the tsar's personal entourage; the fact that he served as an officer within the regular guards regiments formed during these military maneuvers testifies to his position as a trusted member of the tsar's inner circle. Indeed, in his unfinished exposé of the court intrigues during the reign of Peter the Great, written a few years after the death of the first Russian emperor, Kurakin even flaunted his status as a knowledgeable insider who was "brought up at court alongside [the tsar] and was always with him. . . . , even until the battle of Poltava."[68]

Prince Kurakin devoted extraordinary attention to the origins of the tsar's Yuletide amusements, and in particular to the ordination of the first mock patriarch. Recording his impressions nearly twenty-five years after the event, he deliberately conflated several similar ceremonies to produce a vivid (and scathing) description of the pastimes indulged in by the tsar's entourage in the early 1690s. Despite its late appearance and its polemical intent, his exposé remains the most detailed eyewitness account of this political sacrament, and deserves to be quoted in full:

> Now I must not forget to describe the manner in which the mock patriarch, metropolitans, and other ecclesiastical ranks were established from among the distinguished courtiers who surrounded His Majesty. . . . Boyar Matvei Filimonovich Naryshkin, a drunk and foolish old man, was designated patriarch.

66. Kurakin was married to K. F. Lopukhina, the sister of tsar Peter Alekseevich's first wife. See Lavrov, *Regentstvo*, 162.

67. Ibid., 162–63. Prince Kurakin and his two brothers all served as privy chamberlains (*komnatnye stol'niki*) at the court of the young tsar Peter Alekseevich. See Airapetian, "Feodal'naia aristokratiia," 99–100.

68. Kurakin, "Gistoriia," 56.

A few other boyars were given the [titles of] members of the higher orders of clergy [such as bishops, archbishops, and metropolitans] from different provinces. The royal chamberlains [served in the capacity of] deacons and various other [clerical] ranks. The garb [of the mock patriarch] was made to be somewhat waggish, and not exactly on the model [of the vestments] of the [real Russian Orthodox] patriarch. He had a tin miter, in the shape of the miters worn by Catholic bishops, which was engraved with the figure of Bacchus [astride] a cask; playing cards[?] were sewn onto his attire; and in place of the pectoral crosses [traditionally worn around the neck by Orthodox bishops], he wore earthenware flasks trimmed with little bells. Finally, a book that contained several phials of vodka was constructed in place of the Gospels. And all of this constituted [the accoutrements available] there [for the enactment of] the ceremonies [in honor of] the festival of Bacchus.[69]

"There" in the last sentence referred to the little fortress that served as the royal residence of the mock tsar and sovereign of Pressburg. Over the course of the reign, the mock capital of Generalissimo Friedrich served as the site where "the ordination of these mock patriarchs and members of the higher orders of clergy usually took place." Here the tsar and his courtiers composed the entire mock ceremonial. According to Kurakin, it was couched "in such terms that I dare not repeat them, beyond saying briefly that it [enjoined the initiates] to drunkenness, lechery, and all kinds of debauches."[70]

While Gordon found it more prudent to keep his evaluation of the situation to himself, the logic of the political exposé necessitated that Kurakin offer his intended readers an explanation for this strange ceremony. However, even during the short and relatively more liberal reign of Catherine I, Peter's imperial consort and successor, Kurakin chose not to finish the thought. He noted, almost in passing, that distributing mock clerical ranks among the courtiers was aimed "more toward the destruction [*unichtozheniiu*] of those ranks" than, presumably, to their maintenance, support, and efflorescence. But his analysis, written several years after the official abolition of the patriarchate and the establishment of the Ecclesiastical College, is clearly more of a retrospective judgment than an assessment of the tsar's actual motives. Furthermore, Kurakin's use of the passive voice in describing the allocation of roles and the authorship of the mock ceremonial is striking for the heavy-handed way in which it seems to ignore the question of the role played by the tsar himself. This obvious omission was part of Kurakin's literary strategy: he avoided a direct attack on the person and memory of the recently deceased tsar by characterizing Peter by the supposedly unsavory company he kept.[71]

One of those unsavory characters was V. A. Sokovnin, the young royal

69. Ibid., 79–80.
70. Ibid., 80.
71. For some insightful comments about the literary strategy of Kurakin's political exposé, see the editor's introduction, ibid., 55.

chamberlain whom Kurakin blamed for "introducing" and "inaugurating" these and other unseemly "Yuletide pastimes" (*zabavy sviatoshnye*) at the court of Peter Alekseevich.[72] As the nephew of the infamous Old Believer sisters F. P. Morozova and E. P. Urusova, Sokovnin was already suspect in the eyes of Prince Kurakin, who, like most seventeenth-century Muscovite courtiers, willingly accepted the liturgical reforms introduced during the reign of Tsar Aleksei Mikhailovich.[73] The fact that Kurakin attributed Peter's crude amusements to the "fanciful invention" (*vymysel*) of Sokovnin therefore put these games in the context of the heretical "fabrications" of the schismatic opposition movement directed against the Russian Orthodox Church. Indeed, Kurakin made sure that a knowledgeable reader would put Sokovnin's blasphemous "invention" in the same camp as the "devilish" amusements of the "common rabble" by underscoring the plebeian origins of Peter's mock ecclesiastical council. Kurakin preceded an explanation of its origins with an ethnographic digression that placed the tsar's Yuletide amusements squarely in the context of traditional Russian winter games:

> The Russian people have an old custom, according to which, before and after the Nativity of Christ, they celebrate Christmastide [*igraiut svitaki*]. That is, friends gather together in [someone's] home at night and, among the common rabble, themselves don masquerade dress, while more distinguished people have their servants stage all manner of comical theatrical productions. And according to that habit, His Highness also celebrated Christmastide with the chamberlains of his court. And one [of those chamberlains] . . . , Vasilii Sokovnin . . . , an evil man who was full of all kinds of dirty tricks, was elected leader and inventor of that amusement [and] nicknamed "The Prophet" [*prorok*].

Sokovnin's "fanciful invention" is indeed remarkably similar to the Yuletide amusements favored by Russian peasants and townsfolk, who habitually "designate[d] some of their number saints, invent[ed] their own monasteries, and name[d] for them an archimandrite, a cellarer, and elders."[74] However, the prominence of the Roman god of wine in Kurakin's account of the tsar's Yuletide amusements demonstrates that the religious parody attributed to Sokovnin owed as much to the didactic and allegorical culture of the seventeenth-century Muscovite court as to the popular customs of the Russian folk.[75] As I have already had occasion to remark, this

72. For the career of V. A. Sokovnin, see Airapetian, "Feodal'naia aristokratiia," 334; and Paul Bushkovitch, *Peter the Great: The Struggle for Power, 1671–1725* (Cambridge, 2001), 190, 192, 194–95, 197.

73. On the Sokovnin family, including its connections to Old Belief, see Bushkovitch, *Peter the Great*, 85, 92, 190–97; Airapetian, "Feodal'naia aristokratiia," 62, 326, 105; V. Korsakov, "Sokovniny," in *RBS* 19:48–50; and N. I. Pavlenko, *Petr Velikii* (Moscow, 1990), 62–63.

74. The quotation comes from a 1651 petition addressed to Tsar Aleksei Mikhailovich by an Orthodox religious reformer, who excoriates the "devilish" winter games played "from Christmas Day to the vigils of Epiphany." Cited in Uspenskii, "Tsar and Pretender," 273.

75. On the lack of clear-cut boundaries between popular and elite in Petrine literary culture, see S. I. Nikolaev, *Literaturnaia kul'tura petrovskoi epokhi* (St. Petersburg, 1996), 126–31;

was not the first time that Bacchus had made an appearance at a Yuletide amusement staged for the Muscovite tsar on his suburban estate. The mythological Roman deity was one of the title characters in *The Comedy of Bacchus and Venus*, a "school drama" staged at the Preobrazhenskoe court theater of Tsar Aleksei Mikhailovich at the end of the Christmas fast in 1675. Judging by the list of characters, costumes, and props, as well as the fact that the script (which has not survived) was written by Stepan Chizhinskii, an alumnus of the Orthodox Kiev-Mohyla Academy, this comedy was most likely a morality play about the vices of drunkenness and lust.[76] Ostensibly, Chizhinskii sought to preach about the possibility of leading a good Christian life in the world, as well as to broaden the cultural horizons of his Muscovite patrons, by integrating the contemporary use of Bacchus in European art and literature into the cultural and religious traditions of the Russian Orthodox court.[77]

From the description offered in the list of props, Bacchus was depicted in much the same way as the satyr who appeared on the European stage. Bacchus's oversized head, made of canvas and decorated with horsehair, was ingeniously connected to a wine skin inside the barrel on which he was to be wheeled onstage. His companions, however, were anything but typical. Part of Bacchus's retinue consisted of the "father of drunks" (*otets p'ianits*) and thirteen "drunkards," three of whom stuffed their clothes with pillows in order to look like hunchbacks.[78] Besides Bacchus's lavishly dressed wife, Venus, their son, Cupid, and his votary, the "brothel master," the rest of the characters—four people dressed like bears, two musicians, and a jester—were part of the Muscovite minstrel tradition.[79] Such a scandalous combination of classical mythology and buffoonery for the religious edification of the audience was typical of scholastic "interludes" and had become increasingly common in the later theatrical productions at the court of Tsar Aleksei Mikhailovich.[80] It certainly fitted in well with the carnivalesque atmo-

---

and V. D. Levin, "Petr I i russkii iazyk (K 300-letiiu so dnia rozhdeniia Petra I)," *Izvestiia AN SSSR. Seriia literatury i iazyka* 31, no. 3 (1972): 217n16.

76. Bogoiavlenskii, *Moskovskii teatr*, 14. For a biography of Stepan Chizhinskii and his role in producing *The Comedy of Bacchus and Venus*, see Vsevolodskii-Gerngross, *Russkii teatr*, 116–21.

77. On the image of Bacchus in Renaissance and Baroque Europe, see the two-volume study by Andreas Emmerling-Skala, *Bacchus in der Renaissance*, Studien zur Kunstgeschichte, 83 (Hildesheim, 1994); and Martine Vasselin, "Des fastes de Bacchus aux beuveries flamandes: L'iconographie du vin de la fin du XVᵉ siècle a la fin du XVIIᵉ siècle," *Nouvelle revue du seizième siècle* 17, no. 2 (1999): 219–51. For the Russian appropriation of the Bacchus myth, see Andreas Ebbinghaus, "Obraz bakhusa v kontekste russkoi kul'tury XVIII–nachala XIX vekov," in *Reflections on Russia in the Eighteenth Century*, ed. Ioakim Klein, Simon Dixon, and Maarten Fraanje (Cologne, 2001), 186–99.

78. Bogoiavlenskii, *Moskovskii teatr*, 14–15.

79. Derzhavina, "Teatr i dramaturgiia," 126–27.

80. On the function of interludes in Muscovite and Ukrainian school drama, see P. N. Berkov, *Istoriia russkoi komedii XVIII v.* (Leningrad, 1977), 9–11, 17–22; Paulina Lewin, "Vostochnoslavianskie intermedii," in *Drevnerusskaia literatura i ee sviazi s novym vremenem*, ed. O. A. Derzhavina, 194–205 (Moscow, 1967); and N. K. Gudzii, "Ukrains'ki intermedii XVII–XVIII st.," in *Ukrains'ki intermedii XVII–XVIII st.: Pam'iatniki davn'oi ukrains'koi literaturi*, 5–30 (Kiev, 1960).

sphere of the twelve days between Christmas and Epiphany, during which the play was staged.[81]

The appearance of a "father of drunks" and his thirteen drunken disciples preceded by some two decades the ordination of a mock patriarch and his council at the court of Tsar Peter Alekseevich. Although there is little evidence of direct borrowing, the similarities between the religious parodies staged before Tsar Aleksei Mikhailovich and his son are a striking illustration of the way Peter's entourage adapted the discursive practices of the earlier reign to their own purposes. Both of these theatricalized court spectacles took place during Yuletide, on the grounds of the royal estate named for the Transfiguration. Both of them made reference to mythological as well as stock characters. Both included parodies of religious rites: in the case of Chizhinskii's comedy, the actors ostensibly enacted a parody of Christ and his disciples during the Last Supper, the historical model for the sacrament of Communion; similarly, during the ordination of the mock patriarch of the Transfigured Kingdom, the entourage of Tsar Peter Alekseevich parodied the sacrament of holy orders. Finally, in both cases these sacred parodies served as dramatic rhetorical devices in the pursuit of some higher didactic or political goal. During the ordination of the mock patriarch, however, the tsar and his courtiers personally participated in the organization, staging, and execution of a burlesque that had earlier been left to lowborn actors. This change in the social makeup as well as the relationship between actor and audience entailed a concomitant change in the nature of the political relations underlying the theatrical experience at the court of Peter Alekseevich.

As we have seen, Peter's theatrical innovation was noted by Prince Kurakin in his indignant account of Sokovnin's "invention." In order to understand how Kurakin could argue that these Yuletide amusements constituted an insidious assault against the honor of the Muscovite elite, one must pay careful attention to the way this titled prince differentiated between the Yuletide celebrations of the "distinguished people" and those of the "base rabble."[82] Foreign travelers to Russia had already noted that seventeenth-century Muscovite elites "consider it improper for an honest man to dance. . . . 'An honest man,' they say, 'ought to sit in his place and be amused only at the jester's contortions, he should not himself be the jester for the amusement of others.'"[83] But in Kurakin's polemical reading that is precisely what the tsar's Yuletide amusements succeed in doing: with the aid of "evil" and even "heretical" royal favorites such as Sokovnin, the tsar transformed the distinguished nobles who attended Peter Alekseevich into

81. On the interpenetration of official and lay spirituality during seventeenth-century Yuletide celebrations, see N. V. Ponyrko, "Russkie sviatki XVII veka," *Trudy otdela drevnerusskoi literatury* 32 (1977): 84–99; and her contribution to Likhachev et al., *Smekh v drevnei Rusi*, 154–74.

82. Kurakin, "Gistoriia," 81.

83. S. Maskevich (1611) in *Skazaniia sovremennikov o Dimitrii Samozvantse* (St. Petersburg, 1834), 5:61–62, cited in Iu. M. Lotman and B. A. Uspenskii, "New Aspects in the Study of Early Russian Culture," in Shukman, *Semiotics of Russian Culture*, 51–52n15.

base servants who performed humiliating skits for the amusement of their lord and master (as well as his entire court). Kurakin's insight into the broad definition and the political significance of jesters at the court of Peter the Great will be explored more fully in Chapter 3; for now, it is sufficient to point out that knowledgeable contemporaries perceived serious political consequences in such seemingly unimportant amateur theatricals.[84] Keeping this in mind will help us to unravel the reasons why a courtier whom Kurakin derisively dismissed as a "drunk and foolish old man" was ordained the patriarch of the Transfigured Kingdom.

The election of M. F. Naryshkin to the position of patriarch during Yuletide of 1691–92 tapped into the royal entourage's knowledge of history and genealogy, as well as traditional Yuletide symbolism, to evoke the birth of a new, Petrine Transfigured Kingdom from the passing of the old Alekseevan one. Boyar M. F. Naryshkin (d. 1692)—known by the coarse yet affectionate nickname of Patriarch Deary (*Milak*)[85]—was Peter Alekseevich's first cousin twice removed and the oldest living male of the tsar's maternal relatives.[86] According to the Muscovite laws of family precedence, this old courtier represented the generation of the fathers, a superior place vis-à-vis the one occupied by the young tsar within the Naryshkin clan. In the days before the abolition of precedence ranking, this position would have given him significant authority over his younger relatives.[87] Indeed, judging by the stern glance of the pastoral-staff-bearing courtier depicted in a contemporary portrait of Patriarch Deary—the first in a series commissioned specifically for the dining hall of the royal palace in Novo-Preobrazhenskoe (see Figure 1)[88]—even now the elevation of this old kinsman to the rank of spir-

---

84. For a discussion of amateur theatricals and more broadly the theatricalization of court culture in the reign of Peter the Great, see A. Kriuger, "Samodeiatel'nyi teatr pri Petre I," in *Starinnyi spektakl' v Rossii. Sbornik statei,* ed. V. N. Vsevolodskii-Gerngross, Russkii teatr, 2 (Leningrad, 1928), 358–85; and A. N. Robinson, "Dominiruiushchaia rol' russkoi dramaturgii i teatra kak vidov iskusstva v epokhu petrovskikh reform," in *Slavianskie kul'tury v epokhu formirovaniia i razvitiia slavianskikh natsii XVIII–XIX vv. Materialy mezhdunarodnoi konferentsii IuNESKO,* 176–82 (Moscow, 1978), esp. 181–82.

85. For the various shades of meaning of the word "dear" (*milyi*) and its derivatives, including the vulgar *milakha,* see V. I. Dal', *Tolkovyi slovar' zhivogo velikorusskogo iazyka* (Moscow, 1955), 2:325–26.

86. For a brief biography of M. F. Naryshkin, see "Naryshkiny," in *RBS* 11:94–95 (St. Petersburg, 1914); and L. N. Semenova, *Ocherki istorii byta i kul'turnoi zhizni Rossii, pervaia polovina XVIII v.* (Leningrad, 1982), 176–77. For the genealogy of the Naryshkin clan, see Aleksandr [A.] Vasil'chikov, "Rod Naryshkinykh," *Russkii arkhiv* 9 (1871): 1487–519, 1960–61; and A. B. Lobanov-Rostovskii, *Russkaia rodoslovnaia kniga,* 2nd ed. (St. Petersburg, 1895), 2:6.

87. On the familial terminology of Muscovite precedence ranking, see E. A. Vasilevskaia, "Terminologiia mestnichestva i rodstva," *Trudy istoriko-arkhivnogo instituta* 2 (1946): 155–79, esp. 170; D. [A.] Valuev, "Vvedenie. Razriadnaia kniga ot 7067 [1559] do 7112 [1604]," *Sinbirskii sbornik. Istoricheskaia chast'* (Moscow, 1845), 1:36, 72; and Nancy Shields Kollmann, *By Honor Bound: State and Society in Early Modern Russia* (Ithaca, 1999), chaps. 1 and 4.

88. For the attribution of the portrait of Patriarch Deary, see E. I. Gavrilova, "O metodakh atributsii dvukh grupp proizvedenii Petrovskoi epokhi (zhivopis', risunok)," in *Nauchno-issledovatel'skaia rabota v khudozhestvennykh muzeiakh* (Moscow, 1975), pt. 2, 45–75. On the Preobrazhensk series in general see N. M. Moleva and E. M. Beliutin, *"Zhivopisnykh del mas-*

Figure 1. Patriarch Deary. Anonymous portrait, late seventeenth century. (State Russian Museum, St. Petersburg [zh 3935].)

itual elder may have signaled that he still wielded some kind of moral authority at the court of Peter Alekseevich. If so, then during the parodic ceremony staged at Yuletide of 1691–92 the Naryshkin patriarch would have served in the capacity of spiritual father to the young Naryshkin candidate: a fictive diarchy between this father and son that would have recapitulated the original Romanov diarchy—that of Patriarch Filaret and his son,

tera." *Kantseliariia ot stroenii i russkaia zhivopis' pervoi poloviny XVIII veka* (Moscow, 1965), chap. 1; N. M. Moleva, "Persony vseshuteishego sobora," *Voprosy istorii* 10 (1974): 206–11; and V. G. Chubinskaia, "Novoe ob evoliutsii russkogo portreta na rubezhe XVII–XVIII vv.," in *Pamiatniki kul'tury. Novye otkrytiia. 1982* (Leningrad, 1984), 317–28.

Mikhail Fedorovich, the first Romanov tsar—while poking fun at the current diarchy between Peter and his lame half brother, Tsar Ivan Alekseevich.[89]

In pointed contrast to the idealized symphony between the first Romanov tsar and patriarch, the unequal relationship between Peter Alekseevich and his older relative(s) embodied a critique of patriarchal authority in both its ecclesiastical and genealogical senses. Seeking to distance themselves from the factions that had organized the coup in favor of the Naryshkin candidate, the tsar and his intimates attacked not only his maternal relatives but also the court of Tsar Ivan Alekseevich and the entourage of the Russian Orthodox patriarch. Indeed, the ordination of Patriarch Deary seems to have been something of a declaration of independence from the paternalism of the political coalition that had put the young Peter Alekseevich on the throne. As a political commentary on the faction that had dominated the formal organs of government since the coup of 1689, the ordination of M. F. Naryshkin emphasized the distinction between those men who, bound by familial ties and personal ambitions, had put the young tsar on the throne and those who came to profess their belief in the tsar's personal charisma and his vision of a new Transfigured Kingdom. The fact that the tsar's old kinsman could not translate familial power into political power may well have been intended to demonstrate the way the tsar's entourage felt about the unprecedented inflation of honors that accompanied the succession struggle, when the formerly restricted membership of the Muscovite royal council swelled with the supporters and hangers-on promoted first by one and then another court faction.[90] Indeed, M. F. Naryshkin's own relatively recent promotion to the Boyar Duma only underlined the fact that, like this once-powerful advisory body, he had been reduced to the status of a living link between the past and the future. Increasingly, important political decisions were made in the tsar's inner council, which gathered at Novo-Preobrazhenskoe rather than in Moscow.[91] In fact, since the symbolic inauguration of the Transfigured Kingdom, participation in the suburban military maneuvers had became at least as important as Muscovite clan politics in determining access to the tsar. While this was still a far cry from the meritocratic thrust of the Table of Ranks of 1722, the organization of the tsar's entourage seemed to have shifted the emphasis away from pedigree to professional expertise. In this sense, the parodic ordination of Patriarch

89. This historical parallel is suggested by the fact that one of the courtiers who participated in the earliest Yuletide amusements adopted the title of Patriarch of Palestine, possibly in imitation of the hierarch who had ordained Filaret (Romanov) in 1619. For the ordination of Filaret by Patriarch Feofan III of Jerusalem, see Uspenskii, *Tsar i Patriarkh*, 95. For the undated (ca. 1690s) letters of Andrei, the mock patriarch of Palestine, see RGADA, f. 9, otd. 2, op. 4, kn. 53, ll. 502–4.

90. On the inflation of honors, see Robert O. Crummey, *Aristocrats and Servitors: The Boyar Elite in Russia, 1613–1689* (Princeton, 1983), 29–31.

91. A. Vostokov, "O delakh general'nogo dvora," in *Opisanie dokumentov i bumag, khraniashchikhsia v Moskovskom arkhive Ministerstva Iustitsii* (Moscow, 1888), 5 (2): 1–11.

Deary reflected the existence of a definite, if still fluid, line of demarcation between Peter's party and the officials of the Naryshkin regime.[92]

As a critique of the policies of Patriarch Ioakim (Savelov), the parodic ordination of a mock pontiff and his Unholy Council challenged the notion that the tsar required the sanction of the church hierarchy to carry out his divine calling, the religious position with which the party of Peter Alekseevich came to power in 1689. By arrogating the right to perform the sacrament of holy orders, if only in jest, the royal entourage asserted that the tsar did not need either the blessings or the approval of the Most Holy Council (*osviashchennyi sobor*), the official ecclesiastical corporate body consisting of higher clergy and headed by the patriarch, traditionally represented at the assemblies of the land, which for most of the seventeenth century were theoretically responsible for confirming Romanov royal rule.[93] This political sacrament even implied that as God's anointed, the tsar was personally responsible for organizing the ceremonies that bestowed grace, a theological position that went one step beyond the arguments voiced by the opponents of Patriarch Ioakim during the Eucharist debate. If we recall the discussion in Chapter 1, Sil'vestr (Medvedev) had justified Tsarevna Sof'ia Alekseevna's claims to be a receptacle of grace, above and beyond the power of the clergy, by citing the biblical Wisdom literature attributed to King Solomon. And now, despite all appearances to the contrary, so did the organizers of the 1691–92 Yuletide ceremonies in honor of the festival of Bacchus. Indeed, by transforming the references to wine in Abbot Sil'vestr's invocation of Wisdom's feast (Prov. 9:1–6)—one of the main tropes in pro-Sof'ia propaganda[94]—into a celebration of their own "sober drunkenness" (*trezvoe p'ianstvo*), Peter and his intimates appeared to have formulated another and no less extraordinary assertion of the tsar's unmediated access to the divine.[95]

92. On the difficulties of distinguishing Peter's nascent company from "those officials who were associated with the court of Tsar Ivan and with the formal organs of government under the control of the Naryshkin faction," see Robert O. Crummey, "Peter and the Boiar Aristocracy, 1689–1700," *Canadian-American Slavic Studies* 8, no. 2 (Summer 1974): 279.

93. On the Most Holy Council, see I. M. Likhnitskii, *Osviashchennyi sobor v Moskve v XVI–XVII vekakh* (St. Petersburg, 1906); and Bogoslovskii, *Petr I*, 1:427, 430.

94. "Wisdom has built her house,/she has hewn her seven pillars./She has slaughtered her animals,/she has mixed her wine, she has also set her table./She has sent out her servant girls,/she calls from the highest places of town,/'You that are simple, turn in here!'/To those without sense she says,/'Come, eat of my bread and drink of the wine I have mixed./Lay aside immaturity, and live,/and walk in the way of insight.'" On Prov. 9:1–6 as one of the foundation texts for Wisdom imagery during the regency of Tsarevna Sof'ia Alekseevna, see Zelensky, "'Sophia the Wisdom of God,'" 106, 122, 279, 309; and A. P. Bogdanov, "Sofiia-Premudrost' Bozhiia i tsarevna Sof'ia Alekseevna: Iz istorii russkoi dukhovnoi literatury i iskusstva XVII veka," *Germenevtika russkoi literatury* 7, no. 2 (1994): 399–428, esp. 402–4.

95. For Prov. 9 as one of the proof texts for the notion of sober drunkenness, see Florence M. Weinberg, *The Wine and the Will: Rabelais' Bacchic Christianity* (Detroit, 1972), 89, 167n29. For an extended discussion of the Hellenistic roots of this mystical trope and its use in allegorical exegesis in both Eastern and Western Christianity, see Hans Lewy, *Sobria ebrietas: Untersuchungen zur Geschichte der antiken Mystik* (Giessen, 1929); B. Krivocheine [Vasilii Krivoshein], "Le thème de l'ivresse spirituelle dans la mystique de Saint Syméon le Nouveau

Substituting the libations of Bacchus for the overflowing of Divine Wisdom, the founding members of Peter's personal "church" initiated select members of the royal entourage into the mystery of the tsar's charismatic authority—the mystery of state at the heart of the Transfigured Kingdom. To the uninitiated, this ceremony looked like a diabolical inversion of the sacraments, particularly that of holy orders, the rite that is supposed to bestow grace upon the clerical successors of Peter the Apostle. Indeed, this is precisely how the tsar's actions appeared to the previously cited author of a late-seventeenth-century denunciation, who mistook Peter's highly stylized, allegorical invocation of Bacchus for a literal renunciation of God.[96] To those courtiers who were familiar with the trope of sober drunkenness, however, the bacchanalian rite accompanying the revelation of the Gospel According to Peter was not blasphemy for its own sake. Rather, this elaborate example of the genre of sacred parody reenacted the apostles' mystical experience at Pentecost (Acts 2), when Christ's divinely inspired followers appeared (to the unbelievers gathered around them) as if they were "filled with new wine," that is, drunk out of their minds. According to this biblical scenario, depicted most sedately in a contemporary print produced by the leading Russian engraver at the court of Peter the Great (Figure 2),[97] Peter and the apostles were not drunk in the base physical sense, but rather in a state of mind akin to euphoria. Illuminated by the Holy Spirit, the apostles are depicted as having "stepped outside" the boundaries of everyday reality (the literal meaning of the Greek *ekstasis*)—an experience that allows them to catch a glimpse of the world as it really is or should be organized in conformity with divine laws. Therein lies the explanation for their strange, seemingly blasphemous acts at Pentecost, as well as the source of their spiritual authority.[98]

Théologien," *Studia Patristica* 5 (1962): 368–76; and Aimé Solignac, "Ivresse spirituelle," in *Dictionnaire de spiritualité ascétique et mystique: Doctrine et histoire* (Paris, 1971), 7 (2): 2312–37. On the importance of this trope in later eighteenth-century Russian literary theory and panegyrics, see V. M. Zhivov, *Iazyk i kul'tura v Rossii XVIII veka* (Moscow, 1996), 252–53.

96. "Otryvok oblicheniia na vseshuteishii sobor. Ok. 1705 g.," in *Materialy dlia russkoi istorii*, ed. S. A. Belokurov (Moscow, 1888), 539; and V. M. Zhivov and B. A. Uspenskii, "Metamorfozy antichnogo iazychestva v istorii russkoi kul'tury XVII–XVIII veka," in *Iz istorii russkoi kul'tury*, ed. A. D. Koshelev (Moscow 1996), 4:482. See also Grigorii Talitskii's account of Prince I. I. the Elder Khovanskii's description of his ordination as mock metropolitan in G. V. Esipov, *Raskol'nich'i dela XVIII stoletiia, izvlechennye iz del Preobrazhenskogo prikaza i Tainoi Rozysknykh del kantseliarii* (St. Petersburg, 1861), 68–69.

97. A. F. Zubov earned his promotion to master engraver status in 1701 after etching a depiction of the descent of the Holy Ghost upon the apostles at Pentecost. Although Zubov copied the illustration from a foreign-made illustrated Bible, the choice of subject matter suggests that he was aware of the significance of this motif at the court of his royal patron. On Zubov and his engraving, see James Cracraft, *The Petrine Revolution in Russian Imagery* (Chicago, 1997), 177–84, esp. 179–81 (figs. 50 and 51).

98. Evidence for the fact that the patristic trope of sober drunkenness (particularly in its Pentecostal redaction) not only entered the homiletic tradition of Eastern Orthodoxy but also found its way to the court of Peter the Great exists in the sermons of Stefan (Iavorskii) and Feofan (Prokopovich), the official preachers at the late Muscovite court. For example, see Stefan (Iavorskii), "Slovo os'moe [:] V nedeliu Piat'desiatnitsy iz temy: Priimite Dukh Sviat. Ioan. gl.

Figure 2. Descent of the Holy Ghost upon the Apostles (1701). Engraving by A. F. Zubov. (From G. V. Esipov, ed., *Sbornik vypisok iz arkhivnykh bumag o Petre Velikom* [Moscow, 1872], vol. 1, endpiece.)

Similarly, upon their induction into Tsar Peter's state of sober drunkenness, the participants in and eyewitnesses of the bacchanalian mysteries staged at Novo-Preobrazhenskoe were supposed to be able to glimpse the Transfigured Kingdom presided over by his chivalrous mock double and to understand what they must do in order to realize the ideals that inspired it. These blasphemous political sacraments would have exposed the rules by which the old world was governed for the conventional, manmade creations that they really were, while making it seem as though the new world were just within reach. Like the apostles, the tsar's new disciples would then feel compelled (sometimes quite literally) to follow through with the transvaluation of values revealed by their encounter with the divine. In this ecstatic state they would venture out into the world to preach about their vision, enjoining other mortals to strive for the deification that was to accompany the imminent transfiguration heralded by V. A. Sokovnin, the "Prophet" of the Transfigured Kingdom.[99]

The symbolism of the accoutrements used during the Yuletide caroling processions (*slavleniia*) that accompanied the Unholy Council's periodic missions to the unbelievers tends to support this interpretation of the political sacrament enacted by Peter's unconsecrated company. According to the previously quoted eyewitness accounts, as well as a few scattered archival references, it is known, for example, that Bacchus appeared on the cover of the "Gospel" (*Evangelie*) carried by the mock patriarch of Peter's Unholy Council. This "Good Book," which was actually a small wooden chest (*larets,* of about 30 by 100 by 60 cm.), served as a portable hamper to hold the religious paraphernalia of the mock ecclesiastical council (such as bottles of vodka and tobacco pipes).[100] On the center of the lid, this mock Bible depicted the infant Bacchus sitting atop a barrel of wine—presumably the "new wine" with which the apostles had been intoxicated during Pentecost. A much larger travel chest, representing the book of Acts and Epistles (*Apostol*), depicted Bacchus on the lid and the twelve apostles on the back.[101] As we can see from the photograph of a Petrine travel chest (Figure

---

k, st. z [John 20:22]," in *Propovedi blazhennyia pamiati Stefana Iavorskogo. . . .* (Moscow, 1804), 1:163–79; and Feofan (Prokopovich), "Panegirikos, ili Slovo pokhval'noe o preslavnoi nad voiskami Sveiskimi pobede . . . ," in his *Sochineniia,* 36. But perhaps the most original reference to the trope of sober drunkenness at the court of Peter the Great can be found in a congratulatory letter written by the first field marshal of the newly reformed Russian army on the birth of Peter's son and heir, Tsarevich Peter Petrovich. See B. P. Sheremetev to Peter, November 27, 1715, in *Pis'ma k gosudariu imperatoru Petru Velikomu, pisannye ot general-fel'dmarshala . . . , Sheremeteva,* 4 vols. (Moscow, 1778–79), 4:120; also in *Russkii arkhiv* 1, no. 2 (1909): 173–74.

99. For a hostile description of the "comical words, jokes and deeds displeasing to God" that accompanied Sokovnin's prophecies (*prorochestva*), see "Delo o podannykh tsariu tetradiakh stroitelia Andreevskogo monastyria Avraamiem. Doprosy Avraamiia, Pososhkova, i dr. [1697]," in B. B. Kafengauz, *I. T. Pososhkov: Zhizn' i deiatel'nost'* (Moscow and Leningrad, 1950), 177–78; and Kurakin, "Gistoriia," 80.

100. This "gospel" is currently housed in the museum of the Moscow Kremlin (inv. DK-1806/1–6). See *Petr Velikii i Moskva: Katalog vystavki* (Moscow, 1998), 52 (nos. 85–86).

101. For a description of this "Book of the Apostles," see I. E. Zabelin, "Istoriia i drevnosti Moskvy," 2:190–91n2.

Figure 3. "The Book of Acts and Epistles *[Apostol],*" a Petrine travel chest, with compartments for flasks and bottles. (Kremlin Armory, Moscow.)

3), the apostles appear to be sitting around a table laden with drinks, perhaps a representation of the Eucharistic meal before Pentecost. If so, then the visual emphasis on the goblets containing the communal wine serves both as a sign of Christ's absent presence and as a declaration of their readiness to receive the outpouring of the Holy Spirit.

In typical Baroque fashion, this startling juxtaposition of the table fellowship of the apostles and a bacchanalian feast could also be expressed in the language of classical mythology. So, for example, in the first book of emblems to be published during the reign of Peter the Great, the image of Ariadne receiving a cup from the hands of Bacchus referred to Psalm 103:15—another of the many proof texts for the notion of sober drunkenness—to express the idea that "wine banishes sorrow and gladdens the heart."[102] The tsar himself frequently expressed similar sentiments in his correspondence with his courtiers. Nowhere, however, did he make his views more explicit than in a letter addressed to the royal favorite, A. D. Menshikov (1673–1729), in the fall of 1706.[103] Congratulating Menshikov

102. A. E. Makhov, ed., *Emblemy i simvoly* (Moscow, 1995), 252 (no. 726). On Ps. 103:15 as one of the sources for the notion of sober drunkenness, see Lewy, *Sobria ebrietas,* 108n1.

103. For a biography of Peter's royal favorite, see Hughes, *Russia,* 432–41, 595; and N. I. Pavlenko, *Poluderzhavnyi vlastelin: Istoricheskaia khronika o zhizni spodvizhnika Petra Pervogo A. D. Menshikova* (Moscow, 1991).

on yet another military victory, Peter confessed that this was the third day that he and his companions were "celebrating" (*prazdnuem*)—a euphemism that, like "making merry" (*veselimsia*), usually referred to the raucous parties that accompanied all courtly festivities. In the last part of this sentence, however, Peter made a veiled allusion to a deeper, almost mystical meaning of these drinking fellowships, in which he would "bring a generous offer of wine to Bacchus, [while] singing the praises of God with [my] soul" (*prinosia zhertvu Bakhusu dovol'nuiu vinom, a dusheiu Boga slavia*).[104] Here, in the tradition of the trope of sober drunkenness, Peter's letter acknowledged the divine origins of the wine that "banishes sorrow and gladdens the heart." Indeed, by juxtaposing the Spirit of God Made Flesh with the spirits of alcohol made divine this letter serves as a perfect illustration of the way the tsar and the members of his unconsecrated company used the idea of sober drunkenness to transform royal festivities into symbols of the coming of a new Transfigured Kingdom.

104. Peter to A. D. Menshikov, November 14–17, 1706, in *PiB*, 4 (1): 438. Peter's formulation of the connection between divine worship and Bacchic mystery echoed the words of another member of his company who once wrote: "Having given thanks to God, I exult [*torzhestvuiu*] with Bacchus." See A. V. Kikin to Peter I, May 19, 1704, ibid., 3:624.

3   Apostles and Apostates

Almost immediately after the young Naryshkin candidate founded the Transfigured Kingdom and informally declared his independence from the political coalition that had put him on the Russian throne, the rituals of inclusion in and exclusion from his entourage began to take on the attributes of a secular religious order. This orientation toward the ideals of an *ecclesia militans*[1] helps to explain why in the spectacles preceding the inauguration of the first Russian Orthodox knightly order (1699), as well as in those accompanying the foundation of its mock chivalrous counterpart (1709), the courtiers of Tsar Peter Alekseevich appeared as both knights and apostles. Precisely by affiliating themselves with a knightly order like those of other contemporary Christian monarchs, the tsar and his courtiers sought to demonstrate their links to the institutions and traditions of the broader, pan-European court society. At the same time, in an effort to actualize the religious imagery associated with these two orders of chivalry, Peter's knights distinguished themselves from their European brethren by appearing as the apostles of the Russian tsar. In fact, only after the idea of discipleship came to be accepted by his circle of intimates could other Muscovite courtiers begin to conceive of Peter as the divinely ordained charismatic leader who was personally responsible for transfiguring his realm and transforming Muscovy into a powerful member of the nascent Concert of Europe.[2]

1. For an argument that the values informing the pillars of the early modern state—the prince, the bureaucracy, and the army—transformed them into an *"ecclesia militans,* a secular religious order, so to speak," see Gerhard Oestreich, *Neostoicism and the Early Modern State* (Cambridge, 1982), 72.

2. For an introduction to the immense bibliography on Russia's role in shaping the emerging pan-European balance of power among Christian monarchs, see Lindsey Hughes, *Russia in the Age of Peter the Great* (New Haven, 1998), chap. 2; and N. N. Molchanov, *Diplomatiia*

At first glance, however, the strange (and estranging) discursive practices by means of which the entourage of Tsar Peter Alekseevich sought to demonstrate his divine gift of grace appear to have very little to do with this monarch's endeavor to raise Muscovy's standing among the ranks of regular Christian kingdoms. After all, what could a pilgrimage to some obscure, unaccredited, and godforsaken Arctic shrine possibly tell us about the tsar's desire to emulate the example of other European princes? What, if anything, does the institution of a mock order of chivalry dedicated to Judas Iscariot reveal about the grandiose imperial ambitions of the tsar and his entourage? Finally, what do these seemingly unrelated events have to do with the humble role that the imperious young monarch adopted in the company of his most trusted advisers? As we shall see, Peter's unexpected visit to the Transfiguration Church of the Pertominsk Monastery, like his decision to create the first Russian knightly order and its mock counterpart, all stemmed from the same source: the desire of the tsar and his supporters to mobilize the loyalties of a committed group of disciples who could attest to the redemptive significance of Peter's personal charisma and help him to realize the ideals first formulated on the grounds of the suburban royal estate of Novo-Preobrazhenskoe during his so-called childhood amusements.

The Accidental Pilgrims

Although some of Peter's closest political advisers had toyed with the idea of building a Russian navy as early as 1688, the young co-tsar did not get a chance to implement this bold new approach to the program of imperial reform until well after the court coup that transformed him into the de facto ruler of Muscovy.[3] Indeed, even after the coup of 1689, the ceremonial duties of his office, as well as the familial and political obligations that he owed to his kinsmen and their supporters, forced Tsar Peter to find ever more elaborate justifications for his avid interest in the unrealized naval projects of his father, Tsar Aleksei Mikhailovich.[4] To get around these restrictions on his freedom of movement, the young tsar hit upon a ploy to which even his mother could not object: whenever he wanted to make a trip to the dockyards of Iauza or the wharves of Pereiaslavl', Peter would offer

---

Petra Pervogo (Moscow, 1986). See also the comments of M. S. Anderson, *Peter the Great,* 2nd ed. (London, 1995), 84; and L. Jay Oliva, *Russia in the Era of Peter the Great* (Englewood Cliffs, NJ, 1969), 29.

3. Hughes, *Russia,* 81–82; and M. M. Bogoslovskii, *Petr I: Materialy dlia biografii* (Moscow and Leningrad, 1940), 1:271–94.

4. For a discussion of the mercantilist naval projects of Tsar Aleksei Mikhailovich, particularly his doomed Caspian flotilla, see Edward J. Phillips, *The Founding of Russia's Navy: Peter the Great and the Azov Fleet, 1688–1714* (Westport, CT, 1995), chap. 1. On Peter's knowledge of his father's projects, see his autobiographical introduction to the Naval Statute of 1720, "Predislovie k morskomu reglamentu," in N. G. Ustrialov, *Istoriia tsarstvovaniia Petra Velikogo* (St. Petersburg, 1858), 2:399.

to make a "pilgrimage" to some nearby monastery. This pious desire was perfectly in keeping with the established Muscovite tradition, according to which Russian tsars had made their political presence known by appearing before their subjects during pilgrimages to the most important holy shrines of the realm. Visits to the hallowed relics of such shrines not only demonstrated the Muscovite rulers' respect for the wonder-working saints of the Orthodox Church but also made an important statement about their own role as intercessors between heaven and earth.[5]

It is not surprising, therefore, that in a letter addressed to his elder half brother and co-ruler, Tsar Peter explained his desire to visit the port city of Archangel—at the time, Muscovy's sole outlet to the sea—by referring to this very tradition. In June 1694, on the way back from his second trip to the White Sea, Peter notified Tsar Ivan Alekseevich that this time he had (finally) fulfilled his earlier promise to visit the famous northern monastery complex of Solovetsk and pray at the shrine of SS. Zosima and Savvatii.[6] He failed to mention that he and his entourage had also paid an unscheduled visit to the (as yet unaccredited) reliquary of SS. Vassian and Iona at the Pertominsk Monastery—a distant outpost (*skit*) of the Solovetsk Monastery. Nor did he ever mention that this unplanned pilgrimage resulted from the fact that the boat in which he was traveling had nearly capsized in the stormy waters directly off the coast fronting the church that housed the relics of the two Arctic saints. As we will see, the tsar's silence about his unexpected detour was motivated by more than a supposed desire to prevent his relatives from worrying about him.[7] Had the powers that be back in Moscow known the meaning of the strange spontaneous spectacle that the tsar staged to commemorate his accidental pilgrimage to the shrine of SS. Vassian and Iona, they would have seen that Peter's pledges of brotherly obedience and paternal respect concealed bold assertions about his independent personal rule. Clearly, then, the unscheduled visit to the Transfiguration Church of the Pertominsk Monastery was meant for an entirely different audience.

The real reasons for Peter's two pilgrimages to Archangel (in 1693 and 1694)—to make contacts with foreign experts, to test the latest technological advances in the field of naval architecture, and to get his first real expe-

5. Nancy S. Kollmann, "Pilgrimage, Procession, and Symbolic Space in Sixteenth-Century Russian Politics," in *Medieval Russian Culture,* ed. Michael S. Flier and Daniel Rowland, 2:163–81 (Berkeley, 1994).

6. Peter to Tsar Ivan Alekseevich, June 14, 1694, in *PiB,* 1:21–22. Tsar Peter and his "hundred-man retinue" first visited Archangel in 1693. See Phillips, *Founding of Russia's Navy,* 34.

7. The hagiographic trope of worrying relatives appears in both Peter's correspondence with his mother and his autobiographical introduction to the Naval Statute of 1720. Lindsey Hughes has recognized the "implicit parallels" with the Lives of the Saints in "the fact that Peter's mother twice tried to dissuade him from his endeavour, first from sailing on a lake [Pereiaslavl'], then from sailing on the White Sea [near Archangel]." She goes on to suggest that Peter's "first visit to the latter [Arctic seaport], and later to the West, is presented as a new sort of pilgrimage, not to holy shrines, but to maritime 'holy places'—harbours, shipyards, and docks" (*Russia,* 81).

rience of sea travel—prefigured his eighteen-month trip to northern and central Europe in 1697–98 and hinted at the form that the tsar and his courtiers imagined his personal rule would take. During his first visit to Archangel, in the summer of 1693, the tsar had an opportunity not only to see but also to sail in the top-of-the-line vessels of the best sea powers in the world. At this time Tsar Peter first sailed on the *St. Peter,* a small armed patrol ship, christened after his heavenly namesake.[8] By mid-September 1693, the tsar had already started making plans for a return trip the following year. Foremost among his reasons was his interest in sailing beyond the White Sea and into the Arctic Ocean with a grandly named, but as yet non-existent White Sea fleet composed of the *St. Peter* and two new ships. The names of these ships, the *St. Paul* and the *Holy Prophecy,* were clearly intended to play off the providential name of the *St. Peter* and to emphasize the fact that the young tsar was predestined for his imperial vocation. The trips to the northern port city of Archangel thus not only offered Peter a chance to try out the best military hardware in the world but also served to highlight the prominent role that the navy—along with the political, ethical, and religious ideals associated with sea travel—was supposed to play in the new economic and foreign policies of the tsar and his entourage.[9]

None of these reasons appeared in the 1694 letter to Tsar Ivan Alekseevich. Instead, the anonymous author of the epistle explained Peter's visit to Archangel by emphasizing the conventional political, religious, and familial obligations of a pious seventeenth-century Muscovite tsar. Even in this politically expedient explanation, however, the letter writer was not willing to discuss Peter's unscheduled pilgrimage to the Pertominsk Monastery, although an account of it would only heighten the impression of the great lengths to which the junior tsar was willing to go to perform his official duties as head of state. For the unofficial saints of Pertominsk were the indirect beneficiaries of the patronage extended by the Russian royal house to the Solovetsk Monastery, and particularly to one of its most powerful abbots, St. Filipp, the sixteenth-century metropolitan of Moscow and the reputed teacher of Vassian and Iona. In fact, in 1652 Tsar Aleksei Mikhailovich and Patriarch Nikon, his top religious adviser and the spearhead behind the controversial reform of the Russian Orthodox liturgy, supervised the posthumous rehabilitation of Metropolitan Filipp, who had been imprisoned and executed for standing up to Ivan the Terrible. Patri-

8. Phillips, *Founding of Russia's Navy,* 34; M. Posselt, *Admiral Russkago flota Frants Iakovlevich Lefort, ili nachalo Russkago flota* (St. Petersburg, 1863), 18–19.

9. For a discussion of the allegorical significance of ships' names in Petrine court culture, see I. D. Chechot, "Korabl' i flot v portretakh Petra I. Ritoricheskaia kul'tura i osobennosti estetiki russkogo korablia pervoi chetverti XVIII veka," in *Otechestvennoe i zarubezhnoe iskusstvo XVIII veka* (Leningrad, 1986), 54–82. For the ideological significance of the navy—and sea travel in general—at the court of Peter the Great, see Evgenii Anisimov, *The Reforms of Peter the Great: Progress through Coercion,* trans. J. Alexander (Armonk, NY, 1993), 23–26; Hughes, *Russia,* 88–89, 66; and G. Kaganov, "'As in the Ship of Peter,'" *Slavic Review* 50 (1991): 354–67.

arch Nikon even accompanied Filipp's relics on their long trip from Archangel to Moscow, where, during an elaborate ceremony, the tsar begged the saint's forgiveness for the "ire of his great-grandfather." Aleksei's ritual contrition, like his deliberate conflation of the Riurikid and Romanov lines of the Russian royal house, thus pointed to the political significance of the transfer of St. Filipp's relics, a calculated move to sanctify the new royal-sponsored program of Orthodox imperial reform.[10]

The historical example provided by Aleksei Mikhailovich's posthumous rehabilitation of Metropolitan Filipp sheds light on the active role played by the tsar's youngest son in the canonization of that saint's disciples. From one point of view, Peter's personal solicitude for the memory of SS. Vassian and Iona during his unscheduled pilgrimage to the Pertominsk Monastery was yet another reminder of the Romanovs' continuing support for the reformist agenda of the Russian Orthodox Church. On the other hand, Peter's visit was also clearly meant to emphasize his legitimacy, by underscoring the reciprocal relation between Peter and the unaccredited Arctic saints, each of whom refracted (and therefore proved) the other's sacrality. For until the retinue of the junior co-tsar visited the Pertominsk Monastery, Vassian and Iona remained saints only in name. According to their vita, sometime in the sixteenth century two dead bodies had washed up on shore near the Pertominsk Monastery—a shrine for the local inhabitants, many of whom made their living by fishing the dangerous icy waters of the Arctic Ocean. Monastic and local tradition immediately identified the bodies with the Solovetsk monks Vassian and Iona, St. Filipp's disciples, who had drowned in 1561 when a storm capsized their boat. The author of the vita described the vision of the fishermen who had found the bodies of the two drowned monks, and recorded the saints' strict instructions about being buried on the spot where they had washed up. He also noted that later a church dedicated to the Transfiguration of the Saviour had been built to house the relics of Vassian and Iona, whom the local population credited with performing miracles. In keeping with this established local tradition, the anonymous chronicler who recorded the details of Peter's unexpected pilgrimage to the shrine of Vassian and Iona attributed the survival of the tsar and his entourage in a storm off the nearby inlet of Unskaia Guba to the intercession of the miracle-working Pertominsk saints.[11]

Relying on a biblical proof text from the Gospel of Matthew (14:24–33), the Pertominsk chronicler made an implicit comparison between the panic that assailed the passengers and crew of the *St. Peter* as they struggled

10. For a discussion of this ceremony, see S. A. Zen'kovskii, *Russkoe staroobriadchestvo: Dukhovnye dvizheniia semnadtsatogo veka* (Moscow, 1995), 182.

11. For the vita of SS. Vassian and Iona, see "Skazanie o poiavlenii i obretenii i o chudesekh prepodobnykh otets nashikh Vasiana i Iony, izhe na Primorii Studenago moria, Velikago Okiiana, v Zatotse, vo Unskikh, naritsaemykh Rogakh Pertominskikh chudotvortsev," RO RNB, "Solovetskoe sobranie" 181–82 (Sbornik zhitii russkikh sviatykh). Thanks to Eve Levin for making available a copy of her notes on this manuscript.

against the storm with the fear and doubt of the apostle Peter as he strode on the waves of the sea of Galilee. Just as the episode of Peter's walk on water served the Gospel author with an allegory of the apostles' faith in the divinity of Jesus, so the Pertominsk chronicler used the story of the near-capsizing of the royal yacht to illustrate the power of Providence in human (as well as royal) affairs. According to the chronicler's account, even the administration of the sacraments of penance and Holy Communion did not succeed in calming either the passengers aboard the royal yacht or the waters of the Arctic Ocean. And although the Pertominsk chronicler recorded that a local pilot finally managed to steer the royal yacht into the bay, he made it clear that the tsar and everyone aboard the *St. Peter* ultimately owed their salvation to God and the intercession of "the two drowned monks who in death still live."[12]

The tsar's actions after this unexpected safe landing demonstrate that he accepted the Pertominsk monks' interpretation of the events and credited his survival to the miraculous intercession of the two Arctic saints. During his four-day layover at the Pertominsk Monastery in June 1694, Peter ordered that the relics of Vassian and Iona be exhumed and examined in the presence of Archbishop Afanasii of Kholmogory, a reform-minded Orthodox cleric who accompanied the tsar on his voyage but had not, at least according to the chronicler, been well disposed toward the monastery or the two saints and even questioned their credentials. To the great joy of the Pertominsk monks, the tsar asked the archbishop to perform an ad hoc ecclesiastical investigation into the status of their (as yet) unattested local miracle cult. Despite the fact that only one body was found, Afanasii of Kholmogory succumbed to royal pressure and agreed to recognize the holiness of the relics, which were laid to rest in the chapel of the monastery. A service of thanksgiving was held and was followed by a solemn liturgy at which the tsar himself sang in the choir and read from the "Book of the Apostles," that is, from the Epistles and Acts. In a final step of the traditional canonization process, the tsar made a gift of money, supplies, land, and fishing rights to the monastery, as well as provision for the extension of its buildings.[13]

The fact that Peter sponsored the immediate investigation into the sanctity of the reputed remains of Vassian and Iona testifies to the political significance that the tsar attached to the personal miracle ostensibly performed for him by these two new saints. Indeed, it appears that the process that resulted, finally, in the recognition of the saintly status of the Pertominsk relics was also meant to affirm his own charisma. In a move that echoed the saints' insistence on being buried where their bodies had been washed ashore, the tsar chose to consecrate the spot where he and his party landed. Using the language and the persona of the "Great Skipper" (*bol'shoi*

12. Ibid., 197–98.

13. On the attestation of the Pertominsk saints, see ibid., 198v–200v; and Eve Levin, "False Miracles and Unattested Dead Bodies: Investigation into Popular Cults in Early-Modern Russia," unpublished MS, 6–8.

ship"ger)—the appellation used by Peter and his intimates in their correspondence during the trip to Archangel[14]—the tsar commemorated his miraculous rescue by carving a four-limbed pinewood cross 10.5 feet (1.5 *sazhen'*) high, on whose crossbeam Peter inscribed the following sentence, in broken Dutch: "This cross was made by Captain Peter in the year of our Lord 1694."[15]

To the monk who chronicled this episode, the unorthodox shape of the cross and its incomprehensible "Roman" (*rimskaia*) inscription highlighted the strangeness of the tsar's behavior on the last day of his visit to the Pertominsk Monastery. The tsar not only stooped to perform the manual work of an ordinary carpenter but also insisted on carrying the wooden cross on his own back before erecting it on the seashore where he and his entourage had disembarked.[16] In an obvious reenactment of Jesus' procession through Jerusalem on the way to Golgotha, Peter appeared literally bowed under the weight of the cross that he had fashioned and willingly took upon himself. Unlike Jesus, however, Peter had not been abandoned by his disciples; the tsar's companions solemnly escorted Peter and helped him carry his burden from the Transfiguration Church of the Pertominsk Monastery down to the shore. Indeed, the conspicuous involvement of some of the leading "clerics" of Peter's Transfigured Kingdom—including N. M. Zotov and T. N. Streshnev, respectively the Prince-Pope and archpriest of the Unholy Council[17]—shows that this ceremony had less to do with re-creating the Way of Sorrows than with celebrating the fact that the royal entourage had survived a test of their faith in the charisma of the tsar. By accompanying the tsar on his pilgrimage to yet another holy shrine named after the Transfiguration of the Saviour, the members of the mock ecclesiastical council sanctified the tsar's undertaking, conveying in jest the serious political message that

14. Posselt, *Admiral Russkago flota*, 37; *PiB*, 1:23–24, 495–96. The tsar even rebuked those courtiers who refused to play by the rules of his company and insisted on using the official royal titles in addressing their letters. See Peter to F. M. Apraksin, December 11, 1696, ibid., 113; cf. 2:97 (October 21, 1702).

15. *PiB*, 1:21, 495; and Bogoslovskii, *Petr I*, 1:181–82. In 1805 Peter's cross was transferred to the main Orthodox cathedral in Archangel. See N. Golubtsov, "Krest Petra Velikogo, khraniashchiisia v Arkhangel'skom Kafedral'nom Sobore," 79–83, and S. Ogorodnikov, "Vtoroe poseshchenie Petrom Velikim Arkhangel'ska v 1694 g.," 28, both in *Petr Velikii na Severe. Sbornik statei i ukazov, otnosiashchikhsia k deiatel'nosti Petra I na Severe*, ed. A. F. Shidlovskii (Archangel, 1909).

16. "Skazanie," 200v–201.

17. For a partial list of the royal suite that visited the Pertominsk monastery, including the *dumnyi d'iak* N. M. Zotov and the boyar T. N. Streshnev, see ibid., 196. It is worth pointing out that the 300-man retinue that accompanied Peter during his second voyage to Archangel in 1694 also included "Sovereign and Admiral" F. Iu. Romodanovskii and "Vice Admiral" (and co-sovereign) I. I. Buturlin, neither of whom had ever been to sea before. During the three-week voyage of the White Sea fleet, Romodanovskii was on board the *Holy Prophecy*, along with "Captain" Franz Lefort and "Skipper" Peter; while I. I. Buturlin was at the helm of the *St. Paul*. General Patrick Gordon, the newly promoted "rear admiral" of the navy, commanded the *St. Peter*. See Peter to F. M. Apraksin, March 5, 1694, in *PiB*, 1:19–20, 493; Franz Lefort to Peter Lefort, February 9, 1694, cited in Bogoslovskii, *Petr I*, 1:188, 173; and Phillips, *Founding of Russia's Navy*, 34–35.

would have been taken as a joke had it been uttered with all the pomp of a royal proclamation back in Moscow.[18]

Taking advantage of their unplanned pilgrimage to the shrine of the Pertominsk saints, Peter and his entourage thus improvised a unique royal spectacle, which was intended for everyone in the group, including the creators of the ceremony. The fact that this ceremony was new, ad hoc, unexpected, is not insignificant either. Indeed, it is a clear illustration of the sociological argument that the charismatic leader's special gift of grace must constantly be demonstrated, at unexpected and unusual times, for his followers to continue believing in his divine election.[19] Such enigmatic assertions of royal charisma demonstrated that the tsar and his entourage sought to foster a particular kind of esprit de corps among those who witnessed and participated in the Pertominsk procession with the cross. Exploiting the fact that the entire royal retinue had personally experienced the near-capsizing of the *St. Peter,* the organizers of this spectacle attempted to transform the relief at their salvation from the storm into a reaffirmation of faith in the coming of a new political dispensation. Although shaken by an unexpected confrontation with their own mortality, the tsar's companions were urged to let go of the past, with all its fears and tribulations, and commit themselves ever more strongly to the tasks set by their divinely appointed leader. Whether or not they actually believed in the ultimate success of the tsar's mission, all of his courtiers had to participate in the procession with the cross, supporting Peter as he carried his burden down to the sea. Thus the ceremony improvised on the last day of the tsar's visit to the Pertominsk Transfiguration Church enacted the scenario of power first articulated just a couple of years earlier on the grounds of Novo-Preobrazhenskoe, the royal estate named after the new Petrine transfiguration.

The procession with the cross—like the fact that at the liturgy following the canonization of Vassian and Iona the tsar chose to read from the Epistles and Acts of the Apostles—thus affirmed the analogy between the tsar's entourage and Christ's disciples. Just as the stormy voyage of the *St. Peter* suggested the biblical proof text from the Gospel of Matthew to the monk who described the royal retinue's miraculous rescue, so the inscription on the cross borne by Captain Peter invited his naval entourage to make an implicit comparison between themselves and the followers of Christ, the divine helmsman.[20] The tsar bolstered that interpretation by carving a crucifix

---

18. For this important point I am indebted to the insightful analysis of the "two-edged language" of a "court coterie" in E. H. Kantorowicz, *Frederick the Second, 1194–1250,* trans. E. O. Lorimer (London, 1931), 522.

19. Max Weber, "The Sociology of Charismatic Authority," in *From Max Weber: Essays in Sociology,* ed. H. H. Gerth and C. Wright Mills (New York, 1958), 246–47.

20. The patristic image of the Orthodox Church as the "ship of Jesus" (*Isusov korabl'*), buffeted by waves but solid as a rock, can be found in the Lives of the Saints (*Velikie Minei Chet'i*) compiled by Metropolitan Macarius in the mid–sixteenth century and revised by Dmitrii (Tuptalo), metropolitan of Rostov, in the reign of Peter the Great. For an insightful discussion of this image, see M. B. Pliukhanova, "O natsional'nykh sredstvakh samoopredeleniia lichnosti:

that looked more like a ship's mast than an eight-limbed Orthodox cross. If we recall that Jesus was also a carpenter, then Peter's personal efforts on the docks of his shipyards, a recurrent motif in the tsar's correspondence with his intimates back in Moscow, suggests that the image of the "artisan tsar" was initially based on a deliberate analogy to Christ, the "New Adam."[21] In this case, working with wood, Peter transformed a poignant reminder of physical suffering and other-worldly redemption into a triumphal sign of earthly salvation for himself and his followers, and—through the projected building of a seaworthy imperial navy—of political salvation for his entire realm. The organizers of this impromptu ceremony thus affirmed that the tsar's mission to make landlocked Muscovy into a major maritime power, the burden that he personally took upon his shoulders, was no less miraculous than the safe landing of the *St. Peter*. To those who had faith in Providence, the miracle-working Orthodox saints, and the divine gifts of the "Great Skipper"—or who, like the anonymous engraver who etched the seascape in Figure 4, commemorated such acts of faith[22]—the unsinkable royal yacht proved that, even on his first ocean voyage, the tsar, like his saintly namesake, could also walk on water.

The Fishermen's Order

By commemorating the debt owed to the two fishermen's saints of Pertominsk, the ceremonial procession staged by the tsar and his entourage recalled those other fishermen who had abandoned their nets to follow a charismatic leader on his mission to transfigure the world as they knew it. Indeed, in light of the playful interchangeability of names and attributes common to the rhetorical conventions of the Moscow Baroque,[23] SS. Vassian and Iona came to stand in for the pair of apostles who first followed

---

samosakralizatsiia, samosozhzhenie, plavanie na korable," in *Iz istorii russkoi kul'tury: XVII–nachalo XVIII veka*, ed. A. D. Koshelev (Moscow, 1996), 408.

21. On Peter's labors as the redemptive work of a new Adam, see the epistolary exchange between the tsar and the "archpriest" T. N. Streshnev, March 6 and 12, 1696, in *PiB*, 1:54, 547–48. On the Christological connotations of Adamite imagery in Russian Orthodox theology, see Vladimir Lossky, *The Mystical Theology of the Eastern Church*, trans. Fellowship of St. Alban and St. Sergius (London, 1957), 136–37. On Adam mysticism and its connection to imperial reform in early modern Europe more generally, see Frances Yates, *Astraea: The Imperial Theme in the Sixteenth Century* (London, 1985), 8, 12.

22. An etching of Jesus walking on the waves before the boat of the apostles introduced a series of seascapes published by the master engravers of the St. Petersburg Typography on September 14, 1718; this engraving served to illustrate the accompanying panegyric, which emphasized the redemptive significance of Peter's naval reforms. See *Kunshty korabel'nye* (St. Petersburg, 1718), 1.

23. Grigorii Amelin, " 'Se Moisei tvoi, O Rossiie!' (O semiotike imeni v 'Slove na pogrebenie Petra Velikogo' Feofana Prokopovicha)," in *V chest' 70-letiia professora Iu. M. Lotmana*, 20–29 (Tartu, 1992); M. P. Odesskii, *Ocherki istoricheskoi poetiki russkoi dramy: Epokha Petra I* (Moscow, 1999), chap. 6; and more generally, L. I. Sazonova, *Poeziia russkogo barokko (vtoraia polovina XVII–nachalo XVIII v.)* (Moscow, 1991).

Figure 4. Allegorical seascape, foregrounding Jesus and the Apostles on the Sea of Galilee (cf. Matt. 14:24–33). Anonymous engraving. (From *Kunshty korabel'nye* [St. Petersburg, 1718]. Rare Books Division, Library of the Russian Academy of Sciences, St. Petersburg [RK BRAN, inv. 267]. Photograph by Alexi Melentiev.)

Jesus. To anyone familiar with the tropes and techniques of courtly panegyrics at the end of the seventeenth century, the implicit evocation of St. Peter in the ceremony honoring the two Pertominsk saints conjured up the image of that apostle's other double—his brother, the apostle Andrew. And while Andrew was also considered the patron saint of travelers and sailors, he was not merely a convenient allegorical substitute for the miracle-working Pertominsk saints. In fact, St. Andrew was more familiar to Russian Orthodox Christians as the apostle who, according to tradition, had introduced Christianity among the eastern Slavs, and therefore as one of the patron saints of Rus'. Reading the story of St. Andrew typologically, Peter and his entourage could invoke this "national" saint to justify the tsar's desire to sail through the whole of Russia and out into the cold waters of the

Arctic Ocean.[24] In such a reading, the tale included in the *Russian Primary Chronicle (Povest' vremennykh let)* had in some sense prefigured the pilgrimage of Peter and his entourage.[25] Just like St. Andrew, the tsar had navigated the Russian river systems in an attempt to find a northern outlet to the sea; and just like the apostle's, the tsar's chance stopover resulted in the recognition of a neglected holy place, a recognition sanctified by the erection of a cross. However, whereas the ancient chronicler used the Andrew legend to highlight Kiev's role in fostering Christianity among the Rus' who inhabited the plains along the trade routes between the eastern and western halves of the Roman Empire, Peter's repeated trips to the port city of Archangel asserted his own grandiose, all-Russian imperial ambitions. Indeed, it was precisely by founding a chivalrous knightly order named for the apostle Andrew that the tsar first attempted to institutionalize his vision of a Transfigured Kingdom.

The tsar's decision (after his return from abroad in 1698) to name the first Russian knightly order after St. Andrew highlights both the imperial aspirations and the polemical thrust of his court's political program. From at least the seventh century, the image of Andrew the Apostle had served as an important point in the debate over precedence between the imperial churches of Rome and Constantinople. The claims of Roman bishops to primacy in the church were based on the fact that they were successors of St. Peter, to whom Christ had entrusted the care of his church. To counter these assertions, Orthodox clerics located a tradition for the apostolic source of the see of Byzantium in the investiture of St. Andrew. Because Andrew was the first apostle to whom Jesus addressed his invitation to become his disciple and because Andrew had introduced his brother to Christ (John 1:37–42), the defenders of Byzantine primacy asserted that they were entitled to regard their episcopal see as equal, if not superior, to that of Rome. By the time the "second Rome" finally fell to the Ottomans (1453), the debate over the apostolic foundations of the see of Byzantium had become moot and both Orthodox and Catholic sides had come to accept the authenticity of the Andrew legend.[26] But so long as Constantinople remained in the hands of the Islamic Ottoman Porte and the Habsburgs continued to claim to be the only Christian ruling house to embody the authority of ancient Rome, it appeared that there could be no *renovatio* of the eastern Roman Empire or the see of St. Andrew. At least from the twelfth century,

24. St. Andrew was, in fact, often invoked alongside Peter and Paul as the tsar's heavenly patron. See G. V. Vilinbakhov, "Gosudarstvennaia geral'dika Rossii kontsa XVII–pervoi chetverti XVIII veka. (K voprosu formirovaniia ideologii absoliutizma v Rossii)" (Avtoreferat diss., kand. ist. nauk, Leningrad State University, 1982), 14; and his "Otrazhenie idei absoliutizma v simvolike petrovskikh znamen," in *Kul'tura i iskusstvo Rossii XVIII veka. Sbornik statei* (Leningrad 1981), 15, 17.

25. *The Russian Primary Chronicle: Laurentian Text*, trans. and ed. Samuel Hazzard Cross and Olgerd P. Sherbowitz-Wetzor (Cambridge, 1953), 53–54.

26. Francis Dvornik, *The Idea of Apostolicity in Byzantium and the Legend of the Apostle Andrew* (Cambridge, 1958).

however, the Andrew legend had been transferred from Byzantium and adopted by Orthodox apologists for the rulers of Russia, who came increasingly to be identified as the founders of a new or "third Rome." Indeed, the growing imperial pretensions of Muscovite rulers from Ivan III on almost guaranteed that the Andrew legend would reappear in Russian political rhetoric. The foundation of the order of St. Andrew "the First-Called" (*Pervozvannyi*) at the court of Tsar Peter Alekseevich thus signaled the revival, in secular and chivalrous guise, of the ancient religious rivalry between the defenders of the Roman Catholic and Greek Orthodox imperial ideas.[27]

The earliest records of its (informal) institution indicate that the order of St. Andrew was intended as an Eastern Orthodox counterpart to the Catholic knightly orders sponsored by the Holy Roman Emperor, and particularly to the crusading order of the seagoing Knights of Malta.[28] In March 1699, boyar F. A. Golovin (1650–1706), the courtier who headed Peter's foreign policy establishment and who had recently led the tsar's Great Embassy to Europe, boasted of his membership in the tsar's new order to Johann Georg Korb, the secretary of the Habsburg ambassador to Moscow.[29] In his diary Korb claimed that the tsar founded this order to reward those servitors who had distinguished themselves in battle against the Turks during the 1695–96 Azov campaigns, when Orthodox Muscovy was part of the Catholic Holy Alliance, consisting of the Holy Roman Empire, Venice, the Polish Republic, and the Knights of Malta. Korb assumed that the turn to chivalry reflected the tsar's desire to imitate the trappings of other European Christian princes, and particularly of Korb's own sover-

27. On the fate of the imperial theme in early modern Europe, see Yates, *Astraea*; and B. N. Floria, ed., *Slaviane i ikh sosedi. Imperskaia ideia v stranakh tsentral'noi, vostochnoi i iugo-vostochnoi Evropy. Tezisy XIV konferentsii* (Moscow, 1995).

28. Although the order of St. Andrew appeared at the end of the seventeenth century (1699), it did not become a true monarchical order until 1720, when it acquired its own set of statutes (monarchical constitution). Until then, it can be classified as a "cliental pseudo order," which has been defined as a "princely order, whose members were bound by an oath of clientship to the prince who bestowed [the order] in the form of a badge." These "pseudo orders" were "in effect glorified retinues, distinguished from other such groupings only by the misleading title 'order' applied to them by the prince who distributed the badge." See D'Arcy Jonathan Dacre Boulton, *The Knights of the Crown: The Monarchical Orders of Knighthood in Later Medieval Europe, 1325–1520* (Woodbridge, 1987), xvii–xx. For the text of the statutes of 1720, see E. E. Zamyslovskii and I. I. Petrov, *Istoricheskii ocherk rossiiskikh ordenov i sbornik osnovnykh ordenskikh statutov* (St. Petersburg, 1892).

29. J.-G. Korb, *Diary of an Austrian Secretary of Legation,* trans. Count MacDonnell (London, 1968), 272–73. For a biography of F. A. Golovin, the first cavalier of the order of St. Andrew, the first general field marshal of the Russian army, the second general admiral of the navy, and a priest in the mock ecclesiastical council of Peter the Great, see Hughes, *Russia,* 420; Paul Bushkovitch, *Peter the Great: The Struggle for Power, 1671–1725* (Cambridge, 2001), 187–88; and N. V. Skritskii, *Pervyi kavaler Ordena Sviatogo Andreia Admiral F. A. Golovin (1650–1706). Biograficheskii ocherk* (Moscow, 1995). For a description of the chivalrous motifs invoked during his elaborate funeral procession, see S. I. Nikolaev, "Rytsarskaia ideia v pokhoronnom obriade petrovskoi epokhi," in *Iz istorii russkoi kul'tury,* ed. A. D. Koshelev, 3:584–94 (Moscow, 1996); and idem, *Literaturnaia kul'tura petrovskoi epokhi* (St. Petersburg, 1996), 38–45. On his mock-ecclesiastical pseudonym, see Appendix 2.

eign, Leopold I the Holy Roman Emperor of the German Nation. As evidence of this desire, the Habsburg diplomat pointed to the special favor shown by the tsar to B. P. Sheremetev (1652–1719), the Russian emissary (and future general field marshal) who had returned from abroad as an honorary member of the Knights of Malta, the crusading Catholic order patronized by the pope and the Holy Roman Emperor.[30] In fact, the motto of the first Russian order, "For Faith and Fidelity" (*za veru i vernost'*), did resemble the one used by the Maltese knights, *Pour la foi*. Even the name of the tsar's new order appeared to have been borrowed from that of two earlier Catholic brotherhoods dedicated to St. Andrew: the old Scottish order also known as the order of the Thistle and the Habsburg order of the Golden Fleece, which was originally dedicated to the Mother of God and Andrew the Apostle.[31]

Despite its similarity to these Catholic brotherhoods, however, the insignia of the Russian order were actually modeled after the first and most ancient European knightly order, reputedly founded by the Byzantine emperor Constantine I (the Great).[32] The fact that Peter Alekseevich chose to emulate this particular emperor was not in itself innovative; even before the collapse of the second Rome, the comparison with Constantine the Great had become a mainstay of the claim that the rulers of Russia had inherited the imperial and religious authority of Byzantium. It was not the traditional image of the pious emperor who legalized Christianity that found favor at Peter's court, however, but that of the divinely ordained, chivalrous warrior-king. In this innovation, as in so many others in Muscovite court culture, the son followed the lead of the father. For during his long and turbulent reign, Tsar Aleksei Mikhailovich had repeatedly invoked the martial imagery associated with the first Christian emperor, particularly the legendary Cross of Constantine—a familiar emblem in medieval European heraldry, representing the cross that had appeared in the sky above the armies of Constantine as a sign that he would defeat the usurper Maxentius. Aleksei Mikhailovich even went so far as to order that the relics of the Cross of Constantine, supposedly housed in an Orthodox monastery on Mount Athos, be transferred to Moscow.[33]

---

30. Korb, *Diary*, 256–57, 274. For a biography of B. P. Sheremetev, see Hughes, *Russia*, 421–22; N. I. Pavlenko, *Ptentsy gnezda Petrova* (Moscow, 1984), 12–108; and esp. A. I. Zaozerskii, *Fel'dmarshal B. P. Sheremetev* (Moscow, 1989). On the geopolitical significance of Sheremetev's trip to Malta, see Zaozerskii, 22–25. On the Knights of Malta, see Boulton, *Knights*, 17.

31. On the Scottish order of St. Andrew, see Boulton, *Knights*, xx, 399, 499–500. For an extensive discussion of the order of the Golden Fleece (*Toison d'or*), see ibid., chap. 13.

32. See the seminal article of G. V. Vilinbakhov, "K istorii uchrezhdeniia ordena Andreia Pervozvannogo i evoliutsii ego znaka," in *Kul'tura i iskusstvo petrovskogo vremeni: Publikatsii i issledovaniia*, 144–58 (Leningrad, 1977).

33. On the Cross of Constantine and its veneration at the court of Tsar Aleksei Mikhailovich, see Vilinbakhov, "Gosudarstvennaia geral'dika," 16–18. On its importance in Muscovite political theology, see M. B. Pliukhanova, *Siuzhety i simvoly Moskovskogo tsarstva* (St. Petersburg, 1995), chap. 3. On the importance of the image of Emperor Constantine the

The cult of the Cross of Constantine, associated with divine protection and victory, was picked up by Aleksei's successors, including his youngest son, who also continued his aggressive policies against the Muslim over-lords of Constantinople. For example, in 1696, during Peter's second attempt to wrest the fortress of Azov from the Crimean Tatars, the Cross of Constantine decorated the standards of a newly organized "naval regiment."[34] After the initial failure (in 1695) to take the fortress by land, the tsar and his military advisers realized the importance of a naval blockade and formed this new regiment in the hope of actualizing the motto on its standard: "By this sign shall you conquer." Indeed, the ideological origins of the insignia for the first Russian order of chivalry can be traced back to the tsar's 1696 triumphal entry into Moscow, during which the royal "captain" walked in the ranks of his naval regiment through an arch whose panels hailed "the victorious return of Tsar Constantine" and "Tsar Constantine's victory over the profane Roman tsar Maxentius."[35] Although both Constantine and Maxentius were called "tsars" in Russian/Church Slavonic, the designers of the banners for the first imperial "triumph" ever staged at the court of Muscovy clearly distinguished the Byzantine *basileus,* the spiritual forefather of the Russian Orthodox tsar, from his profane "Roman" counterpart, who represented the tsar's erstwhile ally, the Catholic kaiser. The decisive role of the tsar's new flotilla in his first major military victory thus provided the impetus for the foundation of an Orthodox order of sea-going knights whose "regular" military organization and Christian valor could rout the "barbarous" hordes of Muslim infidels while at the same time rivaling the Catholic brotherhood sponsored by the Holy Roman Emperor.

By founding Russia's first order of chivalry—a symbolic act that was the institutional equivalent of the 1694 Pertominsk ceremony—the royal "captain" thus transformed the Cross of Constantine into the *Cruz Decussata* of St. Andrew, invoking the protection of the patron saint of sailors for the nascent Russian navy and his own imperial ambitions. As during the procession outside the Pertominsk Monastery, the tsar did not carry this weight solely on his own shoulders. The first cavaliers of the order of St. Andrew included the tsar's most trusted geopolitical allies, particularly those who were involved in the secret diplomacy at the end of the seventeenth century, when Russia was building its coalition against Sweden, while ostensibly still part of the Holy Alliance and its crusade against the Ottoman Empire. Besides the Muscovite foreign minister (F. A. Golovin), the first members of

---

Great in Petrine political culture, see Vilinbakhov, 153–55; and V. M. Zhivov, "Kul'turnye reformy v sisteme preobrazovanii Petra I," in *Iz istorii russkoi kul'tury,* ed. A. D. Koshelev, 3:528–83 (Moscow, 1996); and his "Dopolnitel'nye primechaniia," in *Razyskaniia v oblasti i predistorii russkoi kul'tury* (Moscow, 2002), 427–28.

34. Vilinbakhov, "Gosudarstvennaia geral'dika," 18.

35. For a description of the 1696 triumphal entry into Moscow, see Bogoslovskii, *Petr I,* 1:344–47; V. P. Grebeniuk, "Publichnye zrelishcha petrovskogo vremeni i ikh sviaz' s teatrom," in *Novye cherty v russkoi literature i iskusstve (XVII–nachalo XVIII v.),* 133–45 (Moscow, 1976); and Richard S. Wortman, *Scenarios of Power: Myth and Ceremony in Russian Monarchy,* 2 vols. (Princeton, 1995), 1:42–44.

Figure 5. The Muscovite Order of St. Andrew the First Called. Engraving. (From J. A. Rudolphi, *Heraldica Curiosa* [Frankfurt and Leipzig, 1718].)

the order included I. S. Mazepa, the hetman (Cossack leader) of Left-Bank Ukraine, and Constantine Brancovan, the Orthodox *hospodar* (prince) of Wallachia, the nominal vassal of the Turkish sultan who was covertly involved in recruiting sailors for the imperial Russian navy.[36] Both the honor and the burden of the tsar's personal trust in these men was embodied in the order's badge, a representation of the crucified St. Andrew in the form of the characteristic diagonal cross, which was worn around the neck on a sash or chain (see Figure 5). By accepting the order of St. Andrew, the men empowered to act as Peter's personal representatives on the stage of world politics took on the responsibility of fulfilling the words of the order's motto, "For Faith and Fidelity." Thus, like the courtiers who helped the tsar erect a cross in honor of the Pertominsk saints, the knights of the order of St. Andrew were urged to take up the yoke of faith (Acts 15:10–11) and become the disciples of their royal patron and his heavenly intercessors.

The Uses of Apostasy

The impromptu ceremonies that demonstrated Peter's personal charisma were not confined to the early days of his reign. Indeed, the providential interpretation of Peter's political mission, as articulated during the inaugura-

36. A. V. Viskovatov, "Ob uchrezhdenii ordena sv. Apostola Andreia Pervozvannogo i o pozhalovanii sim ordenom v 1700 g. Multianskogo Gospodaria Brankovana, v kavalerskikh spiskakh nigde ne pokazannogo," in RGAVMF, f. 315, op. 1, ed. khr. 47.

tion of the Transfigured Kingdom in 1691–92 and as reaffirmed during the accidental pilgrimage of 1694, went on to inform the way the tsar and his courtiers handled what was perhaps the most embarrassing episode of the entire Northern War: the unexpected defection of Ivan Mazepa, the second cavalier of the order of St. Andrew, to the side of King Charles XII of Sweden in the fall of 1708. The relative success with which the tsar and his entourage transformed this potentially disastrous foreign policy debacle into the most important turning point of the entire conflict between Russia and Sweden once again serves to underline how easily the tsar and his company could integrate even such a flagrant violation of Peter's new scenario of power into the royalist myth of Russia's anointed one. Playing on the religious and political connotations associated with membership in the tsar's self-styled chivalrous fellowship of believers, Peter and his companions would go on to compare Mazepa's defection with the apostasy of Judas Iscariot, the disciple who betrayed *his* anointed one for thirty pieces of silver. In fact, this analogy would become one of the most prominent motifs in the shaming rituals staged by Russian diplomats after the battle of Poltava, strengthening the impression that Peter's entourage had reorganized itself according to the ideals of a chivalrous religious order so as to demonstrate the charismatic authority of the divinely anointed Russian monarch.[37]

Although they have been obscured by centuries of confessional (and later nationalist) polemics, the reasons for the hetman's breach of faith are not hard to fathom.[38] Over the course of the long and costly conflict among Russia, Sweden, and Poland, Ivan Mazepa had become increasingly worried about the effects of Muscovite wartime exactions on the military organization and morale of the Ukrainian political elite as well as on the security of his own position as hetman of the Cossack host. Doubting that the tsar, beleaguered by the demands of war, would be able to protect Ukraine from the seemingly invincible armies of Charles XII and his Polish protégé, King Stanislaw Leszczynski,[39] Mazepa stunned the Russian leadership by switching sides just a few months before the fateful battle of Poltava. No one in Peter's entourage expected that kind of behavior from the faithful septuagenarian, who had managed to serve the interests of both the Russian crown and the Ukrainian socio-military elite ever since his election as Cossack hetman in 1687. This shock was compounded by the fact that the hetman's de-

---

37. The analogy between Mazepa and Judas also informed the work of Peter's chief apologists, such as Stefan (Iavorskii), "Stikhi na izmenu Mazepy, izdannye ot litsa vseia Rossii," in *Pamiatniki literatury drevnei Rusi: XVII vek* (Moscow, 1994), 3:268; and Feofan (Prokopovich), "Slovo pokhval'noe o preslavnoi nad voiskami Sveiskimi pobede . . . ," in his *Sochineniia*, ed. I. P. Eremin (Moscow and Leningrad, 1961), 28.

38. My interpretation of Mazepa's motives in 1708–9 is indebted to the revisionist studies of Anisimov, *Reforms*, 112–16; and esp. Orest Subtelny, "Mazepa, Peter I, and the Question of Treason," *Harvard Ukrainian Studies* 2, no. 2 (June 1978): 158–83.

39. Stanislaw Leszczynski was installed on the Polish throne by the Swedes after Peter's ally August II "the Strong," the elector of Saxony, was forced to abdicate in 1705. See Molchanov, *Diplomatiia Petra Pervogo*, 188, 195.

fection came at a crucial point in the war between Russia and Sweden, on the eve of what promised to be the final showdown between the armies of Peter and Charles. Mazepa's betrayal caused panic among the Russian leadership, which now had to face the full force of the Swedish invasion without any allies.

News of Mazepa's defection spread very quickly and for months it appeared that this major diplomatic embarrassment would have catastrophic strategic and political consequences, not only for Russia's war effort but also for Peter's whole program of reform. Mazepa had seriously challenged the tsar's authority in Ukraine and had gone unpunished. Worse still (at least from the Russian point of view), he continued to argue his case in numerous proclamations and manifestos that were disseminated throughout Ukraine after October 1708. Clearly the tsar could not let Mazepa and his claims go unanswered. In November 1708 Peter's diplomatic corps mounted an intense campaign to counter the literature produced in the camps of Mazepa and Charles XII.[40] The conclusions that the Cossack elite and the urban inhabitants of Ukraine were supposed to draw from these broadsheets were dramatized during two remarkable ceremonies in which the fugitive Cossack hetman and erstwhile cavalier of the order of St. Andrew figured prominently.

On November 6, 1709, A. D. Menshikov and G. I. Golovkin (1660–1734), the chancellor of Foreign Affairs, hastily gathered the remaining loyal members of the Cossack elite in the town of Glukhov (Hlukhiv).[41] In the midst of the proceedings to elect a new hetman, the Russian military authorities built a large platform and a gallows in the center of town. Accompanied by the sound of rolling drums, a life-size effigy of the treasonous Ukrainian hetman, adorned with the cavalier's medal and the blue sash of the order of St. Andrew, was brought out into the public square. Menshikov and Golovkin waited while the dummy was carried up the steps to the platform. When the effigy of Mazepa was brought before them, these two cavaliers of the order of St. Andrew proceeded to tear up the official certificate that attested to Mazepa's membership in the tsar's knightly order; immediately afterward the effigy was stripped of its insignia. Then, after a public reading of the charges against the ex-hetman, the naked dummy was tossed into the hands of the executioner. The

---

40. For a summary of this propaganda war, see B. Kentrschynskyj, "Propagandakriget i Ukraina, 1708–1709," in *Karolinska Förbundets Årsbok,* 81–124 (Stockholm, 1958); and the English-language summary in *Ukrainian Quarterly* 15 (1959): 241–59.

41. For a brief biography of G. I. Golovkin, see Hughes, *Russia,* 420–21, 591; and D. O. Serov, *Stroiteli imperii: Ocherki gosudarstvennoi i kriminal'noi deiatel'nosti spodvizhnikov Petra I* (Novosibirsk, 1996), 33–34, 51n33, 227. On the genealogy and service career of his clan, see N. P. Likhachev, "Rodoproiskhozhdenie dvorian Golovkinykh," *Izvestiia Russkogo Genealogicheskogo obshchestva* 2 (1903): 103–39; and I. Iu. Airapetian, "Feodal'naia aristokratiia v period stanovleniia absoliutizma v Rossii" (Diss. kand. ist. nauk, M. V. Lomonosov State University, 1987), 71–72, 330. For his rank in Peter's mock ecclesiastical council, see Appendix 2.

dummy was bound with ropes and dragged through the streets to the gallows set up for the occasion. The executioner tore up the Mazepa family seal, broke the sword that still hung at the dummy's side, and finally, without further ado, hanged it from the gallows.[42]

A few days later, on November 12, 1709, in an act timed to coincide with the installation of Ivan Skoropads'kyi, the new Cossack hetman, the Russian tsar and his entourage personally witnessed the official ceremony during which the metropolitan of Kiev thrice anathematized the name of Mazepa. Less than a week later, in Moscow, Mazepa's anathematization in absentia was repeated by Metropolitan Stefan (Iavorskii), the caretaker of the vacant throne of the Russian patriarch, in front of the heir apparent and all the leading political figures of the Russian capital.[43] Like the defamation of Mazepa, this ceremony was undoubtedly part of the propaganda campaign that followed Mazepa's defection; it too was designed to portray the hetman's actions as first and foremost a betrayal of the common Orthodox faith. But apparently for Peter and his entourage it was not enough to exclude Mazepa from the fold of the Orthodox Church and condemn him to eternal damnation. The humiliating ceremony in which Mazepa's effigy was stripped of his cavalier's sash and literally dragged through the mud emphasized the fact that the ex-hetman's personal break with Peter signified the betrayal of the common interest represented by membership in the tsar's knightly order. Peter's charge that Mazepa had "turned traitor and betrayer of his people" thus referred not only to the Ukrainian Cossack elite or the Orthodox Slavs but also to his fellow cavaliers of the order of St. Andrew.[44]

On June 27, 1709, Mazepa was with Charles XII during the clash in which the Swedish army, under the command of the young king himself, was routed by the Muscovite forces near the Ukrainian town of Poltava. While most of the Swedish army eventually surrendered, Charles XII, Mazepa, and a small retinue barely managed to escape from the field of battle. Throughout all of July 1709 the Russian tsar and his military advisers hoped to capture Charles XII and Mazepa before they managed to make their way to the court of the Ottoman sultan, and certainly before the Swedish king and the Ukrainian hetman had succeeded in persuading Ahmed III to enter the fray on their side. To forestall the possibility of a two-front war, on July 1 and 2 Peter sent out two regiments of mounted cavalry, under the commands of Brigadier Kropotkin and Major General Prince G. S. Volkonskoi, in pursuit of the "remnants of Poltava" (*poltavskie nedobitki*). Prince Volkonskoi received detailed written instructions, signed by Menshikov and composed by the tsar himself, about the manner in

42. For a firsthand account of Mazepa's shaming ceremony, see G. I. Golovkin to P. A. Tolstoi, n.d., in *PiB*, 8 (2): 910.

43. For the text of the anathema pronounced by Metropolitan Stefan (Iavorskii), see *Polnoe sobranie zakonov Rossiiskoi imperii* (St. Petersburg, 1830), 4:431–32.

44. Peter to F. M. Apraksin, October 30, 1708, in *PiB*, 8 (1): 253.

which Charles XII and Mazepa were to be transported back to Russia in the event of their capture.[45] In the meantime, Peter and Golovkin began an intensive diplomatic correspondence with the rulers of adjacent territories, encouraging them "diligently to seek out, capture, and put under guard the traitor Mazepa," and implicitly warning them against abetting the fugitives.[46] It is clear that at the beginning of July, the tsar and his closest advisers hoped that Charles and Mazepa would soon be brought to justice.

The attempt to bring the remnants of Poltava to justice, however, necessitated more than a flurry of diplomatic activity. Indeed, this manhunt also led to the creation of a mock counterpart to the first Russian order of chivalry. During the course of the month-long chase across the steppe, A. Ia. Shchukin (c. 1669–1720), the chief secretary of the Ingermanland Chancellery, the department responsible for (among other things) administrating the future site of Russia's new northern capital,[47] received three letters, each more urgent than the last, about the minting of a special silver commemorative medal (like the one depicted in Figure 6). The first letter, written just two weeks after the battle of Poltava, was sent by diplomatic pouch on July 11, 1709. Bearing the seal and signature of the head of the Ingermanland Chancellery, Prince Menshikov himself, the letter contained the following order:

> Upon receipt of this immediately make a silver medal [*moneta,* literally coin] weighing ten pounds and have engraved upon it Judas hanging on an aspen tree, above thirty pieces of silver lying next to a sack; on the reverse the following inscription: "The thrice-cursed [i.e., anathematized] fatal son, Judas, hanging [literally, choking] because of his lust for money." After a two-pound chain is made for that medal, have it sent to us immediately by special courier.[48]

Menshikov repeated his injunction to hurry in two other missives to Shchukin. The last letter, dated August 9, 1709, was written just a week after the retinue of Charles XII had managed to cross the Ukrainian border and evade capture. Although the sultan refused to hand the Swedish king

45. For Peter's instructions see I. I. Golikov, *Deianiia Petra Velikogo, mudrogo preobrazovatelia Rossii, sobrannye iz dostovernykh istochnikov i raspolozhennye po godam* (Moscow, 1789), 13:29–30; and *Trudy Imperatorskogo Russkogo voenno-istoricheskogo obshchestva* (St. Petersburg, 1909), 3:302, 304.

46. *PiB,* 9 (1): 242, (2): 1013; and G. V. Zashchuk, "'Orden Iudy,'" *Voprosy istorii 6,* no. 6 (June 1971): 214.

47. For a brief biography of A. Ia. Shchukin, see Serov, *Stroiteli imperii,* 26n29, 255. For the institutional history of the Ingermanland Chancellery, which was based originally on the royal estate of Semenovsk in Moscow, see ibid., 123n16; N. B. Golikova and L. G. Kisliagina, "Sistema gosudarstvennogo upravleniia," in *Ocherki russkoi kul'tury XVIII veka,* ed. A. D. Gorskii et al. (Moscow, 1987), 2:50–51; and E. V. Anisimov, *Gosudarstvennye preobrazovaniia i samoderzhavie Petra Velikogo v pervoi chetverti XVIII veka* (St. Petersburg, 1997), 48, 90–91.

48. This decree was found in a late eighteenth-century manuscript that was published first in *Trudy Riazanskoi uchenoi arkhivnoi kommissii* 1 (1894): 69; the decree was republished by S. F. Platonov, "Orden Iudy 1709 goda," *Letopis' zaniatii postoiannoi istoriko-arkheograficheskoi komissii* 1 (1927): 194; and Zashchuk, "'Orden Iudy,'" 212.

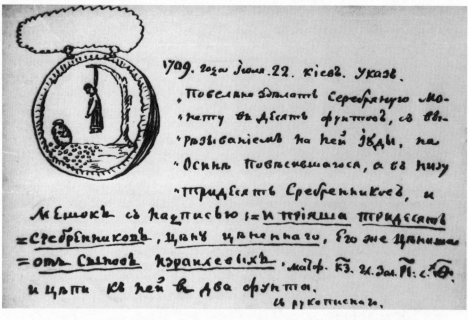

Figure 6. The Order of Judas. Undated ink sketch, early nineteenth century. (I. I. Sreznevskii Collection, Manuscript Division, Library of the Russian Academy of Sciences, St. Petersburg [RO BRAN, Sbornaia rukopis' 24.5.38]. Photograph by Alexi Melentiev.)

over to their mutual enemy, Russian diplomats continued to hold out the hope that the Ukrainian hetman, as the subject of the tsar, would be extradited to answer the charge of treason.[49] Clearly, Peter and his royal favorite believed, even at this late date, that they could still get their hands on him. And the heavy silver chain and medallion of Judas commissioned by Menshikov seems to have figured prominently in their plans to avenge Mazepa's treachery.

According to the instructions later appended to the original decree, upon receipt of Menshikov's commission the staff of the Moscow-based Ingermanland Chancellery contacted a silversmith named Matvei Alekseev and charged him with transforming twelve and a half pounds of silver coin into the medal described in Menshikov's letter.[50] However, in the eleven days between the time Menshikov first commissioned the Judas medal and the time his letter appears to have been rewritten in the form of a royal decree, the reference to the "thrice-cursed fatal son, Judas" was replaced by a

---

49. N. I. Pavlenko, *Petr Velikii* (Moscow, 1990), 320.

50. For the text of the instructions, see Platonov, "Orden Iudy," 194. It is unclear whether this silversmith was related to Fedor Alekseev, the master of the Admiralty Mint and the medallion maker responsible for producing the first commemorative campaign medal of the Northern War. On Fedor Alekseev, see E. S. Shchukina, *Medal'ernoe iskusstvo v Rossii XVIII veka* (Leningrad, 1962), 13.

quote from the Gospel of Matthew (Matt. 27:9).[51] The biblical proof text of the later version of the medal—"And they took the thirty pieces of silver, the price of the one on whom a price had been set, on whom some of the people of Israel had set a price . . ."—comes from Matthew's description of what the chief priests decided to do with the blood money recovered after Judas's death. So as not to sully the temple coffers with tainted funds, the elders decided to use the thirty pieces of silver that Judas received for betraying Christ to buy "potter's field"—a profane place on the outskirts of the Holy City—as a place to bury foreigners. Adapting this biblical story to contemporary events, the new inscription appears to have served as a warning to all of Russia's enemies that if they dared to engage in battle against the army of Russia's divinely anointed monarch, they too would end up in potter's field. In this reading, the Judas medal was intended to offer a prediction: just as Poltava had become a place for burying the Swedes, so any future engagement would end in the defeat of Russia's enemies. Judging by the actions of Menshikov, whose troops had recently razed the capital of the Ukrainian hetman and who was now ordered to invade the territories of the Polish-Lithuanian Commonwealth in order to drive Leszczynski from the Polish throne, this was no idle threat.[52]

The new inscription on the Judas medal also played up the parallel between Christ, "the one on whom a price had been set," and Tsar Peter, the charismatic founder of the order of St. Andrew—a parallel that was fundamental to the chivalrous-religious organization of the Transfigured Kingdom. Like Jesus, the tsar had been betrayed by one of his own chosen people, a disciple who had once belonged, however nominally, to the tight circle of believers in his divine gift of grace. As a result of this fundamental breach of faith, the traitor had become like one of those people of Israel who had set a price on their anointed one. Indeed, by betraying the chivalrous brotherhood committed to the cause of the Russian Orthodox tsar, Mazepa had also betrayed St. Andrew, their patron saint, and by metaphoric extension Christ himself. In retaliation, the Russian royal favorite and the rest of the tsar's disciples—some of whom (such as Chancellor Golovkin) simultaneously served as members of both the mock ecclesiastical council of the Transfigured Kingdom and the chivalrous order of St. Andrew—had enrolled the traitor in a diabolical counterorder representing all the enemies of Christ: an order of Judas.

Judging by the external and internal evidence contained in the original commission, it is not too farfetched to suggest that the heavy silver medal

---

51. The second version of Menshikov's decree was discovered by I. I. Sreznevskii. For the text of the Sreznevskii decree (and the accompanying drawing), see RO BRAN, Sbornaia rukopis'24.5.38, l. 75v.

52. On July 15, 1709, just four days after Menshikov first wrote to Shchukin about the silver medal of Judas, the cavalry divisions of the royal favorite embarked on a new campaign against the remnants of the combined Swedish-Polish forces. See Pavlenko, *Petr Velikii,* 322–23.

and chain were intended as a humiliating replacement for the cross and sash of the order of St. Andrew, of which Mazepa had been stripped in absentia. In this light, the Judas medal would have served as a mock decoration for Mazepa in his new role as the first cavalier of the order of Judas. Indeed, to the extent that the silver medal of Judas was intended as commemoration and commentary on an important aspect of the Russian military victory—Mazepa's betrayal—it served as a satirical counterpart to the campaign decorations for the battle of Poltava. In an ironic extension of the practice of rewarding all the participants of a successful military campaign, the tsar and his advisers thus made sure that even the traitorous ex-cavalier of the order of St. Andrew was to be recognized for his providential contribution not only to the victory at Poltava but also to the apotheosis of Russia's anointed one.[53]

The Cavalier of the Order of Judas

If the primary purpose of the Judas medal was punitive, then the tsar and his advisers failed to reach their objective. Indeed, despite all their efforts, Mazepa permanently escaped Russia's grasp. Broken by his defeat and his headlong flight across the border, the old Cossack hetman died just a few months after finding asylum in the fortress town of Bendery. With him went all hope of stripping the real Poltava traitor, not just his dummy, of the insignia of the order of St. Andrew and hanging the twelve-pound silver medal and chain of the order of Judas around his neck. However, the mock order did not die with the Ukrainian hetman. Indeed, the fate of the Judas medal after the death of Mazepa only confirms the enduring connection between the idea of a knightly order, the tsar's geopolitical ambitions, and the exercise of charismatic authority at the court of Tsar Peter. Far from losing its raison d'être, the imaginary mock order represented by the silver medallion became, if only for a short time, as much a part of the discourse employed at the Russian court as the annual commemoration of the victory at Poltava.

As early as the winter of 1709, just a few months after it was commissioned, the medal originally intended for Mazepa appeared in an impromptu skit staged by the tsar in front of Joost Jules, the newly appointed Danish extraordinary envoy to the court of Muscovy, who was sent to negotiate a new alliance between Denmark and Russia. During his first meeting with the Russian tsar, which took place in the recently reconquered city of Narva, Jules saw the badge of the order of Judas around the neck of a "Prince Jacobskoy," one of the titled court jesters whom the tsar habitually

53. On the Muscovite practice of awarding campaign medals to all participants, see Shchukina, *Medal'ernoe iskusstvo,* 11–12; and V. A. Durov, "Russkie boevye nagrady za Poltavskoe srazhenie," *Numizmatika i sfragistika* 5 (1974): 63–64.

kept in his personal retinue and whom he jokingly referred to as "patriarchs."[54] In his diary the Danish diplomat recorded a story that he claims to have heard from the tsar himself about the origins of this mock chivalric order:

> The tsar told me that this jester is one of the wisest men in Russia, but despite that fact, he is seized with a spirit of rebellion. Once, when the tsar began a conversation with him about how the traitor Judas betrayed the Saviour for thirty pieces of silver, Jacobskoy objected that the price was too low and that Judas should have asked for more. Then, in order to poke fun at Jacobskoy as well as to punish him—for it seemed from his words that had the Saviour been alive today, he would not have been averse to betraying him either, only for a bigger price—the tsar immediately commanded that the above-mentioned order of Judas be made, with a depiction of the latter preparing to hang himself.[55]

As will immediately become apparent to anyone familiar with the actual circumstances surrounding the origins of this commemorative silver medallion, the anecdote innocently recorded by the Danish envoy was much more than an amusing explanation of how an impudent royal jester wound up wearing the Judas medal.

The jester's joke, as retold by the tsar at an informal diplomatic meeting at which the battle of Poltava was in fact the main topic of conversation, had a contemporary political resonance.[56] The anecdote recalled the actions of Hetman Mazepa, whose betrayal had almost resulted in the death of Russia's savior and the loss of his crown. By hinting at the exorbitant price he had nearly paid for his misplaced trust, the tsar made an implicit comparison between the inconstancy of the former Cossack hetman and that of Russia's potential new ally, the Danish king. The very fact that the badge of the Order of Judas was first shown to the Danish ambassador in Narva, the site of the disastrous defeat that Russia suffered immediately after Denmark capitulated to Charles XII in 1700, emphasized the inconstant actions of Frederick IV, who had already, at the very beginning of the Northern War, betrayed the confidence of the Russian leadership by withdrawing from the secret alliance against Sweden and leaving Russia to face Charles's army alone. By their insistence that the first meeting between the Danish diplomat and the Russian tsar should take place at Narva, after Peter had returned from reaping the diplomatic fruit of the victory of Poltava, the tsar and his advisers meant to instill the belief that the Muscovites had overcome their initial problems and were capable of handling Sweden by themselves. If the Danes wanted to join in the dismemberment of the Swedish Empire, they

54. Iu. N. Shcherbachev, ed. and trans., "Zapiski Iusta Iulia, datskogo poslannika pri Petre Velikom (1709–1711)," in *Chteniia Moskovskogo obshchestva istorii i drevnostei Rossiiskikh* 189, no. 2 (1899): 91, 93.

55. Ibid., 92–93.

56. Ibid., 91.

had to act on the terms set by the tsar and his representatives, or else remain on the sidelines (if not in the camp of the enemy and of the traitors).

What Jules actually recorded in his diary was therefore a subtle dig at the honor of his king orchestrated at the expense of the Danish diplomat by Peter and his court jester. However, whether the Danish envoy misunderstood the political significance of the tsar's practical joke or simply decided not to record its real import in his diplomatic diary, it seems clear that he was not the primary intended audience for this impromptu little skit about faith, honor, and betrayal. In fact, if we analyze who "Prince Jacobskoy" was and why the tsar chose this particular Russian courtier to succeed Mazepa as the first cavalier of the order of Judas, we will see that the full significance of this satirical performance could be understood only by Muscovite insiders. Those courtiers who were able to recall the history of the complicated relationship between the Russian royal family and the Shakhovskoi princely clan and understood the role of jesters at the Muscovite court would surely have grasped that the "spirit of rebellion" that supposedly had characterized the new cavalier of the order of Judas referred as much to events in his family's past as to the treachery of the former Cossack hetman or to the inconstancy of the Danish king.

The Shakhovskois were a princely clan with a family history of rebellion against the house of Romanov. One incident in particular seems to have left a lasting impression in the collective memory of the Muscovite political elite. In the summer of 1620, several members of the Shakhovskoi family staged a parody of the election of Tsar Mikhail Fedorovich. During a private gathering at the Moscow residence of a family acquaintance, Prince Matvei Fedorovich Shakhovskoi, the great-uncle of the future cavalier of the order of Judas, was named "tsar" and invested with royal authority in what Muscovite officials later described as an "intricate and rebellious manner" (*zateinym vorovskim obychaem*); meanwhile, his brothers and cousins styled themselves as top-ranking members of the mock tsar's royal council (*boiare*).[57] This political burlesque, which recalled the installation of Mikhail Fedorovich by the 1613 *zemskii sobor,* underlined the fact that the relatively lowly Romanovs were not God-ordained but men-made rulers, and hence could be replaced, especially by a princely family like the Shakhovskois. This was no idle threat, since another Prince Shakhovskoi, Grigorii Petrovich, was actively involved in organizing the Bolotnikov uprising during the Time of Troubles immediately before the installation of the first Romanov on the Russian throne.[58] In 1620, after an official investigation, one of the first of its kind, into the Shakhovskoi princes' "words

57. A. I. Timofeev, ed., "Zapisnye knigi Moskovskogo stola. 1633 sentiabr'–1634 avgust," *Russkaia istoricheskaia biblioteka* (St. Petersburg, 1884), 9:550.

58. E. Likhach, "Shakhovskie," in *RBS* (St. Petersburg, 1905), 571, 578–79. For a genealogy of the Shakhovskoi clan, see A. A. Dolgorukov, *Rossiiskaia rodoslovnaia kniga* (St. Petersburg, 1854), 1:168–69; and P. N. Petrov, "Kniaz'ia Shakhovskie," *Istoriia rodov russkogo dvorianstva* (St. Petersburg, 1886), 1:73.

and deeds against the sovereign,"[59] the mock tsar and his company were found guilty of treason and demonstratively condemned to death by the royal council of Mikhail Fedorovich Romanov. However, at the request of Patriarch Filaret, Mikhail's father and chief political adviser, the Shakhovskois' death sentence was commuted to exile and imprisonment in the towns of the lower Volga and Siberia. The Shakhovskois were finally allowed to return to Muscovite court society fourteen years later, and then only after Prince Matvei Shakhovskoi and his mock royal council solemnly promised to "pay off their great faults with service" to the real tsar, the God-ordained representative of the Romanov dynasty.[60]

His family was still working its way back into prominence by means of faithful service to the Romanov dynasty when Prince Iu. F. Shakhovskoi (c. 1671–1713) received the Judas medal from Tsar Mikhail's grandson. With this promotion to the imaginary order of Judas, Prince Shakhovskoi acquired more than yet another in a long series of mock titles by which he was jokingly referred to at the court of Tsar Peter Alekseevich. Indeed, if we now turn to Shakhovskoi's service career, we will see that despite the opinions of hostile contemporary witnesses, he was much more than a court jester. The prince spent his entire political career at the Muscovite court, where he was an important (and relatively well paid) member of the royal household.[61] He began his career as an ordinary courtier in the retinues of various members of the Muscovite royal family. In 1687 Prince Iurii and his younger brother were transferred from the entourage of Tsaritsa Praskov'ia Fedorovna (*née* Saltykova, the wife of Tsar Ivan Alekseevich) to that of the younger co-tsar. In 1696, after the successful second campaign to capture the fortress of Azov, he was appointed to the position of privy chamberlain by Tsar Peter Alekseevich himself.[62] Even before this promotion, however, Prince Iurii Fedorovich was already part of Peter's inner circle. Sometime in the early 1690s, immediately after the formation of the mock ecclesiastical council of the Transfigured Kingdom, Prince Iurii Fedorovich adopted the title Archdeacon Gideon, the pseudonym by which he was known among the tsar's personal entourage, many of whose members also assumed mock ecclesiastical titles in their intimate correspondence with the tsar. In this new "ecclesiastical" capacity, Prince Shakhovskoi was the courtier responsible for drawing up the lists of participants in the tsar's annual Yuletide

59. For a work that places this skit in the context of other cases of lèse-majesté in seventeenth-century Muscovy, see I. I. Polosin, " 'Igra v tsaria' (Otgoloski Smuty v moskovskom bytu XVII veka)," *Izvestiia Tverskogo pedagogicheskogo instituta* 1 (1926): 59–63.

60. Timofeev, "Zapisnye knigi Moskovskogo stola," 9:551.

61. Shakhovskoi received substantial annual sums from the state budget for his upkeep: 223 rubles in 1702 and 700 in 1704. See P. N. Miliukov, *Gosudarstvennoe khoziaistvo Rossii v pervoi chetverti XVIII stoletiia i reforma Petra Velikogo* (St. Petersburg, 1905), 100, cited in Hughes, *Russia*, 424–25, 554n73.

62. For the service career of Iu. F. Shakhovskoi see Airapetian, "Feodal'naia aristokratiia," 432, 336; and M. G. Spiridov, *Sokrashchennoe opisanie sluzheb blagorodnykh Rossiiskikh dvorian* . . . (Moscow, 1810), 1:252–53.

caroling processions,[63] in effect reenacting the role of the divinely inspired biblical judge whose trumpet called the righteous to their duty (Judg. 6:34–35).

Judging by the admittedly fragmentary evidence about his career from the period of the Northern War, Shakhovskoi also seems to have served as a personal liaison between Peter and two of his closest political advisers, A. D. Menshikov and I. A. Musin-Pushkin. Besides heading up one of the departments in Menshikov's Ingermanland Chancellery[64]—the office responsible for minting the silver commemorative medal of Judas—Prince Shakhovskoi also acted as a personal intermediary between the tsar and Musin-Pushkin, the courtier who headed the Moscow-based Monastery Chancellery (while simultaneously playing the part of "His Meekness Ianikii of Kiev and Galicia" in the mock ecclesiastical council of the Transfigured Kingdom).[65] In fact, Shakhovskoi seems to have spent the entire Northern War en route between the old capital and the new, and his constant travels, whether as part of the tsar's personal retinue or as Peter's personal emissary, may explain why so few of his letters have come to light.[66] Be that as it may, Shakhovskoi continued to serve in his capacity of privy chamberlain until 1710, when Peter bestowed upon him the highest (boyar) rank in the Muscovite royal council.[67] Despite its prestige value, it was clear that this appointment was more an honorary promotion than an actual advance in service rank. In fact, this was one of the last promotions to the Muscovite royal council, whose aging membership was undergoing a natural decline and whose political authority was being usurped by new, foreign-sounding institutions, such as the Novo-Preobrazhenskoe "consilium" presided over by Prince-Caesar Romodanovskii.

Prince B. I. Kurakin, the author of a scathing exposé of the "mediocrities" who composed the royal entourage of Tsar Peter at the end of the seventeenth century, characterized Prince Shakhovskoi as the ultimate political creature, a man who was totally dependent on the good graces of his royal patron and willing to do anything for him. According to Kurakin, Prince Shakhovskoi was "a highborn court fool" who allegedly earned his daily bread by spying on, denouncing, and humiliating the respectable members

63. B. I. Kurakin, "Gistoriia o tsare Petre Alekseeviche," in *Petr Velikii. Vospominaniia. Dnevnikovye zapisi. Anekdoty,* ed. L. Nikolaeva et al. (Moscow, 1993), 81.

64. An unpublished document dated August 16, 1710 (Menshikovskii arkhiv, *BAN, karton* 13-i, kn. 211), lists the *blizhnii boiarin* Prince Iu. F. Shakhovskoi as serving at the Ingermanland Chancellery. See Platonov, "Orden Iudy," 196.

65. See the letters from Prince Shakhovskoi to A. D. Menshikov and I. A. Musin-Pushkin in *Opisanie dokumentov i bumag, khraniashchikhsia v Arkhive Ministerstva Iustitsii* (Moscow, 1888), 8:169–73. On Musin-Pushkin's mock-ecclesiastical pseudonym, see Appendix 2.

66. For a reference to the going-away party thrown in honor of "Archdeacon Gideon's" departure for the front, where he was supposed to join the tsar, see "His Meekness Anikit" (N. M. Zotov) to Peter, n.d., RGADA, f. 9, otd. II, op. 3, chap. 1 (ca. 1710 g.), ed. khr. 11, ll. 189r–v. Despite the archival date, internal evidence suggests that this letter was written before F. A. Golovin's death in 1706.

67. Airapetian, "Feodal'naia aristokratiia," 319, 110.

of the Muscovite elite during court festivities. Unlike some other jesters in Peter's retinue, however, Prince Shakhovskoi was not weak-minded. In fact, according to Kurakin, Prince Shakhovskoi possessed "not a small intellect", and was "a reader of books." Coming from such a cosmopolitan polyglot as Prince Kurakin, this was indeed high, if backhanded, praise. Nevertheless, Kurakin immediately went on to qualify this already ambivalent characterization by describing Shakhovskoi as one of the "most drunken and malicious vessels" in the tsar's entourage, a man "who acted villainously toward everyone, from the lowest person to the highest." As the unofficial eyes and ears of the tsar, Shakhovskoi was the "channel" through which Peter was able to "know everything." In fact, Kurakin dubbed him "Prince Sticking Plaster" (*lepen'-prilipalo*), presumably because Shakhovskoi would spy on important government officials, bring up their misdeeds during dinner, and reproach them in front of the tsar in the way that a sticking plaster, suddenly peeled off, draws out all the filth in a boil unto the surface of the skin.[68] By this disgusting metaphor Kurakin alluded to Shakhovskoi's idiosyncratic role in implementing what we would now call the anticorruption thrust of Petrine legislation. For like the more formal guardians of probity at Peter's court, such as the procurator general and the fiscals, in his unofficial capacity as the tsar's spy Shakhovskoi made sure that courtiers were really loyal, doing their business, not embezzling, slacking off, or worse, plotting behind the tsar's back.[69]

In view of his family's history, as well as his work in the capacity of the tsar's private investigator, it appears likely that Prince Shakhovskoi was given the badge of the order of Judas back in 1709 to expiate his family's sins against the Romanovs. By serving to ferret out traitors, Judases against the Lord's anointed, Shakhovskoi not only made up for his family's checkered past but also made sure that other courtiers would never take the tsar's name in vain. This hypothesis is strengthened by the fact that in 1711, two years after Shakhovskoi received the Judas medal, Peter appointed him to the newly created post of general gevaldiger, or head of the military police.[70] In this capacity, Shakhovskoi was responsible for all the military policemen and executioners in every division of every regiment of the Russian army, as well as the instruments of their trade, such as the gallows, shack-

68. Kurakin, "Gistoriia," 80–81.

69. Later Petrine legislation eventually replaced sporadic raids by the tsar's trusted courtiers with the institution of government inspectors (*fiskaly*) and the office of the procurator general, who was officially referred to as the "sovereign's eye." On the Procuracy and the state fiscals, see A. A. Preobrazhenskii and T. E. Novitskaia, eds., *Zakonodatel'stvo Petra I* (Moscow, 1997), 133–35.

70. On June 2, 1711, the "highborn Prince, Privy Counselor and General Gevaldiger" received a copy of the seven articles according to which he was to exercise his new function. On June 30, 1711, Prince Shakhovskoi's new commission was confirmed by a royal decree sent to all the field commanders of the Russian army. A copy can be found among the papers of the personal chancellery of General A. A. Weide, who headed an army division under General Field Marshal B. P. Sheremetev. See "Chernovye zhurnaly, reliatsii i pism' a kasaiushchiesia kak do voennykh deistv, tak i do ministerskikh negotsiatsii, 1711-go g.—Zhurnal iskhodi-

les, and armed mounted escorts. His most important duties, however, consisted in judging, sentencing, and if necessary organizing the execution of traitors, deserters, and anyone who caused disorder in the ranks during the Pruth campaign against the Ottoman Empire. In particular, Shakhovskoi was charged with investigating breaches of discipline during the planned military marches through the Balkans and with "hanging, without any show of mercy," anyone who "willfully" deserted from the Russian ranks in the face of the enemy.[71] As the chief hangman of the Russian expeditionary army, the cavalier of the order of Judas—who, it must be remembered, wore a medal showing Judas hanging on a tree—was thus put in charge of the division responsible for executing deserters by hanging them on the gallows, in front of the troops, to teach potential deserters a lesson. Obviously, this was no longer merely playful parody. Shakhovskoi's responsible position was deadly serious. And this, in turn, suggests that the role played by jesters at Peter's court should be redefined. Indeed, the example of Prince Shakhovskoi, the second cavalier of the order of Judas, demonstrates that jesters provided more than just royal amusement. Or rather, these so-called amusements were, in fact, part of the very spectacle of power—a way of demonstrating and enacting the tsar's charismatic authority.[72]

Prince Shakhovskoi played out the last years of his political career as a living representative of the order of Judas, an institution that existed only symbolically, in the discourse employed at the court of Peter the Great, as a parodic counterpart to (and reflection of) the values informing the order of St. Andrew. As the courtier actually entrusted with the task of locating and executing traitors to the Russian cause, this mock cavalier enforced obedience to the ideals of faith and fidelity associated with the tsar's knightly order. Even on the day of his funeral, Shakhovskoi was charged with performing the leading role in a ceremony that affirmed the chivalrous fellowship of believers in the tsar's charisma. The second cavalier of the order of Judas was buried in St. Petersburg on December 30, 1713, with all the pomp and circumstance worthy of his rank in the mock ecclesiastical council of the Transfigured Kingdom. The coffin of Archdeacon Gideon was escorted by the "entire [mock] Holy Council [*osviashchennyi sobor*]," which reconvened in the new imperial Russian capital to honor the memory of one of its founding members. Prince-Pope Zotov, the mock pontiff of the Transfigured Kingdom, headed up this Yuletide funeral procession. He was fol-

ashchikh dokumentov [iz kantseliarii generala] A. A. Veide," SPb F IRI RAN, f. 83, op. 3, ed. khr. 3, ll. 3r–v, 5r–v.

71. Ibid., 5v. On the duties of the general gevaldiger, and the Petrine military police in general, in keeping order within the ranks, see Preobrazhenskii and Novitskaia, *Zakonodatel'stvo Petra I*, 185–86; and John L. H. Keep, *Soldiers of the Tsar: Army and Society in Russia, 1462–1874* (Oxford, 1988), 108.

72. The thrust of this argument is echoed in Lindsey Hughes's analysis of the career of another of Peter's court jesters. See her " 'For the Health of the Sons of Ivan Mikhailovich': I. M. Golovin and Peter the Great's Mock Court," in *Reflections on Russia in the Eighteenth Century*, ed. Joachim Klein, Simon Dixon, and Maarten Fraanje, 43–51 (Cologne, 2001).

lowed by the Anti-Caesar (Prince F. Iu. Romodanovskii) and other "spiritual dignitaries" (*dukhovnye osoby*).[73]

The advent of the Anti-Caesar and the Prince-Pope, who represented the ostensible patrons of the mock order of Judas, recalled the fact that the order of St. Andrew was intended as an Orthodox counterpart to the chivalrous brotherhoods sponsored by the Holy Roman Emperor and the pope. Thus the organizers of the grotesque funeral procession that escorted the coffin of Prince Shakhovskoi employed the corpse of the cavalier of the order of Judas in much the way the tsar had once used the relics of the Pertominsk saints, or as he would eventually use the bones of St. Aleksandr Nevskii[74]—to sanctify the places visited by Peter's peregrinating entourage and to restate the imperial pretensions and the polemical thrust behind the chivalrous religious organization of the Russian court.

73. See the entry for December 30, 1713, in *Pokhodnyi zhurnal 1713 goda* (St. Petersburg, 1854), 53.

74. On the cult of St. Aleksandr Nevskii, whose victory over the Swedes (1240) near the future site of St. Petersburg was taken to prefigure Peter's own victories in the Northern War, see Hughes, *Russia*, 276–78; Iu. M. Lotman and B. A. Uspenskii, "Echoes of the Notion 'Moscow the Third Rome' in Peter the Great's Ideology," in *The Semiotics of Russian Culture*, ed. Ann Shukman (Ann Arbor, 1984), 57; and O. G. Ageeva, *"Velichaishii i slavneishii bolee vsekh gradov v svete"—grad sviatogo Petra: Peterburg v russkom obshchestvennom soznanii nachala XVIII veka* (St. Petersburg, 1999), 284–86.

4 *Unholy Matrimony*

In a letter dictated on February 13, 1715, just one month after Peter and the members of his unconsecrated company had celebrated the carnivalesque wedding of the Prince-Pope of the Transfigured Kingdom—until that point, the most elaborate public parody of the sacrament of marriage ever staged in St. Petersburg—the tsar articulated his ideas about the civilizing role of the new-style weddings that he had instituted at his court. The letter was addressed to "First Senator and Minister" Prince Ia. F. Dolgorukov (1639 [or 1650]–1720), the powerful grandee and government official whose own wedding in 1712 had served as the symbolic foil for that of another of Peter's intimates, P. I. Buturlin, the mock Metropolitan of St. Petersburg.[1] Contrary to the tsar's wishes, Prince Dolgorukov had sought to prevent the logical extension of Peter's matrimonial policies by blocking the tsar's attempt to marry off Dolgorukov's niece to a foreigner. Reiterating the comments he had already made to the prince in private, the tsar explained that the reason a marriage between a Russian noblewoman and a non-Orthodox Christian was essential to his reformist vision was that "we have a great need to have all kinds of intercourse [*vsiakimi obrazy so-obshchatsa;* literally, to have all manner of communication] with other Eu-

---

1. For a biography of Prince Ia. F. Dolgorukov, one of the oldest and most powerful supporters of the former Naryshkin candidate, see I. Iu. Airapetian, "Feodal'naia aristokratiia v period stanovleniia absoliutizma v Rossii" (Diss., kand. ist. nauk, M. V. Lomonosov State University, 1987), 77, 96, 330, 317; D. O. Serov, *Stroiteli imperii: Ocherki gosudarstvennoi i kriminal'noi deiatel'nosti spodvizhnikov Petra I* (Novosibirsk, 1996), 231 (disputed date of birth); Lindsey Hughes, *Russia in the Age of Peter the Great* (New Haven, 1998), 268, 367, 410, 442, 459, 489, 490; and Paul Bushkovitch, *Peter the Great: The Struggle for Power, 1671–1725* (Cambridge, 2001), 155n55, 470. He first appears with the title "first senator and minister" during Peter's wedding to Catherine. See *Pokhodnyi zhurnal 1712 goda* (St. Petersburg, 1854), 3, 14.

ropean peoples [*s drugimi Evropskimi narodami*], not only in great but also in minor affairs, so that by this [means], the crudeness of old customs [*grubost' starykh obychaev*] gradually disappears."[2] According to Peter's reasoning—which was later codified in various royal decrees on the issue—although such a union could still technically be considered an unequal marriage, the inequality would work in favor of the Russian crown, and therefore serve the general good.[3]

If there is an element of truth in every joke, then the tsar's crude double entendre about all kinds of "intercourse" with "European peoples" may be said to have captured not only the essence of the changes introduced in his own royal house but also the didacticism of the matrimonial spectacles staged at Peter's court. For intermarriages and unequal weddings—such as that between the lowborn and aging Prince-Pope and his noble young bride (1715), or even that between Peter and his own mistress, a foreign-born commoner named Marta Skavronska (1711)—were an important part of the tsar's efforts to reform the marriage-based clan system while simultaneously polishing the manners and policing the morals of the Muscovite elite. In fact, as we will see, the wedding of the Prince-Pope marked the apogee of the court-sponsored program that was first revealed with utmost clarity in the jester weddings staged on the fields outside Novo-Preobrazhenskoe at the end of the seventeenth century. Together with other measures designed to create a cosmopolitan service elite—such as the 1718 decree on "assemblies," which pointedly listed the Prince-Pope as the first host of the new-style soirees—the 1715 masquerade wedding served to demonstrate, in the most public way possible, the close relationship between travesty and "good order" at the court of Peter the Great.[4]

2. Peter to Prince Ia. F. Dolgorukov, February 13, 1715, in SPb F IRI RAN, koll. 277, op. 2, ed. khr. 6, ll. 3r–v.

3. For the text of the most important decree regarding intermarriages, see "Poslanie Sviateishego Sinoda k pravoslavnym o besprepiatstvennom im vstuplenii v brak s inovertsami (Avgusta 18 dnia 1721 goda)," in *Zakonodatel'stvo Petra I*, ed. A. A. Preobrazhenskii and T. E. Novitskaia, 719–25 (Moscow, 1997). See also the elaborate justification of the utility and orthodoxy of mixed marriages by Feofan (Prokopovich), *Razsuzhdenie sv. Sinoda o brakakh pravovernykh s inovernymi* (St. Petersburg, 1721). For an insightful discussion of these and other documents that enacted Peter's reforms of the marriage law, see James Cracraft, *The Church Reform of Peter the Great* (London, 1971), 216–17.

4. The words in quotation marks come from the preamble to the Military Statute of 1716, which included the following formulation about the didactic role of parody: "But when (with the Almighty's help) the army was brought to order, then what great progress was made with the Almighty's help against glorious and regular nations. Anyone can see that this occurred for no other reason than the establishment of good order. For all disorderly barbarian practices are worthy of ridicule [*dostoiny smekha*] and no good can come of them." Quoted in Hughes, *Russia*, 122–23. For the text of the decree of November 26, 1718, instituting the St. Petersburg assemblies, see *Polnoe sobranie zakonov Rossiiskoi imperii*, 55 vols. (St. Petersburg, 1830–84), 5:597–98 (no. 3246). The list of the courtiers scheduled to act as hosts of the first assemblies appears as sec. 8 of the rough draft (*korrekturnyi ekzempliar*) of the decree. See O. G. Ageeva, "Obshchestvennaia i kul'turnaia zhizn' Peterburga I chetverti XVIII v." (Diss., kand. ist. nauk, Institut istorii Akademii nauk SSSR, 1990), 288. The first assembly under the new regulations was held November 27, 1718, at the home of P. I. Buturlin, the reigning Prince-Pope of the Transfigured Kingdom. See Hughes, *Russia*, 268.

Muscovite Travesties

In the old capital Peter had already set a precedent for using the marriage ceremony as a way of travestying Muscovite politics in the name of the ideals of his Transfigured Kingdom. The first matrimonial spectacles organized by the members of Peter's company sought to sharpen the contrast between the idea that the Muscovite court was a microcosm of outmoded clan politics and the ostensibly novel conception that described the relationship between tsar and courtier as predicated on personal service. The exaggeration of this contrast was a matter of political rhetoric, self-consciously enacted in carnivalesque ceremonies in which the subjects of the Transfigured Kingdom were the leading actors. Assigning the role of jester-groom to some particular member of his entourage, the tsar and his courtiers would periodically take part in theatricalized pageants modeled on traditional Russian wedding banquets. Like the wisecracking, picaresque harlequins (*gaery*) of the comical "interludes" in contemporary school dramas,[5] royally appointed jester-grooms would become both the instigators and the butts of the court's laughter—a position that was captured most clearly by the anonymous author of the explanatory key to the list of wedding guests of the "most ferociously witty" (*ostroumnoliutneishii*) F. P. Shanskii, a member of Peter's company who appeared as both a "buffoon and a laughingstock" (*shut i smekhotvorets*) in the engraving officially commissioned to commemorate his marriage to a Russian princess (see Figure 7).[6]

5. For the texts of three interludes of the Petrine period, see "Skazanie o gaere garlikine Rossiiskom. Starinnye deistva i komedii Petrovskogo vremeni, izvlechennyia iz rukopisei i prigotovlennyia k pechati I. A. Shliapkinym," *Sbornik Otdeleniia russkogo iazyka i slovesnosti Rossiiskoi Akademii Nauk* 97, no. 1 (1921): 200–212; "Intermediia," in *Russkiia dramaticheskiia proizvedeniia, 1672–1725 gg.,* ed. N. S. Tikhonravov, 2:485–98 (St. Petersburg, 1874); and "Shutovskaia komediia," in *Pamiatniki russkoi dramy epokhi Petra Velikogo,* ed. V. N. Peretts, 493–558 (St. Petersburg, 1903).

6. For the text of the key to the series of engravings produced by Adrian Schoonebeck, see M. A. Alekseeva, *Graviura petrovskogo vremeni* (Leningrad, 1990), 31–32. In the *Trilingual Lexicon* of F. P. Polikarpov, the Muscovite printer whose publishing activities were instrumental in defining and spreading the new ideals enacted by Peter's royal entourage, "jester" (*shut* or *koshchun*) was synonymous with "mocking joker" (Lat. *ioculator,* Rus. *glumitel'* or *glumnik*), someone who could actually learn to be virtuous just by mocking something (*glumliusia znachit i pouchaiusia vo blagoe*). As an example of this paradoxical notion, Polikarpov offered the following quote from the Psalms: "As [King] David says, 'I exult [lit. play, exercise] in your miracles' [*Az zhe poglumliusia v chudesekh tvoikh*] instead of saying 'I learn from [them]' [*vmesto reshchi pouchusia*]." See *Leksikon treiazychnyi . . .* (Moscow, 1704), 73v. Whether Polikarpov's definition of the didactic role of mockery had anything to do with his observations of the travesties staged at the court of Peter Alekseevich, or, more likely, whether such didactic ideas were part of his rhetorical training as a pupil of Moscow's Slavonic-Greco-Latin Academy, we would do well to remember this reference to King David, the "humble Psalmist," when we analyze the typological symbolism invoked at the 1715 wedding of the Prince-Pope.

Figure 7. The Wedding of the Most Ferociously Witty Royal Jester Feofilakt Shanskii (1702). Engraving by Adrian Schoonebeck. (Rare Books Division, Library of the Russian Academy of Sciences, St. Petersburg [RK BRAN, inv. 1]. Photograph by Alexi Melentiev.)

Poking fun at the conventional morality of an older generation of Muscovite courtiers, Peter Alekseevich, his jester-grooms, and their guests enacted the ideals of a new masculine fellowship—one manifestly based on a sense of belonging to the chivalrous community of believers in the charismatic authority of the divinely ordained warrior tsar. For example, in January 1694 Peter organized the wedding of Ia. F. Turgenev, a low-ranking noble courtier and clerk in the chancellery responsible for administering the royal play regiments, as a way of mocking elite Muscovite conventions of honor.[7] Staged as the denouement of the "Kozhukhov campaign," the war

7. Information on the service career of Ia. F. Turgenev comes from Airapetian, "Feodal'naia aristokratiia," 67, 328, 421; and L. N. Semenova, *Ocherki istorii byta i kul'turnoi zhizni Rossii, pervaia polovina XVIII v.* (Leningrad, 1982), 180–81. The conventional belief that Turgenev died immediately after (and as a result of) his wedding is based on a nineteenth-century editor's misreading of a contemporary Russian diary. See Paul Bushkovitch, "Aristocratic

games organized by General Patrick Gordon soon after the tsar's return from his accidental pilgrimage to the Transfiguration Church of the Pertominsk Monastery, the winter wedding had all the qualities of a Yuletide mummers' skit.[8] Like the carolers and entertainers making their rounds of Christmas visits, the Muscovite courtiers who followed in Turgenev's wedding train wore "comical dress: bast sacks, bark hats, multicolored kaftans lined with cat fur . . . in shoes made out of straw, with mouse-lined mitts." They rode bulls, goats, pigs, and dogs—barnyard animals that were often anthropomorphized in the lewd ditties traditionally sung by Yuletide mummers.[9] I. A. Zheliabuzhskii, the old Muscovite courtier who left a record of this carnivalesque matrimonial spectacle in his daily log, dismissed Turgenev as a jester, intimating that the ceremony had only an incidental comic effect. At the same time, however, Zheliabuzhskii understood that the Turgenev wedding procession effectively turned existing distinctions in rank on their head: Turgenev and his undistinguished bride—"a chancellery clerk's wife"—rode "in the sovereign's own best velvet-lined carriage," while the members of the most venerable clans of Trubetskoi, Sheremetev, Golitsyn, and Gagin rode behind him, just ahead of the wedding procession.[10] The topsy-turvy world of this carnivalesque wedding procession thus hinted at the reformist thrust of Peter's developing political agenda by means of an ironic commentary on the private and public lives of the "famed old warrior and Kievan commander," Turgenev's facetious title during the "Kozhukhov campaign."[11]

In a similar way, the parodic origins of Turgenev's portrait—which, together with the previously mentioned portrait of Patriarch Deary (M. F. Naryshkin) was one of the first in a series of pictures to adorn the walls of the tsar's palace in Novo-Preobrazhenskoe—accounted for its innovative realism. The tsar commemorated Turgenev's role in the spectacles of the

---

Faction and the Opposition to Peter the Great: The 1690s," *Forschungen zur Osteuropäischen Geschichte* 50 (1995): 97n45. In fact, as late as 1700, the "jester" Iakov Turgenev was listed in the personnel records of Peter's court (*v dvortsovom shtate*) as receiving a salary of 50 rubles. See I. E. Zabelin, *Domashnii byt russkikh tsarei v XVI i XVII st.*, 2 vols. (Moscow, 1915), 1 (1): 267.

8. M. I. Semevskii, ed., "Kozhukhovskii pokhod, 1694. (Sovremennoe opisanie)," *Voennyi sbornik* 11, no. 1 (1860): 49–106. For an insightful discussion of this mock military campaign, see Richard H. Warner, "The Kozuchovo Campaign of 1694; or, The Conquest of Moscow by Preobrazhenskoe," *Jahrbücher für Geschichte Osteuropas* 13 (1965): 487–96.

9. On traditional Yuletide processions, see N. V. Ponyrko, "Russkie sviatki XVII v.," *Trudy otdela drevnerusskoi literatury* 32 (1977): 84–99; idem, "Sviatochnyi i maslenichnyi smekh," in D. S. Likhachev et al., *Smekh v drevnei Rusi*, 154–202 (Leningrad, 1984); and, in general, Larisa Ivleva, *Riazhen'e v russkoi traditsionnoi kul'ture* (St. Petersburg, 1994).

10. I. A. Zheliabuzhskii, "Zapiski Ivana Afanas'evicha Zheliabuzhskogo," in *Rossiiu podnial na dyby*, ed. N. I. Pavlenko (Moscow, 1987), 1:413–14. On his service career, see Airapetian, "Feodal'naia aristokratiia," 321; and B. Ussas, "Zheliazbuzhskii, Ivan Afanas'evich," in *RBS* 7:25–26 (New York, 1962).

11. For a contemporary reference to Turgenev's mock title, as well as a description of his "old-fashioned noble seal," representing a nanny goat (*starobytnyi ego shliakhovetskii gerb: koza*), see Semevskii, "Kozhukhovskii pokhod," 62.

Transfigured Kingdom by commissioning a portrait that repudiated the extravagant stylistic features of the *parsuna,* a form of portraiture that was fashionable at the Muscovite court since at least the middle of the seventeenth century, in favor of what may be described as a civic icon.[12] The anonymous artist who painted Turgenev's portrait dispensed with the elaborate inscriptions, coats of arms, and architectural props that accompanied stylized depictions of late seventeenth-century Muscovite courtiers and showed Turgenev warts and all, armed with a colonel's mace and dressed simply in the uniform of the regiment that he led during the mock Kozhukhov campaign (see Figure 8). Thus the portrait celebrated not a lowly noble jester with pretensions to *parsuna* greatness but a royal servitor defined exclusively by the instruments of his function in the Transfigured Kingdom and his role in the ceremonies dramatizing the inversion of the old order while solidifying the cultural and political foundations of the new.

In January 1702 the nuptials of another member of Peter's company, Feofilakt (or Filat) Pimenovich Shanskii, a member of the ecclesiastical entourage of "Patriarch Andrei of Palestine," became the first royal-sponsored wedding celebration self-consciously to pit the traditional Muscovite standard of precedence ranking against the ideal of the court as a quasi-religious order of knights devoted to the charismatic person of the tsar. The unequal marriage between this relatively ordinary courtier and a Russian princess played out the transformation of roles at court by challenging elite notions of rank and family honor.[13] As in the Turgenev wedding, every aspect of this three-day celebration was choreographed by Peter and his company. Cornelius de Bruyn, a Dutch explorer and artist who, along with several other foreigners, received an invitation to take part in the celebration of the nuptials of the tsar's favorite "jester," noted that during the first two days of this royal spectacle "all of the invited guests were commanded to appear at the wedding in the ancient attire" of Muscovy. The tsar himself donned a long Muscovite robe,

12. For a description and history of the portrait and its place in the so-called Preobrazhenskoe series, see N. M. Moleva, "Persony vseshuteishego sobora," *Voprosy istorii* 10 (1974): 206–11; E. I. Gavrilova, "O metodakh atributsii dvukh grupp proizvedenii petrovskoi epokhi (zhivopis', risunok)," in *Nauchno-issledovatel'skaia rabota v khudozhestvennykh muzeiakh* (Moscow, 1975), 2:54–55; and, more generally, James Cracraft, *The Petrine Revolution in Russian Imagery* (Chicago, 1997), 190–220, esp. 192–93. On its parodic, anti-*parsuna* origins, see V. G. Chubinskaia, "Novoe ob evoliutsii russkogo portreta na rubezhe XVII–XVIII vv.," *Pamiatniki kul'tury. Novye otkrytiia, 1982* (Leningrad, 1984), 323–25.

13. For Shanskii's career as equerry (*striapchii*) and royal chamberlain (*stol'nik*), see Airapét'ian, "Feodal'naia aristokratiia," 431; and P. [P.] Ivanov, *Alfavitnyi ukazatel' familii i lits, upominaemykh v boiarskikh knigakh* (Moscow, 1853), 464. According to Moleva, "Persony vseshuteishego sobora," 208, he was also one of the Russian "volunteers" sent abroad for further education in 1697–98. Shanskii's bride was actually the sister of Prince Iu. F. Shakhovskoi, the cavalier of the order of Judas described in Chapter 3. See *Pokhodnyi zhurnal 1713 goda* (St. Petersburg, 1854), 53n(c).

АКОВЪ : ТУРЗГЕНЕВЪ ;

Figure 8. Iakov Turgenev. Anonymous portrait, late seventeenth century. (State Russian Museum, St. Petersburg [zh 5657].)

"intermixed with many figures and of several colors," as well as a "great red fur cap," for the first half of the wedding celebration.[14] Indeed, for the duration of the Shanskii-Shakhovskoi wedding the tsar seemed to have lifted the formal injunction against wearing the old Muscovite garments by the noble elite, which he had officially introduced just two

14. Cornelius de Bruyn, *Travels into Muscovy, Persia, and Part of the East Indies; Containing an Accurate Description of What Is Most Remarkable in Those Countries* (London, 1737), 1:26, cited in Hughes, *Russia,* 362; in Russian, *Puteshestvie cherez Moskoviiu Korniliia de Bruina,* trans. P. P. Barsov, ed. O. M. Bodianskii (Moscow, 1873), 47–48. For another contemporary description of this matrimonial spectacle, see John Perry, *The State of Russia under the Present Tsar* (London, 1716), 237–41.

years earlier.[15] As if to underline the traditional nature of this event, the newlyweds were seated in different rooms and chaperoned by members of their own sex. As befits the temporary elevation of status assumed by the bride and groom at a Muscovite wedding—when they are tradition-ally referred to as "Prince" and "Princess," or alternatively as *Boiar* and *Boiarynia*[16]—both Shanskii and his betrothed sat in the company of mock royalty: the two "monarchs" (Prince F. Iu. Romodanovskii and I. I. Buturlin) and the "patriarch" of the Transfigured Kingdom (N. M. Zotov) presided over the male half of the celebrations (see Figure 9), while the royal wives occupied a parallel position over the female half.[17] So while this travesty of royal and ecclesiastical authority may have been intended as a deliberate subversion of tradition, it also accentuated the sanctity of those members of Peter's company who, like the groom him-self, belonged to the mock ecclesiastical council of the Transfigured Kingdom.

On the third and final day of the festivities surrounding the Shanskii-Shakhovskoi wedding, it became apparent that the organizers of the event considered Muscovite habits—both clothes and customs—to be the ragtag equivalent of those Yuletide mummers who had followed in Turgenev's wedding train; for on that day the guests were required to appear dressed in the latest foreign fashions. The mandate to change their old clothes for the new "German dress" officially prescribed by the tsar went hand in hand with a new code of courtly etiquette. For the first time ever the public segre-gation of male and female guests was abandoned. Now, as Bruyn recorded, the wedding party, both the men and the women, "sat at table together, as the custom is with us; and there was dancing and skipping about, after the

15. *Polnoe sobranie zakonov Rossiiskoi imperii*, vol. 4, nos. 1741 (January 4, 1700) and 1887 (August 20, 1700); and "Peter's Decree on Wearing German Clothes, 1701," in *Major Problems in the History of Imperial Russia*, ed. James Cracraft, 110–11 (Lexington, MA, 1994).

16. R. O. Jacobson, "While Reading Fasmer's Dictionary," in *Selected Writings* (The Hague, 1971), 2. On the nomenclature and semiotics of the wedding ranks temporarily as-sumed by the newlyweds, their families, and their guests in Russian popular culture, see P. S. Bogoslovskii, "K nomenklature i topografii svadebnykh chinov (Po dannym etnograficheskoi literatury i rukopisnym materialam Geograficheskogo Obshchestva)," in *Permskii kraevedch-eskii sbornik*, 1–64 (Perm, 1927); and A. K. Baiburin and G. A. Levinton, " 'Kniaz' i 'kni-aginia' v russkom svadebnom velichanii (k semantike obriadovykh terminov)," *Russkaia filologiia* 4 (1975): 58–76, esp. 58, 62–63.

17. For a depiction of the separate men's and women's sides on the first two days of the Shanskii wedding, see the (unfinished) triptych by Adrian Schoonebeck in Alekseeva, *Grav-iura*, 31–32. According to the key attached to the first engraving, the three mock dignitaries occupied the first table, on a dais near the entrance to the main banquet hall (*bol'shaia stolo-vaia palata*) of the Lefort palace. Prince F. Iu. Romodanovskii and I. I. Buturlin were "dressed like monarchs" (*v oblachenii, podobno monarsheskogo*), while N. M. Zotov ap-peared in "the guise of a patriarch" (*v vide patriarkha*). Ibid., 31; R. Podol'skii, "Petrovskii dvorets na Iauze," *Arkhitekturnoe nasledstvo* 1 (1951): 27. According to the key attached to the second engraving of the Shanskii wedding, the wife of I. I. Buturlin presided over the women's side "in the dress of a tsaritsa (*vo oblachenii podobnaia tsrtsna*)." See Alekseeva, *Graviura*, 32.

Figure 9. Detail of *The Wedding of the Most Ferociously Witty Royal Jester Feofilakt Shanskii* (Figure 7), depicting the center table, with two mock tsars and the mock patriarch of the Unholy Council. (Photograph by Alexi Melentiev.)

entertainment, to the great satisfaction of the Czar himself, as all his guests."[18] The appearance of Russian women during the wedding of Peter's "most ferociously witty jester" thus broke with the seventeenth-century tradition of keeping elite Muscovite women confined to their quarters and anticipated by almost fifteen years the royal decree on assemblies, which codified such behavior as a court norm.[19] However, the fact that it took nearly a decade and a half for these new courtly conceptions to become official royal policy demonstrates that the carnivalesque wedding of Peter's comical bridegroom, like carnival itself, could only suspend the conventions of everyday life; it could not abolish them. Apparently, only when Peter and his advisers felt strong enough to enforce such changes could these temporary liberties be transformed into permanent laws. As we will see, this transformation took place very gradually over the tumultuous fifteen years that witnessed the transplantation of Peter's Transfigured Kingdom from the

18. Bruyn, *Travels,* 53.
19. Nancy Shields Kollmann, "The Seclusion of Elite Muscovite Women," *Russian History* 10, no. 2 (1983): 170–87; and Ageeva, "Obshchestvennaia i kul'turnaia zhizn'," 135–45, esp. 138–39.

grounds of the suburban royal estates of Moscow to the banks of the Neva River.

The Petrine Round Table

Like other suburban royal amusements, therefore, the jester weddings of 1694 and 1702 turned the clannish politics of the old capital upside down in order to juxtapose the social relations in Moscow with those supposedly institutionalized in the chivalrous-religious organization of Peter's peregrinating court. The nomadic lifestyle of the recently divorced tsar (1699), who led a series of military campaigns against the Ottomans and the Swedes, traveled to Europe, and repeatedly crisscrossed his extensive realm, only bolstered the importance of matrimonial spectacles as unifying events for his company. Indeed, the founding of St. Petersburg in 1703 opened up a new realm of possibilities for the realization of the ideals elaborated at Novo-Preobrazhenskoe. Unencumbered by the institutional and political constraints placed on the royal person by life in Moscow, the intimate circle of believers in the tsar's charisma gave free play to their imaginations. And marriage ceremonies—especially those associated with Peter's own second wedding—would be one of the most important ways of bringing these dreams to fruition.

Seeking to loosen the hold of a dynastic marriage system that relied on endogamy to bind the elite to the crown, the tsar and his intimates sought to transform Muscovite royal weddings into tools of geopolitics, not simply of domestic factionalism.[20] Taking advantage of the opportunities presented after the victory at Poltava, Peter began to challenge the conventions of the Muscovite system of dynastic marriage and to elevate the royal house above the fray of traditional matrimonial politics by marrying off members of his family to foreign royalty. This step was not totally unprecedented, for both Kievan princes and Muscovite grand dukes had married outside of native elites in order to secure foreign allies. After one disastrous attempt at the beginning of the seventeenth century, however, the Romanovs gave up trying to make equal marriages. Instead, the new Russian ruling house and the rest of the Muscovite oligarchy elaborated a complicated process in which royal brides were chosen mainly from military clans of middling rank. This practice ensured the integration of new families into the elite without upsetting the existing balance of power between the tsar and the most influential political clans at court. Peter's intention to marry members of his family to foreign royalty therefore flew in the face of the "traditional" structures of political authority, which were maintained by controlling the marital choices

---

20. The following analysis of Muscovite matrimonial politics owes much to the work of Edward L. Keenan, "Muscovite Political Folkways," *Russian Review* 45 (1986): 115–81; and Russell Edward Martin, "Dynastic Marriage in Muscovy, 1500–1729" (Ph.D. diss., Harvard University, 1996).

of the new (and still relatively insecure) Russian royal house. By reinstituting the practice of equal marriage between heads of state, the tsar was able to establish tactical diplomatic alliances for his ambitions in the Baltic and at the same time demonstrate the power of the Romanov dynasty over the boyar clans that had once brought it to the throne.

Peter's elevation of a young Livonian peasant woman to the status of royal consort reflected the same political and dynastic concerns as those that urged him to favor intermarriage with European royalty for his blood relations. After confining his first wife, Tsaritsa Evdokiia Fedorovna Lopukhina, in a convent at the end of the seventeenth century, Peter spent nearly a decade as a bachelor—a very unusual status for an adult tsar.[21] He had chosen bachelorhood in order to maintain his independence from the parties that had arranged his marriage to Lopukhina. Once freed from his in-laws and their political allies, Peter attempted to mold the only surviving male child from this marriage, Tsarevich Aleksei Petrovich, into a suitable heir to his vision of a reformed Russian empire. As the relationship between the tsar and his only son grew strained, however, Peter began to construct an alternative dynastic scenario, in which he could legitimate any possible future male heirs without abandoning his hard-won political independence. Marriage to Marta Skavronska (1683–1727), his longtime mistress and the mother of his numerous illegitimate children,[22] presented an opportunity to bypass the presumptive heir and ensure that Peter's successors—those who were not tainted by their association with the Lopukhin line of the house of Romanov—would continue his policies. A foreign bride who brought no domestic or diplomatic entanglements and was wholly dependent on the favor of her royal husband thus appeared to be the best candidate for the achievement of this goal.

In anticipation of her new status, Marta Skavronska was received into the Orthodox faith. During this ceremony her future stepson, Tsarevich Aleksei Petrovich, was forced to act as her godfather. Although it was typical for a member of the royal family to preside over such sacraments as the baptism of a child of the royal house, this was hardly a typical Romanov event and Marta was hardly a child. Even more shocking was the fact that the tsar compelled his son to participate in the attempt to displace Aleksei's own mother and implicitly to challenge the tsarevich's claim to the throne. Marta's new given name demonstrated her full if problematic incorporation

21. On Tsaritsa Evdokiia see S. V. Efimov, "Evdokiia Lopukhina—posledniaia russkaia tsaritsa XVII veka," in *Srednevekovaia Rus': Sbornik nauchnykh statei k 65–letiiu . . . R. G. Skrynnikova,* ed. S. V. Lobachev and A. S. Lavrov, 136–65 (St. Petersburg, 1995).

22. By the time Peter married his mistress, they had already had five children together. See the dispatches of Charles Whitworth, the British ambassador to St. Petersburg, in *Sbornik Imperatorskogo russkogo istoricheskogo obshchestva* 61 (1888), 146. For a biography of Marta/Catherine, see Hughes, *Russia,* 394–98; M. I. Semevskii, *Tsaritsa Katerina Alekseevna, Anna i Villim Mons', 1692–1724,* 2nd rev. ed. (St. Petersburg, 1884); and John Alexander, "Catherine I, Her Court and Courtiers," in *Peter the Great and the West: New Perspectives,* ed. Lindsey Hughes, 227–49 (Houndmills, 2001).

into the Romanov dynastic line. Following traditional Orthodox practice, the newly baptized Catherine Alekseevna took the name of the saint commemorated on the same day as her conversion and the Christian name of the godfather as her patronymic. By name she became the spiritual child of her stepson, as well as his stepmother.[23] And since her husband had the same patronymic, Catherine in effect also became one of the children of Tsar Aleksei Mikhailovich. Around the same time, in her intimate correspondence Catherine also adopted Peter's pseudonymous last name, Mikhailov, which the tsar used to distinguish his service in the ranks from his dynastic role as the grandson of Tsar Mikhail Fedorovich, the first Romanov to wear the crown of Russia.[24] By this pseudonym the tsar's lowborn foreign bride metaphorically underscored her connection to the founder of the house of Romanov while underlining her own role as the wife of the chivalrous warrior-tsar who was intent on restoring the territories lost to the Swedes during his grandfather's reign.

The public celebration of Peter's second wedding—like his bride's second baptism, a political sacrament that was intimately connected to the tsar's dynastic policies—constituted a pivotal moment in the integration of a new service elite into the court's reformist project.[25] The tsar's insistence that the public ceremony be termed an "old wedding,"[26] a reference to the fact that the nuptials had already been solemnized in secret, before Peter had left for the front in March 1711, reflected ironically on the nontraditional, secular character of the celebrations, particularly their location in the new port city of St. Petersburg. The city most closely associated with Peter's navy and his involvement in European diplomacy served as the stage on which the tsar dramatized the link between his new dynastic policy and his old company. The tsar appeared at his wedding, which took place on February 10, 1712, in the guise of a rear admiral (*kontr-admiral*). Peter self-consciously masked his royal persona by assuming a rank that he awarded himself, through the offices of the royal mock double, "Prince-Caesar" F. Iu. Romodanovskii, for the Russian victory in the battle of Poltava.[27] This masquerade advanced the chivalric ethos according to which feats of skill and valor in battle

23. Hughes, *Russia*, 397, 450–51, 560n40; and B. A. Uspenskii, "Historia sub specie semioticae," in *Soviet Semiotics: An Anthology*, ed. and trans. Daniel P. Lucid (Baltimore, 1977), 108–9.

24. S. M. Solov'ev, *Istoriia Rossii s drevneishikh vremen*, 15 vols. (Moscow, 1993), 8:356–57. For references to this pseudonymous last name, see "Patent dannoi Ego Imperatorskomu Velichestvu v obuchenii bombardirskago dela, i pri tom s onago perevod, 1698 g.," RGADA, f. 9, otd. i, op. 2, chap. i, ed. khr. 37, ll. 1–3; "Rospiska v poluchenii zhalovan'ia (January 29, 1701), in *PiB*, 1:424; cf. 1:453, 765, 847, 859; 3:31–32; Hughes, *Russia*, 98, 488n45; and N. I. Pavlenko, "Petr I (K izucheniiu sotsial'no-politicheskikh vzgliadov)," in *Rossiia v period reform Petra I* (Moscow, 1973), 44–46, 56–60.

25. My analysis of the symbolism and politics surrounding Peter's second wedding is indebted to Hughes, *Russia*, 261–62; and Martin, "Dynastic Marriage," 254–59.

26. Peter to Gavrilo Menshikov, February 20, 1712, in *PiB*, 12 (1): 86; Whitworth, *Sbornik*, 144.

27. For the correspondence related to Peter's 1709 "promotions," see *PiB*, 9 (1): 242–43, 342; and the discussion in Pavlenko, "Petr I," 44–45.

would be rewarded by royal recognition and matched by the social affirmation of one's masculinity. Acting out a new standard of gentlemanly conquest, both sexual and military, the tsar could be said to have challenged, confronted, and defeated those who scorned his intention to marry outside the Muscovite clan network.

The organization of Peter's second wedding reflected a new style of public ceremony, which had originated in the jester weddings that the tsar had staged at the end of the seventeenth century and which had first been demonstrated in St. Petersburg, in 1710, during the nuptials of his niece, Anna Ioannovna, to the Duke of Courland.[28] As in the earlier ceremonies, during his own wedding the tsar dispensed with the traditional functionaries, ceremonies, and fertility rituals associated with Muscovite matrimonial celebrations. Instead, Peter personally composed the list of participants, assigning the most important ceremonial posts, often with new, foreign-sounding titles such as *Marshal, Schaffer,* and *Vorschinder,* to his trusted advisers and companions, most of whom served in the tsar's cherished navy.[29] As in Muscovite royal weddings, the bride and groom were chaperoned by their proxy mothers and fathers. However, whereas these honorific posts were traditionally occupied by blood relatives of the Russian royal house, at Peter's wedding three of the four proxy parents were foreigners— Count de Buss, rear admiral in command of Peter's galley fleet; Cornelius Cruys, vice admiral in command of the Baltic fleet; and Cruys's wife. The fourth, Tsaritsa Praskov'ia Fedorovna (*née* Saltykova), widow of Tsar Ivan Alekseevich, was a Romanov only by marriage. The proxy brothers were F. M. Skliaev, one of Peter's childhood companions and an energetic shipbuilder, and I. M. "the Shipwright" (*Bas*) Golovin, a courtier who was the nominal head of Peter's shipbuilding industry.[30] Thus the leading actors in this carnivalesque matrimonial spectacle complemented Peter's fictional identity as a rear admiral and sustained the drama of transformation that was being enacted at court and in the new imperial city.

The arrangement of guests in the banquet hall of Prince Menshikov's newly constructed Petersburg palace likewise contributed to the sense of a new community, both spiritual fellowship and knightly order, affirmed

28. For a description of Tsarevna Anna Ioannovna's marriage to the Duke of Courland, as well as an insightful analysis of this new-style wedding ceremony, see Martin, "Dynastic Marriage," 268–72; Ageeva, "Obshchestvennaia i kul'turnaia zhizn'," 141–42; and idem, "Novye iavleniia v obshchestvennoi zhizni i bytu Peterburga pervoi chetverti XVIII veka: Na primere tsarskikh svadeb," in *Russkai kul'tura v perekhodnoi period ot srednevekov'ia k novomu vremeni. Sbornik statei* (Moscow, 1992), 98, 102n9.

29. For Peter's handwritten list, see *PiB,* 12 (1): 83; for the official list of wedding guests, see *Pokhodnyi zhurnal 1712 goda* (St. Petersburg, 1854), 1–7.

30. For an extended discussion of I. M. Golovin's place in Peter's company, see Hughes, *Russia,* 364–65; and her " 'For the Health of the Sons of Ivan Mikhailovich': I. M. Golovin and Peter the Great's Mock Court," in *Reflections on Russia in the Eighteenth Century,* ed. Joachim Klein, Simon Dixon, and Maarten Fraanje, 43–51 (Cologne, 2001).

through the celebration of the tsar's second wedding.[31] According to the engraving created by A. F. Zubov, the artist commissioned to immortalize the wedding of Peter and Catherine (see Figure 10),[32] the most important guests at the banquet sat at a large ring-shaped table with an open space in the center and a passage through which guests seated on the inside edge of the table could reach their seats. A smaller square table was placed in the middle of the open space at the center of the round one. Seated at this center table, in full view of the other wedding guests, were three bewigged "spiritual personages" (*dukhovnye persony*): Prince-Pope N. M. Zotov, Arch-Hierarch P. I. Buturlin, and Archdeacon Prince Iu. F. Shakhovskoi (Figure 11).[33] The prominent presence of the Prince-Pope and the leading members of his Unholy Council at the wedding of Peter and Catherine, like the placing of civil servants and foreigners in posts formerly occupied by royal relatives—as well as the conspicuous absence of the heir apparent[34]—signaled the tsar's intention to celebrate his wedding in the company of his own creation, independent of the traditional demands placed by family and faith. Instead the cavaliers and ladies sitting around the Petrine round table enacted a new chivalrous code of conduct, one that bound them to the Russian monarch and his bride by a commitment to common goals, the obligations of service, and a belief in his charismatic authority.

As if to emphasize the fact that the chivalrous code of conduct displayed during the tsar's second wedding applied to the entire Russian political elite, all three of the "spiritual personages" sitting at the center of Peter's round table soon appeared in their own public *parodia sacra*. We have already seen the prominent role that Archdeacon Gideon played (even after his death) in trumpeting the court's commitment to Peter's charisma and the ideals of Christian chivalry. What remains to be demonstrated is the extent to which the carnivalesque spectacles associated with the weddings of his mock brethren contributed to the same project. As we shall see, the court's celebration of P. I. Buturlin's marriage in June 1712 not only captured the transformation of values revealed by the tsar's nuptials but also set the stage

31. For a reconstruction of the seating arrangements at Peter's second wedding, see G. A. Mikhailov, "Graviura A. Zubova 'Svad'ba Petra I': Real'nost' i vymysel," *Panorama iskusstv* 11 (1988): 20–55, esp., 25–38.

32. Note that Zubov depicted only the third (and final) day of the festivities associated with Peter's new-style wedding, thereby eschewing Adrian Schoonebeck's attempt to depict (sequentially) the carnivalesque transformation of Muscovite habits. According to Zubov's (much more static) rendition of this same process, carnivalesque royal play—represented by the three mock clerics—is located at the very center of the political project symbolized by the Petrine round table. For a detailed analysis of the origins of this engraving, see Alekseeva, *Graviura*, 122–24; and Mikhailov, "Graviura," 20–21, 51–53. On Zubov, a student of Adrian Schoonebeck and perhaps the most famous Russian engraver of the entire reign, see Cracraft, *Petrine Revolution*, 177–84.

33. *Pokhodnyi zhurnal 1712 goda*, 5–6.

34. During his father's wedding, Tsarevich Aleksei Petrovich was (conveniently) abroad. See Mikhailov, "Graviura," 39, 55n29.

Figure 10. The Wedding of Peter I and Catherine Alekseevna (1712). Engraving by A. F. Zubov. (Courtesy of Richard S. Wortman and the Pushkin Museum of Fine Arts, St. Petersburg.)

for the much more elaborate masquerade-wedding of the Prince-Pope of the Transfigured Kingdom. Taking advantage of the northern location of Russia's new port city, Peter and his advisers staged a carnivalesque spectacle intended to parallel on an emotional and aesthetic level the extraordinary effect produced by the famous St. Petersburg white nights. Presiding over this topsy-turvy world of black-and-white contrasts was the boyar P. I. Buturlin (d. 1723), in his capacity as the mock Arch-Hierarch of St. Petersburg.[35] As in the jester weddings organized nearly a decade earlier on the

35. For information on P. I. Buturlin, an ordinary courtier from a large noble family who was promoted to the top rank (boyar) of the obsolescent royal council only in 1711, see Airapetian, "Feodal'naia aristokratiia," 98, 110, 347, 316; and M. I. Semevskii, "Petr Velikii kak iumorist [1690–1725]," in *Ocherki i razskazy iz russkoi istorii XVIII v.: Slovo i delo! 1700–1725*, 2nd rev. ed., 278–334 (St. Petersburg, 1884), esp. 286–87. See also *Pokhodnyi*

Figure 11. Detail of *The Wedding of Peter I and Catherine Alekseevna*, depicting the center table, with three mock hierarchs of the Unholy Council.

outskirts of Moscow, travesty was the order of the day. On June 3, 1712, immediately after the conclusion of the new-style festivities surrounding the nuptials of "First Senator and Minister" Prince Ia. F. Dolgorukov, the tsar "appointed a wedding to be kept after the old fashion"—a deliberate polemical attempt to juxtapose the old and the new.[36] Everyone invited to this event, "from the royal family even to the footmen," was obliged to come in the long-skirted Muscovite smocks that Charles Whitworth, the British ambassador, described as both "very extraordinary" and "inconvenient." While the tsar sent out the appropriate habits to the resident foreigners, members of the Russian elite and their wives donned the clothes that "they or their ancestors had worn about thirty years ago." Furthermore,

zhurnal 1723 goda, 21, 36–37; and N. F. Samarin, "Buturliny i Iushkovy. Zametki iz bumag semeinogo arkhiva N. F. Samarina," *Russkaia starina* 6 (1872): 560.

36. Dolgorukov's wedding took place in St. Petersburg on June 1–2, 1712, just a year after he escaped from Swedish captivity (1700–1712). According to the British ambassador, Prince Dolgorukov "was married to a sister of Prince Cercasky [Cherkasskii]" in a ceremony at which "the Czar officiated as marshal." See Whitworth's dispatch to London, June 8/19, 1712, in *Sbornik*, 214. Prince Dolgorukov married Princess I. M. Cherkasskaia, the daughter of Prince M. Ia. Cherkasskii (d. 1712). See *Pokhodnyi zhurnal 1712 goda*, 3, 14.

"so that all might be of a piece," the tsar had sent for "his father's old musicians from Moscow."[37] The staging of these festivities thus evoked the fashions at the court of Tsar Aleksei Mikhailovich in order to symbolize the generational and cultural transformation under way at the court of his son.

Dressed in these period pieces, the wedding party escorted the bride and groom to the church in which they were to be married in the traditional Orthodox fashion. According to the log kept by the tsar's personal secretary, Buturlin's wedding train was led off by the Russian royal family, followed by "the Admiral [of the imperial navy, F. M. Apraksin], the Generals, the Senators, the foreign Ambassadors and Residents, as well as the leading figures of St. Petersburg and their wives."[38] After they had been to church "in this masquerade,"

> the whole company embarked on board a sort of hoy or old Russian vessel, very heavy and clumsy, which could sail before the wind, and that being contrary, was towed by a half-galley to Petershoff, a pretty country house His Majesty has built midway between this place and Cronschloss, where they arrived about eleven in the evening (for here is no night now) and found a very handsome entertainment ready. The Czar all the way took a particular delight in exposing the old methods of the country, but it was very plain that several others acted their part with regret, and wished themselves in their former condition.[39]

Both the ancient Muscovite dress and the poorly maneuverable vessel that carried the wedding party represented the "old methods of the country," which the tsar took such delight in exposing. According to the tsar and the organizers of these festivities, neither had a place in the new commercial, administrative, and maritime center on the shores of the Neva. Their appearance during the carnivalesque wedding of the mock Metropolitan of St. Petersburg brilliantly captures the highly charged polemical nature of the travesties that transformed the old habits of Muscovite courtiers into disguises for newly fashioned royal servitors.

The "masquerade" that accompanied the wedding of the metropolitan of St. Petersburg was therefore only the latest in a series of elaborate matrimonial spectacles arranged by Peter for members of the royal family and his intimates during the construction of St. Petersburg. Like the new-style wedding that immediately preceded it, this raucous celebration of unholy matrimony symbolized a movement away from wedlock as a tool of clan politics toward marriage as a way of integrating the Russian elite into the broader European court society. As such, it tends to support the thesis that Petrine matrimonial spectacles were among the chief symbolic acts that es-

---

37. Whitworth, *Sbornik,* 214.
38. *Pokhodnyi zhurnal 1712 goda,* 14.
39. Whitworth, *Sbornik,* 215–16. In the official court record of this event, the old Russian vessel (*sudno*) was called the "Raft of Novgorod" (*Novgorodskaia luma*), after the regional term for a string of wooden rafts. See *Pokhodnyi zhurnal 1712 goda,* 14.

tablished Muscovy's parity abroad while institutionalizing the tsar's charisma at home. Indeed, this proposition can elucidate the significance of the 1715 wedding of Prince-Pope Zotov, which until now has been seen simply either as an attack on the Russian Orthodox church by an overzealous secularizer or as the prime example of Peter's dark and demented sense of humor. Once the historical context and the biblical subtext of this baroque court spectacle have been taken into account, we will be in a better position to understand how the marriage of the mock pontiff of the Transfigured Kingdom could possibly make a powerful statement about Russia's new imperial capital and the charisma of the monarch who founded it.

A Marriage of Convenience

The origins of this particular matrimonial spectacle go back to the end of the summer of 1713, when Peter began making plans for the winter festivities that would follow the end of the first Finnish campaign—a highly successful land and sea invasion of the remote province that was the southern breadbasket of Sweden's Baltic empire.[40] On August 30, 1713, the scribes from the tsar's personal chancellery sent out a standard communiqué concerning the Russian victory in Äbo (Turku) to all of Peter's top courtiers, including N. M. Zotov.[41] This form letter, however, included a handwritten postscript from the tsar, addressing his old servitor in the joking style to which Zotov had become accustomed: "We hope that Your Holiness will not forget us with his visit."[42] Judging by the letters later sent to Peter's mock double, His Majesty Prince F. Iu. Romodanovskii, and Princess A. P. Golitsyna (*née* Prozorovskaia), a member of the female half of the mock ecclesiastical council, the tsar intended to gather his entire company in St. Petersburg for the projected (and by now obligatory) tri-

40. For an analysis of the Finnish campaigns of 1713–14, see Hughes, *Russia,* 52; Pavlenko, *Petr Velikii,* 369–73; and E. V. Tarle, *Russkii flot i vneshniaia politika Petra I* (St. Petersburg, 1994), 68–80.

41. For Zotov's career after the 1689 court coup in favor of the Naryshkin candidate, see V. Korsakov, "Zotov, gr. Nikita Moiseevich," in *RBS* 7:476–81 (New York, 1962). On Zotov as head of the Moscow-based Privy Chancellery (*Blizhniaia kantseliariia*), the institutional predecessor of the College of State Accounting (*Revizion-kollegia*), see [N. Tokarev], "Blizhniaia kantseliariia pri Petre Velikom i eia dela," in *Opisanie dokumentov i bumag khraniashchikhsia v Moskovskom arkhive Ministerstva Iustitsii,* 5 (2): 43–75 (Moscow, 1888); N. P. Eroshkin, *Istoriia gosudarstvennykh uchrezhdenii dorevoliutsionnoi Rossii,* 3rd ed. (Moscow, 1983), 74; and E. V. Anisimov, *Gosudarstvennye preobrazovaniia i samoderzhavie Petra Velikogo v pervoi chetverti XVIII veka* (St. Petersburg, 1997), 22–25. For Zotov's official appointment as state fiscal (*gosudarstvennyi fiskal*), the courtier responsible for supervising the proper functioning of the administrative apparatus, see the royal decree of August 22, 1711, in *PiB,* 11 (2): 100, 409. Although the position of state fiscal was soon made redundant by the reorganization of the entire system of state control (*fiskalitet*), the expansion of Zotov's responsibilities was a natural consequence of his job as general-president of the Privy Chancellery, the central auditor of the realm.

42. SPb F IRI RAN, f. 270, kn. 73, l. 149.

umphal entry.[43] But to Peter's surprise, the septuagenarian balked at the prospect of relocating to St. Petersburg and instead broached the subject of his retirement to a monastery.

The tsar responded to Zotov's unilateral attempt to end his service career by ordering him to get married—a retort that sought to forestall any future thoughts of retirement once and for all by taking advantage of the fact that the vows of marriage and those of the monastic life were mutually incompatible.[44] Zotov's attempts to postpone the inevitable drew a curt response from the tsar, who dropped the comical tone (though not the mock title) of the previous summons and insisted on Zotov's arrival in St. Petersburg.[45] Even before Zotov received this sharply worded missive, however, he had hit on another delaying tactic. In a letter to his "most kind and gracious sovereign" dated October 2, 1713, the old courtier acknowledged that he was as powerless to refuse the tsar's wishes as he was capable of going against the will of the Almighty.

> I report to your highness, like unto God himself[:] From your sovereign lips I have received your will, along with a true affirmation that you do not wish to release me to enter a monastery and become a monk; instead, in order to take care of my house, you ordered me to get married, having chosen a good, middle-aged woman to cherish [me in] my old age. Now, according to your gracious sovereign charity, for tending my old age, I have been ordered to live in Moscow until the [roads are once again passable in] winter. But if, Sovereign, one of these days there shall be found a wife fit for my marriage, allow me, our gracious sovereign, to be wed here in Moscow without any fanfare and concealed from the machinations of the malicious people in Petersburg. Later, Sovereign, when we arrive in Petersburg, whatever public [festivities] you wish to arrange for your sovereign entertainment, I will happily be ready to amuse you. Marriage [is probably the only thing capable of] dragging an old woman away from Moscow; without it, no widow will want to ride with a groom on her frozen shame.[46]

Couching his reluctance in the phrase "one of these days," Zotov expressed his hope that a marriage ceremony was only in the planning stages and that the tsar might still be persuaded to abandon it. This implicit refusal belied

43. Peter to F. Iu. Romodanovskii, October 4, 1713, ibid., ll. 211–12; Peter to Princess A. P. Golitsyna, October 4, 1713, ibid., l. 216.

44. Peter had already used this tactic to good effect in the case of General Field Marshal B. P. Sheremetev, who was bribed into several more years of service by this expression of the tsar's favor, a sizable dowry, and a rather tenuous marital connection with the royal family (his bride was the twenty-six-year-old widow of Peter's maternal uncle, L. K. Naryshkin). For a discussion of Sheremetev's second wedding, see N. I. Pavlenko, *Ptentsy gnezda Petrova* (Moscow, 1984), 90–91; and esp. A. I. Zaozerskii, *Fel'dmarshal B. P. Sheremetev* (Moscow, 1989), 128–29, 228–29, 281.

45. Peter to N. M. Zotov, October, 1713, SPb F IRI RAN, f.270, kn. 73, l. 215.

46. RGADA, f. 9, otd. 2, op. 3, ch. 1, d. 17, ll. 518r–v, 521v; and in Semevskii, "Petr Velikii," 291–92.

the eagerness with which the old courtier asserted his readiness to perform his role as the main character in the projected royal amusement. In this light, the weak pun with which he ended the letter was perhaps a better reflection of the courtier's unwillingness to live up to his duties than an old man's misogynous comment on the frigidity of his potential bride.

In this case, however, neither attestations of faith nor obscene jokes could dissuade Peter from his intentions. In his reply to Zotov's letter, Peter pretended to take the old courtier's hesitant acquiescence as an affirmation of the Prince-Pope's zeal to get married:

> We have received Your Holiness's letter, in which you express your desire to enter into legal matrimony. No one can be forbidden that. But we cannot allow you surreptitiously [lit. like a thief or robber] to perform the seventh sacrament [i.e., marriage] in the ancient barbaric custom. For as the Apostle says, "If I build up again the very things that I once tore down, then I demonstrate that I am a transgressor." Also, it is impossible in that matter to deprive us, and this place, of your celebration. As for [the excuse] that she does not have anyone to ride with from Moscow, tell my sister [Tsarevna Natal'ia Alekseevna] to take her along (and show her this letter [to prove] that I ordered her to do it) and it will immediately be done. As for making your trip before the winter, I would like you [to arrive] before the 20th of next month, although I leave that up to you; just be here before Christmas.[47]

Seeking to forestall any more evasive tactics, the tsar branded Zotov's request for a private wedding in Moscow as tantamount to a criminal act—a characterization that was based on an explicit invocation of the apostle Paul's injunction against "transgressors" (Gal. 2:18). Peter's seemingly offhand allusion to the Bible immediately brings up two questions: Why did the tsar quote the Scriptures in this heated epistolary exchange with his old tutor? And why did he invoke this particular passage of Paul's Epistle to the Galatians? An answer to these questions might shed light on the reason the tsar insisted that the Prince-Pope celebrate his nuptials in St. Petersburg.

When the tsar playfully chided his mock father superior for attempting "to build up the very things" that Zotov himself had helped "to tear down," he was making a statement that applied as much to his own transgressions as to those of the mock patriarch. In fact, Peter's comments about the "ancient barbaric customs" associated with the performance of the "seventh sacrament" must be seen against the background of the innovative matrimonial spectacles staged by the tsar and his courtiers both in Moscow and St. Petersburg. The tsar's polemical, if implicit, distinction between the old and the new echoed the apostle Paul's discussion of the difference between

---

47. Peter to N. M. Zotov, c. October 21, 1713, in SPb F IRI RAN, f. 270, kn. 73, l. 256; *Materialy dlia istorii Gangutskoi operatsii* (Petrograd, 1914), 1 (1): 68; and Semevskii, "Petr Velikii," 291–92.

a righteous life, lived in anticipation of Jesus' imminent return, and a hypocritical one, lived by paying lip service to the tenets of the faith.[48] In his epistle to the Galatians, Paul rebuked the apostle Peter—the disciple to whom
Christ had left his church—for espousing ancient customs that would have
eased the transition to Christianity for Jewish converts. Denouncing Peter's
apparent inability to recognize the radical break heralded by Jesus' death
and resurrection, Paul insists that for those who have truly come to believe
in justification through faith, there is no going back to the works of the law.
To believe in the divine grace of the Anointed One is to be beyond the law—
the *nomos* as defined under the old dispensation—and in the realm of the
coming kingdom of God.

A secular version of this eschatologically oriented antinomianism under-
lies Peter's reference to the Pauline epistles in his letter to the Prince-Pope.
Addressing his own mock pontiff as the comical foil for St. Peter, the tsar
apparently invoked Paul's rebuke to emphasize the irreversible break heralded by the relocation of the Muscovite capital to the banks of the Neva
River.[49] For the mock spiritual leader of his Transfigured Kingdom to get
married according to the "ancient barbaric custom" was as great a transgression under the new political dispensation proclaimed by the tsar as the
Galatians' reliance on the works of the law during the messianic age heralded by the death and resurrection of Christ. Thus, by specifying that he
intended Zotov's wedding to take place in St. Petersburg, at the end of the
most successful campaign season since Poltava, Peter sought to capitalize on
the millenarian moment afforded by the current strength of Russian arms
and to underline the imminent realization of his lifelong attempt to institute
his vision of paradise on earth.[50]

At this point, however, the tsar's ambitious preparations for Yuletide
1713 came to a temporary halt. The culprit for this unexpected change of
plans appears to have been none other than Anna Stremoukhova (*née*
Pashkova)—daughter of a Muscovite nobleman suspected of supporting
prominent Old Believers and the woman the tsar had personally picked to
be Zotov's bride.[51] As early as November 8, 1713, Peter had informed his

48. For several examples of Peter's well-documented obsession with hypocrisy (*khanzh-estvo*), see Cracraft, *Church Reform*, 24–25.

49. Although the fortress of St. Petersburg was founded in 1703, it did not become the tsar's *Residenzstadt* until well after the victory at Poltava. Since Peter never issued an official decree proclaiming St. Petersburg the capital of the Russian Empire, the de facto relocation of the Sen-ate in late 1713 is conventionally taken to mark the *translatio capitalii*. See Hughes, *Russia*, 215; and N. I. Pavlenko, *Petr Velikii* (Moscow, 1990, 525).

50. For the tsar's explicit analogy between St. Petersburg and paradise, see Peter to A. D. Menshikov, April 7, 1706, in *PiB*, 4:209. For an insightful analysis of Peter's epistolary refer-ences to "edenic" St. Petersburg, see Hughes, *Russia*, 211–13. For a suggestive attempt to place this utopian theme in a broader context, see Stephen L. Baehr, *The Paradise Myth in Eighteenth-Century Russia: Utopian Patterns in Early Secular Russian Literature and Culture* (Stanford, 1991), ix, 1, 31–33, 38–40, 65, 153, 184n2.

51. Anna's father, an assistant military governor of a distant Muscovite outpost in eastern Siberia, where Avvakum had been exiled from 1656 to 1662, became the archpriest's spiritual son. Although Anna's grandfather, A. F. Pashkov, governor of Dauria, disapproved of his son's religious convictions, Avvakum seems to have been secretly patronized by most of the gover-

friend Lieutenant General I. I. Buturlin—a distant relative of P. I. Buturlin, the mock Metropolitan of St. Petersburg[52]—about the "desire" of "the most blessed father, the Prince-Pope," to "be wed." In this letter the tsar first mentioned the name of Zotov's intended bride, "a widow from the Pashkov clan, who had previously been married to an officer of our regiment, Ivan Stremoukhov," before his untimely death in 1708, during the battle of Lesnaia.[53] In a matter of weeks, Peter's intimate knowledge about the affairs of the Preobrazhensk regiment allowed him to locate someone who could not possibly object to going along with his plans for another of his Yuletide weddings. However, the widow of Ivan Stremoukhov was not as eager to make a spectacle of herself as the tsar had imagined. Although he expected Zotov and Stremoukhova "here soon," when the Prince-Pope finally did arrive in St. Petersburg, at the end of November 1713 (as the tsar had instructed), he came without his betrothed. So, although Zotov participated in the court's winter festivities—including the funeral of Archdeacon Gideon (Prince Iu. F. Shakhovskoi)—his wedding had to be postponed.[54]

After the start of the new campaign season in Finland, the tsar entrusted the task of organizing the Zotov wedding to G. I. Golovkin, a member of Peter's company and (since the death of F. A. Golovin in 1706) the new head of the Chancellery of Foreign Affairs. By handing the task of staging a jester wedding over to the institution traditionally responsible for organizing all official royal spectacles, particularly, royal weddings, Peter had in effect put the projected royal amusement on a regular bureaucratic foot-

---

nor's family, including his wife and daughter-in-law. Avvakum even baptized one (at least) of Anna's brothers. See "Life of Avvakum by Himself," trans. Jane Harrison and Hope Mirrlees, in *Medieval Russia's Epics, Chronicles, and Tales*, ed. Serge A. Zenkovsky, 2nd ed. (New York, 1974), 412, 417, 421–24. On the service career of A. F. and E. A. Pashkov, see the respective entries by N. Voronkov in *RBS* (St. Petersburg, 1902), 12:444–45. For a brief genealogy of the Pashkov clan, see A. B. Lobanov-Rostovskii, *Russkaia rodoslovnaia kniga*, 2nd ed. (St. Petersburg, 1895), 2:77–78. Biographical information on Anna Stremoukhova can be found in *Pokhodnyi zhurnal 1720 goda*, 22, 48; and S. Liubimov, *Opyt istoricheskikh rodoslovii: Gundorovy, Zhizhemskie, Nesvitskie, Sibirskie, Zotovy i Ostermany* (Petrograd, 1915), 83.

52. For a biography of I. I. Buturlin, see *RBS* (New York, 1962), 3:549–51; and P. V. Albin, "Ivan Ivanovich Buturlin, general-anshef (1661–1738)," *Russkaia starina* 23 (1878): 161–86, esp. 163–64.

53. SPb F IRI RAN, f. 270, kn. 73, l. 302. On Ivan Stremoukhov, see Liubimov, *Opyt istoricheskikh rodoslovii*, 83.

54. Despite this temporary setback, Peter continued making the requisite preparations. Acting on his declared intention to put his sister in charge of the arrangements for conveying the reluctant bride to St. Petersburg, the tsar personally contacted Tsarevna Natal'ia Alekseevna, who still lived in Moscow, in Novo-Preobrazhenskoe. In an addendum (*v tsydulke*) to a letter written two months after the projected wedding failed to materialize, Peter passed on a "request" from the mock spiritual leader of the Transfigured Kingdom: "The Prince-Pope has asked that you take his bride along with you. Announce [this] to her. When she receives a letter from him [calling her to St. Petersburg], bring her along with you." Peter to Tsarevna Natal'ia Alekseevna, January 24, 1714, in SPb F IRI RAN, f. 270, kn. 75, l. 59. For an analysis of Natal'ia Alekseevna's special role as cultural intermediary at her brother's court, see Lindsey Hughes, " 'Between Two Worlds': Tsarevna Natal'ia Alekseevna and the 'Emancipation' of Petrine Women," in *A Window on Russia*, ed. M. di Salvo and L. Hughes, 29–36 (Rome, 1996).

ing.[55] In the months leading up to the masquerade wedding of the Prince-Pope, the staff of Golovkin's chancellery compiled muster rolls of all the people who were expected to take part in the celebrations, registered the costume that each participant was supposed to wear, and even kept a record of the musical instrument and noisemaker that each member of the wedding train would carry.[56] At the end of September 1714, the staff of the Foreign Affairs Chancellery oversaw the implementation of a royal decree that announced the call-up of the projected wedding guests, both men and women, all of whom were instructed to assemble at the appointed time and place to sign up for a mask, a costume, and an appropriate musical instrument.[57] Closer to the date of the masquerade, Golovkin's chancellery also oversaw a general dress rehearsal, where the participants were ordered to keep their outfits concealed by their long cloaks, so as to maintain an element of surprise for the other maskers.[58]

According to the register of sleighs produced by the staff of the Foreign Affairs Chancellery, originally there were to be only thirteen floats: those of the groom, "[His] Royal Highness [Peter]," Governor A. D. Menshikov, Admiral Count F. M. Apraksin, Count G. I. Golovkin, Count I. A. Musin-Pushkin, Prince Ia. F. Dolgorukov, Prince G. F. Dolgorukov, Prince V. V. Dolgorukov, the "local Metropolitan" (P. I. Buturlin), the Metropolitan of Novgorod (T. N. Streshnev), General James Bruce, and General Adam Weide.[59] A later version of this list transferred Menshikov's sleigh behind those of Admiral Apraksin and Tsar Peter, who was now listed in his new capacity as "Vice Admiral" of the Imperial Navy, a promotion he received for his bravery at the battle of Hangö, the naval victory that capped the 1714 campaign season.[60] This list also included two new additions: the sleighs of the foreign ministers and of Prince M. A. Cherkasskii, the head of the chancellery responsible for supervising the construction of Peter's "edenic" city by the sea.[61] If we assume that each float carried its total complement of maskers, the wedding train of the Prince-Pope would have included about 150 people; doubling this number (to take into account the wives of these men) would make the total number of maskers around

55. On the role of the Foreign Affairs Chancellery in drawing up and storing the muster rolls for royal weddings, see Martin, "Dynastic Marriage," 293–94, 318, 325, 339–40.

56. Most of these documents have been collected in an archival file titled "Zapiski kasaiushchiisia do shutoshnoi svad'by kniaz' papy tainogo sovetnika Nikity Moiseevicha Zotova v Sankt-Peterburge [1714^{go.} Sent. po fevr: 1715^{go.}]," in RGADA, f. 156, op. 1, ed. khr. 129.

57. See the royal decrees dated September 21, 1714, ibid., ll. 1–4. For the preliminary register of the main courtiers and their wives, see ibid., ll. 8r–9v,12.

58. Prince A. D. Menshikov to G. I. Golovkin, December 10, 1714, ibid., ll. 13–14; and the royal decree (December 11, 1714) based on this letter, ibid., ll. 15–21v, 94–95.

59. Ibid., l. 14. For the identity of the two mock prelates, see ibid., l. 22.

60. Hughes, *Russia*, 52–53, 99.

61. Ibid., ll. 81, 89v. On Prince M. A. Cherkasskii and his chancellery (*Prikaz kamennykh del*), see O. G. Ageeva, *"Velichaishii i slavneishii bolee vsekh gradov v svete"—grad sviatogo Petra: Peterburg v russkom obshchestvennom soznanii nachala XVIII veka* (St. Peterburg, 1999), 99.

300—a figure that corresponds fairly closely to the "four hundred people of both sexes" mentioned by Friedrich Christian Weber, the Hanoverian resident at the court of Peter the Great, in his eyewitness account of the St. Petersburg masquerade.[62]

The deliberate inclusion of Weber and other foreign ambassadors in the 1715 masquerade wedding suggests, however, that this spectacle was intended for a much broader audience than the one the tsar and his chief advisers had mustered in St. Petersburg. Judging by the costumes commissioned by the Foreign Affairs Chancellery, the projected royal spectacle contained a message that would be of interest to the courts of other Christian monarchs, especially anyone who was still dealing with the consequences of the recently concluded Peace of Utrecht (1714). Indeed, if we consider why the old groom appeared in the crimson cassock and red skullcap of a Roman Catholic cardinal and why his young bride wore a long black dress "in the Spanish manner," we may see the wedding of the Prince-Pope as a scurrilous commentary on the real losers of the conflict known as the War of the Spanish Succession (1701–14)—the Holy Roman Emperor of the German Nation, Habsburg Spain, and the Papacy.[63]

When viewed in the context of the anti-Catholic and anti-Habsburg propaganda produced during the War of the Spanish Succession, the masquerade costumes of the Prince-Pope and his "Spanish" bride acquire a distinctively polemical coloration. In her long black dress, the widow Stremoukhova could be said to have presented the spectacle of a widowed Spain, who, despite the recent death of her husband (Charles II) and her properly mournful appearance, was in reality open to the advances of her many covetous neighbors. Similarly, the ecclesiastical vestments of her new beau, the Prince-Pope, hinted at the impure political motives for the courtship between Catholic Spain and the Vatican. The wedding between the Prince-Pope and his Spanish bride could thus be said to have embodied a critique of the unholy union between the papacy and the Spanish Habsburgs—a ruling house that by the end of the war had become synonymous with overweening imperial ambition and religious intolerance, as well as political impotence.[64] As we will see when we analyze the costumes of Peter

---

62. RGADA, f. 156, op. I, ed. khr. 129, ll. 57–62, 67–72v, esp. 60v and 73; and 75r–v, 78r–v, 90r–v. For Weber's figure, see F.-Ch. Weber, *The Present State of Russia* (London, 1723), 1:89.

63. Hughes, *Russia*, 30–31; N. N. Molchanov, *Diplomatiia Petra Pervogo* (Moscow, 1986), 100–103, 108–9, 168, 316. The attire of the bride and groom is described in RGADA, f. 156, op. I, ed. khr. 129, ll. 65–66, 93r–v.

64. Both sides of the conflict over the Spanish succession published pamphlets that lampooned their political and confessional opponents and sought to discredit them in the eyes of the European public. Even the Russian government joined in the game, commissioning the translation of a 1706 Polish broadside that represented the geopolitical players as card sharks. For the text of the pamphlet, see T. K. Krylova, "Poltavskaia pobeda i russkaia diplomatiia," in *Petr Velikii: sbornik statei*, ed. A. I. Andreev (Moscow and Leningrad, 1947), 111–12; cf. RGADA, f. 9, otd. 2, op. 4, chap. 3, kn. 95, ll. 378–81, and kn. 93, ll. 251–54v. For an insightful analysis of the playful language of royal propaganda during the War of the Spanish

and his mock double, this playful commentary on the religious and political pretensions of the Holy Roman Emperor and the pope appears to have served as a deliberate counterpoint to the supposedly more tolerant but no less ambitious imperial vision of the tsar. In this respect, the anti-Habsburg bias of the St. Petersburg masquerade of 1715 echoed the polemical thrust of the war games attending the foundation of "Pressburg," the Moscow-based capital of the Transfigured Kingdom.

A Royal Charivari

On January 15, 1715, on the eve of the Zotov-Stremoukhova wedding, the tsar issued a decree detailing the order of ceremony for the long-awaited St. Petersburg masquerade.[65] On the following morning, the participants were to listen for a three-gun salute, a signal to don their costumes and go immediately to their muster places, making sure to hide their fancy dress under their cloaks, "as during the inspection." The gentlemen maskers were reminded to take along the musical instruments assigned to them during the dress rehearsal, while the women were commanded to bring red piccolos. The men were to gather at the house of Count Golovkin, while the women were to assemble at the house of D. G. Rzhevskaia (*née* Sokovnina), the Abbess of the mock ecclesiastical council of the Prince-Pope and a distant relative of V. A. Sokovnin, the onetime Prophet of the Transfigured Kingdom.[66] The tsar, who had paid personal visits to the houses of both courtiers at the start of the annual Yuletide caroling season, just a few weeks before this decree was promulgated, had already assured himself that the prospective hosts were ready to receive their many guests.[67] The banks of the Neva River in front of their houses were already icy, so that the drivers of the specially commissioned ten-man floats and the large sledges set

---

Succession, see Jean-Pierre Etienvre, "Du jeu comme métaphore politique: Sur quelques textes de propagande royale diffusés en Espagne à l'avènement des Bourbons," *Poétique* 56 (1983): 397–415.

65. For the text of this royal decree, see RGADA, f. 156, op. I, ed. khr. 129, ll. 55–56.

66. D. G. Rzhevskaia was the first cousin of A. P. Sokovnin, one of the Muscovite courtiers executed during the so-called Tsykler plot (1697) against the life of the tsar. Like other members of the Sokovnin family, including V. A. Sokovnin, she fell into disfavor after this affair. In the early eighteenth century she appears to have become a lady-in-waiting to Peter's second wife, who employed her as a female jester—and a spy. In 1714 the Arch-Abbess was assigned to supervise the tsar's foreign daughter-in-law, Princess Charlotte of Wolfenbüttel, and charged with reporting on any "irregularities" in the household of Tsarevich Aleksei Petrovich. For a brief biography of D. G. Rzhevskaia, see Petr Dolgorukii, *Rossiiskaia rodoslovnaia kniga* (St. Petersburg, 1857), 4:31–35; P. F. Karabanov, "Stats-damy i freiliny russkogo dvora v XVIII stoletii," pt. 2, *Russkaia starina* 2 (1870): 482; and Hughes, *Russia*, 253; on her brief stint as a royal spy, see D. G. Rzhevskaia to Peter, July 8, 1714, in N. G. Ustrialov, *Istoriia imperatora Petra Velikogo* (St. Petersburg, 1859), 6:322.

67. See the entries for December 23–25, 1714, in *Pokhodnyi zhurnal 1714 goda*, 150–51.

aside for the ladies had no problem finding parking space while they waited for the maskers.[68]

After dining at Golovkin's on January 16, 1715, Peter joined the costumed women and men to escort the Prince-Pope and his bride to the Trinity Cathedral.[69] The Hanoverian resident's colorful eyewitness account deserves to be quoted at length, if only to get a sense of the spectacle afforded by the wedding procession:

> Preparations having been made by the whole Court during three Months for a *great Masquerade,* the same was at length kept on the 27th and 28th of *January* [January 16–17, 1715]. I will relate the main Particulars, the World never having heard, for ought I know, of the like before. The occasion of this Masquerade was a Wedding. One *Sotoff,* who had been the Czar's Writing-Master in his Majesty's younger years, was in the 70th [*sic*] Year of his Age advanced to be his Jester, or merrymaking *Privy-Counsellor,* and afterwards *Mock-Patriarch.* Moreover, for Humor sake he was raised to the Dignity of a *Prince* and at length declared *Pope.* Invested with those imaginary Characters, and being now in the 84th [*sic*] Year of his Age, the Czar married him to a buxom Widow of thirty-four, and the Nuptials of this extraordinary Couple were solemnized by the Court in Masks, or Mock-show. The Company consisted of about four hundred persons of both sexes. Every four Persons had their proper Dress and peculiar musical Instruments, so that they represented a hundred different sorts of Habits and Music, particularly of the Asiatic Nations. . . . The *Mock-Tsar of Moscow,* who represented King *David* in his Dress, instead of a Harp had a Lyre covered with a Bear-skin, to play upon. He being the Chief of the Company, was carried on a sort of Pageant placed on a Sled, to the four Corners of which were tied as many Bears, which being pricked with Goads by Fellows purposely appointed for it, made such a frightful roaring as well suited the confused and horrible Din raised by the disagreeing Instruments of the rest of the Company. The *Czar* himself was dressed like a Boor [*Bauer,* peasant] of *Frizeland* and skillfully beat a Drum in Company with three Generals. In this manner, Bells ringing everywhere, the ill-matched Couple were attended by the Masks to the Altar of the great Church, where they were joined in Matrimony by a priest a hundred Years old, who had lost his Eyesight and Memory, to supply which Defect a pair of Spectacles were put on his Nose, two Candles held before his Eyes, and the Words sounded into his Ears, which he was to pronounce.[70]

---

68. RGADA, f. 156, op. 1, ed. khr. 129, l. 55.

69. *Pokhodnyi zhurnal 1715 goda,* 47.

70. Weber, *Present State of Russia,* 1:89–90. See also the firsthand account of Jacob de Bie (b. 1681), the Dutch resident at the court of Peter the Great and yet another foreign participant in the masquerade wedding of the Prince-Pope. In a letter of February 1, 1715, de Bie notified the States General that the wedding of the "soi-disant Patriarch" was "very burlesque: There were several hundreds of disguised wedding guests and a ditto Patriarch, dressed in papal outfit. His Majesty the Tsar himself, together with Prince Trubetskoi and lieutenant-general Buturlin, beat the drum; they were followed by the so-called Tsar of Moscow, who was sitting on a high sledge representing King David, but instead of a harp he was holding a bag-pipe made of a bear's skin under his arm." Quoted in Thomas Eekman, "Seven Years with Peter the

After the blasphemous wedding ceremony staged at the Trinity Cathedral—a performance that prompted one of the chancellery clerks who kept the tsar's daily log to describe the entire affair as an "unlawful marriage" (*neza-konnyi brak*)—the maskers conveyed Zotov and his bride to the spacious palace of the royal favorite across the frozen Neva, on Vasil'evskii Island. Prince Menshikov, who had served as the master of ceremonies at the tsar's own wedding, staged an elaborate wedding feast and provided the newly-weds with a honeymoon suite. In the morning, if one were to judge from the cabinet secretary's brief remark about the matrimonial levee, the wedding guests roused the young couple in a scabrous parody of the customary display of a bride's virginity; although no one seriously expected that this particular bride and groom would ever pass such a test, tradition had to be obeyed.[71] Afterward, the newlyweds and the entire wedding party mounted the floats and sleighs and, once again braving the frozen Neva, crossed over to the St. Petersburg side. After a midday meal at the palace of the "Vice Admiral"—the tsar himself—the company of maskers spent the rest of the day (January 17, 1715) being driven around the snow-packed streets of St. Petersburg. The next night the tsar sailed to Kronshlot, signaling the end of the masquerade, although not of the 1715 winter holiday season.[72]

Everything connected with this carnivalesque spectacle—from the clashing colors worn by the Prince-Pope and his Old Believer bride, to the "Many strange Adventures and comical Accidents" that happened to them, not only during the carnivalesque matrimonial ceremonies but also during "their riding on Sleds throughout the Streets"—served to emphasize that this bride and groom were intended to be "ill-matched."[73] Indeed, whether one judged them in respect to age, social standing, or religious affiliation, the union of a widowed young noblewoman and an ancient chancellery clerk could be described only as an unequal marriage.[74] As befits an unequal marriage, the wedding of this particular couple was to be accompanied by the "rough music" of a charivari, the traditional shaming ceremony im-

Great: The Dutchman Jacob de Bie's Observations," in Hughes, *Peter the Great and the West*, 218–19.

71. *Pokhodnyi zhurnal 1715 goda*, 9, 33, 47. On the custom of displaying the bloodstained bedclothes on the morning after the wedding night, see the contemporary account of J. G. Vockerodt, "Rossiia pri Petre Velikom, po rukopisnomu izvestiiu Ioanna Gottgil'fa Fokkerodta," trans. A. N. Shemiakin, *Chteniia v Imperatorskom obshchestve istorii i drevnostei Rossiiskikh pri Moskovskom universitete* 2 (1874): 104; and the analysis in Eve Levin, *Sex and Society in the World of the Orthodox Slavs* (Ithaca, 1989), 87.

72. *Pokhodnyi zhurnal 1715 goda*, 9, 33.

73. Weber, *Present State of Russia*, 1:90.

74. For a late seventeenth-century comical dialogue directed against unequal marriages, see "Pritcha o starom muzhe," in *Pamiatniki literatury drevnei Rusi. XVII vek* (Moscow, 1989), 2:234–36, 614. Compare the dire consequences described in this dialogue with Peter's reported warning to Zotov not to consummate the marriage with the young widow for health reasons: K. M. Zotov to Peter, June 27, 1720, in RGADA, f. 9, otd. 2, op. 4, chap. 1, kn. 52, l. 340; and with Peter's jokes in his correspondence with his own young wife, particularly the comment that infidelity is "just the sort of thing you daughters of Eve do to us old men." See Peter to Catherine, September 19, 1711, in *PiB*, 11 (2): 140.

posed by the self-appointed guardians of morality on anyone who violated the prevailing social, sexual, or confessional order in early modern Europe.[75] And within the bounds of the Transfigured Kingdom, these self-appointed guardians of order (and rational religion) were none other than Peter and his closest political advisers. In light of her family's heterodox confessional allegiances, therefore, the tsar's decision to unite Anna Stremoukhova and the Prince-Pope in the bonds of holy matrimony within the sacred walls of St. Petersburg's Trinity Cathedral—until the 1730s the most important shrine of the new northern capital[76]—evinced a highly critical attitude toward the old Muscovite dispensation. By conflating the "ancient barbaric customs" of the Orthodox Church with those of its Roman Catholic counterpart and then measuring these against the "heretical" practices of the Old Believers, the tsar and his advisers offered an ironic commentary on the long-standing conflict between the defenders of religious enlightenment and their schismatic opponents, a conflict that presumably could not be resolved harmoniously until Peter's Transfigured Kingdom was relocated to the "edenic" new capital on the Neva. Appropriately enough, the spectacular reconciliation of these two opposing strands of old Muscovite spirituality was to take place in the new imperial "residence" of "Friedrich" Romodanovskii, the Solomonic Prince of Peace who presided over the topsy-turvy world of this sacred parody.[77]

The prominent role played by Prince F. Iu. Romodanovskii, "Chief of the Company" during the St. Petersburg masquerade of 1715, demonstrates that there was more to this court spectacle than the obscene and blasphemous amusements typical of charivaris and Yuletide matrimonial games.[78] Although he preferred to downplay the contemporary political significance of the biblical allusion to the archetype of divine kingship, Weber correctly noted the incongruous detail that the secular counterpart to the mock pontiff of the Transfigured Kingdom appeared in the role of the humble psalmist.[79] To gain insight into why Prince-Caesar Romodanovskii dressed up as King David during the royal charivari, we have to remember that the tsar and his courtiers were very well acquainted with the political and reli-

75. See Natalie Zemon Davis, "The Reasons of Misrule" and "Women on Top," in *Society and Culture in Early Modern France*, 97–151 (Stanford, 1975); E. P. Thompson, "Rough Music," in *Customs in Common: Studies in Traditional Popular Culture*, 467–538 (New York, 1993); and Peter Burke, *Popular Culture in Early Modern Europe* (New York, 1978), 198–99.

76. Hughes, *Russia*, 214, 509n92.

77. For a reference to St. Petersburg as the "residence" of "His Majesty" the "Prince-Caesar," see Peter to Prince F. Iu. Romodanovskii, July 8, 1709, in *PiB*, 9:246.

78. On the eroticism of popular Yuletide rituals in Russia, see V. Ia. Propp, *Russkie agrarnye prazdniki* (Leningrad, 1963), 116–20; and William H. Hopkins, "The Development of 'Pornographic' Literature in Eighteenth- and Early Nineteenth-Century Russia" (Ph.D. diss., Indiana University, 1977), 39–41.

79. Weber, *Present State of Russia*, 90. For the contemporary appropriation of Davidic kingship by both the opponents and the defenders of early modern royal absolutism, see Gerhard Oestreich, *Neostoicism and the Early Modern State*, trans. David McLintock (Cambridge, 1982), chap. 8; and Joseph Anthony Mazzeo, "Cromwell as Davidic King," in his *Renaissance and Seventeenth-Century Studies* (New York, 1964), 189–91.

gious significance of the analogy between the biblical king and his contemporary royal successors.[80] For, in the words of another perceptive foreign observer who visited Muscovy at the beginning of the seventeenth century, according to the Russians, "the word . . . Tzar is to be found in the Holy Scriptures. For wherever mention is made of David, or Solomon, or other kings, they are called 'Zar David' and 'Zar Solomon.' . . . For this reason they maintain that the name of Tzar which it once pleased God to confer on David, Solomon and other rulers of Judah and Israel is the most authentic, and that the words 'Tsisar' [*tsesar'*, Holy Roman Emperor] or 'Kroll' [*korol'*, king] are merely a human invention and acquired by feats of arms."[81]

The invocation of a Davidic persona for Prince-Caesar Romodanovskii suggests that Peter and his advisers sought to make an implicit comparison between the celebrations associated with the royal charivari in St. Petersburg and the jubilation of the Israelites at the ceremonial transfer of the Ark of the Covenant to Jerusalem. The biblical story recounted in II Samuel describes how King David and the entire "house of Israel" conveyed the Ark of the Covenant up to the Temple in Jerusalem, "dancing before the Lord with all their might, with songs and lyres and harps and tambourines and castanets and cymbals" (II Sam. 6:5; cf. I Chron. 15:28). The frenzied dancing of King David and the "rough music" that accompanied his triumphal entry appears to constitute an important (and heretofore unacknowledged) proof text for the choreography of the masquerade staged in Peter's "edenic" city. For in both cases, a raucous and blasphemous example of royal play signaled the bestowal of divine favor on a newly consecrated imperial capital while underlining the ruling monarch's personal gift of grace. The classical statement of this apparent paradox echoes in King David's reply to the sardonic rebuke of Michal, his first wife (II Sam. 6:15–16, 20–23):

> So David and all the house of Israel brought up the ark of the Lord with shouting, and with the sound of the trumpet. And as the ark of the Lord came into the city of David, Michal, Saul's daughter, looked through a window, and saw king David leaping and dancing before the Lord; and she despised him in her heart. . . . And Michal the daughter of Saul came out to meet David, and said, "How glorious was the king of Israel today, who uncovered himself [*vystaviv sebia na pokaz*] today in the eyes of the handmaidens of his servants [i.e., the lowest of the low], as any vulgar fellow [*pliasun*, lit. prancer] might shamelessly uncover himself!" And David said unto Michal, "It was before the Lord,

---

80. For a detailed description of Romodanovskii's Davidic costume, see RGADA, f. 156, op. 1, ed. khr. 129, l. 93v.

81. *Estat de Russie et Grand Duché de Moscovie . . . à sçavoir depuis l'an 1590 jusques en l'an 1606, en septembre par le Capitaine Jacques Margeret* (Paris, 1607), quoted by N. G. Ustrialov, *Skazaniia sovremennikov o Dimitrii Samozvantse*, 3rd ed. (St. Petersburg, 1859), 1:254; and translated by David Budgen in B. A. Uspenskii, "Tsar and Pretender: *Samozvanchestvo* or Royal Imposture in Russia as a Cultural-Historical Phenomenon," in *The Semiotics of Russian Culture*, ed. Ann Shukman (Ann Arbor, 1984), 260–61.

who chose me in place of your father, and before all his house, to appoint me as prince over Israel, the people of the Lord, that I have danced [*veselilsia*, made merry or played] before the Lord. I will make myself yet more contemptible [*umalius'*] than this, and I will be abased [*smirius'*] in my own eyes; but by the maids of whom you have spoken, by them I shall be held in honor." And Michal the daughter of Saul had no child to the day of her death.

In this biblical parable, King David's unseemly prancing serves to underline his humility as well as his direct link to God, the true source of his greatness as a ruler and warrior. Paradoxically, the more this mighty king abased himself before his Creator, the more he elevated himself in the eyes of the Lord and his chosen people.[82] The moral of the royal ceremony in which the king makes a spectacle of himself is clear: those Israelites who understand the sacred significance of this royal merriment and choose to play along with their divinely anointed monarch shall be fruitful, in accord with God's promise to Adam and Eve in the garden (Gen. 1:28); while those prudish unbelievers, such as King David's first wife, who prefer to sit on the sidelines and criticize, shall remain barren and never experience the restoration of Paradise heralded by the transferal of the Ark of the Lord to "David's city." The parallel to the tsar's treatment of his first wife is striking, as is the implication that Peter's city has usurped the prerogatives of Moscow as the spiritual center of the Russian empire.

At this point it is extremely difficult to determine how many participants in the royal charivari of 1715 realized that they were helping the tsar enact an idiosyncratic version of Davidic kingship. However, we do know that both Peter and his mock pontiff were already familiar with the proof text from II Samuel. In fact, just four years before this biblical story came to inform the Davidic scenario of the masquerade that accompanied his own wedding, Zotov had invoked the same imagery to celebrate the tsar's military achievements against the Swedes. In a letter addressed to the "Most Holy Proto-Deacon, Sir Arch-Colonel P. A.," in October 1709, the Prince-Pope congratulated Peter on the recent "God-given victory" at the battle of Lesnaia (September 28, 1708) and notified him about the effect of this news on the morale of the Russian troops stationed in Ukraine. Writing as if he were still under the influence of the large amount of alcohol that he claimed to have consumed at the obligatory celebration dinner, Zotov waxed eloquent about the soteriological implications of the tsar's military success:

82. On the paradoxical self-abasement of King David and its Christian reinterpretation, see Mazzeo, "Cromwell as Davidic King," 189–91, esp. 191. This stress on the negative, apophatic method of understanding the sacred nature of royal authority echoes Russian Orthodox conceptions about the kenotic nature of Christ. On apophatic theology and Christ's kenosis, see Vladimir Lossky, *The Mystical Theology of the Eastern Orthodox Church* (London, 1957), 25, 34, 42, 144, 148; and George Fedotov, "Russian Kenoticism," in *The Russian Religious Mind*, 3:94–131 (Belmont, MA, 1975).

Having received the news . . . from your courier, Mr. Ozerov, we began to re-
joice, body and soul, in ineffable gladness. In everything, every rank and all
ages have perceived as if a renewal in ourselves. Before your many God-given
labors in that victory, our merry feet leap playfully (*veselymi nogami
skachuiushchi igraem*), like David in front of the ark (*iako Davyd pred sennym
kovchegom*). We also pray that God mercifully bestow his munificence upon
you, as he did to David over Goliath, by [allowing you] to defeat and overcome
that second Goliath, the most haughty Swede.[83]

In this tipsy paean to Peter, Zotov makes an explicit comparison between
the deeds of his royal patron and those of the biblical warrior-king in order
to assert the Davidic descent of Russia's divinely anointed tsar. Appealing to
an exegetical tradition according to which King David could serve as a
"type" of Christ, Zotov implied that Peter's "many God-given labors" are
responsible for "renovating" both the "body and soul" of his believers, in
much the way that the crucifixion, death, and resurrection of Jesus is supposed to have done for the followers of this original charismatic "son of
David" (Matt. 1).[84] Finding himself in a state of "ineffable gladness"—the
ecstatic experience of "sober drunkenness" described in Chapter 2—the
mock pontiff of the Transfigured Kingdom thus hinted at the true transcen-
dent genealogy of the tsar, who remained God's anointed even as he assumed a humble role during the course of his royal amusements.[85]

From this perspective, the Davidic attire of the mock tsar only served to
emphasize the sublimity of Peter's humble masquerade costume.[86] For the
duration of the 1715 royal charivari, Peter appeared in the same attire that
he had worn at the lavish masquerade ball held in Vienna by Leopold I of
Austria nearly twenty years before. During the 1698 celebrations of
Wirtschaft, a German holiday reminiscent of Russian Yuletide, Peter had
also donned the dress of a "Boor of Frieseland," that is, of a denizen of the
rough Netherlandish province that produced many sailors—a costume that
was intended to evoke the simple habit of a Dutch ship captain.[87] As we saw

83. N. M. Zotov to Peter, October 6, 1708, in RGADA, f. 9, otd. 2, op. 3, kn. 7 (1707), l.
934r–v.
84. For a good explanation of "typological allegory," as well as a discussion of King David
as *figura Christi,* see Mazzeo, "Cromwell as Davidic King," 183–208; and Steven N. Zwicker,
"The King and Christ: Figural Imagery in Dryden's Restoration Panegyrics," *Philological
Quarterly* 50 (1971): 582–98, esp. 583–84. For the tradition of typological interpretation and
its influence on Russian imperial imagery, see B. A. Uspenskii and V. M. Zhivov, "'Tsar' i
Bog': Semioticheskie aspekty sakralizatsii monarkha v Rossii," in *Izbrannye trudy,* 2nd ed.,
1:205–337 (Moscow, 1996); and L. I. Sazonova, *Poeziia russkogo barokko (vtoraia polovina
XVII–nachalo XVIII v.)* (Moscow, 1991), 53–74, 122–61.
85. For a stimulating discussion of the way Peter's playful renunciation of the "external
signs of his status as Tsar" in favor of a mock pretender actually served to emphasize his "own
authentic right to the royal throne, independent of any formal attributes of kingship," see Uspenskii, "Tsar and Pretender," 271. Compare this argument with Lossky's definition of
Christ's kenosis as the "ineffable descent of the Son who is reduced to the 'form of a slave'
without ceasing to be fully God," in his *Mystical Theology,* 148.
86. For a discussion of the trope of *humilitas/sublimitas* in relation to Davidic kingship, see
Mazzeo, "Cromwell as Davidic King."

in Chapter 3, during the naval exercises staged in the early 1690s, Peter had adopted the nom de guerre of a Dutch skipper ("Piter") not out of humility but rather to demonstrate his divine calling as the charismatic founder of the imperial Russian navy. Like the incognito king of the Gospels, the tsar had taken on a lowly identity in order to create a new community of believers among those who would accompany him on his mission to transfigure the world. Similarly, after the battle of Hangö, the former Skipper (and current Vice Admiral) donned the dress he had worn at the court of the Holy Roman Emperor, underscoring the connection between the successes of the new Russian fleet and Peter's expansionist foreign policy and thereby strengthening his claims to the much-coveted title of emperor.[88] Both the prominent role of the Prince-Caesar and the relatively humble role of the actual tsar therefore underlined the fact that the organizers of the 1715 St. Petersburg masquerade sought to assert, if as yet only in play, Russia's parity vis-à-vis the imperial and confessional claims of the Catholic kaiser. By counterposing the Holy Roman Emperor and Peter's mock Anti-Caesar, the wedding of one court jester (N. M. Zotov) thus repeated the argument made at the funeral of another (Prince Iu. F. Shakhovskoi).

87. M. M. Bogoslovskii, *Petr I: Materialy dlia biografii* (Moscow and Leningrad, 1941), 2:513–20; and Elena Pogosian, *Petr I: Arkhitektor rossiiskoi istorii* (St. Petersburg, 2001), 210–13.

88. For a discussion of the political and diplomatic maneuvering surrounding Peter's adoption of this title, see Isabel de Madariaga, "Tsar into Emperor: The Title of Peter the Great," in her *Politics and Culture in Eighteenth-Century Russia*, 15–39 (London, 1998); and O. G. Ageeva, "Titul 'imperator' i poniatie 'imperiia' v Rossii v pervoi chetverti XVIII veka," *Mir istorii: Rossiiskii elektronnyi zhurnal* 5 (1999): 1–15, available at http://www.tellur.ru /historia/archive/05/ageyeva.htm.

5   *Fathering the Fatherland*

The enforced merriment of the matrimonial spectacles staged at the court of Peter the Great could not conceal the fact that the tsar's attempts to institute a new dynastic scenario—such as the one that was on public display during the 1712 celebration of his marriage to the newly baptized Catherine Alekseevna—failed to resolve the question of royal succession. Having belatedly legitimized the daughters born to him and Catherine, Peter anxiously awaited the birth of a male heir who might replace Tsarevich Aleksei Petrovich, the child from the tsar's unhappy first marriage to Tsaritsa Evdokiia Fedorovna Lopukhina.[1] Despite Catherine's fecundity and relative youth, however, Peter watched two (or three) boys die, one after the other, before their first birthday.[2] The tsar's apparent inability to father a living male heir raised the hopes of Tsarevich Aleksei and his political advisers, who expected and prayed that the son would outlive his father.[3] And since the Romanovs customarily accorded the firstborn son precedence over the children of a second marriage, Aleksei remained the heir apparent, despite his estrangement from his father, long after Peter had confined Aleksei's mother to a convent in distant Suzdal province.

By the second decade of the eighteenth century, therefore, Peter's political

1. On Tsaritsa Evdokiia, see S. V. Efimov, "Evdokiia Lopukhina—posledniaia russkaia tsaritsa XVII veka," in *Srednevekovaia Rus': Sbornik nauchnykh statei k 65–letiiu . . . R. G. Skrynnikova,* ed. S. V. Lobachev and A. S. Lavrov, 136–65 (St. Petersburg, 1995). For a succinct biography of the tsarevich, see Lindsey Hughes, *Russia in the Age of Peter the Great* (New Haven, 1998), 402–11.

2. For an attempt to determine the exact number of Peter's children, see Lindsey Hughes, "A Note on the Children of Peter the Great," *Study Group on Eighteenth-Century Russia Newsletter* 21 (1993): 10–16; and the Romanov family tree in Hughes, *Russia,* xxi, 399–402.

3. During his interrogation under torture, Aleksei's father confessor, Iakov Ignat'ev, alleged that Aleksei "hoped for his father's death with expressions of joy." Quoted in Hughes, *Russia,* 409.

fortunes can be said to have come full circle and to have resembled the situation that he faced at the beginning of his reign. In many ways, the conflict between Peter and Aleksei parallels the struggle that had brought Peter to power during the regency of Tsarevna Sof'ia Alekseevna. This dynastic dispute, too, took the form of a quarrel between the supporters of two different sides of the royal house. And like the earlier contest between the Miloslavskii and Naryshkin candidates, the dispute between Peter and Aleksei was as much about the legitimacy of royal authority—the criteria by which either claimant to the throne could demonstrate divine sanction for his rule—as it was about the legacy of political and religious reform at the Muscovite court. As before, such an unstable political situation could not have lasted indefinitely. And in fact the bloody resolution of this new dynastic standoff—marked by the religiously sanctioned execution of political rivals (in this case, of Tsarevich Aleksei and his alleged accomplices in a plot to seek Austrian aid in overthrowing and assassinating Peter)—resembled the one imposed in 1689 on Fedor Shaklovityi and his co-conspirators by the Naryshkin faction.[4]

However, the victory of Peter and his supporters over the Lopukhin line of the royal house was now signaled not only by the fatal judicial investigation into the treasonous acts of Tsarevich Aleksei Petrovich but also by the staging of an obscene Yuletide parody of the sacrament of holy orders, in which P. I. "Peter-Prick" (*Petrokhui*) Buturlin, the mock Metropolitan of St. Petersburg, assumed the title and honors of His Holiness the Prince-Pope from his late predecessor, N. M. Zotov. Harking back to the private court spectacle that inaugurated the Transfigured Kingdom, the organizers of the sacred parody enacted during Yuletide 1717–18 at Novo-Preobrazhenskoe sought to rally the believers in Peter's personal gift of grace and to mobilize the Russian political elite against the tsar's personal and political opponents. But unlike before, they were now in a position to use the mock election and ordination of the new Prince-Pope to assert Peter's paternal authority at the expense of both his firstborn son and his (as well as Russia's) spiritual father, the patriarch of Moscow.[5] In fact, some of the same members of the unconsecrated company that personally picked Prince-Pope Zotov's successor would eventually go on both to condemn Tsarevich Aleksei and to support the tsar's decision to abolish the patriarchate. From this perspective, the blasphemous anti-rites of Yuletide 1717–18 appear less as a playful illustration of the tsar's dark sense of humor than as the bacchana-

---

4. For reassessments of the affair of Tsarevich Aleksei, see ibid.; Paul Bushkovitch, "Power and the Historian: The Case of Tsarevich Aleksei (1716–1718) and N. G. Ustrialov (1845–1859)," *Proceedings of the American Philosophical Society* 141 (June 1997): 177–205; and his *Peter the Great: The Struggle for Power, 1671–1725* (Cambridge, 2001), chaps. 9–10.

5. For a discussion of Peter's pretensions to "spiritual paternity" (*dukhovnoe otsovstvo*), the prerogative of the patriarch, see B. A. Uspenskii, "Historia sub specie semioticae," in *Soviet Semiotics: An Anthology*, ed. and trans. Daniel P. Lucid (Baltimore, 1977), 109–10, 114n3.

lian mysteries of an antinomian brotherhood of believers in the imperial cult of the divinely ordained Father of the Fatherland.[6]

A Paternal Testament

As in the course of the 1689 coup, a political manifesto thinly disguised as a personal letter captured the stakes of the dynastic conflict currently raging within the house of Romanov. Indeed, judging by its remarkably wide circulation, both before and after it was included in the officially published case against Tsarevich Aleksei, Peter's 1715 letter to his son—much like the 1689 letter to his half brother (discussed in Chapter 1)—served as the opening salvo in the final showdown between two sides of the royal family over the children of the tsar's first and second marriages.[7] Much of the rhetorical power of this epistolary narrative lies in the juxtaposition of two incompatible types of literary texts: the paternal last will and testament and the political broadside. As the tsar's last testament, Peter's first-person "declaration to my son" partakes of the conventions of the ethical will, a didactic literary genre popular with Russian moralists of all political persuasions.[8] However, the royal author transforms the usual fatherly advice—moral and practical—into a self-serving justification of his declared intention to deprive Aleksei of his rightful inheritance. Chief among his reasons is the heir apparent's unwillingness even "to hear anything about military affairs, [even though it is precisely] by this [that] we have come from darkness into light, and from anonymity into world renown." Singling out the art of war as the only way a young, inexperienced monarch can learn about order and defense—the two things he deems absolutely necessary for the divinely appointed task of ruling a well-ordered realm—the tsar acknowledges that, despite Aleksei's royal blood and sacred vocation, the heir apparent is un-

---

6. For the intimate connection between jokes and blasphemous anti-rites, see Mary Douglas, "Jokes," in *Rethinking Popular Culture: Contemporary Perspectives in Cultural Studies,* ed. Chandra Mukerji and Michael Schudson, 291–310 (Berkeley, 1991). For an argument that the events of Yuletide 1717–18 represent the acme of Peter's black humor, see M. I. Semevskii, "Petr Velikii kak iumorist [1690–1725]," in his *Ocherki i razskazy iz russkoi istorii XVIII v.: Slovo i delo! 1700–1725,* 2nd rev. ed., 278–334 (St. Petersburg, 1884).

7. Peter to Tsarevich Aleksei Petrovich, October 11, 1715, in N. G. Ustrialov, *Istoriia tsarstvovaniia Petra Velikogo* (St. Petersburg, 1859), 6:346–48. The correspondence between Peter and his son opens the evidence collected in the Russian version of the case against the heir apparent, titled *Ob"iavlenie rozysknogo dela i suda po ukazu ego tsarskogo velichestva na tsarevicha Alekseia Petrovicha v Sankt"piterburkhe otpravlennago i po ukazu ego velichestva v pechat', dlia izvestiia vsenarodnago, sego iunia v 25 den', 1718, vydannoe* (St. Petersburg, 1718), which came out in a total press run of 4,536 copies. This case was also immediately translated into German and French. For the publication history, see M. V. Nikolaeva, " 'Testament' Petra I tsarevichu Alekseiu," *XVIII vek* 9 (1974): 93–111, esp. 96n2.

8. For two contemporary examples, see I. T. Pososhkov, *Zaveshchanie otecheskoe, k synu svoemu* [1712–1719], ed. E. M. Prilezhaev (St. Petersburg, 1893); and V. N. Tatishchev, "Dukhovnaia [1734]," in *Izbrannye proizvedeniia,* ed. S. N. Valk (Leningrad, 1979), 133–45.

qualified for his future imperial post.[9] In this way, Peter's attempt to depict himself as a ruler who prudently elevates reasons of state above feelings of paternal affection functions polemically to exclude Tsarevich Aleksei and his progeny from the royal succession.

The "joy" with which Peter surveys the lessons that God has deigned to teach him on the battlefield changes into an "all-consuming sadness" when he turns to the succession and sees that his son "is completely useless for the administration of the affairs of the realm." This accusation serves as the leitmotif of the October manifesto and informs the juxtaposition between the tsarevich's "uselessness" (*nepotrebnost'*) and the exemplary service rendered by the tsar himself and the "true sons of imperial Russia."[10] The repeated invocation of Aleksei's "uselessness" suggests that the tsar pushed past the contemporary meaning of the term—which referred primarily to someone's personal faults[11]—toward a much more polemical and highly charged usage. Indeed, throughout the manifesto of 1715, the tsar insists on linking the secular, neo-Stoic ideal of moral development through martial virtue with the religiously sanctioned notion of obedience to divine and paternal authority.[12]

According to the manifesto of 1715, the real reason that Tsarevich Aleksei refused to join his father on the field of battle, expressed such lukewarm interest in the military arts, and did not partake of "the joy come of God to our fatherland" was that he did not believe Peter was Russia's anointed one. Indeed, according to the biblical parable invoked at the end of Peter's paternal testament, Aleksei's real problem was his lack of faith in the tsar's divine gift of grace. After a long excursus summarizing Aleksei's personal faults and demonstrating his inadequacy for assuming the tasks of rule, Peter picked up the thread of the argument against the tsarevich's candidacy for the throne: "And as I am a man and subject to death, to whom shall I leave what, with God's help, has been sown and the little that has already been raised? To him who, in imitation of the lazy slave from the Gospels, buried his talent in the earth (that is, threw away everything that God gave him)?"[13] This rhetorical invocation of the "lazy slave" refers to a parable from Matthew (Matt. 25:14–30; cf. Luke 19:12–27)—a story strategically positioned immediately before Jesus' triumphal entry into Jerusalem on Palm Sunday, and intended to foreshadow the Messiah's imminent death and resurrection. While the obscure language of Jesus' parable—which is

9. Peter to Tsarevich Aleksei Petrovich, October 11, 1715, in Ustrialov, *Istoriia tsarstvovaniia Petra Velikogo*, 6:346–38.

10. Ibid., 346.

11. I. I. Sreznevskii, *Materialy dlia slovaria drevnerusskogo iazyka*, 3 vols. (St. Petersburg, 1895), 2:412.

12. For a discussion of contemporary European notions about the importance of military training for the cultivation of (Roman imperial) virtues, see Gerhard Oestreich, *Neostoicism and the Early Modern State*, trans. David McLintock (Cambridge, 1982), chaps. 2–5.

13. Peter to Tsarevich Aleksei Petrovich, October 11, 1715, in Ustrialov, *Istoriia tsarstvovaniia Petra Velikogo*, 6:348.

addressed to the faithful and can be understood only by those who are already initiated into the Nazarene's messianic mission ("He who has ears to hear, let him hear!" [Matt. 25:30])—hints at the cosmic significance of the tragic events that are about to take place, the story itself is intended to empower his listeners to spread the good news about the coming Kingdom of God. In this respect, the parable of the talents extols the virtues of faith and evangelism, the twin pillars on which the cult of the crucified Messiah rests. Their invocation in Peter's ultimatum to Aleksei suggests that the tsar intended his firstborn son to draw a similar conclusion regarding the need for order and defense, the twin pillars of the new imperial cult.

In the parable of the talents, a wealthy master (Jesus of Nazareth) entrusts his entire fortune (moral and eschatological teachings) to his slaves (disciples) for safekeeping before embarking on a long trip "to a foreign country." Upon his return from abroad (the Second Coming), the lord questions his servants about what each of them has done with his share of the property (Last Judgment). Those good, faithful, and industrious servants who believed that their lord would return from his voyage and prepared for his return by investing the silver coins (talents) allotted to them in profit-making activities (moral acts aimed to bring about the coming of the Messiah, such as evangelism) received a generous reward and "enter[ed] into the joy of [their] master" (Matt. 25:21, 23; cf. Isa. 61:7). However, the lord is chagrined to discover that one wicked and lazy slave had decided to bury his portion in the ground (Matt. 25:25–26). To escape the wrath of his master, whom he characterized as "a harsh man" who "reap[ed] where [he] did not sow, and gather[ed] where [he] did not scatter seed" (Matt. 25:24), the lazy slave simply resolved to play it safe and take no risks. If the master came back, as he promised, the slave could claim to have guarded the master's treasure; if he stayed away indefinitely, he could still claim to be doing the will of his lord (justification by works); and if he never came back, then there was no reason to make the extra effort required to increase his fortune. Appalled by such sloth and hypocrisy, the vengeful lord chastises the "useless" slave, takes away his share of the property, and throws him out of the house, "into the outer darkness, where there will be weeping and gnashing of teeth"—a biblical expression describing the experiences of those tortured souls who, like the "hypocrites" (*litsemery*), are consigned to the fires of hell (Matt. 25:30; cf. Matt. 24:51).

For Peter and his entourage the biblical parable about the lazy slave and his master clearly had a contemporary political resonance. The story of the master's long voyage to a foreign country—an allegory of Jesus' death—served as a memento mori for a tsar whose recurrent health problems prompted him in 1716–17 to go on a long trip, the final destination of which was a European spa.[14] Peter's version of the parable of the talents provided the necessary background against which to see the apotheosis of its charismatic protago-

14. N. I. Pavlenko, *Petr Velikii* (Moscow, 1990), 374–80, esp. 374.

nist. Adopting the position of the wrathful lord, Peter relegated his firstborn son to the unenviable role of the lazy slave. In this analogy, Tsarevich Aleksei appeared as a good-for-nothing, dissimulating ne'er-do-well who refused to learn his royal trade and therefore simply threw away his God-given talents. In the best tradition of an ethical will, Peter offered his advice, based on a relevant biblical passage, about how the tsarevich could correct his behavior. But the choices that the tsar actually provided his son left very little room for maneuver. "Sadly reflecting" on his inability to "turn [Aleksei] to good by any means"—by neither verbal reprimands nor physical chastisements—Peter effectively made the tsarevich an offer he could not refuse:

> I have decided to write you this last testament and wait a little longer, [to see] if *without hypocrisy* [*nelitsemerno*] you convert [*obratish'sia*]. If this does not happen, be advised that I shall cut you off completely from the succession, like a gangrenous member [*ud" gangrennyi*] [cf. Matt. 5:29–30]. And do not think that [because] you are my only son I write this just to scare you: truly (if God so wills it), I shall carry out [the explicit threat]. For since I do not now and never did spare my own life for my fatherland and people, how can I spare [lit. have pity on] you—a good-for-nothing [*nepotrebnago*]? Better a worthy stranger than one's own good-for-nothing [*svoi nepotrebnyi*].[15]

The fact that the only italicized word in the entire testament refers to Aleksei's alleged "hypocrisy" suggests that one of the most weighty reasons why Peter was never satisfied with his son's repeated pledges of allegiance abided in the tsar's skepticism toward the man whom he imagined as the lazy, good-for-nothing slave of the Gospels. Peter did not want Aleksei's formal obedience to the paternal power of the tsar, just as the lord in Jesus' parable would not accept the cautious actions of the faithless servant who buried his God-given gifts in the ground. Instead, the tsar demanded that his son undergo a political conversion.

Although Peter never specified what he meant by such an act, his model of conversion undoubtedly came from the New Testament, which describes in some detail the formal adoption of belief in the messianic status of Jesus by his first followers. In particular, the apostolic Acts and Epistles reveal that Jesus' earliest followers spent many years trying to decide whether accepting the divinity of Jesus required them to abandon the laws and rituals prescribed by the Hebrew Scriptures. The stubborn persistence of the doctrine of justification by works (whether through charity, special dietary laws, or, most emblematically, circumcision), even under the messianic conditions of the new dispensation heralded by the death and resurrection of the crucified Messiah, explains Paul's repeated attacks on the hypocrisy of recent converts (Gal. 2:11–21), as well as his call for a true, spiritual conversion: "For a person is not a Jew [one of the elect] who is one outwardly,

---

15. Peter to Tsarevich Aleksei Petrovich, October 11, 1715, in Ustrialov, *Istoriia tsarstvovaniia Petra Velikogo*, 6:348.

nor is true circumcision something external and physical. Rather, a person is a Jew who is one inwardly, and real circumcision is a matter of the heart—it is spiritual and not literal" (Rom. 2:28–29). The tsar's admonitions to his son emulate the logic of Paul's arguments against hypocrites. Chastising Aleksei in the terms of Christian neo-Stoicism, Peter asked rhetorically: "Do you plead that your weak health prevents you from carrying [the burden] of martial labors [*trudy*]? But this is no excuse! It is not works [*trudov*] that I require, but only the inclination, which no illness can remove."[16] Echoing Paul's emphasis on the primacy of faith, the tsar stressed that actual belief in his imperial mission—not simply external acts of deference to his paternal power—would be the best proof of the tsarevich's personal devotion to Russia's anointed one.

Urging the tsarevich to rise above the accidents of his birth—"for," according to Peter, "everything contrary" to the new imperial order ultimately "derives" from the tsarevich's association with "the other half" (*ot drugoi poloviny*) of his pedigree (the Lopukhin clan)[17]—the tsar sought to define the new criteria by which to determine whether his son truly deserved to inherit his transfigured realm. The tsarevich's prior behavior demonstrated that neither formal obedience to the tsar's decrees nor the ceremonial performance of his duties—the external signs of political loyalty—constituted enough proof to guarantee his place among the new chosen people, the loyal sons of the All-Russian fatherland. For Tsar Peter, as for the apostle Paul, the performance of these "works" did not demonstrate that a convert to the faith truly believed in the new dispensation. That kind of faith was a matter of conscience, a spiritual "inclination" that could come only from within. And, judging by Peter's second and "final ultimatum" of January 1716, he never really believed that his incorrigibly "hardhearted" firstborn son would convert "without hypocrisy"; for as Peter affirmed here, invoking the authority of the humble psalmist David: "Everyone is a liar" (*vsiak chelovek lozh'*) (Ps. 115:2/Ps. 116:11; cf. Rom. 3:4).[18]

The Yoke of Faith

The spiritual admonitions included in the paternal testament of 1715 suggest that the same uncompromising political vision that informed Peter's approach to his son also shaped his view of the projected renewal of the Russian Orthodox Church. Indeed, the tsar's repeated references to the dichotomy between works and faith demonstrate that the doctrinal justifica-

16. Ibid., 347.
17. Ibid., 348.
18. Peter to Tsarevich Aleksei Petrovich, January 19, 1716, ibid., 349.

tion of ecclesiastical reform was as much a part of the succession struggle between Peter and his heir apparent as the question of imperial renovation. After hinting, in the letter of October 11, 1715, that Aleksei's "laziness" could have dangerous consequences not only for the tsarevich himself but also for the realm, Peter quoted the "truth" contained in one of Paul's epistles to Timothy (I Tim. 3:5): "If someone does not know how to manage his own household, how can he take care of God's church?" This citation, which comes in the context of the fatherly excoriation of Aleksei's faults, suggests that Paul's instructions (I Tim. 3:1–10, 12–13) about the qualities of a good bishop or deacon served as another standard against which Peter judged his "good-for-nothing" son. By this analogy, Peter implied that a "worthless slave" like Tsarevich Aleksei could not be trusted with the task of reforming the Orthodox church—a responsibility he would have to take up upon his confirmation as Peter's legitimate successor.

Peter was certainly not the only one to link the reform of the Russian Orthodox Church with the outcome of the dynastic dispute between the tsar and the heir apparent. In fact, by formulating the problem of Aleksei's political loyalty in terms of belief in the divinely ordained authority of his father and sovereign, Peter echoed contemporary debates among Orthodox clerics about the theological notion of justification (*opravdanie*). As even a brief analysis of the views of Feofan (Prokopovich) (1681–1736), the chief architect of Peter's program of religious reform,[19] will demonstrate, the contemporary theological controversy over the problem of works versus faith derived its explosive power (and its political topicality) from the fact that it addressed many of the same kind of concerns that motivated Peter's paternal testament—a document that turned precisely on the question whether the unprecedented hardships and duties imposed by the tsar's new imperial program represented a bearable burden.

At least part of the reason why Feofan faced such stiff opposition to his ordination as bishop of Pskov derived from the way he celebrated the imperial cult. Indeed, in the letters that Feofan wrote to his friends in Kiev, as well as the sermons he preached immediately upon his arrival in St. Petersburg (1716), he connected his struggle against the supporters of Metropolitan Stefan (Iavorskii), the temporary officeholder (*locum tenans*) of the patriarchal see, with the religious questions raised by the tsar's attempt to deprive the heir apparent of his rightful share of royal patrimony, and particularly with the question of justification by faith. Thus, according to a self-serving account Feofan wrote in 1718, shortly after he had been ordained as the bishop of Pskov, a political conspiracy spearheaded by the

---

19. The classic biography of Feofan is I. A. Chistovich, *Feofan Prokopovich i ego vremia* (St. Petersburg, 1868). See also V. M. Nichik, *Feofan Prokopovich* (Moscow, 1977); James Cracraft, *The Church Reform of Peter the Great* (London, 1971), 49–62; and V. G. Smirnov, *Feofan Prokopovich* (Moscow, 1994).

protégés of Metropolitan Stefan almost succeeded in ending his budding political career before it began.[20] And one of the main points against his candidacy for the post of bishop was Feofan's allegedly Protestant theological position on the question of justification.[21]

This was not the first time that Feofan confronted one of his former colleagues from the Kiev Academy on the issue of what he called "justification by grace through Christ" (*opravdanie chrez Khrista tune*). In fact, one of Feofan's early theological treatises—which he described as a "full" if "hurriedly written . . . tractate on justification," composed in 1712 for his academic course on theology—had already elicited a two-volume refutation from one of the leading opponents to his ordination, Feofilakt (Lopatinskii).[22] In his own polemical treatise Feofan had offered an extended commentary on Paul's repeated confrontations with Peter over the question whether the gentiles needed to be circumcised in order to enter the new covenant heralded by Jesus' death and resurrection (Gal. 2:1–14).[23] Adopting the persona of the "apostle to the uncircumcised," Feofan cast his academic opponents in the roles of the "Judaizers," the early Christian sect that confronted Paul in Galatia, Antioch, and Jerusalem.[24] According to Feofan, his colleagues misinterpreted Peter's words about the "yoke" of the law (Acts 15:10–11) in the same way as had the defenders of the Judaizing

20. See Feofan's letter to the professors of the Kiev Academy (after June 8, 1718), in *Epistolae illustrissimi ac reverendissimi Theophanis Procopovitsch, variis temporibus et ad varios amicos datae*, ed. Samuil (Mislavksii) (Moscow, 1776), no. 6; trans. into Russian by Chistovich, *Feofan Prokopovich*, 33–34, 41–43.

21. In particular, see objections 1–4 in Stefan (Iavorskii), "Poslanie mestobliustitelia patriarsheskogo prestola, riazanskogo mitropolita, Stefana Iavorskogo k preosviashchennomu Varlaamu tverskomu i kashinskomu, 1718," in I. A. Chistovich, *Reshilovskoe delo. Feofan Prokopovich i Feofilakt Lopatinskii. Materialy dlia istorii pervoi poloviny XVIII stoletiia* (St. Petersburg, 1861), app. I.

22. Feofan to Ia. A. Markevich, 1716, in Smirnov, *Feofan Prokopovich*, 187; Feofilakt (Lopatinskii), *Igo Gospodne blago i bremia Ego legko, si est' zakon Bozhii s zapoved'mi svoimi ot prizrachnykh novoiizmyshlennykh osvobozhdaet* (Kiev, 1712), cited in Chistovich, *Feofan Prokopovich*, 19n2.

23. Feofan's 1712 treatise was first published at the end of the eighteenth century in his collected works, *Bogoslovskiie sochineniia* (St. Petersburg, 1774), 4:83–242; it was printed separately as *Knizhitsa, v nei zhe Povest' o raspre Pavla i Varnavy s iudeistvuiushchimi, i trudnost' slova Petra apostola O neudobnonosimom zakonnom ige prostranno predlagaetsia*, ed. N. I. Novikov (Moscow, 1784). For an extensive inventory of Feofan's works, see James Cracraft, "Feofan Prokopovich: A Bibliography of His Works," *Oxford Slavonic Papers* 8 (1975): 1–36.

24. The Greek verb "to Judaize" is found only in the New Testament, in the context of Paul's rebuke of Peter (Gal. 2:14). In the ancient sources, the noun "Judaizer" and the verb "to Judaize" refer primarily to the actions of gentiles. While the verb can be used to designate the forced conversion of gentiles to Judaism, it normally refers to the adoption of Jewish customs by gentiles without conversion. However one defines the profile of these Judaizers, it is clear that their "different gospel" (Gal. 1:6) included such Jewish practices as circumcision (Gal. 5:1–6), the celebration of feasts according to the Jewish calendar (Gal. 4:10), and the keeping of Jewish dietary laws. See James W. Aageson, "Judaizing," in *The Anchor Bible Dictionary*, ed. David Noel Freedman et al. (New York, 1992), 3:1089; and Karl P. Donfried, "Peter," ibid., 5:251–63.

heresy.[25] In both cases, the pedantic insistence on the performance of the law—whether through the compulsory circumcision of converts or, (as in the case of Kiev), through the veneration of unattested Orthodox relics and icons—only serves to conceal the fact that God's grace is given freely (*tune*) to all who believe in Christ. The conclusion that Feofan wanted people to draw was that true religious enlightenment occurs when the diligent student of theology realizes the truth contained in his rational exposition of the facts and learns to distinguish sincere piety from the hypocritical and scholastic religion of "our own Latinizers" (*latinshchiki*)—Feofan's derogatory term for the alleged admirers of the Roman Catholic Church among the other graduates of the Kiev Academy called to serve in the Russian church.[26] Thus what mattered to the Ukrainian monk who would soon become the tsar's ecclesiastical protégé was the spiritual inclination toward the Lord, not the extravagant display of personal piety.

In his very first St. Petersburg sermon, Feofan quickly conflated his critique of unenlightened hypocrisy—which came out of his doctrinal position on the question of justification by faith—with the tsar's views about the purely formal, external obedience of his firstborn son. Under the guidance of A. D. Menshikov and several unnamed "senators" who favored the tsar's plan to exclude Tsarevich Aleksei from the inheritance, Feofan grasped the crux of the succession struggle and tailored his speech to fit the occasion.[27] On October 29, 1716, just five days after his arrival in the new imperial capital, Feofan delivered a panegyrical oration in honor of the birth of Tsarevich Peter Petrovich, the long-awaited issue of Peter's second marriage and the "universally acknowledged hope" for the continuation of his reformist legacy.[28] This birthday sermon gave Feofan the opportunity to present himself as the "one and seemingly the only" ecclesiastical leader willing to take up the burden of defending Peter's reforms and in particular of justifying the tsar's new dynastic scenario by catechizing the St. Petersburg political elite during the tsar's second trip abroad.[29] From the pulpit of the St. Petersburg Trinity Cathedral, Feofan publicly acknowledged the hereditary claims of the one-year-old Peter Petrovich, the "royal seed" that promised to take

25. Addressing a council of church elders who had gathered in Jerusalem to decide whether to accept the proposition that "unless you are circumcised according to the custom of Moses, you cannot be saved" (Acts 15:1), Peter asks: "Why are you putting God to the test by placing on the neck of the disciples a yoke that neither our fathers [the Jews] nor we [the Jewish Christians] have been able to bear. On the contrary, we believe that we will be saved through the grace of the Lord Jesus Christ, just as they [the uncircumcised gentiles] will." The opinion recorded by Luke coincides with Paul's position in Gal. 2:7–9. See Donfried, "Peter," 254.

26. Feofan to Ia. A. Markevich, 1716, in Chistovich, *Feofan Prokopovich*, 38.

27. For a description of Feofan's first meeting with Prince Menshikov, see ibid., 25–26.

28. Feofan (Prokopovich), "Slovo pokhval'noe v den' rozhdestva blagorodneishago gosudaria tsarevicha i velikogo kniazia Petra Petrovicha" (October 29, 1716), in his *Sochineniia*, ed. I. P. Eremin (Moscow and Leningrad, 1961), 38–48, 463.

29. For Feofan's exaggerated and self-aggrandizing claims, see Feofan to Ia. A. Markevich, 1716, in Chistovich, *Feofan Prokopovich*, 26.

root and the only hope for the future "bliss of the All-Russian realm." Significantly, Feofan mentioned Tsarevich Aleksei only once, at the end of the sermon, and then only in a clause in which the female members of the Russian royal family are urged to recognize the divine favor visited upon them through the birth of their new brother, Tsarevich Peter Petrovich.[30] Feofan's polemical juxtaposition of the tsar's two sons thus echoed Paul's argument (Rom. 9:8) that "it is not the children of the flesh who are the children of God, but the children of the promise who are counted as descendants."

Feofan drove home this point early in 1718, in a "Sermon on royal power and authority, how it is established in the world by God himself, and how men are obliged to honor tsars and obey them, and who the people are who oppose them, and how great is the sin they have," delivered in front of the tsar and the entire political elite of St. Petersburg on Palm Sunday.[31] In the course of his defense of the tsar's campaign of terror against anyone suspected of supporting Aleksei, Feofan also scored a victory against his own ecclesiastical rivals, who had accused him of Protestant heresy in the theological controversy over justification. Thanks to his rhetorical strategy, he not only successfully defended himself against the charges but also managed to declare his own (and to enjoin others to declare their) wholehearted commitment to the tsar's new dynastic scenario, as spelled out in the manifesto of February 3, 1718—the document that officially deprived Tsarevich Aleksei of the inheritance and named Tsarevich Petr Petrovich as the heir apparent.[32]

Without mentioning their names, Feofan's Palm Sunday sermon relegated Stefan (Iavorskii) and his protégés to the ranks of those hypocritical, ungrateful, and politically unreliable clerics who had allegedly supported Aleksei's challenge to his father's God-given authority. Using the story of Jesus' triumphal entry into Jerusalem to make a contemporary political reference to the widespread support that Aleksei enjoyed in clerical circles, Feofan placed the fault for these developments squarely on the shoulders of all those who refused to recognize the Davidic pedigree of the divinely anointed "King of Israel," simply because their reason had been "obscured by rabbinic [scholastic] traditions."[33] Here, as in the 1712 treatise on justification, Feofan's old rivals appeared in the guise of their evil biblical prototypes, the "Judaizers," "arch-hierarchs," "scribes," and "holy Pharisees." Hinting at the typological comparison that would form the basis for the official interpretation of the case of Tsarevich Aleksei—the "new Absalom"

30. "Slovo pokhval'noe," in Feofan (Prokopovich), *Sochineniia*, 38–39, 48.

31. For the text of this Easter sermon, see Feofan (Prokopovich), "Slovo o vlasti i chesti tsarskoi . . . ," ibid., 76–93 (hereafter "Slovo"); and "Sermon on Royal Authority and Honor . . . ," trans. Horace G. Lunt, in *Russian Intellectual History: An Anthology*, ed. Marc Raeff, 14–30 (New York, 1966) (hereafter "Sermon").

32. For the text of this manifesto, see Ustrialov, *Istoriia tsarstvovaniia Petra Velikogo*, 6:443–44.

33. "Sermon," 27, 14–16; "Slovo," 90, 76–77.

of imperial Russian history[34]—Feofan argued that those clerics who had supposedly supported the fugitive tsarevich rebelled against the divine basis of royal rule, as embodied in King David; and like his disobedient and ungrateful son, they deserved to die at the hands of their lord and master.

Feofan's refutation of those who cited the Gospel of Luke (16:15) to excuse political disobedience reveals that he was keenly aware of previous comparisons between Peter and the humble psalmist, who was himself a "type" of Christ. In the Palm Sunday sermon, Feofan attacked those "hypocritical" clerics whose "outward poverty, . . . gloomy faces, and . . . whole Pharisee hide" arouse "admiration in men" solely in order to "deceive the hearts of the innocent." Countering their assertions, Feofan argued that God's word was not directed at the "high esteem of government authorities, for the lowliness that God loves is found also in purple robes when a king confesses before God that he is sinful and places his hopes solely in God's mercy, as did David, Constantine, Theodosius, and the rest. On the contrary, the Pharisee's high esteem lives even in a beggar's dress."[35] Feofan's imperial genealogy suggested not only that Peter—like the first Christian rulers of the Eastern Roman Empire—had inherited the God-given responsibility for reforming the church, but also that, like King David, he embodied the paradoxical combination of humility and sublimity typical of the kenotic Christ. As we saw in Chapter 4, precisely such an oxymoronic combination of opposites characterized the choice of costumes selected for Peter and his mock double during the 1715 masquerade that accompanied the carnivalesque wedding of the Prince-Pope of the Transfigured Kingdom.

Invoking the highly charged anti-Catholic rhetoric unveiled against the Latinizers back in his days as the rector of the Kiev-Mohyla Academy, Feofan implied that his Orthodox rivals were infected with the "papist spirit" (*papezhskii dukh*)—the dangerous and erroneous belief that unlike all the other orders of society, the clergy was exempt from the duties of service and loyalty to the tsar.[36] Foreshadowing the point he was to make just a few years later, in the *Ecclesiastical Regulation* of 1721, Feofan argued that regardless of whether this Orthodox "papalism" issued from a sense of

---

34. Aleksei's new sobriquet was based on the biblical story (II Sam. 15–18) about the rebellion and death of King David's son, Absalom. For an explicit reference to the "example of Absalom" (*Avessalomov priklad*), see the royal decree of June 13, 1718, addressed to the clergy, as well as their collective verdict (June 18, 1718) against Tsarevich Aleksei, both in Ustrialov, *Istoriia tsarstvovaniia Petra Velikogo*, 6:516, 518–19, 520, 522–23. This biblical reference is also implicit in the manifesto of February 3, 1718, depriving Aleksei of the throne; the royal decree of June 13, 1718, addressed to the secular ranks, and their collective verdict (June 24, 1718), all ibid., 438–44, 516, 529–36. Aleksei's "Absalom-like malice" (*Avesalomskaia zlost'*) is also cited in the new imperial law on succession, "Ustav o nasledstvii prestola rossiiskogo" (February 5, 1722), in *Zakonodatel'nye akty Petra I*, ed. A. Voskresenskii (Moscow and Leningrad, 1945), 175. On the story of Absalom and David as the official point of view on the affair of Tsarevich Aleksei, see Nikolaeva, " 'Testament,' " 96.

35. "Sermon," 18–19; "Slovo," 80–81.

36. "Sermon," 25; "Slovo," 88.

puffed-up pride in their own exalted spiritual calling, a "misanthropic" disdain "for anything wondrous, merry, great, and glorious," or a mistaken belief that nothing useful can be accomplished without the Russian Orthodox patriarch, the philosophizing of the Latinizers sowed the seeds of heresy, treason, and domestic unrest. Seduced by the "mellowed words" and affected "emotional countenance" of Baroque preachers, good Christians—not to mention the "simple and ignorant" rabble—could easily be led astray into the belief that the Russian Orthodox patriarch (or his *locum tenans*) was a "second sovereign."[37] Drawing on his earlier attacks against the homiletic style of Jesuits, Uniates, and their Orthodox imitators, Feofan's renewed attack against the so-called Latinizers thus took on the contours of the argument he would later use to justify the tsar's decision to abolish the patriarchate and institute an Ecclesiastical College in its stead.[38]

Summarizing the points he had already made in his 1712 treatise on Paul's confrontation with the Judaizers, Feofan also argued that the failure to understand the fundamental difference between the conventions associated with paying respect to Orthodox clerics and the immutable laws regarding the authorities—that is, between "ritual" and "moral" law—led the Latinizers and their ignorant followers to misinterpret the apostle Peter's words about the yoke of the law. In turn, this fundamental theological error caused them to reject the "truth" contained in Feofan's sermon: that a well-ordered realm could have only one supreme law, the divinely inspired natural law that was "written in the hearts of men" (Rom. 2:14–15) and that commanded all Orthodox believers to obey the decrees of Russia's "anointed one" (*khristos*).[39] And since man had a conscience, "which itself is also the seed of God," in the final analysis, that obedience could not be coerced; in other words, political loyalty, like religious belief, had to come straight from the heart. By citing fully most of the biblical allusions of Peter's paternal testament, Feofan's Palm Sunday oration thus argued that true "Christian freedom" lay precisely in the inner burden of faith.[40] The invocation of justification in the context of a defense of royal authority demonstrates Feofan's awareness of the important role of this question in the succession struggle between Peter and Aleksei. It also lends credence to the hypothesis that Feofan used the opportunity provided by the investigation into the affair of Tsarevich Aleksei to silence his longtime rivals by associating them with the recently uncovered clerical opposition. Feofan's

37. "Sermon," 17–18, 23–25; "Slovo," 79–80, 86, 88. According to Feofan, this explains the ease with which the ignorant "common people" could be enticed into heresy, or worse, into treasonous "words and deeds" against the tsar. See Alexander V. Muller, ed., *The Spiritual Regulation of Peter the Great* (Seattle, 1972), 10–11.

38. For Feofan's criticism of "Polish eloquence," see Chistovich, *Feofan Prokopovich*, 9–13, 39; and James Cracraft, "Feofan Prokopovich and the Kiev Academy," in *Russian Orthodoxy under the Old Regime*, ed. Theofanis George Stavrou and Robert L. Nichols (Minneapolis, 1978), 53–54.

39. "Sermon," 22, 16, and "Slovo," 84–85.

40. "Sermon," 17–19; "Slovo," 79.

panegyric therefore not only branded his theological rivals as dangerous papists; it also presented Feofan himself as the spokesman of a new, more rational Orthodoxy and as the most ardent defender of Peter's God-given authority.

After explaining the reasons why the tsar's subjects must obey him as God's anointed, Feofan went on to explain why they must also heed him as Father of the Fatherland. Echoing the tsar's letter to his son, Feofan argued that "our monarch, [like] all monarchs," expects his subjects to fulfill their filial duty "to honor the authorities sincerely and conscientiously"—"un-hypocritically," as Peter had written in his paternal testament—in accordance with God's injunction to "honor thy father" (Exod. 20:12). "For," the preacher asked rhetorically, "if Christians have to be subject even to willful and pagan rulers, how much more must they be utterly obligated to true-believing and true-judging sovereigns?" The answer is clear: while the former are merely despotic "masters," who administer their patrimony like an estate populated by serfs—that is, for their own personal benefit and perhaps for the benefit of their own house—the latter are also "fathers," who are responsible for the general welfare of the entire realm. Entrusted with the God-given authority to ensure "the life, the integrity, and the welfare of a whole great people," the Orthodox sovereign possesses "the primary and ultimate degree of fatherhood."[41] Feofan's attempt to distinguish between patrimonial and legal rule—one of the first self-conscious efforts in Russian political thought to locate sovereignty outside the person of the monarch—here transcends the sordid realities of the moment to make a more general observation about the religious and political ideals embodied in the notion of a Russian imperial "fatherland" (*otechestvo*). His discussion of the difference between pagan and imperial Christian rule also hints at the honorific title by which the Romans addressed their emperor (*pater patriae*). Indeed, the appearance of the Russian translation of the Latin term for "Father of the Fatherland" (*otets otechestva*) in Feofan's Easter sermon foreshadowed by more than three years the tsar's decision to accept that very title from the official representatives of imperial Russia.[42]

At the end of his sermon, Feofan invoked the elite's sense of honor, as well as its fear of earthly punishment and eternal damnation, to hammer home the point about the honors due to the founding father of imperial Russia.[43] Focusing on the same twin aspects of imperial rule that the tsar had outlined in the 1715 letter to his son—order and defense—Feofan iden-

41. "Sermon," 25; "Slovo," 87.

42. Feofan had referred to Peter by this Roman epithet as early as 1709, in a panegyric on the victory at Poltava. See Hughes, *Russia*, 97. For an even earlier reference, see V. M. Zhivov, "Kul'turnye reformy v sisteme preobrazovanii Petra I," in *Iz istorii russkoi kul'tury*, ed. A. D. Koshelev (Moscow, 1996), 3:549–50.

43. "Slovo," 91–92; "Sermon," 28–29. The phrase about "hammering home" his point derives from Feofan's description of the way Paul the Apostle repeats his message that there is no power except from God, "as though pounding with a hammer" (*aki mlatom tolchet*). Feofan's

tified the "renewal" of the "fatherland" with the man (*sei;* cf. *Ecce homo*) who had "given birth" (*otrodil*) to the new Russia, both literally, in the person of the new heir apparent, and metaphorically, in the new patriotic ideal acknowledged by the assembled representatives of the political nation. Implicitly addressing his listeners as the true sons of the fatherland, the court preacher appealed to contemporary notions about the procreative powers of fathers, the classical Roman ideals of patriotism, and the imperatives of divine and natural law to shame the congregation into realizing that "the doctrine presented here about [the divine nature of] royal authority is indeed the truth," and therefore must be conscientiously obeyed, on pain of eternal punishment of their immortal souls.[44] By urging his audience to receive the earthly tsar with the same awe and respect with which the people of Jerusalem received the heavenly Tsar, the new official court preacher thus made a very deliberate parallel between the redemptive suffering of the son of God and the personal tribulations experienced by Russia's Father of the Fatherland.[45] In both cases only those chosen few who "walked near the light" of Mount Tabor would ever be able to recognize the gift of grace possessed by their divinely anointed leader and participate fully in the imminent transfiguration of the world.[46] And in both cases those chosen few constituted the intimate inner circle of the royal disciples.

High Priests

As the only group within the Muscovite political elite who even came close to matching the zeal with which Feofan extolled the virtues of obedience to the tsar, the members of Peter's Transfigured Kingdom—including the high priests of its mock ecclesiastical council—formed a crucial linchpin in the tsar's attempt to father the Fatherland. Although by the first decade of the eighteenth century the members of this unconsecrated company had become important political players in the expanding bureaucracy of the

words about the rhetorical strategy of the "apostle to the uncircumcised" sheds light on the way he saw his own mission in Muscovy. See "Sermon," 22; "Slovo," 84.

44. "Sermon," 29; "Slovo," 93.

45. On Feofan's self-conscious use of the homology of the earthly and heavenly kings, see the translator's comment in "Sermon," 15n1. Despite Feofan's protestation that he had no intention of making a direct comparison between "the earthly tsar [*zemnogo tsaria*] and the heavenly one," he proceeded to argue that "we have models in God's Word for taking God's honor and love to be a reason for man's love and honor, not in equality [*v ravenstvo*] but as an example [*v priklad*]." See ibid., 15; "Slovo," 76–77. In an earlier sermon, Feofan had already played up the comparison between the divinely anointed "suffering servant" (Isa. 53:11–12) and Russia's warrior-tsar. See Feofan (Prokopovich), "Slovo v nedeliu osmuiunadesiat' . . ." (October 23, 1717), in his *Sochineniia,* 67; and the translation in Nicholas V. Riasanovsky, *The Image of Peter the Great in Russian History and Thought* (New York, 1985), 12–13.

46. I am here putting a positive spin on Feofan's reference to the "blindness" (*slepota*) of the apostles, as well as on his excoriation of all those "chosen people" whose "theology was blind, filled with many foolish fables, so it knew not the Messiah either by his person or by his deeds." See "Sermon," 15; "Slovo," 76–77.

well-ordered police state, with their own relatively independent administrative bailiwicks, Peter never missed an opportunity to remind them that they owed their livelihoods (and their lives) to the unrestrained, unrestricted, and uncodified charisma of the divinely anointed warrior tsar. So while the mechanisms of state administration did undergo an unmistakable process of bureaucratization, at the end of Peter's reign, as at the beginning, his intimates continued to derive their legitimacy from their close association with the royal person (as was the case elsewhere in Europe).[47] And participation in the rituals of the Transfigured Kingdom was as central to the tsar's style of rule as to his courtiers' sense of election. This is part of the reason why the blasphemous ceremonies staged at Yuletide 1717–18 offer such a good way of analyzing how Peter's company could successfully integrate the political execution of Russia's heir apparent and the abolition of the patriarchate into the court's charismatic authority structure. By putting the mock election and ordination of Prince-Pope P. I. Buturlin and Prince-Caesar I. F. Romodanovskii into the context of the political practices and allegorical language by which the tsar and his advisers (secular and religious) justified the excision of Aleksei's "gangrenous member" from the Russian body politic, we can thus attempt to understand some of the mechanisms by which an important segment of the Russian political elite came to accept Peter's grandiose claims to greatness.

The way the tsar and his unconsecrated company chose to cope with the almost simultaneous deaths of Prince F. Iu. Romodanovskii and N. M. Zotov demonstrated Peter's eagerness to resolve his own succession question once and for all.[48] At the beginning of October 1717, immediately upon his arrival in St. Petersburg after an eighteen-month voyage to Western Europe, the tsar was informed of the newest political developments from "Pressburg," the capital of his play world. His source of information was none other than Prince Ivan Fedorovich (c. 1678–1730), the last surviving heir of the Romodanovskii clan.[49] In a letter written September 21,

47. For an insightful discussion of the ways in which access to the person of the monarch determined one's position at court and in the state bureaucracy, see David Starkey, "Representation through Intimacy: A Study in the Symbolism of Monarchy and Court Office in Early Modern England," in *Symbols and Sentiments: Cross-Cultural Studies in Symbolism*, ed. Ioan Lewis, 187–224 (London, 1977); and his "Court History in Perspective," in *The English Court: From the Wars of the Roses to the Civil War*, ed. Starkey, 1–24 (London, 1987); as well as John Adamson, "The Making of the *Ancien-Régime* Court, 1500–1700," in *The Princely Courts of Europe: Ritual, Politics and Culture under the* Ancien Régime, *1500–1750*, ed. Adamson (London, 1999), 7–10. For the Russian case, see Bushkovitch, *Peter*, passim; and John P. LeDonne, "Ruling Families in the Russian Political Order, 1689–1825," *Cahiers du monde russe et soviétique* 28, no. 3–4 (1987): 233–322.

48. Prince Romodanovskii died in Moscow on September 17, 1717, just six days before Zotov. See *Pokhodnyi zhurnal 1717 goda* (St. Petersburg, 1855), 36.

49. Biographical information on Prince I. F. Romodanovskii, including his approximate age, can be found in A. Petrov, "Romodanovskii, kn. Ivan Fedorovich," *RBS* 17:120–24 (New York, 1962); and M. D. Khmyrov, *Grafinia Ekaterina Ivanovna Golovkina i ee vremia (1701–1791 gg.). Istoricheskii ocherk po arkhivnym dokumentam* (St. Petersburg, 1867), 52, 77.

1717, four days after his father's death, Prince Romodanovskii notified his "Most Merciful Great Sovereign" of their mutual loss:

> By the will of the Almighty, at one o'clock in the afternoon of September 17, death struck down my father, Prince Fedor Iur'evich. Until Your Royal Highness commands, his body has been placed in the Church of the Three Prelates, which is located near the Earthen City, on Butcher's [Street in Moscow]. With the most bitter tears of a complete orphan, I run to Your protection. Reminding Your Tsarist Highness of my father's services with respect to Your Most Luminous Majesty [*maestatu*], I beg that Your Highness's merciful commands and charity will not abandon me, a complete orphan. Your Tsarist Highness's slave, Ivan Romodanovskii.[50]

In this carefully crafted letter, Prince Romodanovskii combined the formulaic language of a petition with the emotional appeal of a supplication. Indeed, the figurative language of Romodanovskii's epistle evokes the "tearful" prayers of pious Orthodox believers—the "orphans" and "slaves" who pour into the church on the feast of the Protective Veil (*Pokrov*) of the Virgin to beg for the intercession of the Mother of God.[51] However, adopting the kind of language favored by Peter and his company, this knowledgeable Muscovite courtier addressed his prayers not to the heavenly Mary but to the earthly Peter, the only authority who could guarantee the Romodanovskiis' salvation in the here and now.

By using the new Russian translation of the classical Roman (and contemporary European) term for regal splendor, *maestat,* the young Prince Romodanovskii sought to underline his father's career as the anti-Caesar, the mock sovereign whose antics only served to emphasize the true majesty and imperial pedigree of the tsar. The tsar's response to Romodanovskii's pathetic attempt to curry royal favor revealed just how much Peter valued the personal contribution of the Prince-Caesar: "I received your letter of 21 September upon arrival in which you inform me of the death of your father, for which I offer deepest condolences that he did not lose his life as a result of old age but from an attack of gangrene; still, there goes everyone one way or another by God's will, bear this in mind and don't give in to grief. And please don't imagine that I have abandoned you, or forgotten your father's good deeds. I shall write to you anon about the time and place of the burial."[52] So, for more than a month after his death, the body of Prince F. Iu. Romodanovskii, the dreaded investigator of Peter's secret police chancellery and mock tsar of "Pressburg," lay in state in the Moscow Church of the Three Prelates. The delay, however, was less a sign of Peter's indifference to the fate of this old princely family than of his frantic preparations for the criminal investigation into the case of his firstborn son. In fact, as we will

---

50. RGADA, f. 9, otd. 2, op. 3, ch. 2 (1717), kn. 33, ll. 445r–v.
51. For a discussion of the symbolism associated with this Orthodox feast day, see M. B. Pliukhanova, *Siuzhety i simvoly Moskovskogo tsarstva* (St. Petersburg, 1995), chap. 1.
52. SPb F IRI RAN, f. 270, d. 84, l. 179, as quoted in Hughes, *Russia*, 373, 543n159.

see, despite the tsar's apparent neglect, Romodanovskii *fils et père* were never far from Peter's thoughts at this time.

During the investigation into the affair of Tsarevich Aleksei, Prince I. F. Romodanovskii became as important to the fulfillment of Peter's dynastic scenario as Prince F. Iu. Romodanovskii had been to the articulation of the tsar's imperial project. In both cases, the Romodanovskiis acted as the tsar's personal doubles, doing things that Peter would not or perhaps could not do for himself. Primary among them was administering the chancellery entrusted with investigating all cases of lèse-majesté. Although Peter handed over the responsibility of trying Aleksei to the special investigative commission headed by P. A. Tolstoi (1653–1729)—the wily diplomat who succeeded in enticing the tsar's prodigal son back to Russia—Prince Romodanovskii played a role consistent with his heritage.[53] Soon after the tsar dispatched his letter of condolence, he had a private chat with the grieving prince. In the course of this unrecorded conversation, Peter promised to allow Ivan Fedorovich to inherit the important administrative position once occupied by his father. In addition, Peter vowed to treat him with the same half-joking formality with which he had treated his father. Although the tsar did not send a written confirmation of this verbal agreement until February 21, 1718, almost immediately Peter began referring to Ivan Fedorovich by the mock royal title of his late predecessor.[54] A private conversation on the eve of the investigation into the case of Tsarevich Aleksei Petrovich thus inaugurated the reign of Prince-Caesar Ivan Fedorovich Romodanovskii.

The tsar's acceptance of the principles of primogeniture and administrative continuity with respect to the Romodanovskii heir contrasted sharply with his efforts to deprive Tsarevich Aleksei of the right to the throne.[55] The tsar's unconsecrated company had long ago come to identify Prince Ivan Fedorovich as the heir apparent to Prince-Caesar F. Iu. Romodanovskii. For example, as early as June 21, 1706, the tsar, in his capacity as the dutiful

53. For the career of P. A. Tolstoi, the great-grandfather of the nineteenth-century novelist, see N. I. Pavlenko, *Ptentsy gnezda Petrova* (Moscow, 1984), 109–232, esp. 188–204; N. Tolstoy, *The Tolstoys: Twenty Generations of Russian History, 1353–1983,* 2nd ed. (New York, 1985), 83–90; and D. O. Serov, *Stroiteli imperii: Ocherki gosudarstvennoi i kriminal'noi deiatel'nosti spodvizhnikov Petra I* (Novosibirsk, 1996), 29n50, 113–16, 129n60, 251.

54. By couching his decision in the form of a humble request more typical of a plaintiff's petition or subordinate's report, Peter's five-line note confirmed his intention to reestablish the playful hierarchical relationship that he had cultivated with the previous Prince-Caesar. See Peter to Prince I. F. Romodanovskii, February 21, 1718, in RGIA, f. 1329, op. 1, d. 65, l. 213; nineteenth-century copy in SPb F IRI RAN, f. 270, kn. 87, l. 185; published by P. Baranov, *Opis' vysochaishim ukazam i poveleniiam, khraniashchikhsia v Senatskom arkhive, 1704–1725* (St. Petersburg, 1872), 1:48.

55. These principles were consistent, however, with new Petrine legislation on entailed noble estates, particularly the so-called Law of Single Inheritance (March 23, 1714). For a discussion of this important piece of legislation, a precursor of the 1722 decree asserting the monarch's legal right to appoint his own heir as he saw fit, see Hughes, *Russia,* 176–77, 95–96; Lee A. Farrow, "Peter the Great's Law of Single Inheritance: State Imperatives and Noble Resistance," *Russian Review* 55 (1996): 430–47; and the editor's introduction to *Peter the Great and His Law on the Imperial Succession: An Official Commentary,* ed. Antony Lentin (Oxford, 1996).

subject ("Piter"), congratulated "His Highness on this, the name day of your son, and our Sovereign, Tsarevich and Grand Prince Ioann Fedorovich."[56] In the same letter, the tsar went on to inform his mock superior that "your royal uncle, the Right Reverend [Bishop] Mickey [*preosviashchennyi Mishura*]"—the joking episcopal name by which Prince M. G. Romodanovskii (1653–1713), privy counselor, military commander, and future governor general of Moscow, was apparently known to the members of the tsar's company—passed around quite a few "cups," so that everyone could drink to the health of the twenty-eight-year-old "tsarevich."[57] In the current dynastic situation, all such references to the mock tsarevich acquired sinister political connotations. Indeed, the tsar's elevation of Prince-Caesar Romodanovskii's legitimate heir only underlined the illegitimacy of Tsarevich Aleksei.[58]

To make sure that all the courtiers who would be involved in the sensitive investigation into the private lives of Tsarevich Aleksei and his mother understood these allusions, the tsar decided to convene his entire unconsecrated company.[59] At the beginning of December 1717, just one month before the fugitive tsarevich returned to Moscow, Peter asked his personal secretary to begin preparations for the parodic election of a new Prince-Pope. On December 10, 1717, the cabinet secretary A. V. Makarov (c. 1680–1740) dispatched the following missive to A. I. Ushakov (1670/72–1747), an officer of the Preobrazhensk guards regiment and one of the tsar's most trusted adjutants: "His Tsarist Highness has ordered to notify you in writing that he requires you to have his royal mansion [*khoromy*] repaired immediately, so that [it] will be completely ready by his arrival [in Moscow]. Also, be so kind as to repair the mansion on the Iauza, in the little city of Pressburg, where the election of the Caesar and Pope

---

56. *PiB*, 4:305; and Petrov, "Romodanovskii," 121. In an earlier letter, Peter had offered congratulations (as was his "humble duty") on the birth of a son to "our sovereign's son" (i.e., to Prince I. F. Romodanovskii), wishing the boy long life with the increase of his grandfather's reign as Prince-Caesar. See Peter to F. Iu. Romodanovskii, November 21, 1704, in *PiB*, 3:195, cited in Hughes, *Russia*, 99.

57. Peter to Prince F. Iu. Romodanovskii, July 21, 1706, *PiB*, 4:305; and Petrov, "Romodanovskii," 121. For a biography of Prince M. G. Romodanovskii, see B. Modzalevskii's article in *RBS*, 17:126.

58. Despite the fact that it must have underlined his own vulnerability, Tsarevich Aleksei Petrovich played along with his father's companions, even going so far as to address Prince F. Iu. Romodanovskii as "big sovereign" (*bol'shoi gosudar'*) and his son as "little sovereign." See Tsarevich Aleksei Petrovich to Prince F. Iu. Romodanovskii, February 1708, in *PiB*, 7 (1): 24–25, cited in Hughes, *Russia*, 443–44, 551n135.

59. In the course of the investigation into Aleksei's links with his mother, royal investigators discovered that Tsaritsa Evdokiia Lopukhina had not taken the veil, although she had been sent to the Intercession convent in Suzdal nearly twenty years earlier. In essence, by refusing to grant the tsar a proper divorce, she created a situation that threatened not only the validity of Peter's marriage to Catherine but also his entire dynastic scenario. For a discussion of this important point, one of the tsar's main concerns during the investigation into the so-called Suzdal affair, see Efimov, "Evdokiia Lopukhina," 136–65; Bushkovitch, "Power and the Historian," 388–90, 396–401; and Serov, *Stroiteli imperii*, 60–61n75.

usually takes place."[60] Since Peter and his suite left St. Petersburg on December 15, just as soon as the post roads were once again passable in winter, Major Ushakov did not have much time to fix up the dilapidated wooden structures before the tsar's arrival. By Christmas Eve, Peter was already in Novo-Preobrazhenskoe, writing a letter to A. D. Menshikov, who was left behind to maintain order in the new capital while Peter dealt with his son in the old one.[61] Thus at the height of the Yuletide season of 1717–18, in the tense days immediately preceding the arrival of Tsarevich Aleksei and the start of the investigation into the reasons for his treasonous flight to the Holy Roman Empire, the tsar proceeded to stage the election of a new Prince-Pope in the old mock capital of his Transfigured Kingdom.

Despite a wealth of (mostly undated) documents about the ceremonial election and ordination of the Prince-Pope who succeeded N. M. Zotov (some of them in Peter's own hand), the archival file that contains a description of this particular carnivalesque spectacle does not allow us to reconstruct the events that took place in "Pressburg" at Yuletide 1717–18 with any degree of certainty.[62] Our only piece of solid evidence for the events of the time in question consists of a letter from P. I. Buturlin, the former "Metropolitan of St. Petersburg" and Zotov's first successor to the (in)dignity of Prince-Pope. In this obscene missive, dated December 28, 1717, and addressed to the "Princess Abbess of St. Petersburg," the "Most Drunken and Most Foolish Mother, beloved mother-in-law of Bacchus"—D. G. Rzhevskaia—the new mock pontiff announced that

> on the 28th day of this month, by the will of the universal Prince-Caesar and the entire Extravagant Council, yours truly, unworthy that I am, was elected, and on the 29th elevated to the most high throne of the Prince-Pope. And because Our Intemperance has always promised to take good care of Our flock, that is why I have not forgotten about you, our ancient nun-prick [*monakhuinia*, combining *monakhinia*, nun, and *khui*, prick] and mentor. I have presented your exploits to His Highness, the Prince-Caesar, and to the entire Council, which is why [they] have deigned [to accept my suggestion about your promotion]. So, standing up with my body and witnessing with my soul, by the power vested in me by Bacchus, I promote you from the degree of Princess

60. RO RNB, f. 874, op. 2, kn. 207, ll. 38, 55 (two nineteenth-century copies of the original letter, located in RGADA, f. 9, otd. 2, ch. 1). For a biography of A. V. Makarov, see Pavlenko, *Ptentsy gnezda Petrova*, 233–308. On the career of A. I. Ushakov, see Hughes, *Russia*, 427; Serov, *Stroiteli imperii*, 79, 96n62, 252; and I. Iu. Airapetian, "Feodal'naia aristokratiia v period stanovleniia absoliutizma v Rossii" (Diss. kand. ist. nauk, M. V. Lomonosov State University, 1987), 121. Earlier in the year, Ushakov was charged with drawing up an inventory (*opis'*) of the property and personal effects left in the palace at Novo-Preobrazhenskoe on the death of Prince-Caesar F. Iu. Romodanovskii. For Ushakov's commission, see RGADA, f. 9, otd. 2, op. 4, ch. 3, kn. 34, ll. 364–68v; for the text of the actual inventory compiled by Ushakov, October 19, 1717, see RGADA, f. 9, otd. 2, ch. 3, kn. 34 (1717), ll. 466–520v.

61. Peter to A. D. Menshikov, December 24, 1717, SPb F IRI RAN, f. 270, kn. 85, l. 319.

62. For the undated texts of "ceremonials" (*chiny*) for the election of the Prince-Pope, see RGADA, f. 9, otd. 1, kn. 67.

Abbess to that of Arch-Abbess and, as if I were present [at your consecration],
I pronounce [the final words of the sacramental liturgy]: "Holy, Holy, Holy."
Upon your promotion, the nun Anastasia [Princess A. P. Golitsyna], who has
come from the faraway hermitages, has been elevated to your [former] position. Given in Pressburg, on the 28th day of the month of December, in the
year 1717 [by] the universal Prince-Pope Peter-Prick.[63]

According to the confused chronology of this mock letter of patent, at the
request of the "universal Prince-Caesar," Buturlin was "elevated to the
Most High Throne of the Prince-Pope" on December 29, 1717. Because
the letter exists in two copies, however, only one of which is actually
signed by "Prince-Pope Peter-Prick" himself, it is very difficult to determine to what extent the events really occurred in the way the decree describes. The fact that this mock epistle is actually dated "Pressburg, December 28, 1717"—one day before the events recounted by Buturlin were
supposed to take place—further compromises the truth status of the
source, though not its significance as the script for the day's festivities.

Although we have no reliable evidence that the events described in Buturlin's epistle actually took place, we now have an unimpeachable source
for the 1717–18 ceremony—a letter from its organizer, the tsar himself. On
January 12, 1718, the tsar informed Menshikov that on January 9 a courier
named Tanaev arrived with the news that "my offspring"—*izchadie,* a deliberate conflation of *chado,* child, and *ischadie ada,* the curse invoking the
Devil incarnate[64]—"has left imperial territory. . . . I expect him, along with
his chaperons, here soon." Only after describing the actual whereabouts of
his prodigal son—the "devilish" offspring who was still wandering in the
Holy Roman Empire as if in the nether regions of hell—did Peter notify
Menshikov about the latest developments in "Pressburg":

A letter of patent regarding the election of the P. Pope has been sent to the new
Arch-Abbess. [In this document you will find] an extensive description of when
and in what manner [this ceremony] was staged. [I don't know what kind of]
government this will be, but the selection [process itself] was quite spiritual
[*dukhonosen,* lit. spirit-bearing]. On the fifth of this month P. Caesar was
anointed as the Prince Abbot [alongside] the termagant [who] was ordained [as
the new Princess Abbess]. I have nothing else to report, besides, thank God,
everything is fine.[65]

The ordination of the "termagant" Princess A. P. Golitsyna, a noblewoman
who had fallen out of favor because of her alleged dealings with Aleksei's
supporters, including an émigré relation who was suspected of abetting

63. RGADA, f. 9, otd. 1, kn. 67, ll. 64 (rough draft), 65r–v (clean copy); an expurgated version of the clean copy was published by Semevskii, "Petr Velikii kak iumorist," 311.
64. For the difference in meaning between the more neutral, traditional Russian word for
"offspring" and the "devilish" evocative word used by the tsar, see V. I. Dal', *Tolkovyi slovar'
zhivogo velikorusskogo iazyka,* 4 vols. (Moscow, 1955), 2:65, 4:580.
65. SPb F IRI RAN, f. 270, kn. 87, l. 22.

Aleksei's attempt to emigrate from Peter's "edenic" kingdom—underscored that the tsar and his entourage used the blasphemous ceremonies surrounding the election of the new Prince-Pope to demonize Tsarevich Aleksei and all his supporters, whether in the Holy Roman Empire or in Russia.[66]

Peter's letter to Menshikov suggests that the tsar and his closest political advisers saw a direct connection between the successful completion of the covert operation to return the fugitive tsarevich and the court's blasphemous parody of the sacrament of ordination. Under the aegis of a newly anointed anti-Caesar, the mock conclave of courtiers nominated and ordained a new pontiff in a "spirited" ceremony that recalled the Yuletide bacchanal that inaugurated the state of sober drunkenness at the Transfigured Kingdom. After this sacred parody, sometime between December 28, 1717, and January 12, 1718, the new Prince-Pope forwarded the documents intended for the other members of the tsar's company to St. Petersburg to signal that, with God's help, everything would be fine from now on. In this way, Peter took advantage of the brief span of time between the death of Prince-Pope Zotov and the arrival of Tsarevich Aleksei to prepare the brotherhood of believers in his dynastic scenario for the trials and revelations yet to come. And when these difficult times did come, the unconsecrated company was there in full force. For like other members of the tsar's entourage, both P. I. Buturlin and Prince I. F. Romodanovskii were among those dignitaries (lay and ecclesiastical) who had been called to the main banquet hall of the Moscow Kremlin to hear the reading of the manifesto depriving Aleksei Petrovich of the throne in favor of Peter Petrovich.[67] And they were also among those members of the elite who attended the reading of the manifesto of March 5, 1718, about the "crimes" of the tsar's first wife, the "former tsaritsa Evdokiia."[68] During the reading of these manifestos, only those courtiers who were in on the joke would have noted that Prince-Pope Buturlin and the mock clerics of his Unholy Council appeared in the same hall as the patriarchless Holy Council.[69]

66. On Princess A. P. Golitsyna (*née* Prozorovskaia), see *Zapiski o rode kniazei Golitsynykh*, ed. Evgenii Serchevskii (St. Petersburg, 1853), 57, 292; G. V. Esipov, "Kniaginia-igumen'ia," *Russkaia starina* 1 (1870): 400–403; P. F. Karabanov, "Stats-damy i freiliny russkogo dvora v XVIII stoletii," pt. 1, *Russkaia starina* 2 (1870): 478–79; and Hughes, *Russia*, 194, 201, 253, 261, 291, 504n254, 516–517nn42–46. On Peter's suspicions about the Prozorovskii clan's involvement in the case of Tsarevich Aleksei, see S. F. Platonov, "B. I. Kurakin i A. P. Prozorovskii (1697–1720)," in *Doklady Akademii Nauk SSSR, Seriia istorii i filosofii* 12 (1929): 236–43, esp. 241, 243. For Princess Golitsyna's conviction and punishment, see Ustrialov, *Istoriia tsarstvovaniia Petra Velikogo*, 6:221, 221n78, 222n80, 225; and Bushkovitch, "Power and the Historian," 400n40.

67. "Spisok lits, zasvidetel'stvovavshikh v sovete 3 fevralia, 1718 goda," in M. P. Pogodin, "Tsarevich Aleksei Petrovich, po svidetel'stvam vnov' otkrytym," *Chteniia v Imperatorskom Obshchestve Istorii i Drevnostei Rossiiskikh pri Moskovskom universitete* 3, pt. 2 (1861): 318, 319.

68. "Povestka o sobranii 5 marta [1718]," ibid., 321–23, 325.

69. For the circumstances of these public readings, and particularly for an explicit reference to the attendance of the Muscovite Holy Council, see Ustrialov, *Istoriia tsarstvovaniia Petra Velikogo*, 6:143–44, 477–87, esp. 477.

The Royal Phallus

The repeated use of the obscene Russian term for the male organ (*khui*) in the mock epistles and letters of patent sent out to the St. Petersburg branch of the Most Foolish and All Drunken Council lends further support to the contention that there was an intimate connection between the court's scatological parody of the sacrament of holy orders and the political emasculation of Tsarevich Aleksei Petrovich and his "papist" supporters. The fact that the "servants of the Arch-Prince-Pope" referred to each other as "pricks" suggests that all the members of the tsar's mock ecclesiastical council (both male and female) metaphorically partook of the virility of the royal phallus.[70] Indeed, their ribald clerical pseudonyms reveal that the tsar and his company quite literally sought to embody the connection between religious charisma and political potency. In turn, this strategy was as much a product of the succession struggle between Peter and his son as of the theological dispute between Feofan (Prokopovich) and the Latinizers. In fact, the figurative importance of circumcision in the debate about justification through faith provides the crucial link for understanding why Peter decided to draw up the mock ceremonials for the election and installation of Prince-Pope Peter-Prick at the very moment that the succession struggle between the tsar and his son reached a critical stage. For only those courtiers who had sided with the tsar could be said to have undergone a conversion experience comparable to Paul's "circumcision of the heart"; and therefore only those members of the royal entourage who had publicly declared their wholehearted commitment to the tsar could have the dubious privilege of being referred to by the obscene word for the *membrum virile*.

The fact that those foreigners who were most closely affiliated with Peter's court also extolled the power of the royal phallus suggests that this trope reached beyond the members of the tsar's immediate entourage to embrace everyone on intimate terms with the tsar. This may explain why, for example, a picture of a giant ejaculating phallus (Figure 12) graced the back cover of the handwritten booklet containing the statutes, rules, and membership list of a mock religious order known as the British Monastery (*Velikobritanskii slavnyi monastyr'*) or, alternatively, as the Bung College (*Bengo-kollegiia*) of St. Petersburg.[71] Judging by the activities described in

70. For a list of the "servants of the Arch-Prince-Pope" (*sluzhiteli arkhi kniaz' papy*), which was probably written sometime before Buturlin's second wedding (September 10, 1721), see RGADA, f. 9, otd. 1, kn. 67, l. 73; published, heavily expurgated, in Semevskii, "Petr Velikii kak iumorist," 313–14.

71. Research on the membership of the British Monastery has demonstrated that these men were foreign financiers, merchants, and professionals who were on the most intimate terms with the tsar and served him in some personal capacity. So, for example, "*medicus* William Horn," the surgeon who was to perform an operation on the tsar in 1725, shortly before his death from a urological disorder, was a member of the British Monastery. So was Peter's official historiographer and panegyrist ("fame-sow"), Baron Heinrich von Hüyssen. As Hüyssen's

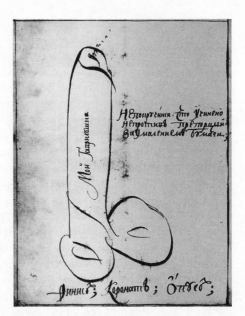

Figure 12. Little Gabriel. Undated sketch (c. 1720), illustrating the motto "At the end, you see the work" (Lat. *finis coronat opus*). (Manuscript Division, Library of the Russian Academy of Sciences, St. Petersburg [RO BRAN, kn. 17.7.12, l. 110].)

the booklet, the British Monastery was a foreign subsidiary of the Most Comical and All-Drunken Council of Peter the Great. Like the mock clerics of the latter fraternity, the "wild brotherhood" of the British Monastery had supposedly vowed to live together according to the rules of the Roman god of wine. Like Bacchus's Russian followers, they were formally subordinated to the mock pontiff of the Transfigured Kingdom, who resided literally across the street from the premises of the British Monastery, on Bol'shaia Dvorianskaia ulitsa, in St. Petersburg. And like other members of the Prince-Pope's ecclesiastical entourage, they were also supposed to take part in the annual Yuletide caroling processions, which formed such an important part of the court's winter holiday season.

In view of some of their by-laws, as well as the designations of some officeholders, the members of the British Monastery shared their Russian counterparts' "preoccupation with private parts," a preoccupation symbolized most eloquently by the drawing of "My Little Gabriel" (*moi*

example demonstrates, some of these people—actually, according to Anthony Cross's calculation, perhaps as many as a third of the members (18 of 46)—were not even British. The original booklet is in RO RNB, MS 17.7.12, ll. 104–11v. This text was first published and analyzed by S. F. Platonov, "Iz bytovoi istorii Petrovskoi epokhi. I. Bengo-Kollegiia ili Velikobritanskii monastyr' v S.-Peterburge pri Petre Velikom," *Izvestiia Akademii Nauk SSSR* 7–8 (1926): 527–46. See also M. P. Alekseev, *Russko-angliiskie literaturnye sviazi (XVIII vek—pervaia polovina XIX veka)* (Moscow, 1982), 74–76; and A. G. Cross, "The Bung College or British Monastery in Petrine Russia," *Newsletter of the Study Group on Eighteenth-Century Russia* 12 (1984): 14–24; and his *By the Banks of the Neva: Chapters from the Lives and Careers of the British in Eighteenth-Century Russia* (Cambridge, 1997), 31–34.

Gavrilushka).[72] S. F. Platonov, who first published and analyzed the statutes of the British Monastery, interpreted the "indecent drawing" that he found on the back cover of the ceremonial booklet as a sign of how crude the amusements of the British community of St. Petersburg really were at the beginning of the eighteenth century and of how unworthy such amusements were of the respected names of Baron Heinrich von Hüyssen and the future academician Johann Werner Paus (in whose personal file the statutes were found).[73] I do not dispute the fact that this image is obscene, but I do not think it is obscenity for obscenity's sake. In fact, this phallic image may perhaps best be understood as a politically relevant Baroque emblem.

Like more traditional examples of *picta poesis*—a rhetorical technique that became popular at the Muscovite court as early as the mid–seventeenth century—this phallic emblem must be approached as a compositional unity of three elements: the drawing itself (*pictura, imago, icon*), the obligatory Latin inscription (*motto, lemma*), and the prose caption (*subscriptio, explicatio*).[74] When read in conjunction with the Latin motto ("Finis coronat opus") and the Russian caption ("Ne pokruchinisia chto uchineno ne protiv preportsyi za umaleniem bumagi"), the phallic image is supposed to reveal the hidden meaning of the whole emblem. And in accordance with the essential feature of the Baroque emblem—namely, wit (*acumen*)—this hidden meaning must be both instructive and amusing, especially for those in the know. Now, those in the know were certainly well informed about the predicament in which the tsar found himself after the mysterious death (under torture) of Tsarevich Aleksei and the unexpected death, in April 1719, of Peter's handpicked heir apparent, Tsarevich Peter Petrovich.[75] By the spring of 1720, when the mock statutes of the British Monastery were drawn up, the tsar faced an intractable problem that was both biological and political: he now had no male heir.[76] And unless Peter was able to pro-

---

72. Cross, "Bung College," 33–34.

73. On Johann Werner Paus (1670–1735), a German scholar who came to Moscow at the beginning of the eighteenth century as a Pietist missionary and ended his career in St. Petersburg as the chief translator for the newly founded Russian Academy of Sciences, see the article in *Slovar' russkikh pisatelei XVIII veka* (St. Petersburg, 1999), vol. 2; see also the review by M. Schippan in *Study Group for Eighteenth-Century Russia Newsletter* 27 (November 1999): 71–75, esp. 75; V. N. Toporov, "Gliuk i 'nemetskaia' russkaia poeziia pervoi treti XVIII v.," in *M. V. Lomonosov i russkaia kul'tura*, 11–16 (Tartu, 1986); and esp. V. N. Peretts, *Istoriko-literaturnye issledovaniia i materialy* (St. Petersburg, 1902), 3:143–246.

74. For a discussion of the genre of emblems in the Russian Baroque, see A. A. Morozov, "Emblematika barokko v literature i iskusstve petrovskogo vremeni," *XVIII vek* 9 (1974): 184–226; L. I. Sazonova, "Obshcheevropeiskie cherty vostochnoslavianskogo barokko. Iz nabliudenii nad poetikoi: *Acumen, poesia artificiosa, emblema, picta poesis*," *Slavianovedenie* 2 (2002): 107; and, more generally, her *Poeziia russkogo barokko (vtoraia polovina XVII–nachalo XVIII v.)* (Moscow, 1991).

75. For a discussion of the circumstances surrounding the death of Tsarevich Aleksei Petrovich, see Bushkovitch, "Power and the Historian," 420–21; and Hughes, *Russia*, 410; Hughes discusses the death of Tsarevich Peter Petrovich on 400–401.

76. According to the anonymous compiler, this "publication was written on April 20th in the year [1]720," i.e., the Wednesday of Easter week. See Platonov, "Iz bytovoi istorii," 530.

duce one soon, he would be put in the unenviable position of having to decide whether to leave the throne to Aleksei's son or to one of the women in his own royal household. For Peter, who had personally lived through the troubled regency of a female ruler and had worked hard to shape a successor in his own image, this was not the outcome he favored. In this fraught dynastic context, the drawing of "Little Gabriel" begins to take on a much more serious meaning than it has previously been given.

In fact, the Latin motto turns out to be one of the keys to the larger political meaning of the whole emblem—a meaning that was to be realized in October 1721, during the elaborate fireworks display staged to celebrate the peace treaty that ended the long Northern War between Russia and Sweden. In the first book of emblems ever to be published in Russia—the *Emblemy i simvoly* of 1705—the motto "Finis coronat opus" was translated into three languages: in Russian it read as "Konets uvenchal delo"; in German it was "Das Ende krönt die Arbeit"; and in English, "At the end you see the work." In Peter's emblem book, however, this motto accompanied a different picture, an image of a storm-tossed ship entering a harbor. Like its sister emblem, representing a hunting dog killing a rabbit that he has just captured, the ship emblem conveyed the idea of bringing an enterprise to a triumphant conclusion. However, whereas the hunting dog emblem represented the idea that "the end is glory" (*gloria finis*), the ship emblem suggested that how you got to the end didn't matter, so long as you finished.[77]

It is in its nautical incarnation that this motto appeared in the elaborate fireworks display staged on October 22, 1721, in honor of the Nystadt peace treaty.[78] According to Friedrich Wilhelm von Bergholz, a Holstein diplomat who left an invaluable eyewitness account of these events, one of the pyrotechnical devices was a giant illuminated shield depicting a ship entering a harbor, below a motto reading "Finis coronavit opus."[79] As an allegorical commentary on Russia's long-awaited victory, this fireworks display pointed to the link between Russia's military victory and the new titles Peter had accepted a little earlier that day: Emperor, Father of the Fatherland, and "the Great." In fact, looking at this illuminated shield, a politically savvy spectator such as Bergholz was supposed to see a visual representation of how the end (of the war) truly crowned the work (of reform). Inas-

77. A. E. Makhov, ed., *Emblemy i simvoly* (Moscow, 1995), 95–96 (no. 103), 218–19 (no. 591).

78. For an analytical description of these celebrations, see Hughes, *Russia*, 272–74; O. G. Ageeva, "Obshchestvennaia i kul'turnaia zhizn' Peterburga pervoi chetverti XVIII v." (Diss. kand. ist. nauk, Institute of History, Russian Academy of Sciences, 1990), 72–77; Elena Pogosian, *Petr I: Arkhitektor rossiiskoi istorii* (St. Petersburg, 2001), 149–63, 220–29; V. N. Vasil'ev, *Starinnye feirverki v Rossii (XVII–pervaia chetvert' XVIII veka)* (Leningrad, 1960), 46–50; and Richard S. Wortman; *Scenarios of Power: Myth and Ceremony in Russian Monarchy*, 2 vols. (Princeton, 1995, 2000), 1:60.

79. Friedrich Wilhelm von Bergholz, *Dnevnik kamer-iunkera F. V. Berkhgol'tsa*, trans. I. F. Ammon (Moscow, 1902–3), 1:140.

much as the statutes of the British Monastery ended with the same motto, it appears that the (as yet unidentified) authors of that booklet were also aware of the meaning of the ship emblem. However, they obviously reworked this emblem to suit their creative fancy. Making an obscene pun on the verb "to finish," the inventors of the British Monastery substituted the drawing of an ejaculating phallus for the image of a boat entering a harbor—an image that may itself be interpreted as a kind of sexual innuendo. Like some giant pyrotechnical device shooting off its charge, the phallus offered a public display of potency—a potency that was only highlighted by the ironic aside about the "disproportion" (*uchineno ne protiv preportsyi*) between the smallness of the drawing and the greatness that it represents. From all we know about Peter's dynastic difficulties, the phallic emblem thus appears to have been both a talisman and an assertion of power. As an assertion of power, "Little Gabriel" delivered a compelling message about Peter's ability to bring the long Northern War to a satisfactory conclusion; as a talisman, it offered a forthright declaration of faith in Peter's ability to secure the royal succession, echoing perhaps the words uttered by the Archangel Gabriel: "You will conceive . . . and bear a son . . . ; He will be great . . . , and the Lord God will give him the throne of his ancestor David" (Luke 1:31–33).

Indeed, from this perspective "Little Gabriel" can be said to have represented the (pro)creative power of the royal phallus itself—the power to bring Peter's personal political vision to life, as if from scratch; or, in other words, the power to father the Fatherland. As such, the obscene emblem on the statutes of the British Monastery recapitulated the phallocentric fantasies that informed the rhetoric of Petrine panegyrists such as Feofan (Prokopovich), who, as we have seen, had already extolled the potency of the monarch who gave Russia a new birth (*otrodil*). Of course, these fantasies have about as much relation to reality as the classical myths in which they were sometimes couched. The new Russia did not spring fully grown from Peter's head, like Athena from the head of Zeus; nor was she fashioned, Galatea-like, by Russia's royal Pygmalion, despite the prevalence of this particular classical image in Petrine iconography.[80] Nevertheless, much like the Greek and Roman myths, these male fantasies have a life and significance of their own. Perhaps most important, they shed light on how the men who founded imperial Russia imagined their political project. For

---

80. V. Iu. Matveev, "K istorii vozniknoveniia i razvitiia siuzheta Petr I—vysekaiushchii statuiu Rossii," in *Kul'tura i iskusstvo Rossii XVIII veka,* 26–43 (Leningrad, 1981); and Hughes, *Russia,* xii–xiii, 470. Similarly, yet another reason why the tsar and his courtiers appeared in the guise of drunken followers of the satyr god of wine may be the putative connection between alcohol and virility—a commonplace in Renaissance medical manuals best captured by a line from the Roman poet Terence: "Without Bacchus, Venus waxeth cold." On the connection between wine and semen in contemporary medical manuals, see Thomas Laqueur, *Making Sex: Body and Gender from the Greeks to Freud* (Cambridge, 1990), 116. On Peter's awareness of this medical literature, see the reference to the ideas of Hippocrates and Galen in G. I. Golovkin to Peter, May 14, 1696, in *PiB,* 1:570.

Peter and his most ardent sympathizers, both Russian and foreign, reforming Russia was not just a matter of importing rational bureaucratic techniques of government. It was also a matter of political will. And that political will was definitely gendered male.

That Peter would have found this kind of wit both flattering and amusing is suggested by the lewd pseudonym he adopted as a member of the mock ecclesiastical council of the Transfigured Kingdom. In a list of "servants of the Arch-Prince-Pope" dating from the early 1720s—that is, from around the same time as the composition of the statutes of the British Monastery—Peter appeared as "Archdeacon Pachomius Crams-with-his-Prick Mikhailov" (*Pakhom pikhai khui Mikhailov*)—an alliterative pun based on the clerical name Pachomius and the dative case of the Russian word for groin (*pakh*).[81] The royal Archdeacon's humble rank in the brotherhood of believers in the potency of the divinely ordained Father of the Fatherland marked the tsar's desire to embody the most active generative principle. Indeed, Peter's pseudonym suggests that the use of the Russian "three-letter word" (*khui*) before the pseudonymous name of a particular mock cleric may have been intended as much more than an obscene pun on the polite form of address (*kir*) conventionally used by Orthodox clergymen in their correspondence. Peter's decision to use the Christian name of his paternal grandfather—Tsar Mikhail Fedorovich—as his own last name suggests that these principles referred to the procreative power of the imperial persona. By assuming the name Mikhailov, Peter presented himself as the only Romanov male who could fulfill his duties to the royal house—whether those duties included restoring his grandfather's patrimony in the Baltic, fathering a worthy successor to the throne, or renovating the Orthodox Church.[82]

Similarly, the lowly rank of deacon—a rank that Peter maintained for his entire career as a member of the mock ecclesiastical council of the Prince-Pope—only served to underline the tsar's divine calling.[83] Judging by the evidence gathered by B. A. Uspenskii, it appears that Peter played the part of deacon because this clerical rank denoted the position of Byzantine emperors in relation to the patriarch of Constantinople. According to Uspenskii, this ecclesiastical title allowed the tsar to underline his special charismatic status as the doubly anointed Orthodox tsar—the only layman allowed to receive Communion like a priest, directly from a chalice, behind the Royal

81. For Peter's obscene pseudonym, see RGADA, f. 9, otd. 1, kn. 67, l. 73; Semevskii, "Petr Velikii kak iumorist," 313–14.

82. On the Muscovite practice of using a grandfather's Christian name as one's last name (*dedichestvo*), see V. B. Kobrin, *Vlast' i sobstvennost' v srednevekovoi Rossii (XV–XVI vv.)* (Moscow, 1985), 25–26. On Peter's appropriation of this practice, see T. Maikova, "Petr I i pravoslavnaia tserkov'," *Nauka i religiia* 7 (1972): 44, 46.

83. Around 1710, Peter-Prick (P. I.) Buturlin, the mock "Metropolitan of Izhorsk and St. Petersburg," promoted the tsar from the rank of "Proto-Deacon . . . of the eparchy of the Most Foolish Patriarch" to that of "Archdeacon . . . of Our eparchy." See Buturlin to Peter, c. 1710, in RGADA, f. 9, otd. 2, op. 3, chap. 1, kn. 11 (1710), l. 188.

Gates.[84] Peter's embrace of his lowly clerical position, like that of the persona of humble skipper, thus served to underline his exalted imperial dignity. Furthermore, the very fact that the mock pontiff of the Transfigured Kingdom could be referred to either as "Patriarch" or as "Pope" suggests that the tsar asserted the charismatic authority of the Christian emperor against Catholicism as a whole, represented either by the head of the Eastern (Apostolic) church or by his Western (Latin) counterpart. According to this interpretation, Peter's carnivalesque performance of the role of deacon turned all arguments about the predominance of clergy over empire on their head.

Thus, even before a secret investigative chancellery uncovered evidence of widespread sympathy for the fate of the luckless tsarevich among prominent clerics, and certainly before the tsar ordered Feofan (Prokopovich) to devise a plan to reassert royal control over top-level ecclesiastical appointments, Peter and his closest advisers had moved one step closer to the "correction" of the Russian Orthodox Church mandated by the *Ecclesiastical Regulation* of 1721.[85] So, while the tsar probably did not decide to abolish the patriarchate until the end of 1718, the increasingly anti-Catholic thrust of the mock ecclesiastical council hinted that Peter was moving toward a radical solution to both of the questions plaguing him at the beginning of the 1720s—the questions of the patriarchal and the royal successions.

84. See B. A. Uspenskii, *Tsar' i patriarkh: Kharizma vlasti v Rossii (Vizantiiskaia model' i ee russkoe pereosmyslenie)* (Moscow, 1998), 156n5; cf. M. V. Zazykin, *Patriarkh Nikon: Ego gosudarstvennye i kanonicheskie idei. V trekh chastiakh* (Moscow, 1995), 1:191.

85. On the tsar's God-given obligation to "reform [*ispravit'*, lit. correct] the clerical estate," see Muller, *Spiritual Regulation*, 3; P. V. Verkhovskoi, *Uchrezhdenie dukhovnoi kollegii i dukhovnyi reglament: K voprosu ob otnoshenii Tserkvi i gosudarstva v Rossii. Izsledovanie v oblasti istorii russkago tserkovnago prava* (Rostov-on-Don, 1916), 2:6; and Cracraft, *Church Reform*, 60–62, 135, 147–53.

Conclusion

By tracing the history of the Transfigured Kingdom—a heretofore neglected aspect of Petrine political theology—I have tried to demonstrate the
proposition that behind the court's antinomian spectacles lay not a mission
to secularize Muscovy, but rather a belief in the divine gift of grace
(charisma) reputedly possessed by Peter Alekseevich, the man whom royal
panegyrists hailed as Russia's "God and Christ." In the memorable words of
Chancellor G. I. Golovkin—the courtier who was given the prestigious job
of petitioning Peter to accept the titles of All-Russian Emperor, Father of
the Fatherland, and "the Great" on behalf of the Senate, the Synod, and all
the chivalrous sons of the fatherland (1721)—this extraordinary monarch
was personally responsible for bringing his realm "from the darkness of Ig-
norance into the Theater of the World, so to speak from nothingness into
being, into the company of political peoples."[1] This oft-quoted line echoed
what one Petrine scholar has described as perhaps the most important
prayer in the Russian Orthodox liturgy—a prayer that, not coincidentally,
stresses the Creator's role in separating light from darkness and being from
nonbeing.[2] And it is doubly appropriate that the courtier who was chosen

---

1. For the full text of Golovkin's speech, see *Rech', kakova . . . ego imperatorskomu velichestvu . . . ot gospodina kantslera grafa Golovkina govorena v 22 den' oktiabria 1721 godu* (St.
Petersburg, 1721); reprinted in *Opisanie dokumentov i del, khraniashchikhsia v archive Sviateishego Pravitel'stvuiushchego Sinoda*, 49 vols. (St. Petersburg, 1869–1914), 1: 458–59. For
insightful analyses of this speech, see Lindsey Hughes, *Russia in the Age of Peter the Great*
(New Haven, 1998), 56, 272–74; O. G. Ageeva, "Titul 'imperator' i poniatie 'imperiia' v
Rossii v pervoi chetverti XVIII veka," in *Mir istorii: Rossiiskii elektronnyi zhurnal* 5 (1999):
1–15; and esp. Richard S. Wortman, *Scenarios of Power: Myth and Ceremony in Russian
Monarchy* (Princeton, 1995), 1: 63–64.
2. On the biblical and liturgical sources of this line, see Hans-Joachim Härtel, *Byzantinisches Erbe und Orthodoxie bei Feofan Prokopovic* (Würzburg, 1970), 86; and esp. V. M.
Zhivov, "Kul'turnye reformy v sisteme preobrazovanii Petra I," in *Iz istorii russkoi kul'tury*,
ed. A. D. Koshelev (Moscow, 1996), 3: 550.

to deliver this line was not only Russia's top diplomat, whose job it was to elevate the prestige of his royal master on the international stage, but also a leading member of Peter's company and the "truly drunk proto-deacon" of the mock ecclesiastical council of his Transfigured Kingdom. For, as we have seen, the discursive practices adopted by such companions as Golov-kin helped the tsar to create the Baroque rhetoric of authority that sustained his charismatic scenario of power.

The original members of Peter's company were responsible for organizing the spectacles, devising the rituals, and supervising the induction of other courtiers into the bacchanalian mysteries of state at the heart of the Trans-figured Kingdom. But while the actual authors of these sacred parodies as-sumed relatively minor ranks within the mock hierarchy of the Unholy Council, the leading actors—the ones who were given the most prominent roles and were forced to play the most demeaning parts in the successive elections and ordinations of the Prince-Popes—were usually older men who were often ambivalent about the changes introduced by the young tsar and his entourage.[3] Their adherence to what the company defined as outmoded Muscovite values only heightened the polemical charge of the rituals meant to evoke their humorous discomfort. And, as we saw in respect to the cul-tural significance of Petrine matrimonial politics, this discomfort frequently took center stage in the ever more lavish public spectacles in which the other courtiers inducted into the mock ecclesiastical council of the Prince-Pope served both as the supporting cast and as the main spectators for the drama of Muscovy's transfiguration. Thus, long before the acclamation cer-emony of 1721, Peter's company had succeeded in transforming the public rituals of the late Muscovite court into celebrations of the coming of a new political dispensation—one in which Peter had become the metaphorical rock on which Russia's future imperial greatness was to be built (cf. Matt. 16:18).[4]

As it soon became apparent, however, the very success of Peter's project

---

3. A prime example of this type is "Metropolitan" I. I. Khovanskii the Elder (d. 1702), a courtier tainted by his familial ties to the reputed leaders of the Moscow mutiny of 1682. Kho-vanskii was alleged to have described his induction into Peter's mock ecclesiastical council as follows: "God had given me a [martyr's] crown, but I lost it. They took me to the General Yard at [Novo-]Preobrazhenskoe, Nikita Zotov ordained me as a metropolitan, and for the renunci-ation [of God (*Bog*) in favor of Bacchus (*Bag*)] they gave me a scroll, and in accordance with that writ I made my renunciation. During the renunciation they asked me 'Do you drink?' in-stead of 'Do you believe [in the Father, Son, and Holy Ghost]?' And with my renunciation I lost more than the beard I disputed. It would have been better for me to receive the crown of martyrdom than to have effected such a renunciation." See the testimony of Grigorii Talitskii (1700), in G. V. Esipov, *Raskol'nich'i dela XVIII stoletiia, izvlechennye iz del Preobrazhen-skogo prikaza i Tainoi Rozysknykh del kantseliarii* (St. Petersburg, 1861), 68–69. For an in-sightful discussion of the ritual and textual parallels between the mock and real ceremonies of ordination, see Zhivov, "Kul'turnye reformy," 563–66, esp. 565–66n21.

4. Not surprisingly, the image of Peter as the bedrock of Russia's imperial greatness re-mained central to the political legitimation of his successors. See Wortman, *Scenarios of Power*; Karen Rasmussen, "Catherine II and the Image of Peter I," *Slavic Review* 37 (March

undermined the accessible style of rule that shaped the relations among the members of his unconsecrated company. The tsar's attempt to transform the cabal that had put him on the throne into a polished elite ruling over a well-ordered police state resulted in the simultaneous rationalization and dispersion of his personal charisma.[5] Although the empire continued to be run by the tsar's intimates and royal favorites, their repeated attempts to adapt the Muscovite chancellery system to the demands of almost continuous warfare brought the Russian administrative and military machines closer to the ideals of government espoused and at least to some extent embodied by Muscovy's northern European contemporaries.[6] Thus the larger the number of agents and governmental offices that could claim to exercise the will of the charismatic warrior-tsar and the more elaborate and hierarchical the structure of civil and military subordination, the less accessible Peter became, both to his subjects and to his acolytes. The legislation that resulted in the formation of the office of Request Master (*Reketmeister,* from Fr. *maître de requêtes*) and that required people to petition the emperor only through proper channels was paradigmatic of the changing policy of royal access.[7]

This shift in the policy of access accompanied and found justification in the simultaneous redefinition of Peter's royal authority.[8] Led by Feofan (Prokopovich), the tsar's official court preacher and one of the ghost writers of the speech delivered by Chancellor Golovkin in 1721, apologists for Russian monarchical absolutism increasingly came to depict the last Muscovite

1978): 57–69; and Cynthia H. Whittaker, "The Reforming Tsar: The Redefinition of Autocratic Duty in Eighteenth-Century Russia," *Slavic Review* 51 (Spring 1992): 77–98.

5. By "rationalization" I mean to invoke Weber's definition of "rational-legal" or "bureaucratic" authority, as enshrined in such founding documents of the well-ordered police state as the Military Statute (1716), the decree instituting the office of Police Master (1718), the General Regulation (1720), the statutes of the Chief Magistracy (1721), and the Table of Ranks (1722). For the text of these documents see A. A. Preobrazhenskii and T. E. Novitskaia, eds., *Zakonodatel'stvo Petra I* (Moscow, 1997), 155–231, 630–33, 99–124, 393–402. For the notion of the dispersion and attenuation of charisma, see Edward Shils, "Charisma," in his *Constitution of Society* (Chicago, 1982), 110–18, esp. 117–18.

6. For an extensive discussion of the Swedish and German models of Petrine administrative reform, see Marc Raeff, *The Well-Ordered Police State: Social and Institutional Change through Law in the Germanies and Russia, 1600–1800* (New Haven, 1983); Claus Peterson, *Peter the Great's Administrative and Judicial Reforms: Swedish Antecedents and the Process of Reception* (Stockholm, 1979); A. N. Medushevskii, *Utverzhdenie absoliutizma v Rossii* (Moscow, 1994); and Evgenii Anisimov, *Gosudarstvennye preobrazovaniia i samoderzhavie Petra Velikogo v pervoi chetverti XVIII veka* (St. Petersburg, 1997).

7. For the text of the decree, see "O generale reket-meistere. Ukaz iz Senata" (February 23, 1722), in Preobrazhenskii and Novitskaia, *Zakonodatel'stvo Petra I*, 86–88. On the office of *reketmeister* and the growing importance of the Privy Cabinet and its secretary as a filter for royal correspondence, see Hughes, *Russia*, 94, 112–13, 128, 493n263; and Anisimov, *Gosudarstvennye preobrazovaniia*, 282–86.

8. For an insightful description of the theological implications of this shift in the policy of royal access, see Michael Cherniavsky, "The Old Believers and the New Religion," in *The Structure of Russian History: Interpretive Essays,* ed. Cherniavsky (New York, 1970), 177–78, 188n178.

tsar as the first all-powerful Father of the Fatherland—the original embodiment of natural sovereignty and the ultimate source of power for settling disputes within the multiethnic and multiconfessional ruling class that governed the Russian empire.[9] Particularly after the bloody resolution of the succession struggle between Peter and Tsarevich Aleksei—which, as we saw in Chapter 5, had also served notice to anyone who dared to question the burdens of faith in Russia's anointed one—the tsar's military, civilian, and even clerical servitors were increasingly urged to identify with the heroic figure of the suffering royal servant, depicted as the paragon of patriotism, self-discipline, and rational obedience to God. Indeed, as Archbishop Feofan insisted, it was only by becoming conscientious, skilled, and socially responsible subjects that the new chosen people could ever hope to live up to the tremendous personal sacrifices that Russia's charismatic leader made for the sake of the common good. The routinization of Peter's personal charisma was thus accompanied by the intensification, not diminution, of references to the redemptive significance of the divinely anointed monarch, "by whose labors we rest, by whose campaigns we stand unshakable," and "by whose many deaths we live."[10]

The way in which an informal political movement in favor of the Naryshkin candidate was transformed into an organized religion centered on the person of the charismatic monarch—a veritable cult of Peter the Great—can most readily be seen in the evolution of the Unholy Council of the Transfigured Kingdom. Over the course of the reign, as the core group of Peter's supporters became dispersed to all corners of the empire, the mock ecclesiastical council of the Prince-Pope expanded its membership base and spawned imitators.[11] Both trends were encouraged by the fact that after St. Petersburg was founded, the semiprivate bacchanalian mysteries associated with the Transfigured Kingdom became an important part of Petrine public celebrations. Thus, whenever the court would get together to

---

9. On the broader imperial implications of Peter's new scenario of power, see Wortman, *Scenarios of Power*, 1: 41, 44; and James Cracraft, "Empire versus Nation: Political Theory under Peter I," *Harvard Ukrainian Studies* 10 (December 1986): 524–40. For a non-Marxist definition of the notion of ruling class, see John P. LeDonne, *Absolutism and Ruling Class: The Formation of the Russian Political Order, 1700–1825* (New York, 1991).

10. Feofan (Prokopovich), *Sochineniia Feofana Prokopovicha*, ed. I. P. Eremin (Moscow and Leningrad, 1961), 67; and Nicholas V. Riasanovsky, *The Image of Peter the Great in Russian History and Thought* (New York, 1985), 12–13. For an important corrective to Max Weber's analysis of charismatic authority, which amends his description of the "routinization of charisma" by stressing its immanence, even in supposedly modern bureaucratic regimes, see Shils, "Charisma"; and Clifford Geertz, "Centers, Kings, and Charisma: Reflections on the Symbolics of Power," in *Rites of Power: Symbolism, Ritual, and Politics since the Middle Ages,* ed. Sean Wilentz, 13–38 (Philadelphia, 1985).

11. Two institutions of note are what may be described as a ladies' auxiliary based on the court of Catherine Alekseevna and her ladies-in-waiting; and the so-called British Monastery or Bung College, analyzed in Chapter 5. For a list of the predominantly foreign members of this mock institution, see S. F. Platonov, "Iz bytovoi istorii Petrovskoi epokhi." Pt. 1, "Bengo-Kollegiia ili Velikobritanskii monastyr' v S.-Peterburge pri Petre Velikom," *Izvestiia Akademii Nauk SSSR* 7–8 (1926): 527–46.

celebrate Yuletide, the launching of a ship, or yet another military victory, the far-flung members of the tsar's company would bring with them the "clerics" (local officials, junior officers, etc.) whom they had inducted into the royalist cause. However, these trends also unintentionally subverted the original purpose of the mock ecclesiastical council of the Prince-Pope, so that by the end of the reign, the antinomian travesties associated with the promulgation of a new Gospel According to Peter became no more important than the other carnivalesque elements of the lavish masquerades celebrating the advent of the Transfigured Kingdom. In this way, even before Peter's death, the Unholy Council had become just another (if still prominent) element within the imperial Russian court's new St. Petersburg–based social calendar—an institutionalized artifact of Peter's youth, when his position at the Muscovite court and Muscovy's position within the concert of Christian nations were still in flux.[12]

However, unlike other artifacts of Peter's youthful zeal for reform—such as the so-called Granddaddy (*dedushka*) of the Russian Fleet, a little dinghy (*botik*) that the tsar claimed to have discovered in a barn at Izmailovo and on which he first learned to sail—the Unholy Council never attained the status of a venerated Petrine relic.[13] Despite the fact that by the end of the reign the informal, semiprivate spectacles associated with Peter's mock synod had become regularly scheduled three-day events including hundreds of masked protagonists and costing thousands of rubles, the carnivalesque processions of the Most Foolish and All-Drunken Prince-Pope and his conclave disappeared along with Proto-Deacon Pachomius Crams-with-His-Prick Mikhailov, their producer, director, and guiding spirit. In that respect, the mock ecclesiastical council of the Transfigured Kingdom shared the fate of Novo-Preobrazhenskoe, where it was first created. Indeed, as Richard Wortman has so amply demonstrated, immediately after the death of the first Russian emperor, Peter's royal successors quickly consigned Novo-Preobrazhenskoe to the dustbin of history in favor of other realms of memory that were more significant to the articulation of their particular scenarios of power.[14]

---

12. On the Drunken Council as an institutionalized artifact of Peter's youth, see Paul Hollingsworth, "Carnival and Rulership in the Reign of Peter the Great" (paper presented at the Annual Convention of the American Historical Association, December 1985), 13. For an analysis of the development of the new imperial court calendar, see Hughes, *Russia*, xxix, 270–79; idem, "The Petrine Year: Anniversaries and Festivals in the Reign of Peter I (1682–1725)," in *Festive Culture in Germany and Europe from the Sixteenth to the Twentieth Century*, ed. Karin Friedrich, 149–68 (Lewiston, NY, 2000); and esp. Elena Pogosian, *Petr I: Arkhitektor rossiiskoi istorii* (St. Petersburg, 2001), 23–182, 287–327.

13. For Peter's autobiographical (and highly didactic) version of the story about the finding of the toy boat, see the introduction to the Naval Statutes (1720) in N. G. Ustrialov, *Istoriia tsarstvovaniia Petra Velikogo* (St. Petersburg 1858), 2: 399–400. For the ceremonial transfer of the relics of the Grandfather of the Russian Fleet, see Hughes, *Russia*, 80–81, 87, 224, 265, 374, 463.

14. In that respect, Wortman's decision to underemphasize the significance of sacred parodies at Peter's court in *Scenarios of Power* mirrors the deliberate forgetfulness of the authors of his sources on eighteenth-century Russian court spectacles. For an insightful discussion of the

During Peter's lifetime, however, this estate was crucial to the elaboration of his reformist political vision. The fact that the tsar and his courtiers recognized Novo-Preobrazhenskoe as an important site of memory can be seen most clearly in the unusual fireworks display staged on its grounds during Shrovetide of 1723. In that year Peter and his entourage spent the Christmas holidays in Moscow, where the tsar had urgent business to attend to regarding a corruption case involving several high-ranking members of his new regime, as well as the arrangements for his daughter Anna's marriage to Karl-Friedrich, Duke of Holstein. During the court's annual winter outings, Peter had made a special point of visiting Pressburg, the little city whose name (as we saw in Chapter 2) made an oblique reference to his pretensions to titular parity with the Holy Roman Emperor and which served as the original location of the bacchanalian ceremonies staged in honor of the Prince-Pope and the Prince-Caesar of the Transfigured Kingdom.[15] In keeping with the carnivalesque spirit of the season, Peter organized a three-day masquerade that included, among other exotic spectacles, a triumphal entry into Moscow aboard specially designed sleighs representing various naval vessels—a device first used for the Nystadt peace celebrations the previous December. (Rumors to the effect that the tsar had allegedly thrown live fish from the deck of his "ship" to signal to the assembled crowd how many souls this apocalyptic "fisher of men" [Matt. 4:19; Mark 1:17] had already ensnared remain unsubstantiated, if completely in the spirit of the impromptu Christological spectacle analyzed in Chapter 3).[16] On the last day of that masquerade, February 24, 1723, immediately before the tsar and his court returned to St. Petersburg, Peter staged yet another of those monarchical rites of power that shocked contemporaries while at the same time affirming his charisma.[17]

On this occasion Peter had personally set fire to a perfect replica of the palace of Novo-Preobrazhenskoe, the original locus of the new, Petrine (as

---

"narrative of forgetting" vis-à-vis Peter's parodies, see V. M. Zhivov, "O prevratnostiakh istorii, ili o nezavershennosti istoricheskikh paradigm," in *Razyskaniia v oblasti i predistorii russkoi kul'tury* (Moscow, 2002), esp. 713–16. For the notion of "realms of memory," see *Realms of Memory: Rethinking the French Past,* trans. Arthur Goldhammer, 3 vols. (New York, 1996–98).

15. See the entries for Epiphany (January 6, 1723) and for January 27, 1723, in *Pokhodnye zhurnaly Petra I, 1695–1726* (St. Petersburg, 1853–55), 2–3, 6.

16. See the testimony of Ivan Pavlov, a former soldier and chancellery official turned Old Believer, in K. I. Arsen'ev, "Stradalets po svoei vole za dvoeperstnoe krestnoe znamenie (1737)," ed. P. P. Pekarskii, *Sbornik otdeleniia russkogo iazyka i slovesnosti Imperatorskoi Akademii nauk* 9 (1872): 123–24. For Pavlov's outraged remarks about other masquerades (*mushkaraty*) and caroling processions (*slavleniia*), especially those that included the mock ecclesiastical council of Peter the Great, see ibid., 121–22. For a detailed eyewitness account of the Moscow masquerade of 1722, which did in fact include a triumphal boat entry (but no references to live fish), see Friedrich Wilhelm von Bergholz, *Dnevnik kamer-iunkera F. V. Berkhgol'tsa,* trans. I. F. Ammon (Moscow, 1902–3), 2:45–56.

17. For a contemporary eyewitness description of the Moscow masquerade of 1723, see Bergholz, *Dnevnik,* 2: 22–29; and Jean-Jacques Campredon to the French king, March 13, 1723, in *Sbornik imperatorskogo russkogo istoricheskogo obshchestva* 49 (1885): 321–23.

opposed to the old, Alekseevan) transfiguration.[18] Representatives of foreign courts who had been invited to witness what one of them candidly described as a rather "strange" fireworks display received oral explanations from the tsar himself about the meaning of this royal spectacle—a practice that was employed on other important occasions of state, such as the elaborate fireworks display staged earlier that year to commemorate the wedding anniversary of Peter and Catherine.[19] According to the contemporary eyewitness accounts of the French and Holstein ambassadors to Muscovy, Peter deliberately burned his "old wooden palace" in order to create a spectacle that would allow him to depict his childhood retreat as the cradle of the royal lifeguard regiments and, by implication, of the military victories he had achieved as an adult. Indeed, according to F. H. von Bassewitz, the tsar himself had described the rapid transition from the "most beautiful fireworks display" to the "most shocking conflagration" as the very "image of war," in which "brilliant deeds" are almost invariably followed by "destruction and havoc." Descending from such lofty allegorical heights, the tsar supposedly made the following comment to the Duke of Holstein over a glass of fine Hungarian wine: "Together with this house, in which I worked out my first plans for war against Sweden, may there disappear any idea that might make me take up arms against that state and may it be the most true ally of my empire"—a toast that contained a topical message for his future son-in-law, who also happened to be a candidate for the Swedish throne.[20] Whether or not this conversation actually took place is less important than the fact that the representatives of two hostile diplomatic factions at the Muscovite court received more or less the same message, namely, that this spectacular fireworks display marked the sacred spot from which Peter's radiance first shone forth upon a waiting world, like that of the transfigured Christ at Mount Tabor; a location that, in the words of the French ambassador, served as the "beginning of everything marvelous" that the Russian monarch later accomplished during his reign.[21] Like other Baroque magician kings, therefore, Peter used the latest in modern technol-

18. For a description of the 1723 Novo-Preobrazhenskoe fireworks display, see Bergholz, *Dnevnik,* 3:28–29; and H. F. von Bassewitz, "Zapiski Golshtinskago ministra grafa Bassevicha (o Petre Velikom), 1713–1725," trans. I. F. Ammon, *Russkii arkhiv* 5 (1865): 583. For a discussion of the fate of the real Novo-Preobrazhenskoe, which the tsar intended (but never managed) to renovate along the well-ordered architectural lines of the royal estates outside of St. Petersburg, see D. Zheludkov, "Novye materialy o dvortsovom stroitel'stve v Moskve petrovskogo vremeni," in *Tsarskie i imperatorskie dvortsy. Staraia Moskva* (Moscow, 1997), 126.

19. For a discussion of the way this particular fireworks display, like Petrine fireworks in general, served to inform contemporaries about forthcoming events, see V. N. Vasil'ev, *Starinnye feirverki v Rossii (XVII–pervaia chetvert' XVIII veka)* (Leningrad, 1960), 52.

20. Campredon to French king, 322–23; Bassewitz, "Zapiski," 583; Bergholz, *Dnevnik,* 28–29.

21. Campredon to French king, 322; for a brief summary of Peter's "superhuman" efforts on behalf of his realm and the "marvels" (*des prodiges*) accomplished during his reign, see ibid., 309–13, esp. 309.

ogy to produce seemingly supernatural marvels that transformed ephemeral pyrotechnics into royal epiphanies.[22]

The fireworks display set off in the winter of 1723 at Novo-Preobrazhenskoe shows that by the end of his reign, Peter still had not abandoned the notion of staging amazing ceremonies at unexpected times and in unusual places to demonstrate the notion that he was predestined for his imperial vocation. Indeed, such court spectacles constituted one of the primary discursive practices by means of which the tsar and his advisers cultivated a belief in Peter's personal election for the task of transfiguring the Russian realm. Over the course of the eighteenth century this belief in the personal and charismatic basis of royal authority—a belief inextricably associated with the image of Peter the Great—found expression in the ideal of the reforming tsar surrounded by a group of loyal disciples and freed from all institutional and legal constraints.[23] Even as the formal apparatus of imperial administration continued to expand, every one of Peter's successors would rely on his or her own unconsecrated company, a group of intimates who derived their power from proximity to the monarch, who dedicated themselves to the monarch's reforming projects, and whose administrative role transcended the framework of existing ruling bodies. Indeed, the paradoxes of the Petrine project—which demanded both the institutionalization of sovereignty and the cultivation of charisma—continued to shape the scenarios of power staged by the supporters of royal absolutism long after Peter's bacchanalian mysteries of state were either forgotten or selectively subsumed into the master narrative of Russia's imperial greatness.

22. For an insightful discussion of the way fireworks (and other ephemera connected to royal amusements) could actually deify the Baroque magician king, see Louis Marin, *Portrait of the King,* trans. Martha M. Houle (Minneapolis, 1988), 193–205, esp. 202–3; and, for the Russian case, Wortman, *Scenarios of Power,* 1: 7, 17, 45–46.

23. For the evolution of the idea of the tsar as reformer, from Peter the Great to Mikhail S. Gorbachev, see Whittaker, "Reforming Tsar," 77–98.

APPENDIX I

Chronology

1598–1613	Time of Troubles, a period of foreign invasion and civil war, follows the death of the last surviving member of the Riurikid dynasty
1613	Election of Mikhail Fedorovich Romanov as tsar puts a symbolic end to the Time of Troubles, but Muscovy fails to recapture territories lost to the Poles and Swedes
1645–76	Reign of Tsar Aleksei Mikhailovich Romanov
1657	Birth of Sof'ia Alekseevna to Tsar Aleksei Mikhailovich and Tsaritsa Mariia Il'inichna Miloskavskaia
1661	Birth of Fedor Alekseevich
1666	Birth of Ivan Alekseevich
1666–67	Church council ratifies liturgical reforms introduced during the patriarchate of Nikon, inaugurating the schism between the Russian Orthodox establishment and the Old Believers
1669	Death of Tsaritsa Mariia Il'inichna
1671	Tsar Aleksei Mikhailovich weds Natal'ia Kirillovna Naryshkina
1672	*May 30* Birth of Peter Alekseevich, Tsar Aleksei Mikhailovich's only son by his second marriage
1676–82	Reign of Tsar Fedor Alekseevich, Tsar Aleksei Mikhailovich's eldest son by his first marriage
1682	*April 27* Death of Fedor Alekseevich; the lame Ivan Alekseevich is passed over in favor of Peter, who is proclaimed tsar
	May 15–17 Musketeer mutiny in Moscow
	May 26 Proclamation of dual tsardom of Ivan and Peter
	May 29 Declaration of regency of Peter's half sister, Tsarevna Sof'ia Alekseevna
	June 25 Coronation of Ivan and Peter as joint tsars

1684   *Jan. 9* Tsar Ivan Alekseevich marries Praskov'ia Fedorovna Saltykova

1689   *Jan. 27* Tsar Peter Alekseevich marries Evdokiia Fedorovna Lopu-
        khina

        Aug. 6–7 Peter's flight from Novo-Preobrazhenskoe on the eve of the
        feast of the Transfiguration signals the beginning of the court coup
        against the regency of Tsarevna Sof'ia Alekseevna

        Sept. 7 Tsarevna Sof'ia Alekseevna excluded from royal titles; confined
        in Novodevich'i Convent, under the supervision of F. Iu. Ro-
        modanovskii, future head of Peter's secret police

        Sept. 11 Execution of F. L. Shaklovityi and his alleged co-conspirators
        signals the overthrow of the regency of Tsarevna Sof'ia Alekseevna

        Sept. 16 On the day before Tsarevna Sof'ia's birthday, Peter and his
        supporters stage a "field ballet military" on the grounds of Aleksan-
        drovskaia sloboda, the site of Ivan the Terrible's countercourt
        (*oprichnina*)

1690   *Feb. 19* Birth of Tsarevich Aleksei Petrovich, Peter's firstborn son and
        heir apparent

        March 17 Death of Patriarch Ioakim (Savelov)

1691   *Oct. 6–9* War games (a.k.a. Semenovskoe campaign) on the fields out-
        side Novo-Preobrazhenkoe mark the conclusion of the military re-
        organization of the court; Peter serves in the new model army of the
        King of Pressburg (F. Iu. Romodanovskii), the mock monarch of the
        Transfigured Kingdom

1691–92 *Dec. 27–Jan. 1* Election and ordination of Patriarch Deary (M. F.
        Naryshkin), the first mock pontiff of the Transfigured Kingdom

1693   *Summer* Peter and his company first visit Archangel, at the time Rus-
        sia's only outlet to the sea

1694   *Jan. 25* Death of Tsaritsa Natal'ia Kirillovna, Peter's mother

        June Near-capsizing of the royal yacht *St. Peter,* next to the site of the
        Transfiguration Church of the Pertominsk Monastery, offers the
        tsar an unexpected opportunity to demonstrate the charisma of
        "Captain Peter"

        September–October War games (a.k.a. Kozhukhovo campaign) led by
        King Jochann of Poland (I. I. Buturlin) and King Friedrich of Press-
        burg (F. Iu. Romodanovskii), the respective heads of the two newly
        founded royal guards regiments, enact the defeat of the Moscow
        musketeers and, more broadly, the conquest of Moscow by the
        Transfigured Kingdom; ceremonies also include the carnivalesque
        wedding of Ia. F. Turgenev, demonstrating the importance of faith-
        ful service over clan honor

1695   *Summer* Failure of the first Azov campaign against the Crimean Tatars

1696   *Jan. 29* Death of Tsar Ivan Alekseevich leaves Peter as both de facto
        and de jure ruler of Russia

May The use of a newly built Russian flotilla results in the successful siege of Azov

September 30 Triumphal entry into Moscow, first imperial triumph ever organized in Russia; Peter walks in the ranks of the newly created "Naval Regiment"

1697–98   Peter's Great Embassy to northern and western Europe; Peter returns to quash another mutiny by Moscow musketeers; public executions signal the de facto disbandment of the musketeer forces

1699   *May* Peter divorces Tsaritsa Evdokiia Fedorovna and confines her in a convent in Suzdal province

Nov. 30 Informal institution of the order of St. Andrew "the First-Called"

Dec. 19–20 Decrees on calendar reform, initiating a new century with New Year celebrations on Jan. 1

1700   *Jan. 4* Decree making foreign fashions obligatory at court

Aug. 19 Russia's declaration of war against Charles XII of Sweden marks the start of the Great Northern War

Oct. 16 Death of Patriarch Adrian; Peter and his advisers choose not to organize the election of another Russian Orthodox patriarch; instead, they appoint Metropolitan Stefan (Iavorskii) as temporary caretaker of the patriarchal see

Nov. 19 Russian defeat at the Battle of Narva

1701   *January* Reestablishment of the Monastery Chancellery, abolished during the ascendancy of Patriarch Ioakim; I. A. Musin-Pushkin, Ioakim's nephew-in-law (as well as a member of Peter's mock ecclesiastical council), assumes de facto control over all property of the Russian Orthodox Church

Dec. 30 Russian victory at Erestfer marks the first major defeat of the previously unbeaten Swedish army

1702   *Jan. 11* Display of fireworks in Moscow in honor of the first Russian victory in the Northern War

Jan. 26 Winter holiday season also includes the staging of the carnivalesque wedding of F. P. Shanskii, marking the change of habits (both clothes and manners) among Peter's companions

1703   *May 1* Russian victory at Nienshants

May 16 Foundation of St. Petersburg

1704   *July 4* Death of Tsarevna Sof'ia Alekseevna

Aug. 9 Russian victory at Narva

Dec. 22 Decree on foreign dress reissued

1708   *Sept. 28* Russian victory at Lesnaia

October I. S. Mazepa, Ukrainian hetman and cavalier of the order of St. Andrew, defects to the Swedes

Oct. 31 A. D. Menshikov, Peter's favorite, sacks Baturin, Mazepa's capital

1709   *Nov. 6* Mazepa stripped of his knightly insignia and hanged in effigy

Nov. 11 Mazepa anathematized and excommunicated in absentia

June 27 Russian victory at Poltava

July 11 In anticipation of the capture of Mazepa, Menshikov orders the minting of a heavy silver chain and medal depicting Judas Iscariot's suicide

1711   *Feb. 22* Russia declares war on the Ottoman Empire; Peter establishes the Senate

Mar. 6 On the eve of his departure for the front, Peter declares Marta Skavronska (future Catherine I) his consort

June 2 Iu. F. Shakhovskoi, a member of Peter's mock ecclesiastical council and the mock Cavalier of the Order of Judas, appointed chief hangman of the Russian expeditionary army during the Pruth campaign against the Ottoman Empire

Oct. 14 Wedding of Tsarevich Aleksei Petrovich to Princess Sophia-Charlotte of Brunswick-Wölfenbüttel

1712   *Feb. 10* Peter's second wedding, a naval-themed celebration that includes the participation (and blessing) of members of the mock ecclesiastical council, including Prince-Pope N. M. Zotov, Arch-Hierarch P. I. Buturlin, and Archdeacon Iu. F. Shakhovskoi

June Carnivalesque wedding of P. I. Buturlin, Arch-Hierarch of St. Petersburg

1713   *April* Peace of Utrecht ends War of the Spanish Succession and marks the resumption of western diplomatic involvement in the Northern War

Apr. 25 Beginning of successful Russian campaign in Finland

October Peter starts making plans for the carnivalesque wedding of Prince-Pope N. M. Zotov, but is frustrated by the reluctance of the designated bride, A. E. Stremoukhova (*née* Pashkova)

Senate's move to St. Petersburg marks the de facto relocation of the Russian capital

1714   *Mar. 17* Decree about the permanent settlement in St. Petersburg by selected merchants and nobles

Mar. 23 Promulgation of Law on Single Inheritance

July 27 Battle of Hangö, first Russian naval victory

1715   *Jan. 16–17* Long-delayed wedding of Prince-Pope Zotov marks the translation of the Transfigured Kingdom to the banks of the Neva River and celebrates St. Petersburg's ascendancy over Moscow

Oct. 12 Birth of Peter's grandson, Tsarevich Peter Alekseevich

Oct. 29 Birth of Peter's second son, Peter Petrovich

1716   *February* Peter begins second major tour of western Europe

Aug. 26 Peter sends ultimatum to Tsarevich Aleksei Petrovich

Sept. 26 Under the pretext of joining his father at the front, Tsarevich Aleksei flees to Vienna and seeks asylum at the court of his brother-in-law, the Holy Roman Emperor, Charles VI

1717   *July 10* Peter coaxes Tsarevich Aleksei to return to Russia

Sept. 17 Death of Prince F. Iu. Romodanovskii, first mock Tsar of the Transfigured Kingdom

Sept. 23 Death of N. M. Zotov, second Prince-Pope of the Transfigured Kingdom

Oct. 4 Tsarevich Aleksei agrees to return to Russia

Oct. 10 Peter returns to St. Petersburg after more than a year and a half abroad

Dec. 11–15 Planned reorganization of the Russian central government administration leads to the creation of collegiate boards (*kolegii*)

Dec. 21 Peter arrives in Moscow after making arrangements for the fixing up of his mansion in Novo-Preobrazhenskoe and the fortress of Pressburg, where previous elections of the Prince-Pope and Prince-Caesar took place

Dec. 28–29 P. I. Buturlin, mock Metropolitan of St. Petersburg, elected and ordained as the third Prince-Pope of the Transfigured Kingdom

1718   *Jan. 5* Prince-Caesar I. F. Romodanovskii elected to the mock ecclesiastical rank of Prince Abbot, having already inherited his father's post as head of the secret police

Jan. 31 Tsarevich Aleksei arrives in Moscow

Feb. 3 Promulgation of the manifesto depriving Aleksei of the succession and naming Peter's second son, Tsarevich Peter Petrovich, as heir apparent

June 26 Death of Tsarevich Aleksei

November Beginning of new provincial reform on the Swedish model

Nov. 26 Decree instituting French-style assemblies in high society

1719   *Apr. 25* Death of Peter's second son and heir apparent, Tsarevich Peter Petrovich

1720   *Jan. 13* Naval Statute issued

April Unofficial publication of the statutes of the mock British Monastery or Bung College

May 30 Death of Prince-Pope Buturlin's wife

July 27 Russian naval victory at Grengham

1721   *Jan. 25* Ecclesiastical Regulation abolishes the Russian patriarchate

Feb. 14 Holy Governing Synod founded

Aug. 30 Peace of Nystadt ends the twenty-one-year Northern War between Russia and Sweden, consolidating territorial gains made by Russia in the Baltics and recouping the losses incurred during the Time of Troubles

Sept. 10 The masquerade wedding of Prince-Pope Buturlin and A. E. Stremoukhova-Zotova inaugurates celebrations to mark the signing of the Nystadt peace treaty and St. Petersburg's triumph over Stockholm

Oct. 22 The second stage of the peace celebrations, during which Chancellor G. I. Golovkin, Russia's foreign minister (and member of the mock ecclesiastical council) asks Tsar Peter to accept the titles of All-Russian Emperor, Father of the Fatherland, and Great in the name of the Senate and Synod

Oct. 24–30 The third and final stage of the Nystadt peace celebrations takes place in Moscow, during Shrovetide; the Unholy Council participates in the masquerade

1722   *Jan. 24* Creation of the Table of Ranks

Feb. 5 Law on Succession to the Throne gives Peter sole discretion over choice of next tsar

1723   *Shrovetide* While in Moscow, Peter visits Pressburg and organizes the ceremonial demolition of his old palace at Novo-Preobrazhenskoe, the cradle of Petrine military reforms

May 30 Peter and his court stage the ceremonial transfer of the relics of the "Grandfather of the Russian Fleet" from Moscow to St. Petersburg

Aug. 28 Ceremonial funeral procession for the late Prince-Pope Buturlin

1724   *May 7* Catherine, Peter's second wife, crowned as empress-consort

Nov. 8 Arrest of William Mons, Catherine's reputed lover

Nov. 16 Execution of William Mons signals the beginning of a major government shake-up

Yuletide Election and installation of Prince-Pope Stroev, fourth and final mock pontiff of the Transfigured Kingdom

1725   *Jan. 28* Death of Peter I; accession of Catherine I

Mar. 10 Peter entombed in the Peter-Paul Cathedral of St. Petersburg

1727   *May 6* Death of Catherine I

APPENDIX 2

Members of the Unholy Council

The history of Peter's court is, to a large extent, the history of his company, and the story of his company cannot be written without at least mention of the Unholy Council of the Transfigured Kingdom.[1] This obvious parody of the Muscovite Holy Council of the Russian Orthodox patriarch constituted an integral part of the countercultural play world created on the grounds of the suburban royal estate of Novo-Preobrazhenskoe at the end of the seventeenth century. Indeed, all of the "clerics" listed below had also at one time or another pledged allegiance to Prince-Caesar F. Iu. Romodanovskii, the mock King of Pressburg, who served as the secular counterpart to His Most Foolish and All-Drunken Highness the Prince-Pope. More important, all of these individuals also held some other rank within the official military, civilian, and court hierarchies of the evolving well-ordered police state. It is this fact that justifies the effort to identify the courtiers concealed behind the frequently obscene pseudonyms and to reconstruct the social composition of Peter's company. This catalog of all known members of the Unholy Council of Peter the Great is the first and admittedly preliminary step in that direction.

I say "preliminary" because my list of members is incomplete, for two major reasons. First, there was never an official roll of members of the Unholy Council; surviving lists are not the staff registers of a real institution but the occasional ephemera produced for royal spectacles or invoked in

---

1. For a pioneering attempt to define the membership of Peter's company, see A. I. Zaozerskii, *Fel'dmarshal B. P. Sheremetev* (Moscow, 1989), 200–206. For a prosopographical study of Peter's court, see Robert O. Crummey, "Peter and the Boyar Aristocracy, 1689–1700," and Brenda Meehan-Waters, "The Russian Aristocracy and the Reforms of Peter the Great," both in *Canadian-American Slavic Studies* 8 (Summer 1974): 275–87 and 288–99, respectively; John P. LeDonne, "Ruling Families in the Russian Political Order," pt. 1, "The Petrine Leadership, 1689–1725," *Cahiers du monde russe et soviétique* 28, no. 3–4 (1987): 233–322; and esp. I. Iu. Airapetian, "Feodal'naia aristokratiia v period stanovleniia absoliutizma v Rossii" (Diss. kand. ist. nauk, M. V. Lomonosov State University, 1987).

private correspondence. Second, because these sacred parodies were produced mostly for an internal audience at court, the writers did not bother to reveal the names of many individuals concealed behind the pseudonyms (a fact recognized by M. M. Shcherbatov, the first cataloger of the correspondence associated with the Unholy Council of the Prince-Pope).[2] In compiling this list, I have tried to identify as many members of Peter's mock synod as was possible with the present state of knowledge, but full identification is a task for the future, as we learn more about the changing composition of his company.[3]

However, the fact that some leading figures of the reign are not mentioned as having pseudonyms within Peter's mock ecclesiastical council does not mean that none of them had one (since some of the people on the list have not been identified) or that they did not participate in the bacchanalian mysteries of state practiced at his court. As an example of the first problem, consider the "sacristan" Apraksin in Table 1. The Apraksins were a long-time boyar family with marital links to the royal house and with easy access to the quarters of Tsar Peter Alekseevich. All three Apraksin brothers served as Peter's privy chamberlains; two of them, Petr Matveevich and Fedor Matveevich, even reached the highest rank (boyar) in the Muscovite royal council (in 1710 and 1713, respectively), although by that time the appointment was largely ceremonial.[4] They also held some of the most prominent positions in Peter's administration, as well as in his company. Petr, the eldest of the Apraksin brothers, served as the governor of Kazan province (from 1711); while his more famous younger brother Fedor served as the governor of Voronezh and the titular head of the Russian imperial navy.[5] At the same time, a portrait of the third (and last) Apraksin brother, A. M.

---

2. RO RNB, f. 450, ll. 10–11.

3. A preliminary qualitative analysis of the admittedly fragmentary evidence makes it clear, for example, that the number of "prelates" (i.e., bishops, archbishops, metropolitans, abbots, abbesses, and archimandrites) who attended the St. Petersburg masquerade of 1723 was more than four times higher than the number mentioned in Peter's 1698 letter about his Unholy Council. For a list of the prelates and other mock clerics who took part in the 1723 masquerade, see "Kompaniia mashkarada v Sankt Piter Burkhe 1723 goda" (August 20–September 6, 1720), in RGADA, f. 156, op. 1, ed. khr. 186, ll. 30v, 27v. Cf. Peter to A. A. Vinius, July 9, 1698, in *PiB*, 1:265, 741. In addition to "His Holiness" [Ianikit, the Patriarch of Pressburg] Peter mentions three arch-hierarchs (Tikhon, Misail, and Aleksei), Presbyter Aleksandr the Hirsute, and Deacon Gavrill the Long-Lived. Even if one includes Andrei, the Patriarch of Palestine alongside the three metropolitans mentioned in this letter, it is clear that by the end of Peter's reign the top echelons of the mock ecclesiastical hierarchy had increased dramatically. This increase corresponds to the veritable explosion in the number of lower-ranked "servitors of the Arch-Prince-Pope." For a partial list of those servitors (c. 1722), see V. I. Semevskii, "Petr Velikii kak iumorist (1690–1725)," in his *Ocherki i razskazy iz russkoi istorii XVIII v.: Slovo i delo! 1700–1725*, 2nd rev. ed., 278–334 (St. Petersburg, 1884).

4. See Airapetian, "Feodal'naia aristokratiia," 99, 329, 321, 316.

5. On Petr Matveevich Apraksin (1659–1728), see A. Kh. Gorfunkel', "Andrei Belobot-skii—poet i filosof kontsa XVII–nachala XVIII veka," *Trudy otdela drevnerusskoi literatury* 18 (1962): 191; and Lindsey Hughes, *Russia in the Age of Peter the Great* (New Haven, 1998), 115. For a biography of "General-Admiral" Fedor Matveevich (1661–1728), see Hughes, *Russia*, 115, 418–19; *RBS*, 2:256–58; S. I. Dmitriev, *General-Admiral graf F. M. Apraksin. Spodvizhnik Petra Velikogo* (Petrograd, 1914); and P. Belaventsev, *General-Admiral graf Fedor Matveevich: Kratkii biograficheskii ocherk* (Revel, 1899).

Apraksin (a.k.a. *Andrei Besiashchii*), dressed in the vestments of a high priest of the mock ecclesiastical council, hung in the picture gallery of the royal palace in Novo-Preobrazhenskoe.[6] It is possible that Andrei Matvee-vich is the Apraksin referred to as sacristan (though that is rather a lowly rank for someone who was already known as a high priest); however, we cannot be certain of that attribution until further evidence becomes available. Indeed, despite the amount of information that we do have about this family, it is still extremely difficult to determine which of the three Apraksin brothers was referred to by this pseudonym.

As for the issue of those high-placed courtiers who supposedly did not participate in the bacchanalian mysteries of state celebrated by members of the tsar's inner circle, I point the reader to the collective "epistle" that was drafted by Prince-Pope N. M. Zotov before 1706, during a gathering held at the home of Prince Menshikov to toast Archdeacon Gideon (Iu. F. Shakhovskoi) on his departure for the front. In addition to the signatures of several mock priests (such as "His Meekness Anikit of Kiev and Galicia" [I. A. Musin-Pushkin], the "Drunken Protopresbyter Fedor Golovin," and "Gavrilo [Golovkin], the Truly Drunk Proto-Deacon of [the Metropolitan of] Kiev"), this example of sacred parody included the signatures of P. P. Shafirov (vice chancellor of foreign affairs); Jacob Bruce (head of the artillery chancellery); Johann Georg, Baron von Keyserling (the Prussian ambassador); and the illiterate Prince Menshikov himself.[7] What is significant here is the almost seamless way in which the playful personae associated with the Prince-Pope's ecclesiastical council melded into the entourage of Peter's top policy makers and advisers—the men who helped him imagine and build the Transfigured Kingdom that was imperial Russia. Ultimately, whether or not these people held mock ecclesiastical ranks in the Unholy Council is less significant than the fact that they all took part in the bonding rituals that allowed Peter to enact his charismatic scenario of power.

6. On the portrait of *Andrei Besiashchii*, see N. M. Moleva, " 'Persony' vseshuteishego sobora," *Voprosy istorii* 10 (October 1974): 209.

7. D. O. Serov, *Stroiteli imperii: Ocherki gosudarstvennoi i kriminal'noi deiatel'nosti spodvizhnikov Petra I* (Novosibirsk, 1996), 30–68, 254; Hughes, *Russia*, 423, 429–30; I. N. Kolkina, "Iakov Vilimovich Brius," in *Soratniki Petra*, ed. N. I. Pavlenko et al., 433–76 (Moscow, 2001). For the original text of the letter, see RGADA, f. 9, otd. 2, op. 3, ch. 1 (1710 g.), ed. khr. 11, ll. 189–90v; for a nineteenth-century copy, see RO RNB, f. 824, op. 2, kn. 200, ll. 20r–v, 26.

Table 1. Members of the Unholy Council

	Name	Official rank/position	Mock title
1	P. A. Romanov (1672–1725)	Tsar	Humble deacon Petr;[1] Proto-Deacon Piter;[2] Proto-Deacon Pitirim;[3] Proto-Deacon Pachomius, Crams-with-His-Prick Mikhailov (*pakhom pikhai khui Mikhailov*), servant (*sluzhitel*) of the Arch-Prince-Pope[4]
2	V. A. Sokovnin	Privy chamberlain (*komnatnyi stol'nik*) to Peter (1683–97);[5] governor of Iaroslavl, Rostov, and Pereiaslavl (1692–94) during Peter's boat-building in Pereiaslavl[6]	Prophet (*prorok*)[7]
3	T. N. Streshnev (1649–1719)	Tutor (*diad'ka*) to Peter; boyar (from 1688), head of *Sysknoi*, Vladimir Judicial, Equerry Chancelleries, and *prikaz Bol'shogo dvortsa;* head of *Razriadnyi prikaz* (from 1690), the main war chancellery; administrative head of Moscow province (from 1708); senator (from 1711)[8]	Right Reverend Tikhon;[9] Metropolitan of Novgorod[10]
4	Prince F. Iu. Romodanovskii (1640–1717)	Privy chamberlain (*komnatnyi stol'nik*) at Peter's court; head of *Preobrazhenskaia poteshnaia izba* (from 1686), reorganized in 1695 as *Preobrazhenskii prikaz,* Peter's secret police[11]	Generallissimus Friedrich (*Fridrikh*); King of Pressburg;[12] Prince-Caesar (*Kniaz''-Kesar'*); Anti-Caesar (*Anti-Tsesar'*)[13]
5	M. F. Naryshkin (d. 1692)	Privy chamberlain (*komnatnyi stol'nik*) at Peter's court, *okol'nichii* (1688–90); boyar (1690–92)[14]	Patriarch Deary (*Patriarkh Milak*)[15]
6	I. A. Musin-Pushkin (1661–1729)	*Okol'nichii* (from 1682); governor of Smolensk and Astrakhan (from 1683); boyar (from 1692); head of Monastery Chancellery (from 1701), de facto administrator of church property; *tainyi sovetnik* (from 1709); count (from 1710); senator (from 1711); president of *Shtatskontor collegium* (from 1717); member of *Vysshii sud* (from 1723); head of the Senate's Moscow branch (from 1725)[16]	Iannikii, Metropolitan of Kiev and Gaditsiia;[17] His Meekness Anikit of Kiev and Galicia[18]

Table 1.—cont.

Name	Official rank/position	Mock title
7 F. A. Golovin (1650–1706)	Boyar and count; head of Moscow Armory and associated court workshops (from 1697); second head of Peter's Great Embassy (1697–98); head of Marines Chancellery (*Voinskogo morskogo flota*); first cavalier of order of St. Andrew (1699); second general-admiral of the navy (1699); from 1700, head of Foreign Affairs Office and all associated chancelleries; first general field marshal of the army (1700)[19]	Priest (*pop*) Fetka;[20] Clergyman (*sviashchennik*) Fedor;[21] Protopresbyter (*protopresviter*) Fedor Golovin[22]
8 G. I. Golovkin (1660–1734)	Privy chamberlain (*komnatnyi stol'nik*) of Peter (from 1686); *postel'nichii* and *verkhovnyi komnatnyi* (from 1689); head of *Kazennyi prikaz* (1689–94); head of *Masterskaia palata* (1689–1712); knight of order of St. Andrew (from 1703); head of Foreign Affairs Chancellery (from 1706); count (from 1707); president of Foreign Affairs Collegium (from 1717); senator (from 1718)[23]	Deacon Gavriil the Long-Lived (*diakon Gavriil Dolgoveshchnyi*);[24] Gavriil the Truly Drunk Proto-Deacon (*gei p'iannyi protodiakon*)[25]
9 N. M. Zotov (1643/44–1717)	Tutor to Peter; *dumnyi diak* (1683–98); head of Peter's traveling chancellery (1695–96); *dumnyi dvorianin i pechatnik* (1698–1701); head of Privy Chancellery (*Blizhniaia kantseliariia*) (from 1701), institutional precursor of College of State Accounting (*Revizion-kollegiia*); count and *general-prezident* of Privy Chancellery (from 1710); state *fiskal* (from 1711)[26]	Most Holy Patriarch (*sviateishii patriarkh*);[27] Great Sovereign, His Holiness, Sir Ianikit, Archbishop of Pressburg and Patriarch of all Iauza and Kokui;[28] Prince-Pope (*Kniaz'-Papa*) (ca. 1693–1718)
10 I. I. Buturlin the Elder (d. 1710)	Privy chamberlain (*komnatnyi stol'nik*) at Peter's court (1682–1710); head of *Semenovskii prikaz*, later *Semenovskaia kantseliariia prikaza Zemskikh del*, charged with overseeing law and order in Moscow[29]	Generalissimus Johann (*Iagan*) of Semenovsk regiment;[30] King of Semenovsk; Polish King
11 A. P. Protas'ev	*Okol'nichii*; governor of Mangazeia, Siberia (1686–90); head of Vladimir Judicial Chancellery (1692–95, 1697–1700); *admiralteets* during Azov campaign (1696)[31]	Presbyter Aleksandr the Hirsute (*presviter Aleksandr Volosatyi*)[32]

Table 1.—cont.

	Name	Official rank/position	Mock title
12	Prince M. F. Zhirovoi-Zasekin	*Okol'nichii*[33]	Right Reverend [Metropolitan] Misail (*preosviashchennyi Misail*);[34] His Meekness the Right Reverend Misail, Metropolitan of Kazan and Sviazhsk (*Smirennyi Preosviashchennyi Mitropolit Misail Kazanskii i Sviazhskii*)[35]
13	F. P. Shanskii	Equerry (*striapchii*) (1692); rank-and-file chamberlain (*stol'nik*) [1694–99][36]	Bailiff (*pristav*) and parishioner (*soborian*) of Patriarch Andrei of Palestine[37]
14	Prince Iu. F. Shakhovskoi (ca. 1672–1713)	Rank-and-file courtier (*riadovoi stol'nik*) (from 1687); privy chamberlain (*komnatnyi stol'nik*) at Peter's court (1696–1710); boyar (1710–13); *general-gevaldiger,* head of military police during Pruth campaign (1711)[38]	Archdeacon Gideon (*arkhidiakon Gedeon*);[39] Cavalier of the Order of Judas (1709–13)[40]
15	I. I. Khovanskii the Elder (d. 1701)	Boyar	Metropolitan[41]
16	Prince M. G. Romodanovskii (1653–1713)	Boyar, head of *Razboinyi*, later Vladimir judicial chancelleries; governor of Pskov (1685–87) and Kiev (1689–92); head of *Proviantskii prikaz* (1705–7) and commander of Belgorod regiment; governor of Moscow (1712–13)[42]	Right Reverend [Metropolitan] Mickey (*Preosviashchennyi Mishura*)[43]
17	Prince I. F. Romodanovskii (ca. 1678–1730)	*Blizhnii stol'nik;* picked to replace his father as head of Preobrazhenk chancellery (from 1718); *deistvitel'nyi tainyi sovetnik* and knight of order of St. Andrew (1725); governor general of Moscow[44]	Second Prince-Caesar; Prince Abbot (*knez' igumen*) (both from 1718)[45]
18	P. I. Buturlin (d. 1723)	Boyar (from 1711)[46]	Metropolitan Peter-Prick (*Petrokhui*) of Izhorsk and St. Petersburg;[47] Bishop (*arkhierei*) of St. Petersburg;[48] third Prince-Pope (from 1718)[49]
19	I. M. Golovin (1672–1737)	Chief surveyor (*obor-sarvair*) of the navy	Prince Jochann (*Ioagan*), Master Craftsman (*kniaz'-Bas*)[50]
20	D. G. Rzhevskaia (*née* Sokovnina)	Lady-in-waiting (*stats-dama*) to Catherine I[51]	Princess Abbess; Arch-Abbess (*arkhi-igumen'ia*)[52]
21	Princess A. P. Golitsyna (*née* Prozorovskaia) (1655–1729)	Lady-in-waiting (*stats-dama*) to Catherine I[53]	Princess Abbess (*kniaz'-igumen'ia*) (1718–29)[54]

Table 1.—cont.

Name	Official rank/position	Mock title
22 Stepan Vasil'ev Medvedev (d. 1722)	Watchman at Sergeants' Yard (*storozh Serzhantskogo dvora*) in Novo-Preobrazhenskoe; rank-and-file soldier in Preobrazhensk guards regiment; member of tsar's personal household staff (*sluzhitel' v dome tsarskogo velichestva*)[55]	The Bear (*medved'*); Crozier-Bearer (*pososhnik*); Subdeacon (*ipodiakon*)[56]
23 S. Ia. Turgenev	Rank-and-file courtier (*riadovoi stol'nik*, 1692–1710); *dumnyi dvorianin* (from 1711); member of tsar's personal household staff[57]	*Groznyi* and Subdeacon (*ipodiakon*)[58]
24 [*N. N.*]		Bishop (*arkhierei*) Andrei;[59] Andrei, Patriarch of Palestine (*Andrei Palestinskii* or *patriarkh Palestinskii*)[60]
25 [*N. N.*]		Right Reverend [Metropolitan] Aleksii[61]
26 [*N. N.*]		Right Reverend [Metropolitan] Gedeon of Kiev and Galicia[62]
27 [*N. N.*]		Nominee (*naminat*) Kuska; Confessor (*dukhovnik*) Koz'ma[63]
28 [*N. N.*] Streshneva		Arch-Abbess[64]
29 [*N. N.*] Mukhanov		Servant (*sluzhitel'*) of Arch-Prince-Pope[65]
30 [I. I.?] Buturlin		Deacon John (*Ion*), servant (*sluzhitel'*) of Arch-Prince-Pope
31 [*N. N.*] Apraksin		Sacristan (*kliuchar'*)
32 [*N. N.*] Khilkov		Sacristan
33 [*N. N.*] Subbota		Sacristan
34 [*N. N.*] Musin-Pushkin		Sexton (*rizhnichii*)
35 [*N. N.*] Repnin		Canon (*ustavshchik*)
36 [*N. N.*] Shusherin		Priest Feofan
37 [*N. N.*] Golovin		Deacon
38 [A. M.?] Voeikov[66]		Deacon
39 [*N. N.*] Ronov		Deacon
40 [*N. N.*] Shemiakin		Deacon
41 [*N. N.*] Prozorovskii		Subdeacon Filaret
42 [*N. N.*] Iushkov		Provost (*blagochinnoi*) and Subdeacon
43 [*N. N.*] Koltovskii		Gerfalcon keeper (*krechetnik*) and Subdeacon
44 [*N. N.*] Palibin		*Lopatchik* and Subdeacon (*ipodiakon*)

Table 1.—cont.

Name	Official rank/position	Mock title
45 [N. N.] Gubin		Subdeacon
46 [N. N.] Vasil'ev		Subdeacon
47 [N. N.] Timashev		Subdeacon
48 [N. N.] Kliucharev		Subdeacon
49 [N. N.] Likharev		Subdeacon
50 [N. N.] Kozyrev		Novgorodian scribe (*pod"iachii*) and Subdeacon
51 Grigorii [N.] Kashnin		Siberian commandant and Subdeacon
52 Prokopii Ushakov	*Dumnyi dvorianin*	Little Jester (*shutik*) or fool [-prick] (*durachik* [*khui*]*chok*)[67]
53 [N. N.] Trokhaniantov		Subdeacon
54 Ivan Losev		Clerk (*d'iak*)
55 Osip Metlin		Clerk
56 F. P. Sheremetev		Prelate (*arkhierarkh*)[68]
57 Prince Iu. F. Shcherbatov (1686–1737)	*Okol'nichii*; brigadier (from 1704);[69] assistant (*tovarishch*) to Prince Iu. F. Shakhovskoi at Ingermanland Chancellery (1710);[70] hosted tsar and company at one of the first assemblies in St. Petersburg[71]	Prelate
58 M. V. Kolychev		Prelate
59 Mikhailo [N.] Sobakin		Prelate
60 Prince Ia. I. Lobanov-Rostovskii (1660–1732)	Privy chamberlain (*komnatnyi stol'nik*) [1676–82]; sent abroad as "volunteer" (1696); served as major in Semenovsk regiment and as corporal of a Cossack regiment[72]	Prelate
61 Matvei Golovin		Prelate
62 Vasilii Rzhevskoi		Prelate
63 Anton Savelov		Prelate
64 Ivan Denisov, son of Subota, a.k.a. Danilov		Sacristan (*kliuchar'*)
65 Fedor Protas'ev		Sacristan
66 Prince M. M. Obolenskoi	*Stol'nik* at court of Tsar Ivan Alekseevich (since 1687); sent abroad as "volunteer" (1696)[73]	Priest (*pop*)
67 Vasilii, a.k.a. Samoila, Glebov		Priest
68 I. R. Streshnev		Priest
69 Lev Voeikov		Deacon

Table 1.—cont.

Name	Official rank/position	Mock title
70 [N. N.] Stroev	Commissariat officer[74]	Archdeacon (*arkhidiakon*), servant (*sluzhitel'*) of Arch-Prince-Pope;[75] Archdeacon Fuck Off (*idi na khui*) Stroev;[76] last Prince-Pope[77]

[1]Peter to F. M. Apraksin, ca. April 1695, in *PiB*, 1:28.

[2]Collective "epistle" to A. D. Menshikov, March 1706, ibid., 4:184.

[3]Ibid., 2:126–28.

[4]Undated list of the "servants [*sluzhiteli*] of the Arch-Prince-Pope [*arkhi kniaz-papy*]" (c. 1722), in V. I. Semevskii, "Petr Velikii kak iumorist (1690–1725)," in his *Ocherki i razskazy iz russkoi istorii XVIII v.: Slovo i delo! 1700–1725*, 2nd rev. ed. (St. Petersburg, 1884), 313–14.

[5]I. Iu. Airapetian, "Feodal'naia aristokratiia v period stanovleniia absoliutizma v Rossii" (Diss. kand. ist. nauk, M. V. Lomonosov State University, 1987), 334.

[6]Paul Bushkovitch, *Peter the Great: The Struggle for Power, 1671–1725* (Cambridge, 2001), 197.

[7]See Chapter 2.

[8]D. O. Serov, *Stroiteli imperii: Ocherki gosudarstvennoi i kriminal'noi deiatel'nosti spodvizhnikov Petra I* (Novosibirsk, 1996), 250; Lindsey Hughes, *Russia in the Age of Peter the Great* (New Haven, 1998), 418.

[9]Peter to A. A. Vinius, July 9, 1698, in *PiB*, 1:265, 741.

[10]RGADA, f. 156, op. 1, ed. khr. 129, l. 22.

[11]Hughes, *Russia*, 423–24; N. B. Golikova, *Politicheskie protsessy pri Petre I: Po materialam Preobrazhenskogo prikaza* (Moscow, 1957), 10, 12.

[12]*PiB*, 1:29–30.

[13]*Pokhodnyi zhurnal 1713 goda* (St. Petersburg, 1854), 53 ("*Antitsesar*").

[14]Airapetian, "Feodal'naia aristokratiia," 101, 103–4, 317, 323, 333; "Naryshkiny," in *RBS*, 11: 94–95.

[15]See Chapter 2.

[16]Serov, *Stroiteli imperii*, 241; Hughes, *Russia*, 418.

[17]*PiB*, 2:126–28; V. M. Zhivov, "Kul'turnye reformy v sisteme preobrazovanii Petra I," in *Iz istorii russkoi kul'tury*, ed. A. D. Koshelev (Moscow, 1996), 3:555n14.

[18]N. M. Zotov to Peter (before 1706), in RGADA, f. 9, otd. 2, op. 3, ch. 1 (1710 g.), ed. khr. 11, ll. 189–90v; and RO RNB, f. 824, op. 2, kn. 200, ll. 20r–v, 26.

[19]Serov, *Stroiteli imperii*, 226–27.

[20]F. A. Golovin to Peter, February 1700, in *PiB*, 1:788.

[21]"Patriarch Andrei of Palestine" to Peter, ca. 1690s, in RGADA, f. 9, otd. 2, op. 4, ch. I, kn. 53, l. 504, also mentions "clergyman [*sviashchennik*] Fedor" as one of his "parishioners" (*soboriane*).

[22]N. M. Zotov to Peter (before 1706), RGADA, f. 9, otd. 2, op. 3, ch. 1 (1710 g.), ed. khr. 11, ll. 189–90v; and RO RNB, f. 824, op. 2, kn. 200, ll. 20r–v, 26.

[23]Serov, *Stroiteli imperii*, 227; Hughes, *Russia*, 420–21.

[24]*PiB*, 1:265, 741.

[25]N. M. Zotov to Peter (before 1706), RGADA, f. 9, otd. 2, op. 3, ch. 1 (1710 g.), ed. khr. 11, ll. 189–90v; and RO RNB, f. 824, op. 2, kn. 200, ll. 20r–v, 26.

[26]Hughes, *Russia*, 423; V. Korsakov, "Zotov," in *RBS*, 7:476–81; S. Liubimov, "Zotovy," in *Opyt istoricheskikh rodoslovii: Gundorovy, Zhizhemskie, Nesvitskie, Sibirskie, Zotovy i Ostermany*, 80–90 (Petrograd, 1915); [N. Tokarev], "Blizhniaia kantseliariia pri Petre Velikom i eia dela," in *Opisanie dokumentov i bumag khraniashchikhsia v Moskovskom arkhive Ministerstva Iustitsii*, 5:43–75 (Moscow, 1888); and Evgenii Anisimov, *Gosudarstvennye preobrazovaniia i samoderzhavie Petra Velikogo v pervoi chetverti XVIII veka* (St. Petersburg, 1997), 22–25.

[27]Peter to F. M. Apraksin, October 11, 1693, in *PiB*, 1:17–18, 491. Judging by this letter, just one year after the death of Patriarch Deary, the *dumnyi diak* N. M. Zotov had taken his place as the head of the mock ecclesiastical council of the Transfigured Kingdom.

[28]Peter to Prince F. Iu. Romodanovskii, June 10, 1695, in *PiB*, 1:31–32, refers to "*otets nash velikii gospodin sviateishii kir Ianikit, arkhiepiskup Preshpurskii i vseia Iauzy i vsego Kokuiu patriarkh*," a pun on the full title of the Russian Orthodox patriarch, "*vsesviateishii kir Adrian, Bozhieiu milost'iu arkhiepiskop Moskovskii i vseia Rossii i vsekh severnykh stran patriarkh.*" See Peter to Patriarch Adrian, July 19, 1695, ibid., 41. New geographical references could be added at will to Zotov's patriarchal title; see, for example, ibid., 520–21 ("Archbishop of Paris") and 532–33 ("Ianikit of

Pressburg and Azov and Patriarch of all the Lower Lands from Down There [in the Crimea] [*vsekh tamoshnikh ponizovykh stran patriarkh*]."

[29]Airapetian, "Feodal'naia aristokratiia," 77, 98, 329, 347; Anisimov, *Gosudarstvennye preobrazovaniia,* 26; SPB F IRI RAN, f. 276, op. 1, ed. khr. 108, ll. 57, 35–36, 115–16; *PiB,* 1:60, 493, 506, 530–33, 652, 683–84, 814–15, 835; Golikova, *Politicheskie protsessy,* 10.

[30]I. I. Buturlin the Elder to Peter, August 1695, in *PiB,* 1:523–24.

[31]Bushkovitch, *Peter the Great,* 180, 186n44.

[32]*PiB,* 1:265, 741.

[33]N. M. Moleva and E. M. Beliutin, *"Zhivopisnykh del mastera." Kantseliariia ot stroenii i russkaia zhivopis' pervoi poloviny XVIII veka* (Moscow, 1965), 15–16, fig. 4, portrait of M. F.(?) Zhirovoi-Zasekin, part of the so-called Preobrazhenskoe series (c. 1690–1700).

[34]*PiB,* 1:265, 631, 632, 644, 741, where he is mistakenly identified with Prince M. N. L'vov. For the correct identification, see *PiB,* 4 (2): 751, 730–31.

[35]N. M. Zotov to Peter (before 1706), RGADA, f. 9, otd. 2, op. 3, ch. 1 (1710 g.), ed. khr. 11, ll. 189–90v; and RO RNB, f. 824, op. 2, kn. 200, ll. 20r–20v, 26.

[36]Airapetian, "Feodal'naia aristokratiia," 431; P. P. Ivanov, *Alfavitnyi ukazatel' familii i lits, upominaemykh v boiarskikh knigakh* (Moscow, 1853), 464.

[37]Patriarch Andrei of Palestine to Peter, ca. 1690s, in RGADA, f. 9, otd. 2, op. 4, ch. 1, kn. 53, l. 504.

[38]Airapetian, "Feodal'naia aristokratiia," 319, 336, 432; SPb F IRI RAN, f. 83, op. 3, ed. khr. 3, ll. 3–5.

[39]Patriarch Andrei of Palestine to Peter, ca. 1690s, in RGADA, f. 9, otd. 2, op. 4, ch. 1, kn. 53, l. 504, mentions "deacon Prince Iurii" as one of his "parishioners."

[40]See Chapter 3.

[41]G. V. Esipov, *Raskol'nich'i dela XVIII stoletiia, izvlechennye iz del Preobrazhenskogo prikaza i Tainoi Rozysknykh del kantseliarii* (St. Petersburg, 1861), 68–69.

[42]Serov, *Stroiteli imperii,* 246; *RBS,* 17:124–26.

[43]*RBS,* 121.

[44]Ibid., 120–24; Serov, *Stroiteli imperii,* 246.

[45]Peter to A. D. Menshikov, January 12, 1718, in SPb F IRI RAN, f. 270, kn. 87, l. 22; see Chapter 5.

[46]Airapetian, "Feodal'naia aristokratiia," 98, 110, 316.

[47]P. I. Buturlin to Peter, January 5, 1709, in Semevskii, "Petr Velikii kak iumorist," 288.

[48]*Pokhodnyi zhurnal 1712 goda,* 5–6; Semevskii, "Petr Velikii kak iumorist," 286–87.

[49]See Chapter 5.

[50]Lindsey Hughes, " 'For the Health of the Sons of Ivan Mikhailovich': I. M. Golovin and Peter the Great's Mock Court," in *Reflections on Russia in the Eighteenth Century,* ed. Joachim Klein, Simon Dixon, and Maarten Fraanje, 43–51 (Cologne, 2001).

[51]For a brief biography of D. G. Rzhevskaia (*née* Sokovnina), see Petr Dolgorukii, *Rossiiskaia rodoslovnaia kniga* (St. Petersburg, 1857), 4:31–35; P. F. Karabanov, "Stats-damy i freiliny russkogo dvora v XVIII stoletii," pt. 1, *Russkaia starina* 2 (1870): 482; and Hughes, *Russia,* 253.

[52]P. I. Buturlin to D. G. Rzhevskaia, December 28, 1717, in RGADA, f. 9, otd. 1, kn. 67, ll. 664–65; Semevskii, "Petr Velikii kak iumorist," 311.

[53]On Princess A. P. Golitsyna (*née* Prozorovskaia), see Evgenii Serchevskii, ed., *Zapiski o rode kniazei Golitsynykh* (St. Petersburg, 1853), 57, 292; G. V. Esipov, "Kniaginia-igumen'ia," *Russkaia starina* 1 (1870): 400–403; P. F. Karabanov, "Stats-damy i freiliny russkogo dvora v XVIII stoletii," pt. 1, *Russkaia starina* 2 (1870): 478–79; and Hughes, *Russia,* 194, 201, 253, 261, 291, 504n254, 516–17nn42–46.

[54]RGADA, f. 156, op. 1, ed. khr. 186, l. 31v.

[55]S. F. Platonov, "Iz bytovoi istorii Petrovskoi epokhi," pt. 2, "Liubimtsy Petra Velikogo: Medved', Bitka i dr.," *Izvestiia AN SSSR,* ser. 6 (1926): 655–78, esp. 659–63; for the date of his death, see ibid., 662.

[56]Undated list of the "servants of the Arch-Prince-Pope" (c. 1722), in Semevskii, "Petr Velikii kak iumorist," 313–14.

[57]Airapet'ian, "Feodal'naia aristokratiia," 67, 328, 421; Platonov, "Iz bytovoi istorii Petrovskoi epokhi," 664.

[58]Undated list of the "servants of the Arch-Prince-Pope" (c. 1722), in Semevskii, "Petr Velikii kak iumorist," 313–14.

[59]Peter to A. A. Vinius, September 17–28, 1696, in *PiB,* 1:110, 606.

[60]Patriarch Andrei of Palestine to Peter, July 23, 1697, ibid., 628.

[61]Peter to A. A. Vinius, July 9, 1698, ibid., 265, 741.

[62]Peter to F. M. Apraksin, August 29, 1694, ibid., 25–26; see also Peter to Apraksin, ca. April 1695, ibid., 28.

⁶³"Patent" to William Peter Loyd, August 10, 1709, in S. F. Platonov, "Iz bytovoi istorii Petrovskoi epokhi," pt. 1, "Bengo-Kollegiia ili Velikobritanskii monastyr' v S.-Peterburge pri Petre Velikom," *Izvestiia Akademii Nauk SSSR* 7–8 (1926): 532. Platonov suggests that "*Nominatus* Kuska" may have been the same person as "priest Koz'ma," who is mentioned in a letter from P. I. Buturlin to Peter in Semevskii, "Petr Velikii kak iumorist," 290–91.

⁶⁴RGADA, f. 156, op. 1, ed. khr. 186, l. 31v.

⁶⁵This and the following names are from the undated list of "servants of the Arch-Prince-Pope" (c. 1722), in Semevskii, "Petr Velikii kak iumorist," 313–14.

⁶⁶Moleva and Beliutin, *"Zhivopisnykh del mastera,"* 16, portrait of Averkii Voeikov ("Aleksei Vasikov"), part of the so-called Preobrazhenskoe series.

⁶⁷"Shutoshnyi patent Petra Velikogo dumnomu dvorianinu Propkopiiu Ushakovu" (n.d.), ed. P. I. Bartenev, *Russkii arkhiv* 5 (1865): 673–74.

⁶⁸This and the following names are from P. I. Buturlin to Vice Governor Voeikov, April 23, 1723, in Semevskii, "Petr Velikii kak iumorist," 312–13.

⁶⁹*RBS*, 24:128–29; "Shcherbatovy," *Dvorianskie rody Rossiiskoi imperii* (St. Petersburg, 1993), 1:210.

⁷⁰Platonov, "Iz bytovoi istorii Petrovskoi epokhi," 196.

⁷¹O. G. Ageeva, "Obshchestvennaia i kul'turnaia zhizn' Peterburga pervoi chetverti XVIII v." (Diss. kand. ist. nauk, Institute of History, Russian Academy of Sciences, 1990), 325.

⁷²M. M. Bogoslovskii, *Petr I: Materialy dlia biografii* (Moscow-Leningrad, 1940), 1:366; "Lobanov-Rostovskie" in *Dvorianskie rody Rossiiskoi imperii*, 1:290–91.

⁷³"Obolenskie," in *Dvorianskie rody Rossiiskoi imperii*, 1:171; Bogoslovskii, *Petr I*, 1:366.

⁷⁴See Eugene Schuyler, *Peter the Great* (New York, 1884), 2:507; and Paul Hollingsworth, "The 'All-Drunken, All-Joking Synod': Carnival and Rulership in the Reign of Peter the Great (Paper presented at the seminar "The Image of Peter the Great in Russian History and Thought," University of California, Berkeley, 1982), 4, 59n13.

⁷⁵Undated list of the "servants of the Arch-Prince-Pope" (c. 1722), in Semevskii, "Petr Velikii kak iumorist," 313–14.

⁷⁶RGADA, f. 156, op. 1, kn. 186, l. 30v.

⁷⁷In 1725 Catherine I commissioned a portrait (*persona*) of, among others, "Prince-Pope Stroev." See Moleva and Beliutin, *"Zhivopisnykh del mastera,"* 9–10, 177.

Bibliography

Unpublished Primary Sources

Moscow

Russian State Archive of Ancient Documents (RGADA)

f. 9   Kabinet Petra I
f. 156   Istoricheskie i tseremonial'nye dela

Russian State Military-Historical Archive (RGVIA)

f. 846   "Zhurnal . . . Generala Patrika Gordona"

St. Petersburg

Manuscript Division, Library of the Russian Academy of Sciences (RO BRAN)

f. 356   Sobranie graviur
MS 24.5.38   Sobranie I. I. Sreznevskogo
MS 17.7.12   Rukopisnyi sbornik . . . I.–V. Pausa

Manuscript Division, Russian National Library (RO RNB)

f. 181/182   Solovetskoe sobranie (Sbornik zhitii russkikh sviatykh)
f. 450   Ermitazhnoe sobranie
f. 874   Arkhiv S. N Shubinskogo

Russian State Historical Archive (RGIA)

f. 1329   Imennye vysochaishie ukazy

Russian State Naval Archive (RGAVMF)

f. 315   Arkhiv Generala-Admirala F. M. Apraksina

St. Petersburg Branch of the Institute of Russian History, Russian Academy of Sciences (SPB F IRI RAN)

f. 279   Kommissiia po izdaniiu "Pisem i bumag Petra I"
koll. 238   Kollektsiia N. P. Likhacheva
koll. 277   Dokumenty Petra I

PUBLISHED PRIMARY SOURCES

Adrianova-Peretts, V. P. *Russkaia demokraticheskaia satira XVII veka.* 2nd ed. Moscow, 1977.

——, ed. *Russkaia sillabicheskaia poeziia XVII–XVIII vekov.* Leningrad, 1970.

Arsen'ev, K. I. "Stradalets po svoei vole za dvoeperstnoe krestnoe znamenie (1737)." Ed. P. P. Pekarskii. *Sbornik otdeleniia russkogo iazyka i slovesnosti Imperatorskoi Akademii nauk* 9 (1872): 114–32.

Avvakum (Petrov). "Life of Avvakum by Himself." Trans. Jane Harrison and Hope Mirrlees. In *Medieval Russia's Epics, Chronicles, and Tales,* ed. Serge A. Zenkovsky, 2nd ed., 399–448. New York, 1974.

Baklanova, N. A. "Tetradi startsa Avraamiia." *Istoricheskii arkhiv* 6 (1951), 143–55.

Baranov, P. *Opis' vysochaishim ukazam i poveleniiam, khraniashchikhsia v Senatskom arkhive, 1704–1725.* St. Petersburg, 1872.

Bartenev, P. I., ed. "Shutoshnyi patent Petra Velikogo dumnomu dvorianinu Prokopiiu Ushakovu." *Russkii arkhiv* 5 (1865): 673–74.

Bassewitz, H. F. von. "Zapiski Golshtinskago ministra grafa Bassevicha (o Petre Velikom), 1713–1725." Trans. I. F. Ammon. *Russkii arkhiv* 1 (1865): 6–54; 2 (1865): 141–204; 5 (1865): 567–636.

Bergholz, Friedrich Wilhelm von. *Dnevnik kamer-iunkera F. V. Berkhgol'tsa.* Trans. I. F. Ammon. Moscow, 1902–3.

Bespiatykh, Iu. N. *Peterburg Petra I v inostrannykh opisaniiakh. Vvedenie. Teksty. Kommentarii.* Leningrad, 1991.

Bruyn, Cornelius de. *Puteshestvie cherez Moskoviiu Korniliia de Bruina.* Trans. P. P. Barsov. Ed. O. M. Bodianskii. Moscow, 1873.

——. *Travels into Muscovy, Persia, and Part of the East Indies; Containing an Accurate Description of What Is Most Remarkable in Those Countries.* London, 1737.

Collins, Samuel. *The Present State of Russia. . . .* London, 1671.

Cross, Samuel Hazzard, and Olgerd P. Sherbowitz-Wetzor, eds. *The Russian Primary Chronicle: Laurentian Text.* Cambridge, 1953.

"Delo o podannykh tsariu tetradiakh stroitelia Andreevskogo monastyria Avraamiem [1697]. Doprosy Avraamiia, Pososhkova, i dr." In B. B. Kafengauz, *I. T. Pososhkov: Zhizn' i deiatel'nost',* 173–81. Moscow and Leningrad, 1950.

Derzhavina, O. A., et al., eds. *Russkaia dramaturgiia poslednei chetverti XVII i nachala XVIII v.* Moscow, 1972.

"Doneseniia frantsuzskago konsula v Peterburge Lavi i polnomochnago ministra pri russkom dvore Kampredona s 1722 po 1724 g." *Sbornik imperatorskogo russkogo istoricheskogo obshchestva* 49 (1885).

Dvortsovye razriady. 4 vols. St. Petersburg, 1855.

Esipov, G. V., ed. *Sbornik vypisok iz arkhivnykh bumag o Petre Velikom.* 2 vols. Moscow, 1872.

Feofan (Prokopovich). *Knizhitsa, v nei zhe Povest' o raspre Pavla i Varnavy s iudeistvuiushchimi, i trudnost' slova Petra apostola o neudobnonosimom zakonnom ige prostranno predlagaetsia.* Ed. N. I. Novikov. Moscow, 1784.

——. *Razsuzhdenie sv. Sinoda o brakakh pravovernykh s inovernymi.* St. Petersburg, 1721.

——. "Sermon on Royal Authority and Honor. . . ." Trans. Horace G. Lunt. In *Russian Intellectual History: An Anthology,* ed. Marc Raeff, 14–30. New York, 1966.

——. *Sochineniia.* Ed. I. P. Eremin. Moscow and Leningrad, 1961.

——. *The Spiritual Regulation of Peter the Great.* Trans. and ed. Alexander V. Muller. Seattle, 1972.

"Grafy Zotovy." In *Gerboved,* ed. S. N. Troitskii, 131–35. September 1914.

Hellie, Richard, ed. *The Muscovite Law Code (Ulozhenie) of 1649.* Irvine, CA, 1988.

"Intermediia." In *Russkiia dramaticheskiia proizvedeniia, 1672–1725 gg*, ed. N. S. Tikhonravov, 2 vols., 2:485–98. St. Petersburg, 1874.

[Jordan, Thomas]. "Bacchus Festival; or, A New Medley Being a Musical Representation at the Entertainment of His Excellency the Lord General Monck, at Vintners'-Hall, April 12, 1660." In *Illustrations of Early English Popular Literature*, ed. J. P. Collier, vol. 2, no. 6. London, 1864.

Juel, Joost. "Zapiski Iusta Iulia, datskogo poslannika pri Petre Velikom (1709–1711)." Ed. and trans. Iu. N. Shcherbachev. *Chteinia Moskovskogo Obshchestva Istorii i Drevnostei Rossiiskikh* 189, no. 2 (1899).

Korb, J.-G. *Diary of an Austrian Secretary of Legation*. Trans. Count MacDonnell. 2 vols. 1863. Rpt. London, 1968.

——. *Dnevnik puteshestviia v Moskoviiu (1698 i 1699 gg)*. Trans. A. I. Malenin. St. Petersburg, 1906.

Kunshty korabel'nye. St. Petersburg, 1718.

Kurakin, B. I. "Gistoriia o tsare Petre Alekseeviche (1682–1694)." In *Petr Velikii. Vospominaniia. Dnevnikovye zapisi. Anekdoty*, ed. L. Nikolaeva, 53–84. Moscow, 1993.

Lentin, Antony, ed. *Peter the Great and His Law on the Imperial Succession: An Official Commentary*. Oxford, 1996.

Lermontova, E. L., ed. *Pokhval'noe slovo Likhudov tsarevne Sof'e Alekseevne*. Moscow, 1910.

Lur'e, Ia. S., and Iu. D. Rykov, eds. *Perepiska Ivana Groznogo s Andreem Kurbskim*. Leningrad, 1979.

Makhov, A. E., ed. *Emblemy i simvoly*. Moscow, 1995.

Materialy dlia istorii Gangutskoi operatsii. 2 vols. Petrograd, 1914.

Matveev, A. A. "Zapiski Andreia Artamonovicha, grafa Matveeva." In *Zapiski russkikh liudei: Sobytiia vremen Petra Velikogo*, ed. N. Sakharov, 1–94. St. Petersburg, 1841.

Ob "iavlenie rozysknogo dela i suda po ukazu ego tsarskogo velichestva na tsarevicha Alekseia Petrovicha v Sankt"piterburkhe otpravlennago i po ukazu ego velichestva v pechat', dlia izvestiia vsenarodnago, sego iunia v 25 den', 1718, vydannoe. St. Petersburg, 1718.

Opisanie dokumentov i del, khraniashchikhsia v archive Sviateishego Pravitel'stvuiushchego Sinoda. 49 vols. St. Petersburg, 1869–1914.

"Opisanie velikogo i strashnogo boiu, kotoryii byl v nyneshnem 200 godu oktiabria 6 i v 7, i v 9 chislekh u ego presvetleishego generalissimusa Fridrikha Romodanovskogo." In N. G. Ustrialov, *Istoriia tsarstvovaniia Petra Velikogo*, 2:486–90. St. Petersburg, 1858. [Cf. RGADA, f. 9, otd. 2, kn. 93.]

Opisanie vysochaishikh povelenii po pridvornomu vedomstvu (1701–1740 gg.). St. Petersburg, 1888.

"Otryvok oblicheniia na vseshuteishii sobor. Ok. 1705 g." In *Materialy dlia russkoi istorii*, ed. S. A Belokurov, 539–40. Moscow, 1888.

Pamiatniki russkogo prava: Zakonodatel'nye akty Petra I. Moscow, 1961.

Perry, John. *The State of Russia under the Present Tsar*. London, 1716.

Pis'ma i bumagi imperatora Petra Velikogo. 13 vols. to date. St. Petersburg, Moscow and Leningrad, 1887–.

Pis'ma k gosudariu imperatoru Petru Velikomu, pisannye ot general-fel'dmarshala, tainogo sovetnika, mal'tiiskogo sv. apostola Andreia, Belogo Orla i Prusskogo Ordena kavalera grafa Borisa Petrovicha Sheremeteva. 4 pts. Moscow, 1778–79.

Pis'ma russkikh gosudarei i drugikh osob tsarskogo semeistva. Vol. 1: *Perepiska Petra I s Ekaterinoi Alekseevnoiu*. Moscow, 1861.

Pleyer, Otto. "O nyneshnem sostoianii gosudarstvennago upravleniia v Moskovii v 1710 godu." *Chteniia v Obshchestve istorii i drevnostei Rossiiskikh* 89, no. 2 (1874): 1–21.

Pokhodnye i putevye zhurnaly Imperatora Petra I. 4 vols. St. Petersburg, 1853–55.

Polikarpov, F. *Leksikon treiazychnyi, sirech rechenii slovenskikh, ellinogrecheskikh i* latinskikh sokrovishche. Iz razlichnykh drevnikh i novykh knig sobrannoe i po slaven-skomu alfavitu v chin raspolozhenoe. Moscow, 1704.

Polnoe sobranie zakonov Rossiiskoi imperii s 1649 goda. 55 vols. St.Petersburg, 1830–84.

Pososhkov, I. T. The Book of Poverty and Wealth. Ed. and trans. A. P. Vlasto and L. R. Lewitter. Stanford, 1987.

——. Zaveshchanie otecheskoe, k synu svoemu. (1712–19.) Ed. E. M. Prilezhaev. St. Petersburg, 1893.

"Predislovie k morskomu reglamentu." [RGADA, f. 9, otd. 1, kn. 38.] In N. G. Ustrialov, Istoriia tsarstvovaniia Petra Velikogo, 6 vols., 2:397–401. St. Petersburg, 1858.

Preobrazhenskii, A. A., and T. E. Novitskaia, eds. Zakonodatel'stvo Petra I. Moscow, 1997.

"Pritcha o starom muzhe." In Pamiatniki literatury drevnei Rusi. XVII vek. 2:234–36. Moscow, 1989.

Rech', kakova . . . ego imperatorskomu velichestvu . . . ot gospodina kantslera grafa Golovkina govorena v 22 den' oktiabria 1721 godu. St. Petersburg, 1721.

Robinson, A. N., et al., eds. Pervye p'esy russkogo teatra. Moscow, 1972.

——, eds. Ranniaia russkaia dramaturgiia (XVII–pervaia polovina XVIII v.). Moscow, 1972.

Rossiiskoe zakonodatel'stvo X–XX vekov. Moscow, 1985.

Rozysknye dela o Fedore Shaklovitom i ego soobshchnikakh. 4 vols. St. Petersburg, 1884–93.

Salmina, M. A., ed. "Uriadnik sokol'nich'ego puti." In Pamiatniki literatury drevnei Rusi. XVII vek, ed. L. A. Dmitrieva and D. S. Likhachev, 2:286–98. Moscow, 1989.

Semevskii, M. I., ed. "Kozhukhovskii pokhod. 1694. (Sovremennoe opisanie)." Voennyi sbornik 11, no. 1 (1860): 49–106.

Shafirov, P. P. A Discourse Concerning the Just Causes of the War between Sweden and Russia, 1700–1721. Trans. and ed. William E. Butler. Dobbs Ferry, NY, 1973.

"Shutovskaia komediia." In Pamiatniki russkoi dramy epokhi Petra Velikogo, ed. V. N. Peretts, 493–558. St. Petersburg, 1903.

Simeon (Polotskii). Izbrannye sochineniia. Ed. I. P. Eremin. Moscow and Leningrad, 1953.

"Skazanie o gaere garlikine Rossiiskom. Starinnye deistva i komedii Petrovskogo vremeni, izvlechennyia iz rukopisei i prigotovlennyia k pechati I. A. Shliapkinym." Sbornik Otdeleniia russkogo iazyka i slovesnosti Rossiiskoi Akademii Nauk 97, no. 1 (1921): 200–212.

Stefan (Iavorskii). "Slovo os'moe [:] V nedeliu Piat'desiatnitsy iz temy: Priimite Dukh Sviat. Ioan. gl. k, st. z." In Propovedi blazhennyia pamiati Stefana Iavorskogo, preosviashchennogo mitropolita Riazanskogo i Muromskogo, byvshago mestobliustitelia prestola patriarshago, vysokim ucheniem znamenitogo, i revnost'iu po blagochestii preslavnogo, 2 vols., 1:163–79. Moscow, 1804.

——. "Stikhi na izmenu Mazepy, izdannye ot litsa vseia Rossii." In Pamiatniki literatury drevnei Rusi: XVII vek, 3:267–69. Moscow, 1994.

Tatishchev, V. N. "Dukhovnaia." In Izbrannye proizvedeniia, ed. S. N. Valk, 133–45. Leningrad, 1979.

"The Testament of Patriarch Joachim, March 17, 1690." In A Source Book for Russian History from Early Times to 1917, ed. George Vernadsky, 2:361–63. New Haven, 1972.

Timofeev, A. I., ed. "Zapisnye knigi Moskovskogo stola. 1633 sentiabr'–1634 avgust." In Russkaia istoricheskaia biblioteka, 9:550–51. St. Petersburg, 1884.

Trudy Imperatorskogo Russkogo voenno-istoricheskogo obshchestva. St. Petersburg, 1909.

Tsvetaev, Dm., ed. Pamiatniki k istorii protestanstva v Rossii. Moscow, 1888.

Vockerodt, J. G. "Rossiia pri Petre Velikom, po rukopisnomu izvestiiu Ioanna Gottgil'fa

Fokkerodta [1737]." Trans. A. N. Shemiakin. In *Chteniia v Imperatorskom obshch-estve istorii i drevnostei Rossiiskikh pri Moskovskom universitete* 2 (1874): 1–120.
Voskresenskii, A., ed. *Zakonodatel'nye akty Petra I.* Moscow and Leningrad, 1945.
Weber, F. C. *The Present State of Russia.* . . . London, 1723.
Zamyslovskii, E. E., and I. I. Petrov. *Istoricheskii ocherk rossiiskikh ordenov i sbornik osnovnykh ordenskikh statutov.* 2 vols. St. Petersburg, 1892.
Zenkovsky, Serge A., ed. *Medieval Russia's Epics, Chronicles, and Tales.* 2nd ed. New York, 1974.
Zheliabuzhskii, I. A. "Zapiski Ivana Afanas'evicha Zheliabuzhskogo." In *Rossiiu pod-nial na dyby,* ed. N. I. Pavlenko, 2 vols., 1:391–460. Moscow, 1987.

UNPUBLISHED SECONDARY SOURCES

Ageeva, O. G. "Obshchestvennaia i kul'turnaia zhizn' Peterburga pervoi chetverti XVIII v." Candidate diss., Institute of History, Russian Academy of Sciences, 1990.
Airapetian, I. Iu. "Feodal'naia aristokratiia v period stanovleniia absoliutizma v Rossii." Candidate diss., M. V. Lomonosov State University, 1987.
Bennett, Douglas Joseph, Jr. "The Idea of Kingship in Seventeenth-Century Russia." Ph.D. diss. Harvard University, 1967.
Chrissidis, Nikolaos A. "Creating the New Educated Elite: Learning and Faith in Moscow's Slavo-Greco-Latin Academy, 1685–1694." Ph.D. diss., Yale University, 2000.
Gainullina, N. I. "Zaimstvovannaia leksika v 'Pis'makh i bumagakh Imperatora Petra Velikogo.' (K probleme osvoeniia slov inoiazychnogo proiskhozhdeniia v petrovskuiu epokhu)." Candidate diss., S. M. Kirov Kazakh State University, 1973.
Herd, G. "General Patrick Gordon of Auchleuchries—a Scot in Seventeenth-Century Russian Service." Ph.D. thesis, Aberdeen University, 1994.
Hollingsworth, Paul. "The 'All-Drunken, All-Joking Synod': Carnival and Rulership in the Reign of Peter the Great." Paper presented at the seminar "The Image of Peter the Great in Russian History and Thought," University of California, Berkeley, June 10, 1982.
——. "Carnival and Rulership in the Reign of Peter the Great." Paper presented at the National Convention of the American Historical Association, December 1985.
Hopkins, William H. "The Development of 'Pornographic' Literature in Eighteenth- and Early Nineteenth-Century Russia." Ph.D. diss., Indiana University, 1977.
Kosheleva, O. E. "Boiarstvo v nachal'nyi period zarozhdeniia absoliutizma v Rossii (1645–1682)." Candidate diss., M. V. Lomonosov State University, 1987.
Levin, Eve. "False Miracles and Unattested Dead Bodies: Investigation into Popular Cults in Early-Modern Russia." Unpublished paper.
Martin, Russell Edward. "Dynastic Marriage in Muscovy, 1500–1729." Ph.D. diss, Harvard University, 1996.
Merguerian, Barbara Joyce. "Political Ideas in Russia during the Period of Peter the Great (1682–1730)." Ph.D. diss, Harvard University, 1970.
Potter, Cathy Jean. "The Russian Church and the Politics of Reform in the Second Half of the Seventeenth Century." Ph.D. diss., Yale University, 1993.
Sadykova, D. M. "Iz istorii massovoi dramaticheskoi literatury XVIII v. Teatr inter-medii." Candidate diss., V. P. Potemkin Pedagogical Institute, 1956.
Sedov, P. V. "Sotsial'no-politicheskaia bor'ba v Rossii v 70kh–80kh gg. XVII v. i otmena mestnichestva." Candidate diss., A. A. Zhdanov State University, 1985.
Smith, Abby Finnogh. "Prince V. V. Golitsyn: The Life of an Aristocrat in Muscovite Russia." Ph.D. diss., Harvard University, 1987.
Strakhov, Olga B. "The Reception of Byzantine and Post-Byzantine Culture and Litera-ture in Muscovite Rus': The Case of Evfimii Chudovskii (1620s–1705)." Ph.D. diss., Brown University, 1996.
Vilinbakhov, G. V. "Gosudarstvennaia geral'dika Rossii kontsa XVII–pervoi chetverti

XVIII veka. (K voprosu formirovaniia ideologii absoliutizma v Rossii)." Candidate diss., Leningrad State University, 1982.

Zelensky, Elizabeth Kristofovich. "Sophia the Wisdom of God as a Rhetorical Device during the Regency of Sof'ia Alekseevna, 1682–1689." Ph.D. diss., Georgetown University, 1992.

PUBLISHED SECONDARY SOURCES

Adamson, John. "The Making of the *Ancien-Régime* Court, 1500–1700." In *The Princely Courts of Europe: Ritual, Politics and Culture under the* Ancien Régime, *1500–1750,* ed. John Adamson, 7–41. London, 1999.

Aercke, Kristiaan P. *Gods of Play: Baroque Festive Performances as Rhetorical Discourse.* Albany, 1994.

Ageeva, O. G. "Novye iavleniia v obshchestvennoi zhizni i bytu Peterburga pervoi chetverti XVIII veka: Na primere tsarskikh svadeb." In *Russkai a kul'tura v perekhodnoi period ot srednevekov'ia k novomu vremeni. Sbornik statei,* ed. A. N. Kopylov, 89–103. Moscow, 1992.

———. "Titul 'imperator' i poniatie 'imperiia' v Rossii v pervoi chetverti XVIII veka." *Mir istorii: Rossiiskii elektronnyi zhurnal* 5 (1999). <http://www.tellur.ru/historia/archive/05/ageyeva.htm>

———. *"Velichaishii i slavneishii bolee vsekh gradov v svete"—grad sviatogo Petra: Peterburg v russkom obshchestvennom soznanii nachala XVIII veka.* St. Peterburg, 1999.

Alabin, P. V. "Ivan Ivanovich Buturlin, general-anshef (1661–1738)." *Russkaia starina* 23 (1878): 161–86.

Alekseev, M. P. *Russko-angliiskie literaturnye sviazi (XVIII vek—pervaia polovina XIX veka).* Literaturnoe nasledstvo, 91. Moscow, 1982.

Alekseeva, M. A. *Graviura petrovskogo vremeni.* Leningrad, 1990.

———. "Zhanr konkliuzii v russkom iskusstve kontsa XVII-nachalo XVIII veka." In *Russkoe iskusstvo barokko. Materialy i issledovaniia,* 7–29. Moscow, 1977.

Alexander, John T. "Catherine I, Her Court and Courtiers." In *Peter the Great and the West: New Perspectives,* ed. Lindsey Hughes, 227–49. Houndmills, 2001.

Amelin, Grigorii. " 'Se Moisei tvoi, O Rossiie!' (O semiotike imeni v 'Slove na pogrebenie Petra Velikogo' Feofana Prokopovicha." In *V chest' 70–letiia professora Iu. M. Lotmana,* 20–29. Tartu, 1992.

Anderson, M. S. *Peter the Great.* 2nd ed. London, 1995.

Anisimov, E. V. *Gosudarstvennye preobrazovaniia i samoderzhavie Petra Velikogo v pervoi chetverti XVIII veka.* St. Petersburg, 1997.

———. *The Reforms of Peter the Great: Progress through Coercion in Russia.* Trans. and ed. John T. Alexander. Armonk, NY, 1993.

———. *Vremia Petrovskikh reform.* Leningrad, 1989.

Asch, Ronald G. "Court and Household from the Fifteenth to the Seventeenth Centuries." In *Princes, Patronage, and the Nobility: The Court at the Beginning of the Modern Age, c. 1450–1650,* ed. Ronald G. Asch and Adolf M. Birke, 1–38. Oxford, 1991.

Astrov, N. P. "Pervonachal'noe obrazovanie Petra Velikogo (po novootkrytym bumagam)." *Russkii arkhiv* 2, no. 8 (1875): 470–88.

———. "Pervonachal'noe obrazovanie Petra Velikogo." Pt. 2, "Mastera Petrovskogo vremeni." *Russkii arkhiv* 3, no. 8 (1875): 90–102.

———. "Pervonachal'noe obrazovanie Petra Velikogo." Pt. 3, "Preobrazhenskoe i poteshnyi gorodok." *Russkii arkhiv* 3, no. 10 (1875): 212–21.

Babushkina, I. K. "Mezhdunarodnoe znachenie Krymskikh pokhodov 1687 i 1689 gg." *Istoricheskie zapiski* 33 (1950): 159–61.

Baehr, Stephen Lessing. *The Paradise Myth in Eighteenth-Century Russia: Utopian Patterns in Early Secular Russian Literature and Culture.* Stanford, 1991.

Bagger, Hans. *Reformy Petra Velikogo: Obzor issledovanii*. Moscow, 1985.

Baiburin, A. K., and G. A. Levinton. "'Kniaz' i 'kniaginia' v russkom svadebnom velichanii (k semantike obriadovykh terminov)." *Russkaia filologiia* 4 (1975): 58–76.

Bakhtin, M. M. *Rabelais and His World*. Trans. Hélène Iswolsky. Bloomington, 1984.

Bantysh-Kamenskii, D. N. *Slovar' dostopamiatnykh liudei Russkoi zemli*. Moscow, 1836.

Belaventsev, P. *General-Admiral graf Fedor Matveevich: Kratkii biograficheskii ocherk*. Revel, 1899.

Belobrova, O. A. "Lichnost' i nauchno-prosvetitel'skie trudy Nikolaia Spafariia." In *Nikolai Spafarii. Esteticheskie traktaty*, ed. A. M. Panchenko. Leningrad, 1978.

Berelowitch, André. "Chasse et rituel en Russie au XVIIe siècle: Le *Règlement de la Fauconnerie* d'Alexis Mixajlovic." In *Russes, Slaves et Soviétiques. Pages d'histoire offertes à Roger Portal*, ed. C. Gervais-Francelle, 85–121. Paris, 1992.

Berger, Peter. *The Heretical Imperative*. Garden City, NJ, 1979.

Berkov, P. N. *Istoriia russkoi komedii XVIII v.* Leningrad, 1977.

——. "Iz istorii russkoi teatral'noi terminologii XVII–XVIII vekov ("Komediia," "intermediia," "dialog," "igrishche," i dr.)." *Trudy otdela drevnerusskoi literatury* 11 (1955): 280–99.

Blanc, Simone. "The Economic Policy of Peter the Great." In *Russian Economic Development from Peter the Great to Stalin*, ed. William L. Blackwell, 21–49. New York, 1974.

Blitzer, Charles. *Age of Kings*. New York, 1967.

Bobrovskii, P. O. *Poteshnye i nachalo Preobrazhenskogo polka (Po ofitsial'nym dokumentam)*. St. Petersburg, 1899.

Bogdanov, A. P. "Fedor Alekseevich." *Voprosy istorii* 7 (1994): 59–77.

——. "Graviura kak istochnik po istorii politicheskoi bor'by v Rossii v period regentstva Sof'i Alsekseevny (Voprosy proiskhozhdeniia)." In *Materialy XV Vsesoiuznoi nauchnoi studencheskoi konferentsii "Student i nauchno-tekhnicheskii progress." Istoriia*, 39–48. Novosibirsk, 1977.

——. "Literaturnye panegiriki kak istochnik izucheniia sootnosheniia sil v pravitel'stve Rossii perioda regentstva Sof'i (1682–1689 gg.)." In *Materialy XVII vsesoiuznoi nauchnoi studencheskoi konferentsii "Student i nauchno-tekhnicheskii progress." Istoriia*, 71–79. Novosibirsk, 1979.

——. *Pamiatniki obshchestvenno-politicheskoi mysli v Rossii kontsa XVII veka. Literaturnye panegiriki*. 2 vols. Moscow, 1983.

——. "Politicheskaia graviura v Rossii perioda regentstva Sof'ii Alekseevny." In *Istochnikovedenie otechestvennoi istorii. Sbornik statei za 1981 g.*, ed. V. I. Buganov, 225–46. Moscow, 1982.

——. "Razum protiv vlasti." In *Pero i krest: Russkie pisateli pod tserkovnym sudom*, 231–383. Moscow, 1990.

——. "Sil'vestr Medvedev." *Voprosy istorii* 2 (1988): 84–98.

——. "Sofiia-Premudrost' Bozhiia i tsarevna Sof'ia Alekseevna: Iz istorii russkoi dukhovnoi literatury i iskusstva XVII veka." *Germenevtika russkoi literatury* 7, no. 2 (1994): 399–428.

Bogoiavlenskii, S. K. *Moskovskii teatr pri tsariakh Aleksee i Petre*. Moscow, 1914.

Bogoslovskii, M. M. "Detstvo Petra Velikogo." *Russkaia starina* 1 (1917): 1–29.

——. *Petr I: Materialy dlia biografii*. 5 vols. Moscow and Leningrad, 1940–46.

Bogoslovskii, P. S. "K nomenklature i topografii svadebnykh chinov (Po dannym etnograficheskoi literatury i rukopisnym materialam Geograficheskogo Obshchestva)." In *Permskii kraevedcheskii sbornik*, 1–64. Perm, 1927.

Boulton, D'Arcy Jonathan Dacre. *The Knights of the Crown: The Monarchical Orders of Knighthood in Later Medieval Europe, 1325–1520*. New York, 1987.

Boureau, Alain. *Le simple corps du roi: L'impossible sacralité des souverains français, XVe–XVIIIe siècle*. Paris, 1988.

Boym, Svetlana. *Common Places: Mythologies of Everyday Life in Russia.* Cambridge, 1994.

Bruseva-Davydova, I. L. "Ob ideinom zamysle Kolomenskogo dvortsa." *Arkhitektura mira* 2 (1993).

——. "Tsarskie usad'by XVII v. v razvitii russkoi arkhitektury." *Russkaia usad'ba. Sbornik Obshchestva izucheniia russkoi usad'by* 1 (1994): 140–44.

Bugrov, A. "Staro-Preobrazhenskii dvorets." *Moskovskii arkhiv. Istoriko-kraevedcheskii al'manakh* 1 (1996): 42–58.

Burke, Peter. *Popular Culture in Early Modern Europe.* New York, 1978.

Bushkovitch, Paul. "Aristocratic Faction and the Opposition to Peter the Great: The 1690s." *Forschungen zur Osteuropäischen Geschichte* 50 (1995): 80–120.

——. *Peter the Great: The Struggle for Power, 1671–1725.* Cambridge, 2001.

——. "Power and the Historian: The Case of Tsarevich Aleksei (1716–1718) and N. G. Ustrialov (1845–1859)." *Proceedings of the American Philosophical Society* 141 (June 1997): 177–205.

——. *Religion and Society in Russia: The Sixteenth and Seventeenth Centuries.* New York, 1992.

Buzzi, Giancarlo. *The Life and Times of Peter the Great.* Trans. Ben Johnson. London, 1968.

Bychkov, V. V. *Russkaia srednevekovaia estetika, XI–XVII veka.* Moscow, 1995.

——., ed. *Khudozhestvenno-esteticheskaia kul'tura Drevnei Rusi XI–XVII veka.* Moscow, 1996.

Bychkova, Margarita E. "Obriady venchaniia na prestol 1498 i 1547 godov: Voploshchenie idei vlasti gosudaria." *Cahiers du monde russe et soviétique* 34, no. 1–2 (1993): 245–56.

Cannadine, David. "Introduction: Divine Rites of Kings." In *Rituals of Royalty: Power and Ceremonial in Traditional Societies,* ed. David Cannadine and Simon Price, 1–19. Cambridge, 1987.

Chechot, I. D. "Korabl' i flot v portretakh Petra I. Ritoricheskaia kul'tura i osobennosti estetiki russkogo korablia pervoi chetverti XVIII veka." In *Otechestvennoe i zarubezhnoe iskusstvo XVIII veka,* 54–82. Leningrad, 1986.

Chernaia, L. A. "Parodiia na tserkovnye teksty v russkoi literature XVII veka." *Vestnik Moskovskogo universiteta,* ser. 8, *Istoriia* 2 (1980): 53–63.

Cherniavsky, Michael. "The Old Believers and the New Religion." In *The Structure of Russian History: Interpretive Essays,* ed. Michael Cherniavsky, 140–88. New York, 1970.

——. *Tsar and People: Studies in Russian Myths.* New Haven, 1961.

Chistovich, I. A. *Feofan Prokopovich i ego vremia.* St. Petersburg, 1868.

——. *Reshilovskoe delo. Feofan Prokopovich i Feofilakt Lopatinskii. Materialy dlia istorii pervoi poloviny XVIII stoletiia.* St. Petersburg, 1861.

Chubinskaia, V. G. "Novoe ob evoliutsii russkogo portreta na rubezhe XVII–XVIII vv." In *Pamiatniki kul'tury. Novye otkrytiia. 1982,* 317–28. Leningrad, 1984.

Cracraft, James. *The Church Reform of Peter the Great.* London, 1971.

——. "Empire versus Nation: Political Theory under Peter I." *Harvard Ukrainian Studies* 10 (December 1986): 524–40.

——. "Feofan Prokopovich: A Bibliography of His Works." *Oxford Slavonic Papers* 8 (1975): 1–36.

——. "Feofan Prokopvich and the Kiev Academy." In *Russian Orthodoxy under the Old Regime,* ed. Theofanis George Stavrou and Robert L. Nichols, 44–64. Minneapolis, 1978.

——. *The Petrine Revolution in Russian Architecture.* Chicago, 1988.

——. *The Petrine Revolution in Russian Imagery.* Chicago, 1997.

——. "Prokopovyc's Kiev Period Reconsidered." *Harvard Ukrainian Studies* 2 (June 1978): 138–57.

——, ed. *Major Problems in the History of Imperial Russia*. Lexington, MA, 1994.

Cross, A. G.. "The Bung College or British Monastery in Petrine Russia." *Newsletter of the Study Group on Eighteenth-Century Russia* 12 (1984): 14–24.

——. *By the Banks of the Neva: Chapters from the Lives and Careers of the British in Eighteenth-Century Russia*. Cambridge, 1997.

——, ed. *Russia in the Reign of Peter the Great: Old and New Perspectives*. 2 vols. Cambridge, 1998.

Crummey, Robert O. *Aristocrats and Servitors: The Boyar Elite in Russia, 1613–1689*. Princeton, 1983.

——. "Court Spectacles in Seventeenth-Century Russia: Illusion and Reality." In *Essays in Honor of A. A. Zimin*, 130–46. Columbus, OH, 1985.

——. "Peter and the Boiar Aristocracy, 1689–1700." *Canadian-American Slavic Studies* 8 (Summer 1974): 274–87.

Curtius, Ernst Robert. *European Literature and the Latin Middle Ages*. Trans. Willard R. Trask. New York, 1953.

Dal', V. I. *Tolkovyi slovar' zhivogo velikorusskogo iazyka*. 4 vols. Moscow, 1955.

Davis, Natalie Zemon. *Society and Culture in Early Modern France*. Stanford, 1975.

De Madariaga, Isabel. "The Staging of Power." *Government and Opposition: An International Journal of Comparative Politics* 31, no. 2 (1996): 228–40.

——. "Tsar into Emperor: The Title of Peter the Great." In Madariaga, *Politics and Culture in Eighteenth-Century Russia: Collected Essays*, 15–39. London, 1998.

Demin, A. S. "Russkie p'esy 1670–kh godov i pridvornaia kul'tura." *Trudy otdela drevnerusskoi literatury* 27 (1972): 273–83.

Derzhavina, O. A. "Russkii teatr 70–90kh godov XVII v. i nachala XVIII v." In *Russkaia dramaturgiia poslednei chetverti XVII i nachala XVIII veka*, ed. O. A. Derzhavina et al., 5–52. Moscow, 1972.

——. "Teatr i dramaturgiia." In *Ocherki russkoi kul'tury XVII v.*, ed. A. V. Artsikhovskii, 126–41. Moscow, 1979.

Dmitriev, S. I. *General-Admiral graf F. M. Apraksin. Spodvizhnik Petra Velikogo*. Petrograd, 1914.

Dolbilov, Mikhail. "The Political Mythology of Autocracy: Scenarios of Power and the Role of the Autocrat." *Kritika: Explorations in Russian and Eurasian History* 2 (Fall 2001): 773–95.

Dolgorukov, A. A. *Rossiiskaia rodoslovnaia kniga*. 2 vols. St. Petersburg, 1855.

Douglas, Mary. "Jokes." In *Rethinking Popular Culture: Contemporary Perspectives in Cultural Studies*, ed. Chandra Mukerji and Michael Schudson, 291–310. Berkeley, 1991.

Duindam, Jeroen. *Myths of Power: Norbert Elias and the Early Modern European Court*. Amsterdam, 1994.

Dukmeyer, Friedrich. *Korbs Diarium itineris in Moscoviam und Quellen, die es ergänzen*. 2 vols. Historische Studien, 70 and 80. Berlin, 1909–10.

Dunning, Chester S. L. *Russia's First Civil War: The Time of Troubles and the Founding of the Romanov Dynasty*. University Park, PA, 2001.

——. "Who Was Tsar Dmitrii?" 60, no. 4 (2001): 705–29.

Durov, V. A. "Russkie boevye nagrady za Poltavskoe srazhenie." *Numizmatika i sfragistika* 5 (1974).

Dushechkina, E. V. *Russkii sviatochnyi rasskaz: Stanovlenie zhanra*. St. Petersburg, 1995.

Dvorianskie rody Rossiiskoi imperii. St. Petersburg, 1993.

Dvorkin, A. L. *Ivan the Terrible as a Religious Type: A Study of the Background, Genesis, and Development of the Theocratic Idea of the First Russian Tsar, and his Attempts to Establish "Free Autocracy" in Russia*. Oikonomia, 31. Erlangen, 1992.

Dvornik, Frances. *The Idea of Apostolicity in Byzantium and the Legend of the Apostle Andrew*. Cambridge, 1958.

Ebbinghaus, Andreas. "Obraz bakhusa v kontekste russkoi kul'tury XVIII–nachala XIX vekov." In *Reflections on Russia in the Eighteenth Century*, ed. Ioakim Klein, Simon Dixon, and Maarten Fraanje, 186–99. Cologne, 2001.

Eekman, Thomas. "Seven Years with Peter the Great: The Dutchman Jacob de Bie's Observations." In *Peter the Great and the West: New Perspectives*, ed. Lindsey Hughes, 206–24. Houndmills, 2001.

Efimov, S. V. "Evdokiia Lopukhina—posledniaia russkaia tsaritsa XVII veka." In *Srednevekovaia Rus': Sbornik nauchnykh statei k 65–letiiu . . . R. G. Skrynnikova*, ed. S. V. Lobachev and A. S. Lavrov, 136–65. St. Petersburg, 1995.

Elias, Norbert. *The Civilizing Process: A History of Manners*. Trans. Edmund Jephcott. New York, 1978.

———. *The Court Society*. Trans. Edmund Jephcott. New York, 1983.

Emmerling-Skala, Andreas. *Bacchus in der Renaissance*. 2 vols. Studien zur Kunstgeschichte, 83. Hildesheim, 1994.

Eroshkin, N. P. *Istoriia gosudarstvennykh uchrezhdenii dorevoliutsionnoi Rossii*. 3rd ed. Moscow, 1983.

Esipov, G. V. "Kniaginia-igumen'ia." *Russkaia starina* 1 (1870): 400–403.

———. *Raskol'nich'i dela XVIII stoletiia, izvlechennye iz del Preobrazhenskogo prikaza i Tainoi Rozysknykh del kantseliarii*. St. Petersburg, 1861.

Etienvre, Jean-Pierre. "Du jeu comme métaphore politique: Sur quelques textes de propagande royale diffusés en Espagne à l'avènement des Bourbons." *Poétique* 56 (1983): 397–415.

Evangulova, O. S. *Dvortsovo-parkovye ansambli Moskvy pervoi poloviny XVIII veka*. Moscow, 1969.

Evans, R. J. W. "The Court: A Protean Institution and an Elusive Subject." In *Princes, Patronage, and the Nobility: The Court at the Beginning of the Modern Age, c. 1450–1650*, ed. Ronald G. Asch and Adolf M. Birke, 481–91. Oxford, 1991.

Farrow, Lee A. "Peter the Great's Law of Single Inheritance: State Imperatives and Noble Resistance." *Russian Review* 55 (1996): 430–47.

Fedotov, George. *The Russian Religious Mind*. 2 vols. Belmont, MA, 1975.

Feigina, S. A. "Inostrannaia literatura o Petre Velikom za posledniuiu chetvert' veka." In *Petr Velikii. Sbornik statei*, ed. A. I. Andreev, 390–423. Moscow and Leningrad, 1947.

Flashar, Miron. "Sobria ebrietas." *Zbornik. Univerzitet u Beogradu. Filozofski fakultet* 4, no. 2 (1959): 287–335.

Floria, B. N., ed. *Slaviane i ikh sosedi. Imperskaia ideia v stranakh tsentral'noi, vostochnoi i iugo-vostochnoi Evropy. Tezisy XIV konferentsii*. Moscow, 1995.

Foucault, Michel. "Truth and Power." In *Power/Knowledge: Selected Interviews and Other Writings, 1972–1977*, ed. Colin Gordon, 109–33. New York, 1980.

Franko, Mark. *Dance as Text: Ideologies of the Baroque Body*. Cambridge, 1993.

Gainulina, N. I. *Epistoliarnoe nasledie Petra Velikogo v istorii russkogo literaturnogo iazyka XVIII veka (Istoriko-lingvisticheskii aspekt)*. Almaty, 1995.

Gavrilova, E. I. "O metodakh atributsii dvukh grupp proizvedenii Petrovskoi epokhi (zhivopis', risunok)." In *Nauchno-issledovatel'skaia rabota v khudozhestvennykh muzeiakh*, 2:45–75. Moscow, 1975.

Geertz, Clifford. "Centers, Kings, and Charisma: Reflections on the Symbolics of Power." In *Rites of Power: Symbolism, Ritual, and Politics since the Middle Ages*, ed. Sean Wilentz, 13–38. Philadelphia, 1985.

———. *Negara: The Theatre State in Nineteenth-Century Bali*. Princeton, 1980.

Gilman, Sander L. *The Parodic Sermon in European Perspective: Aspects of Liturgical Parody from the Middle Ages to the Twentieth Century*. Wiesbaden, 1974.

Girard, René. *Violence and the Sacred*. Trans. Patrick Gregory. Baltimore, 1977.

Girs, I. V., and B. P. Favorov. "Poteshnaia flotiliia Petra." *Sudostroenie* 6 (1972): 72–74.

Golikov, I. I. *Deianiia Petra Velikogo, mudrogo preobrazovatelia Rossii, sobrannye iz dostovernykh istochnikov i raspolozhennye po godam.* 12 vols. Moscow, 1788–89.

——. *Dopolnenie k "Deianiiam Petra Velikogo".* . . . 18 vols. Moscow, 1790–97.

Golikova, N. B. "Organy politicheskogo syska i ikh razvitie v XVII–XVIII vv." In *Absoliutizm v Rossii XVII–XVIII vv. Sb. statei k 70–letiiu B. B. Kafengauza,* 243–80. Moscow, 1964.

——. *Politicheskie protsessy pri Petre I: Po materialam Preobrazhenskogo prikaza.* Moscow, 1957.

Golikova, N. B., and L. G. Kisliagina. "Sistema gosudarstvennogo upravleniia." In *Ocherki russkoi kul'tury XVIII veka,* ed. A. D. Gorskii et al., 2:44–108. Moscow, 1987.

Golitsyn, M. M. "Materialy dlia istorii roda kniazei Prozorovskikh." *Russkii arkhiv* 7 (1899): 21–39.

Golubtsov, N. "Krest Petra Velikogo, khraniashchiisia v Arkhangel'skom Kafedral'nom Sobore." In *Petr Velikii na Severe. Sbornik statei i ukazov, otnosiashchikhsia k deiatel'nosti Petra I na Severe,* ed. A. F. Shidlovskii, 79–83. Archangel, 1909.

Gonneau, Pierre. *La Maison de la Sainte Trinité: Un grand monastère russe au Moyen Age tardif (1345–1533).* Paris, 1993.

Gorchakov, M. *Monastyrskii prikaz (1649–1725).* St. Petersburg, 1868.

Gorfunkel', A. Kh. "Andrei Belobotskii—poet i filosof kontsa XVII–nachala XVIII veka." *Trudy otdela drevnerusskoi literatury* 18 (1962): 188–213.

——. "'Pentateugum' Andreia Belobodskogo. (Iz istorii pol'sko-russkikh literaturnykh sviazei)." *Trudy otdela drevnerusskoi literatury* 21 (1965): 39–64.

Grebeniuk, V. P. "Publichnye zrelishcha petrovskogo vremeni i ikh sviaz' s teatrom." In *Novye cherty v russkoi literature i iskusstve (XVII–nachalo XVIII v.),* 133–145. Moscow, 1976.

——. "Evoliutsiia simvolov rossiiskogo absoliutizma (ot Simeona Polotskogo do N. V. Lomonosova)." In *Razvitie barokko i zarozhdenie klassitsizma v Rossii XVII–nachala XVIII v.,* ed. A. N. Robinson, 188–200. Moscow, 1989.

Grebeniuk, V. P., O. A. Derzhavina, and A. S. Eleonskaia. "Antichnoe nasledie v russkoi literature XVII–nachala XVIII veka." In *Slavianskie literatury. VII mezhdunarodnyi s''ezd slavistov.* Zagreb-Liubliana, sentiabr' 1978 g. Doklady sovetskoi delegatsii, 194–213. Moscow, 1978.

Gudzii, N. K. "Ukrains'ki intermedii XVII–XVIII st." In *Ukrains'kii intermedii XVII–XVIII st.: Pam'iatniki davn'oi ukrains'koi literature,* 5–30. Kiev, 1960.

Härtel, Hans-Joachim. *Byzantinisches Erbe und Orthodoxie bei Feofan Prokopovic.* Das östliche Christentum, 23. Würzburg, 1970.

Hellie, Richard. "The Petrine Army: Continuity, Change, and Impact." *Canadian-American Slavic Studies* 8 (Summer 1974): 237–53.

Hughes, Lindsey. "'Between Two Worlds': Tsarevna Natal'ia Alekseevna and the 'Emancipation' of Petrine Women." In *A Window on Russia: Papers from the Fifth International Conference of the Study Group on Eighteenth-Century Russia, Gargnano, 1994,* ed. M. di Salvo and L. Hughes, 29–36. Rome, 1996.

——. "Biographies of Peter." In *Russia in the Reign of Peter the Great: Old and New Perspectives,* ed. Anthony Cross, 2 vols., 1:13–24. Cambridge, 1998.

——. "'For the Health of the Sons of Ivan Mikhailovich': I. M. Golovin and Peter the Great's Mock Court." In *Reflections on Russia in the Eighteenth Century,* ed. Joachim Klein, Simon Dixon, and Maarten Fraanje, 43–51. Cologne, 2001.

——. "A Note on the Children of Peter the Great." *Study Group on Eighteenth-Century Russia Newsletter* 21 (1993): 10–16.

——. "The Petrine Year: Anniversaries and Festivals in the Reign of Peter I (1682–1725)." In *Festive Culture in Germany and Europe from the Sixteenth to the Twentieth Century,* ed. Karin Friedrich, 149–68. Lewiston, NY, 2000.

——. *Playing Games: The Alternative History of Peter the Great.* SSEES Occasional Papers, no. 41. London, 2000.

——. *Russia in the Age of Peter the Great.* New Haven, 1998.

——. "Shaklovityi, Fedor." In *Modern Encyclopedia of Russian and Soviet History,* ed. Joseph L. Wieczynski, 34:146–48. Gulf Breeze, FL, 1983.

——. *Sophia, Regent of Russia, 1657–1704: "Ambitious and Daring above Her Sex."* New Haven, 1990.

Huizinga, J. *Homo Ludens: A Study of the Play Element in Culture.* Boston, 1970.

Ivanov, P. P. *Alfavitnyi ukazatel' familii i lits, upominaemykh v boiarskikh knigakh.* Moscow, 1853.

Ivleva, L. M. *Riazhen'e v russkoi traditsionnoi kul'ture.* St. Petersburg, 1994.

Jacobson, R. O. "While Reading Fasmer's Dictionary." In *Selected Writings.* The Hague, 1971.

Kafengauz, B. B. *I. T. Pososhkov: Zhizn' i deiatel'nost'.* Moscow and Leningrad, 1950.

Kaganov, G. " 'As in the Ship of Peter.' " *Slavic Review* 50 (1991): 354–67.

Kagarlitskii, Iurii. "Sakralizatsiia kak priem: Resursy ubeditel'nosti i vliiatel'nosti imperskogo diskursa v Rossii XVIII veka." *Novoe literaturnoe obozrenie* 38 (1999): 66–77.

"Kak sdelana istoriia: Obsuzhdenie knigi R. Uortmana." *Novoe literaturnoe obozrenie* 56 (2002): 42–66.

Kaliazina, N. G., and G. N. Komelova. *Russkoe iskusstvo Petrovskoi epokhi.* Leningrad, 1990.

Kameneva, T. N. "Chernigovskaia tipografiia, ee deiatel'nost' i izdaniia." *Trudy Gosudarstvennoi biblioteki im. V. I. Lenina* 3 (1959): 228–84.

——. "Ornamentika i illiustratsii chernigovskikh izdanii XVII–XVIII vv." *Kniga. Issledovaniia i materialy* 29 (1974): 171–81.

Kantorowicz, Ernst H. *Frederick the Second, 1194–1250.* Trans. E. O. Lorimer. London, 1931.

——. *The King's Two Bodies: A Study in Medieval Political Theology.* Princeton, 1957.

——. "Mysteries of State: An Absolutist Concept and Its Late Mediaeval Origins." *Harvard Theological Review* 48 (January 1955): 65–91.

Karabanov, P. F. "Stats-damy i freiliny russkogo dvora v XVIII stoletii." Pt. 1. *Russkaia starina* 2 (1870).

Karlinsky, Simon. *Russian Drama from Its Beginnings to the Age of Pushkin.* Berkeley, 1985.

Kaufmann, Thomas DaCosta. *Court, Cloister, and City: The Art and Culture of Central Europe, 1450–1800.* Chicago, 1995.

Keenan, Edward L. *The Kurbskii-Groznyi Apocrypha: The Seventeenth-Century Genesis of the "Correspondence" Attributed to Prince A. M. Kurbskii and Tsar Ivan IV.* Cambridge, 1971.

——. "Muscovite Political Folkways." *Russian Review* 45 (1986): 115–81.

——. "Royal Russian Behavior, Style, and Self-Image." In *Ethnic Russia in the USSR: The Dilemma of Dominance,* ed. Edward Allworth, 3–16. New York, 1980.

Keep, John L. H. *Soldiers of the Tsar: Army and Society in Russia, 1462–1874.* Oxford, 1985.

Khmyrov, M. D. *Grafinia Ekaterina Ivanovna Golovkina i ee vremia (1701–1791 gg.). Istoricheskii ocherk po arkhivnym dokumentam.* St. Petersburg, 1867.

Khromov, O. R. "Podmoskovnye votchiny Alekseia Mikhailovicha. Predvaritel'nye tezisy k vospriiatiiu stilia tsarskikh usadeb." *Germenevtika drevnerusskoi literatury* 4 (1992): 285–301.

——. " 'Tsarskii dom' v tsikle Simeona Polotskogo na novosel'e." *Germenevtika drevnerusskoi literatury* 2 (1989): 217–43.

Kivelson, Valerie. "Kinship Politics/Autocratic Politics: A Reconsideration of Early-Eighteenth-Century Political Culture." In *Imperial Russia: New Histories for the Empire,* ed. Jane Burbank and David L. Ransel, 5–31. Bloomington, 1998.

Klingensmith, Samuel J. *The Utility of Splendor: Ceremony, Social Life, and Architecture at the Court of Bavaria, 1600–1800*. Chicago, 1993.

Kliuchevskii, V. O. *Sochineniia v deviati tomakh*. 9 vols. Moscow, 1987–90.

Kobrin, V. B. *Vlast' i sobstvennost' v srednevekovoi Rossii (XV–XVI vv.)*. Moscow, 1985.

Kolkina, I. N. "Iakov Vilimovich Brius." In *Soratniki Petra*, ed. N. I. Pavlenko et al., 433–76. Moscow, 2001.

Kollmann, Nancy Shields. *By Honor Bound: State and Society in Early Modern Russia*. Ithaca, 1999.

——. "Pilgrimage, Procession, and Symbolic Space in Sixteenth-Century Russian Politics." In *Medieval Russian Culture*, ed. Michael S. Flier and Daniel Rowland, 2:163–81. Berkeley, 1994.

——. "The Seclusion of Elite Muscovite Women." *Russian History* 10, no. 2 (1983): 170–87.

Korsakov, V. "Sokovniny." In *Russkii biograficheskii slovar'*, 19:48–50. St. Petersburg, 1909.

——. "Zotov, gr. Nikita Moiseevich." In *Russkii biograficheskii slovar'*, 7:476–81. New York, 1962.

Kozlov, O. F. "Delo tsarevicha Alekseia." *Voprosy istorii* 9 (1969): 214–20.

Kozlovskii, I. P. *Sil'vestr Medvedev. Ocherk iz istorii russkogo prosveshcheniia i obshchestvennoi zhizni v kontse XVII veka*. Kiev, 1895.

Krieger, Leonard. *Kings and Philosophers, 1689–1789*. New York, 1970.

Kriuger, A. "Samodeiatel'nyi teatr pri Petre I." In *Starinnyi spektakl' v Rossii. Sbornik statei*, ed. V. N. Vsevolodskii-Gerngross, 358–85. Leningrad, 1928.

Krivocheine, B. [Vasilii Krivoshein]. "Le thème de l'ivresse spirituelle dans la mystique de Saint Syméon le Nouveau Théologien." *Studia Patristica* 5 (1962): 368–76.

Krylova, T. K. "Poltavskaia pobeda i russkaia diplomatiia." In *Petr Velikii: sbornik statei*, ed. A. I. Andreev, 104–66. Moscow and Leningrad, 1947.

Laqueur, Thomas. *Making Sex: Body and Gender from the Greeks to Freud*. Cambridge, 1990.

Lavrov, A. S. *Koldovstvo i religiia v Rossii, 1700–1740 gg*. Moscow, 2000.

——. *Regentstvo tsarevny Sof'i Alekseevny: Sluzhiloe obshchestvo i bor'ba za vlast' v verkhakh Russkogo gosudarstva v 1682–1689 gg*. Moscow, 1999.

LeDonne, John P. *Absolutism and Ruling Class: The Formation of the Russian Political Order, 1700–1825*. New York, 1991.

——. "Ruling Families in the Russian Poitical Order." Pt. 1, "The Petrine Leadership, 1689–1725." *Cahiers du monde russe et soviétique* 28, no. 3–4 (1987): 233–322.

Levin, Eve. *Sex and Society in the World of the Orthodox Slavs, 900–1700*. Ithaca, 1989.

Levin, V. D. "Petr I i russkii iazyk (K 300-letiiu so dnia rozhdeniia Petra I)." *Izvestiia AN SSSR. Seriia literatury i iazyka* 31, no. 3 (1972): 217–27.

Lewin, Paulina. "Jan Kochanowski: The Model Poet in Eastern Slavic Lectures on Poetics of the 17th and 18th Centuries." In *The Polish Renaissance in its European Context*, ed. Samuel Fiszman, 429–43. Bloomington, 1988.

——. "Vostochnoslavianskie intermedii." In *Drevnerusskaia literatura i ee sviazi s novym vremenem*, ed. O. A. Derzhavina, 194–205. Moscow, 1967.

Lewitter, L. R. "Peter the Great, Poland, and the Westernization of Russia." *Journal of the History of Ideas* 19 (October 1958): 493–506.

——. "Peter the Great's Attitude toward Religion: From Traditional Piety to Rational Theology." In *Russia and the World of the Eighteenth Century*, ed. R. P. Bartlett et al., 62–77. Columbus, OH, 1986.

——. "Poland, the Ukraine, and Russia in the Seventeenth Century." *Slavonic and East European Review* 27, no. 68 (1948): 157–71; no. 69 (1949): 414–29.

——. "The Russo-Polish Treaty of 1686 and Its Antecedents." *Polish Review* 9, nos. 3–4 (1964): 5–29, 21–37.

Lewy, Hans. *Sobria Ebrietas: Untersuchungen zur Geschichte der antiken Mystik.* Giessen, 1929.

Likhach, E. "Shakhovskie." In *Russkii biorgaficheskii slovar'*, 22:571, 578–79. St. Petersburg, 1905.

Likhachev, D. S. "Barokko i ego russkii variant XVII veka." *Russkaia literatura* 2 (1969): 18–45.

——. "Byla li epokha petrovskikh reform pereryvom v razvitii russkoi kul'tury?" In *Slavianskie kul'tury v epokhu formirovaniia i razvitiia slavianskikh natsii XVIII–XIX vv. Materialy mezhdunarodnoi konferentsii IuNESKO*, 170–74. Moscow, 1978.

——. "The Petrine Reforms and the Development of Russian Culture." Trans. Avril Pyman. *Canadian-American Slavic Studies* 13, no. 1–2 (1979): 230–34.

——. *Poeziia sadov. K semantike sadovo-parkovykh stilei: sad kak tekst.* 2nd ed. St. Petersburg, 1991.

Likhachev, D. S., et al. *Smekh v drevnei Rusi.* Leningrad, 1984.

Likhachev, N. P. "Rodoproiskhozhdenie dvorian Golovkinykh." *Izvestiia Russkogo Genealogicheskogo obshchestva* 2 (1903): 103–39.

Likhnitskii, I. M. *Osviashchennyi sobor v Moskve v XVI–XVII vekakh.* St. Petersburg, 1906.

Liubimov, S. *Opyt istoricheskikh rodoslovii: Gundorovy, Zhizhemskie, Nesvitskie, Sibirskie, Zotovy i Ostermany.* Petrograd, 1915.

Lobanov-Rostovskii, A. B. *Russkaia rodoslovnaia kniga.* 2 vols. 2nd ed. St. Petersburg, 1895.

Lossky, Vladimir. *The Mystical Theology of the Eastern Church.* Trans. Fellowship of St. Alban and St. Sergius. London, 1957.

Lotman, Iu. M. "Neskol'ko slov o stat'e V. M. Zhivova." In *Iz istorii russkoi kul'tury*, ed. A. D. Koshelev, 4:755–62. Moscow, 1996.

Lotman, Iu. M., and B. A. Uspenskii. "Echoes of the Notion 'Moscow the Third Rome' in Peter the Great's Ideology." Trans. N. F. C. Owen. In *The Semiotics of Russian Culture*, ed. Ann Shukman, 53–67. Ann Arbor, 1984.

——. "New Aspects in the Study of Early Russian Culture." Trans. N. F. C. Owen. In *The Semiotics of Russian Culture*, ed. Ann Shukman, 36–52. Ann Arbor, 1984.

Maikova, T. "Petr I i pravoslavnaia tserkov'." *Nauka i religiia* 7 (1972): 38–46.

Mamyshev, V. N. *General-Fel'dmarshal i General-Admiral graf Fedor Alekseevich Golovin.* St. Petersburg, 1904.

Marin, Louis. *Portrait of the King.* Trans. Martha M. Houle. Minneapolis, 1988.

Marrese, Michelle Lamarche. *A Woman's Kingdom: Noblewomen and the Control of Property in Russia, 1700–1861.* Ithaca, 2002.

Matveev, V. Iu. "K istorii vozniknoveniia i razvitiia siuzheta Petr I—vysekaiushchii statuiu Rossii." In *Kul'tura i iskusstvo Rossii XVIII veka*, 26–43. Leningrad, 1981.

Mazzeo, Joseph Anthony. "Cromwell as Davidic King." In Mazzeo, *Renaissance and Seventeenth-Century Studies*, 189–91. New York, 1964.

McGuckin, John Anthony. *The Transfiguration of Christ in Scripture and Tradition.* Studies in the Bible and Early Christianity, 9. Lewiston, NY, 1986.

Medushevskii, A. N. *Reformy Petra I i sud'by Rossii.* Moscow, 1994.

——. *Utverzhdenie absoliutizma v Rossii.* Moscow, 1994.

Meehan-Waters, Brenda. *Autocracy and Aristocracy: The Russian Service Elite of 1730.* New Brunswick, NJ, 1982.

——. "The Russian Aristocracy and the Reforms of Peter the Great." *Canadian-American Slavic Studies* 8 (Summer 1974): 288–302.

Michels, Georg Bernhard. *At War with the Church: Religious Dissent in Seventeenth-Century Russia.* Stanford, 1999.

Mikhailov, G. A. "Graviura A. Zubova 'Svad'ba Petra I': Real'nost' i vymysel." *Panorama iskusstv* 11 (1988): 20–55.

Miller, David. B. "The Coronation of Ivan IV." *Jahrbücher für Geschichte Osteuropas* 15, no. 4 (1967): 559–74.

M[iller], G.-F. "Izvestie o nachale Preobrazhenskogo i Semenovskogo polkov gvardii." In *Sobranie raznykh zapisok i sochinenii, sluzhashchikh k dostavleniiu polnago svedeniia o zhizni i deianiiakh gosudaria imperatora Petra Velikago,* 299–328. St. Petersburg, 1787.

Modzalevskii, B. "Romodanovskii, kn. Mikhail Grigor'evich." In *Russkii biograficheskii slovar',* 17:124–26. New York, 1962.

Molchanov, N. N. *Diplomatiia Petra Pervogo.* Moscow, 1986.

Moleva, N. M. " 'Persony' vseshuteishego sobora." *Voprosy istorii* 10 (October 1974): 206–11.

Moleva, N. M., and E. M. Beliutin. *"Zhivopisnykh del mastera":* Kantseliariia ot stroenii i russkaia zhivopis' pervoi poloviny XVIII veka. Moscow, 1965.

Monod, Paul Kléber. *The Power of Kings: Monarchy and Religion in Europe, 1589–1715.* New Haven, 1999.

Morozov, A. A. "Emblematika barokko v literature i iskusstve petrovskogo vremeni." *XVIII vek* 9 (1974): 184–226.

——. "Problema barokko v russkoi literature XVII–nachala XVIII veka (sostoianie voprosa i zadachi izucheniia)." *Russkaia literatura* 3 (1962): 3–38.

Morson, Gary Saul. "Parody, History, Metaparody." In *Rethinking Bakhtin: Extensions and Challenges,* ed. Gary Saul Morson and Caryl Emerson, 63–86. Evanston, 1989.

Nekrasov, A. I. *Drevnie podmoskovnye. Aleksandrova sloboda, Kolomenskoe, Izmailovo.* Moscow, 1923.

Nichik, V. M. *Feofan Prokopovich.* Moscow, 1977.

Nikolaev, S. I. *Literaturnaia kul'tura petrovskoi epokhi.* St. Petersburg, 1996.

——. "Rytsarskaia ideia v pokhoronnom obriade petrovskoi epokhi." In *Iz istorii russkoi kul'tury,* ed. A. D. Koshelev, 3:584–94. Moscow, 1996.

Nikolaeva, M. V. " 'Testament' Petra I tsarevichu Alekseiu." *XVIII vek* 9 (1974): 93–111.

Novikov, N. I., ed. *Drevniaia Rossiiskaia Vivliofika.* 2nd ed. Moscow, 1788–89.

Odesskii, M. P. *Ocherki istoricheskoi poetiki russkoi dramy: epokha Petra I.* Moscow, 1999.

Oestreich, Gerhard. *Neostoicism and the Early Modern State.* Trans. David McLintock. Cambridge, 1982.

Ogorodnikov, S. "Vtoroe poseshchenie Petrom Velikim Arkhangel'ska v 1694 g." In *Petr Velikii na Severe. Sbornik statei i ukazov, otnosiashchikhsia k deiatel'nosti Petra I na Severe,* ed. A. F. Shidlovskii, 24–30. Archangel, 1909.

Oliva, L. Jay. *Russia in the Era of Peter the Great.* Englewood Cliffs, NJ, 1969.

Orso, Steven N. *Velásquez, "Los Borrachos," and Painting at the Court of Philip IV.* Cambridge, 1993.

Panchenko, A. M. "Literatura vtoroi poloviny XVII veka." In *Istoriia russkoi literatury X–XVII vekov,* ed. D. S. Likhachev, 372–446. Moscow, 1980.

——. "Nachalo petrovskoi reformy: Ideinaia podopleka." In *Iz istorii russkoi kul'tury,* ed. A. D. Koshelev, 3:503–18. Moscow, 1996.

——. "Russkaia kul'tura v kanun petrovskikh reform." In *Iz istorii russkoi kul'tury,* ed. A. D. Koshelev, 3:11–261. Moscow, 1996.

——. *Russkaia sillabicheskaia poeziia XVII–XVIII vv.* Leningrad, 1970.

——. "Smekh kak zrelishche." In *Smekh v drevnei Rusi,* ed. D. S. Likhachev, 72–153. Leningrad, 1984.

——. "Tserkovnaia reforma i kul'tura petrovskoi epokhi." In *Iz istorii russkoi kul'tury,* ed. A. D. Koshelev, 3:486–502. Moscow, 1996.

Panchenko, A. M., and B. A. Uspenskii. "Ivan Groznyi i Petr Velikii: Kontseptsii pervogo monarkha. Stat'ia pervaia." *Trudy otdela drevnerusskoi literatury* 37 (1983): 54–78.

Pavlenko, N. I. "Idei absoliutizma v zakonodatel'stve XVIII v." In *Absoliutizm v Rossii XVII–XVIII vv. Sb. statei k 70-letiiu B. B. Kafengauza*, 389–427. Moscow, 1964.

———. "Petr I (K izucheniiu sotsial'no-politicheskikh vzgliadov)." In *Rossiia v period reform Petra I*, ed. Pavlenko, 40–102. Moscow, 1973.

———. *Petr Velikii.* Moscow, 1990.

———. *Poluderzhavnyi vlastelin: Istoricheskaia khronika o zhizni spodvizhnika Petra Pervogo A. D. Menshikova.* Moscow, 1991.

———. *Ptentsy gnezda Petrova.* Moscow, 1984.

Pavlova-Sil'vanskaia, M. P. "Annotirovannaia bibliografiia inostrannoi literatury o Petre I (1947–1970 gg.)." In *Rossia v period reform Petra I*, 362–382. Moscow, 1973.

Pavlov-Sil'vanskii, N. P. *Proekty reform v zapiskakh sovremennikov Petra Velikogo.* St. Petersburg, 1897.

Pekarskii, P. P. *Nauka i literatura pri Petre Velikom.* 2 vols. St. Petersburg, 1862.

Peretts, V. N. *Istoriko-literaturnye issledovaniia i materialy.* 3 vols. St. Petersburg, 1902.

Perrie, Maureen. *Pretenders and Popular Monarchism in Early Modern Russia.* Cambridge, 1995.

Peterson, C. *Peter the Great's Administrative and Judicial Reforms: Swedish Antecedents and the Process of Reception.* Stockholm, 1979.

Petr Velikii i Moskva: Katalog vystavki. Moscow, 1998.

Petrov, A. "Romodanovskii, kn. Ivan Fedorovich." In *Russkii biograficheskii slovar'*, 17:120–24. New York, 1962.

Petrov, P. N., ed. *Istoriia rodov russkogo dvorianstva.* 2 vols. St. Petersburg, 1886.

Phillips, Edward J. *The Founding of Russia's Navy: Peter the Great and the Azov Fleet, 1688–1714.* Westport, CT, 1995.

Platonov, S. F. "B. I. Kurakin i A. P. Prozorovskii (1697–1720)." *Doklady Akademii Nauk SSSR. Seriia istorii i filosofii* 12 (1929): 236–43.

———. "Iz bytovoi istorii Petrovskoi epokhi." Pt. 1, "Bengo-Kollegiia ili Velikobritanskii monastyr' v S.-Peterburge pri Petre Velikom." *Izvestiia Akademii Nauk SSSR* 7–8 (1926): 527–46.

———. "Iz bytovoi istorii Petrovskoi epokhi." Pt. 2, "Liubimtsy Petra Velikogo: Medved', Bitka, i dr." *Izvestiia Akademii Nauk SSSR*, ser. 6 (1926): 655–78.

———. "Orden Iudy 1709 goda." *Letopis' zaniatii postoiannoi istoriko-arkheograficheskoi komissii* 1 (1927): 193–98.

Pliukhanova, M. B. "O natsional'nykh sredstvakh samoopredeleniia lichnosti: samosakralizatsiia, samosozhzhenie, plavanie na korable." In *Iz istorii russkoi kul'tury*, ed. A. D. Koshelev, 3:380–459. Moscow, 1996.

———. *Siuzhety i simvoly Moskovskogo tsarstva.* St. Petersburg, 1995.

Pod''iapol'skaia, E. P. "Ob istorii i nauchnom znachenii izdaniia 'Pis'ma i bumagi imperatora Petra Velikogo.'" In *Arkheograficheskii ezhegodnik za 1972 god*, 56–70. Moscow, 1974.

Podol'skii, R. "Petrovskii dvorets na Iauze." *Arkhitekturnoe nasledstvo* 1 (1951): 14–55.

Pogodin, M. P. *Semnadtsat' pervykh let v zhizni imperatora Petra Velikago, 1672–1689.* Moscow, 1875.

———. "Tsarevich Aleksei Petrovich, po svidetel'stvam vnov' otkrytym." *Chteniia v Imperatorskom Obshchestve Istorii i Drevnostei Rossiiskikh pri Moskovskom universitete* 3, no. 2 (1861): i–xxii.

Pogosian, Elena. *Petr I: Arkhitektor rossiiskoi istorii.* St. Petersburg, 2001.

Polosin, I. I. "'Igra v tsaria' (Otgoloski Smuty v moskovskom bytu XVII veka)." *Izvestiia Tverskogo pedagogicheskogo instituta* 1 (1926): 59–63.

Ponyrko, N. V. "Russkie sviatki XVII veka." *Trudy otdela drevnerusskoi literatury* 32 (1977): 84–99.

———. "Sviatochnyi smekh." In *Smekh v drevnei Rusi*, ed. D. S. Likhachev et al., 154–74. Leningrad, 1984.

Pope, Richard W. F. "Fools and Folly in Old Russia." *Slavic Review* 39, no. 3 (1980): 476–81.

Posselt, D. M. *Admiral Russkago flota Frants Iakovlevich Lefort, ili nachalo Russkago flota.* Prilozhenie k Morskomu sborniku, 3. St. Petersburg, 1863.

Propp, V. Ia. *Russkie agrarnye prazdniki.* Leningrad, 1963.

Prozorovskii, A. [A]. *Sil'vestr Medvedev (Ego zhizn' i deiatel'nost'). Opyt tserkovno-istoricheskogo izsledovaniia.* Moscow, 1896.

Pushkarev, L. N. *Obshchestvenno-politicheskaia mysl' Rossii. Vtoraia polovina XVII veka. Ocherki istorii.* Moscow, 1982.

Pushkareva, N. L. *Women in Russian History: From the Tenth to the Twentieth Century.* Trans. and ed. Eve Levin. Armonk, NY, 1997.

Raeff, Marc. "Transfiguration and Modernization: The Paradoxes of Social Disciplining, Paedagogical Leadership, and the Enlightenment in 18th-Century Russia." In *Alteuropa-Ancien Régime-Frühe Neuzeit: Probleme und Methoden der Forschung,* ed. Hans Erich Bödeker and Ernst Hinrichs, 99–115. Stuttgart, 1991.

——. *The Well-Ordered Police State: Social and Institutional Change through Law in the Germanies and Russia, 1600–1800.* New Haven, 1983.

——. "The Well-Ordered Police State and the Development of Modernity in Seventeenth- and Eighteenth-Century Europe: An Attempt at a Comparative Approach." *American Historical Review* 80, no. 5 (1975): 1221–43.

Rasmussen, Karen. "Catherine II and the Image of Peter." *Slavic Review* 37 (March 1978): 57–69.

Realms of Memory: Rethinking the French Past. Trans. Arthur Goldhammer. 3 vols. New York, 1996–98.

Riasanovsky, Nicholas V. *The Image of Peter the Great in Russian History and Thought.* New York, 1985.

Robinson, A. N. *Bor'ba idei v russkoi literature XVII veka.* Moscow, 1974.

——. "Dominiruiushchaia rol' russkoi dramaturgii i teatra kak vidov iskusstva v epokhu petrovsikh reform." In *Slavianskie kul'tury v epokhu formirovaniia i razvitiia slavianskikh natsii XVIII–XIX vv. Materialy mezhdunarodnoi konferentsii IuNESKO,* 176–82. Moscow, 1978.

——, ed. *Pervye p'esy russkogo teatra.* Moscow, 1972.

Rowland, Daniel. "Moscow—The Third Rome or the New Israel." *Russian Review* 55, no. 4 (1996): 591–614.

——. "The Problem of Advice in Muscovite Tales about the Time of Troubles." *Russian History/Histoire russe* 6, no. 2 (1979): 259–83.

Russkii biograficheskii slovar'. 25 vols. St. Petersburg, 1896–1918. Rpt. New York, 1962.

Ryan, W. F. *The Bathhouse at Midnight: An Historical Survey of Magic and Divination in Russia.* University Park, PA, 1999.

Samarin, N. F. "Buturliny i Iushkovy. Zametki iz bumag semeinogo arkhiva N. F. Samarina." *Russkaia starina* 6 (1872): 559–63.

Savelov, L. M. *Rod dvorian Savelovykh (Savelkovy).* Moscow, 1895.

Savluchinskii, P. "Russkaia dukhovnaia literatura pervoi poloviny XVIII veka i ee otnoshenie k sovremennosti (1700–1762)." *Trudy Kievskoi Dukhovnoi Akademii* 4 (1878): 128–90; 5 (1878): 280–326.

Sazonova, L. I. "Obshcheevropeiskie cherty vostochnoslavianskogo barokko. Iz nabliudenii nad poetikoi: *acumen, poesia artificiosa, emblema, picta poesis.*" *Slavianovedenie* 2 (2002): 98–110.

——. *Poeziia russkogo barokko (vtoraia polovina XVII–nachalo XVIII v.).* Moscow, 1991.

Schafly, Daniel L., Jr. "The Popular Image of the West in Russia at the Time of Peter the Great." In *Russia and the World of the Eighteenth Century,* ed. R. P. Bartlett et al., 2–21. Columbus, OH, 1986.

Schaub, Marie-Karine. "Les couronnements des tsars en Russie du XVIᵉ au XVIIIᵉ siècle: Essai d'historiographie." In *La royauté sacrée dans le monde chrétien (Colloque de Royaumont, mars 1989)*, ed. Alain Boureau and C. S. Ingerflom, 137–48. Paris, 1992.

Schuyler, Eugene. *Peter the Great, Emperor of Russia: A Study of Historical Biography.* 2 vols. New York, 1884.

Sedov, P. V. "Detskie gody tsaria Fedora Alekseevicha." In *Srednevekovaia Rus': Sbornik nauchnykh statei k 65–letiiu . . . R. G. Skrynnikova*, 77–93. St. Petersburg, 1995.

Seemann, Klaus-Dieter. "Allegorical-Exegetical Devices in Kievan Literature." *Canadian-American Slavic Studies* 25, no. 1–4 (1991): 27–41.

Semenova, L. N. *Ocherki istorii byta i kul'turnoi zhizni Rossii, pervaia polovina XVIII v.* Leningrad, 1982.

Semevskii, M. I. "Petr Velikii—kak iumorist. (Novye materialy dlia kharakteristike Petra)." *Svetoch. Ucheno-literaturnyi zhurnal*, ed. D. I. Kalinovskii, 9, no. 2 (1861): 1–50 (second pagination).

——. "Petr Velikii kak iumorist (1690–1725)." In Semevskii, *Ocherki i razskazy iz russkoi istorii XVIII v.: Slovo i delo! 1700–1725*, 2nd rev. ed., 278–334. St. Petersburg, 1884.

——. "Shutki i potekhi Petra Velikago. Petr Velikii—kak iumorist." *Russkaia starina* 6 (June 1872): 855–92.

——. *Tsaritsa Katerina Alekseevna, Anna i Villim Mons, 1692–1724.* 2nd rev. ed. St. Petersburg, 1884.

Serchevskii, Evgenii, ed. *Zapiski o rode kniazei Golitsynykh.* St. Petersburg, 1853.

Serman, I. Z. "Literaturno-esteticheskie interesy i literaturnaia politika Petra I." *XVIII vek* 9 (1974): 5–49.

Serov, D. O. *Stroiteli imperii: Ocherki gosudarstvennoi i kriminal'noi deiatel'nosti spodvizhnikov Petra I.* Novosibirsk, 1996.

Serech, J. [Iu. Shevelov]. "On Theofan Prokopovich as Writer and Preacher in His Kiev Period." *Harvard Slavic Studies* 2 (1954): 211–33.

Sharot, Stephen. "The Sacredness of Sin: Antinomianism and Models of Man." *Religion* 13 (1983): 37–54.

Shchukina, E. S. *Medal'ernoe iskusstvo v Rossii XVIII veka.* Leningrad, 1962.

Shils, Edward E. *The Constitution of Society.* Chicago, 1982.

Shmurlo, E. F. "Kriticheskie zametki po istorii Petra Velikogo." Pt. 9, "V chest' kakogo sviatogo Petr Velikii poluchil svoe imia." *Zhurnal Ministerstva Narodnogo Prosveshcheniia* 330 (July–August 1900): 209–22.

——. "Kriticheskie zametki po istorii Petra Velikogo." Pt. 10, "Preobrazhenskoe i Kreml' v zhizni tsarevicha Petra (do 1682 g.)." *Zhurnal Ministerstva Narodnogo Prosveshcheniia* 330 (July–August 1900): 223–34.

——. "Kriticheskie zametki po istorii Petra Velikogo." Pt. 13, "Nachalo uchebnykh zaniatii Petra Velikogo." *Zhurnal Ministerstva Narodnogo Prosveshcheniia* 340 (March–April 1902): 421–39.

——. "Kriticheskie zametki po istorii Petra Velikogo." Pt. 15, "Ob uchastii patriarkha Ioakima v izbranii Petra Velikogo na tsarstvo." *Zhurnal Ministerstva Narodnogo Prosveshcheniia* 341 (May–June 1902): 241–56.

Sinitsyn, P. V. *Preobrazhenskoe i okruzhaiushchie ego mesta: Ikh proshloe i nastoiashchee.* Moscow, 1895.

Skrine, Peter N. *The Baroque: Literature and Culture in Seventeenth-Century Europe.* London, 1978.

Skritskii, N. V. *Pervyi kavaler Ordena Sviatogo Andreia Admiral F. A. Golovin (1650–1706). Biograficheskii ocherk.* Moscow, 1995.

Skrynnikov, R. G. *Samozvantsy v Rossii v nachale XVII veka: Grigorii Otrep'ev.* Novosibirsk, 1987.

Slovar' russkikh pisatelei XVIII veka. St. Petersburg, 1999.

Smentsovskii, M. *Brat'ia Likhudy. Opyt izsledovaniia iz istorii tserkovnogo prosveshcheniia i tserkovnoi zhizni kontsa XVII i nachala XVIII vekov.* St. Petersburg, 1899.

Smirnov, V. G. *Feofan Prokopovich.* Moscow, 1994.

Smith, Johnathan Z. *To Take Place: Toward Theory in Ritual.* Chicago, 1987.

Solignac, Aimé. "Ivresse spirituelle." In *Dictionnaire de spiritualité ascétique et mystique: Doctrine et histoire,* 7 (2): 2312–37. Paris, 1971.

Solov'ev, S. M. *Istoriia Rossii s drevneishikh vremen.* 15 vols. In Solov'ev, *Sochineniia v vosemnadtsati knigakh,* 18 vols. Moscow, 1988–95.

Spasskii, I. G., and E. S. Shchukina, eds. *Medali i monety Petrovskogo vremeni.* Leningrad, 1974.

Spielman, John P. *Leopold I of Austria.* New Brunscwick, NJ, 1977.

Spiridov, M. G. *Sokrashchennoe opisanie sluzheb blagorodnykh Rossiiskikh dvorian. . . . Sobrannoe iz stateinykh, razriadnykh, stepennykh, sluzhebnykh i nekotorykh drugikh rodoslovnykh knig.* Moscow, 1810.

Sreznevskii, I. I. *Materialy dlia slovaria drevnerusskogo iazyka.* 3 vols. St. Petersburg, 1901–3.

Stallybrass, Peter, and Allon White. *The Politics and Poetics of Transgression.* Ithaca, 1986.

Starikova, L. M. "Russkii teatr petrovskogo vremeni, komedial'naia khramina i domashnie komedii tsarevny Natal'i Alekseevny." In *Pamiatniki kul'tury. Novye otkrytiia. Ezhegodnik 1990,* 137–56. Moscow, 1992.

Starkey, David. "Court History in Perspective." In *The English Court: From the Wars of the Roses to the Civil War,* ed. David Starkey, 1–24. London, 1987.

——. "Representation through Intimacy: A Study in the Symbolism of Monarchy and Court Office in Early Modern England." In *Symbols and Sentiments: Cross-Cultural Studies in Symbolism,* ed. Ioan Lewis, 187–224. London, 1977.

Starostina, T. V. "Ob opale A. S. Matveeva v sviazi s sysknym delom 1676–1677 gg. o khranenii zagovornykh pisem." *Uchenye zapiski Karelo-Finskogo Gosudarstvennogo universiteta* 2, no. 1 (Petrozavodsk, 1948).

Stevens, Carol B. "Evaluating Peter's Military Forces." In *Russia in the Reign of Peter the Great: Old and New Perspectives,* ed. Anthony Cross, 2:89–103. Cambridge, 1998.

Stökl, G. "Der zweite Salomon. Einige Bemerkungen zur Herrschervorstellungen im alten Russland." *Canadian-American Slavic Studies* 13, no. 1–2 (1979): 23–31.

Strong, Roy. *Art and Power: Renaissance Festivals, 1450–1650.* Woodbridge, Suffolk, 1984.

Subtelny, Orest. "Mazepa, Peter I, and the Question of Treason." *Harvard Ukrainian Studies* 2 (June 1978): 158–83.

Sumner, B. H. *Peter the Great and the Emergence of Russia.* London, 1958.

Syromiatnikov, B. I. *"Reguliarnoe" gosudarstvo Petra I i ego ideologiia.* Moscow and Leningrad, 1943.

Szeftel, Marc. "The Title of the Muscovite Monarch up to the End of the Seventeenth Century." *Canadian-American Slavic Studies* 13, no. 1–2 (1979): 59–81.

Tarle, E. V. *Russkii flot i vneshniaia politika Petra I.* St. Petersburg, 1994.

Ternovskii, F. [A.] "Imperator Petr I-i v ego otnosheniiakh k katolichestvu i protestantstvu." *Trudy Kievskoi Dukhovnoi Akademii* 1 (1869): 373–403.

——. "Russkoe propovednichestvo pri Petre I-m." *Rukovodstvo dlia sel'skikh pastyrei: Zhurnal izdavaemyi pri Kievskoi Dukhovnoi Seminarii* 3, no. 36 (1870): 13–28; no. 37 (1870): 43–60; no. 39 (1870): 119–29; no. 44 (1870): 290–304; no. 48 (1870): 487–94.

Thompson, E. P. "Rough Music." In *Customs in Common: Studies in Traditional Popular Culture,* 467–538. New York, 1993.

Thyrêt, Isolde. *Between God and Tsar: Religious Symbolism and the Royal Women of Muscovite Russia.* DeKalb, IL, 2001.

Tikhomirov, N. Ia. *Arkhitektura podmoskovnykh usadeb.* Moscow, 1955.

Tikhonov, Iu. A. "Podmoskovnye imeniia russkoi aristokratii vo vtoroi polovine XVII–nachale XVIII v." In *Dvorianstvo i krepostnoi stroi Rossii XVI–XVIII vv. Sbornik statei, posviashchennyi pamiati A. A. Novosel'skogo,* ed. N. I. Pavlenko. Moscow, 1975.

[Tokarev, N.] "Blizhniaia kantseliariia pri Petre Velikom i eia dela." In *Opisanie dokumentov i bumag khraniashchikhsia v Moskovskom arkhive Ministerstva Iustitsii,* 5: 43–75. Moscow, 1888.

Tolstoy, N. *The Tolstoys: Twenty Generations of Russian History, 1353–1983.* 2nd ed. New York, 1985.

Toporov, V. N. "Gliuk i 'nemetskaia' russkaia poeziia pervoi treti XVIII v." In Toporov, *M. V. Lomonosov i russkaia kul'tura,* 11–16. Tartu, 1986.

Trevor-Roper, Hugh. "The Culture of Baroque Courts." In *Europäische Hofkultur in 16. und 17. Jahrhundert,* ed. August Buck et al., 11–23. Hamburg, 1981.

Truvorov, A. N. "Volkhvy i vorozhei na Rusi, v kontse XVII veka." *Istoricheskii vestnik* 6 (1889): 710–15.

Turner, Victor. *Dramas, Fields, and Metaphors: Symbolic Action in Human Society.* Ithaca, 1974.

Uspenskii, B. A. "Antipovedenie v kul'ture drevnei Rusi." In *Izbrannye trudy,* 2nd rev. ed., 1:460–76. Moscow, 1996.

———. "Historia sub specie semioticae." In *Soviet Semiotics: An Anthology,* ed. and trans. Daniel P. Lucid, 107–16. Baltimore, 1977.

———. *Kratkii ocherk istorii russkogo literaturnogo iazyka (XI–XIX vv.).* Moscow, 1994.

———. "The Schism and Cultural Conflict in the Seventeenth Century." In *Seeking God: The Recovery of Religious Identity in Orthodox Russia, Ukraine, and Georgia,* ed. and trans. Stephen K. Batalden, 106–43. De Kalb, IL, 1993.

———. "Tsar and Pretender: *Samozvanchestvo* or Royal Imposture in Russia as a Cultural-Historical Phenomenon." Trans. David Budgen. In *The Semiotics of Russian Culture,* ed. Ann Shukman, 259–92. Ann Arbor, 1984.

———. *Tsar' i patriarkh: Kharizma vlasti v Rossii (Vizantiiskaia model' i ee russkoe pereosmyslenie).* Moscow, 1998.

Uspenskii, B. A., and V. M. Zhivov. "'Tsar' i Bog': Semioticheskie aspekty sakralizatsii monarkha v Rossii." In Uspenskii, *Izbrannye trudy,* 2nd ed., 1:205–337. Moscow, 1996.

———. "Zur Spezifik des Barock in Russland: Das Verfahren der Äquivokation in der russischen Poesie des 18. Jahrhunderts." Trans. A. Kaiser. In *Slavische Barockliteratur II: Gedenkschrift für Dmitrij Tschizewskij (1894–1977),* ed. Renate Lachmann, 25–56. Munich, 1983.

Ussas, B. "Zheliabuzhskii, Ivan Afanas'evich." In *Russkii biograficheskii slovar',* 7:25–26. New York, 1962.

Ustrialov, N. G. *Istoriia tsarstvovaniia Petra Velikogo.* 6 vols. St. Petersburg, 1858–59.

Valuev, D. [A.]. "Vvedenie. Razriadnaia kniga ot 7067 [1559] do 7112 [1604]." In Valuev, *Sinbirskii sbornik. Istoricheskaia chast',* pt. 1. Moscow, 1845.

Vasil'chikov, Aleksandr [A.]. "Rod Naryshkinykh." *Russkii arkhiv* 9 (1871): 1487–519, 1960–61.

Vasil'ev, V. N. *Starinnye feirverki v Rossii (XVII–pervaia chetvert' XVIII veka).* Leningrad, 1960.

Vasilevskaia, E. A. "Terminologiia mestnichestva i rodstva." *Trudy istoriko-arkhivnogo instituta* 2 (1946): 155–79.

Vasselin, Martine. "Des fastes de Bacchus aux beuveries flamandes: L'iconographie du vin de la fin du XVe siècle à la fin du XVIIe siècle." *Nouvelle revue du seizième siècle* 17, no. 2 (1999): 219–51.

Verkhovskoi, P. V. *Uchrezhdenie dukhovnoi kollegii i dukhovnyi reglament: K voprosu ob otnoshenii Tserkvi i gosudarstva v Rossii. Izsledovanie v oblasti istorii russkago tserkovnago prava.* 2 vols. Rostov-on-Don, 1916.

Veselovskii, S. V., et al. *Podmoskov'e: Pamiatnye mesta v istorii russkoi kul'tury XIV–XIX vekov.* 2nd ed. Moscow, 1962.

Vilinbakhov, G. V. "K istorii uchrezhdeniia ordena Andreiia Pervozvannogo i evoliutsii ego znaka." In *Kul'tura i iskusstvo petrovskogo vremeni: Publikatsii i issledovaniia,* 144–158. Leningrad, 1977.

——. "Osnovanie Peterburga i imperskaia emblematika." *Trudy po znakovym sistemam* 18 (1984): 46–55.

——. "Otrazhenie idei absoliutizma v simvolike petrovskikh znamen." In *Kul'tura i iskusstvo Rossii XVIII veka. Sbornik statei,* 7–25. Leningrad, 1981.

Volkov, M. Ia. "Monakh Avraamii i ego 'Poslanie Petru I.' " In *Rossiia v period reform Petra I,* ed. N. I. Pavlenko, 311–36. Moscow, 1973.

Voronkov, N. "Pashkovy." In *Russkii biograficheskii slovar',* 12:444–45. St. Petersburg, 1902.

Vostokov, A. "O delakh general'nogo dvora." In *Opisanie dokumentov i bumag khraniashchikhsia v Moskovskom arkhive Ministerstva Iustitsii.* Moscow, 1888. 5:1–42.

Vsevolodskii-Gerngross, V. N. *Russkii teatr: ot istokov do serediny XVIII v.* Moscow, 1957.

Ware, Timothy. *The Orthodox Church.* Baltimore, 1963.

Warner, Richard H. "The Kozukhovo Campaign of 1694; or, The Conquest of Moscow by Preobrazhenskoe." *Jahrbücher für Geschichte Osteuropas* 13 (1965): 487–96.

Weber, Max. *From Max Weber: Essays in Sociology.* Ed. H. H. Gerth and C. Wright Mills. New York, 1958.

——. *Max Weber on Charisma and Institution Building: Selected Papers.* Ed. S. N. Eisenstadt. Chicago, 1968.

Weinberg, Florence W. *The Wine and the Will: Rabelais' Bacchic Christianity.* Detroit, 1972.

Whittaker, Cynthia H. "The Reforming Tsar: The Redefinition of Autocratic Duty in Eighteenth-Century Russia." *Slavic Review* 51 (Spring 1992): 77–98.

Wilentz, Sean, ed. *Rites of Power: Symbolism, Ritual, and Politics since the Middle Ages.* Philadelphia, 1985.

Wittram, Reinhard. *Peter I, Czar und Kaiser: Zur Geschichte Peters des Grossen in seiner Zeit.* 2 vols. Göttingen, 1964.

——. "Peters des Grossen Verhältnis zur Religion und den Kirchen: Glaube, Vernunft, Leidenschaft." *Historische Zeitschrift* 173 (1952): 261–96.

Wójcik, Z. "From the Peace of Oliwa to the Truce of Bakhchisarai: International Relations in Eastern Europe, 1660–1681." *Acta Poloniae Historica* 34 (1976): 255–80.

Wortman, Richard S. "The Redefinition of the Sacred: Eighteenth-Century Russian Coronations." In *La royauté sacrée dans le monde chrétien (Colloque de Royaumont, mars 1989),* ed. Alain Boureau and C. S. Ingerflom, 149–56. Paris, 1992.

——. "Reply to Mikhail Dolbilov." *Kritika: Explorations in Russian and Eurasian History* 2 (Fall 2001): 797–801.

——. *Scenarios of Power: Myth and Ceremony in Russian Monarchy.* 2 vols. Princeton, 1995, 2000.

Wortman, Richard S., and Edward Kasinec. "The Mythology of Empire: Imperial Russia's Coronation Albums." *Biblion: The Bulletin of the New York Public Library* 1 (Fall 1992): 77–100.

Yates, Frances A. *Astraea: The Imperial Theme in the Sixteenth Century.* London, 1985.

Zabelin, I. E. "Detskie gody Petra Velikogo." In *Opyty izucheniia russkikh drevnostei i istorii. Issledovaniia, opisaniia i kriticheskie stat'i,* 2 vols., 1:1–50. Moscow, 1872–73.

——. *Domashnii byt russkogo naroda.* 2nd ed. 2 vols. Moscow, 1872–73.

——. *Domashnii byt russkogo naroda v XVI i XVII stoletiiakh.* Vol. 2, *Gosudarev dvor, ili dvorets,* ed. A. N. Sakharov, 4th ed. Moscow, 1990.

——. "Istoriia i drevnosti Moskvy." In *Opyty izucheniia russkikh drevnostei i istorii. Issledovaniia, opisaniia i kriticheskie stat'i,* 2 vols., 2:107–53, Moscow, 1872–73.

——. *Preobrazhenskoe ili Preobrazhensk: Moskovskaia stolitsa dostoslavnykh preobrazovanii pervogo imperatora Petra Velikogo.* Moscow, 1883.

Zamyslovskii, E. E., and I. I. Petrov. *Istoricheskii ocherk rossiiskikh ordenov i sbornik osnovnykh ordenskikh statutov.* St. Petersburg, 1892.

Zaozerskii, A. I. *Fel'dmarshal B. P. Sheremetev.* Ed. B. V. Levshin. Moscow, 1989.

——. "Fel'dmarshal Sheremetev i pravitel'stvennaia sreda petrovskogo vremeni." In *Rossiia v period reform Petra I,* ed. N. I. Pavlenko, 172–98. Moscow, 1973.

Zashchuk, G. V. " 'Orden Iudy.' " *Voprosy istorii* 6 (June 1971): 212–15.

Zazykin, M. V. *Patriarkh Nikon: Ego gosudarstvennye i kanonicheskie idei. V trekh chastiakh.* Moscow, 1995.

Zen'kovskii, S. A. *Russkoe staroobriadchestvo: Dukhovnye dvizheniia semnadtsatogo veka.* Moscow, 1995.

Zguta, Russell. "Peter I's Most Drunken Synod of Fools and Jesters." *Jahrbücher für Geschichte Osteuropas* 21 (1973): 18–28.

Zheludkov, D. "Novye materialy o dvortsovom stroitel'stve v Moskve petrovskogo vremeni." In *Tsarskie i imperatorskie dvortsy. Staraia Moskva,* 120–33. Moscow, 1997.

Zheludkov, D., and O. Trubnikova, "Dereviannoe chudo v Kolomenskom." *Moskovskii arkhiv. Istoriko-kraevedcheskii al'manakh* 1 (1996): 12–28.

Zhivov, V. M. "Church Reforms in the Reign of Peter the Great." Trans. W. Gareth Jones. In *Russia in the Reign of Peter the Great: Old and New Perspectives,* ed. Anthony Cross, 1:65–75. Cambridge, 1998.

——. *Iazyk i kul'tura v Rossii XVIII veka.* Moscow, 1996.

——. "Kul'turnye reformy v sisteme preobrazovanii Petra I." In *Iz istorii russkoi kul'tury,* ed. A. D. Koshelev, 3:528–83. Moscow, 1996.

——. *Razyskaniia v oblasti i predistorii russkoi kul'tury.* Moscow, 2002.

Zhivov, V. M., and B. A. Uspenskii. "Metamorfozy antichnogo iazychestva v istorii russkoi kul'tury XVII–XVIII veka." In *Iz istorii russkoi kul'tury,* ed. A. D. Koshelev, 4:449–536. Moscow, 1996.

Zitser, Ernest A. "Ordenonostsy i otstupniki: rytsarskaia ideia v politicheskoi praktike 'kompanii' Petra Velikogo." *Rossiia/Russia* 5/13 (2004).

——. "Politics in the State of Sober Drunkenness: Parody and Piety at the Court of Peter the Great." *Jahrbücher für Geschichte Osteuropas* 51, no. 1 (2003): 1–15.

Zwicker, Steven N. "The King and Christ: Figural Imagery in Dryden's Restoration Panegyrics." *Philological Quarterly* 50 (1971): 582–98.

Index